Health and the Art of Living

HARVARD-YENCHING INSTITUTE MONOGRAPH SERIES 145

Health and the Art of Living

Illness Narratives in Early
Medieval Chinese Literature

Antje Richter

Published by the Harvard University Asia Center
Distributed by Harvard University Press
Cambridge (Massachusetts) and London, 2025

© 2025 by the President and Fellows of Harvard College

All rights reserved. No part of this publication may be reproduced, translated, stored in a retrieval system, or transmitted in any form or by any means, electronic, mechanical, photocopying, recording or otherwise, without prior written permission from the publisher.

Published by the Harvard University Asia Center, Cambridge, MA 02138

The Harvard University Asia Center publishes a monograph series and, in coordination with the Fairbank Center for Chinese Studies, the Korea Institute, the Reischauer Institute of Japanese Studies, and other faculties and institutes, administers research projects designed to further scholarly understanding of China, Japan, Korea, Vietnam, and other Asian countries. The Center also sponsors projects addressing multidisciplinary and regional issues in Asia.

The Harvard University Asia Center gratefully acknowledges the generous support of the Harvard-Yenching Institute, whose funding contributed to the publication of this book.

The Harvard-Yenching Institute, founded in 1928, is an independent foundation dedicated to the advancement of higher education in the humanities and social sciences in Asia. Headquartered on the campus of Harvard University, the Institute provides fellowships for advanced research, training, and graduate studies at Harvard by competitively selected faculty and graduate students from Asia. The Institute also supports a range of academic activities at its fifty partner universities and research institutes across Asia. At Harvard, the Institute promotes East Asian studies through annual contributions to the Harvard-Yenching Library and publication of the *Harvard Journal of Asiatic Studies* and the Harvard-Yenching Institute Monograph Series.

Library of Congress Cataloging-in-Publication Data
Names: Richter, Antje, author.
Title: Health and the art of living : illness narratives in early medieval Chinese literature / Antje Richter.
Other titles: Harvard-Yenching Institute monograph series ; 145.
Description: Cambridge : Harvard University Asia Center, 2025. | Series: Harvard-Yenching Institute monograph series ; 145 | Includes bibliographical references and index. | English ; excerpts in Chinese with English translation.
Identifiers: LCCN 2024049416 (print) | LCCN 2024049417 (ebook) | ISBN 9780674299986 (hardcover ; acid-free paper) | ISBN 9780674301719 (epub)
Subjects: LCSH: Chinese literature—220-589—History and criticism. | Health in literature. | Diseases in literature. | Chinese literature—Themes, motives. | Literature and medicine—China—History. | Buddhist literature—China—History and criticism.
Classification: LCC PL2284.5 .R53 2025 (print) | LCC PL2284.5 (ebook) | DDC 895.109/356109015--dc23/eng/20250129
LC record available at https://lccn.loc.gov/2024049416
LC ebook record available at https://lccn.loc.gov/2024049417

Index by the author

Printed by Books International, 22883 Quicksilver Drive, Dulles, VA 20166, USA (www.books intl.com). The manufacturer's authorized representative in the EU for product safety is LOGOS EUROPE, 9 rue Nicolas Poussin, 17000, La Rochelle, France (e-mail: Contact@logoseurope.eu).

In memory of my parents,
EDITH AND WALDEMAR ZIENER

Literature does its best to maintain that its concern is with the mind; that the body is a sheet of plain glass through which the soul looks straight and clear, and, save for one or two passions such as desire and greed, is null, and negligible and non-existent. On the contrary, the very opposite is true. All day, all night the body intervenes; blunts or sharpens, colours or discolours, turns to wax in the warmth of June, hardens to tallow in the murk of February. . . . But of all this daily drama of the body there is no record. People write always of the doings of the mind; the thoughts that come to it; its noble plans; how it has civilised the universe. . . . Those great wars which it wages by itself with the mind a slave to it, in the solitude of the bedroom against the assault of fever or the oncome of melancholia, are neglected. Nor is the reason far to seek. To look these things squarely in the face would need the courage of a lion tamer; a robust philosophy; a reason rooted in the bowels of the earth.

—Virginia Woolf, "On Being Ill"

CONTENTS

Acknowledgments	xiii
Editorial Conventions	xix

Introduction	1
The Rise of the Health Humanities	3
Concepts and Terminology	8
Health and Illness	8
Illness, Sickness, Disease	11
Scope and Content of This Book	15

PART I. BETWEEN SELF-CARE AND SELF-HARM: HEALTH AND CREATIVITY IN LIU XIE'S "NURTURING THE VITAL BREATH"   23

Writing about Nurturing Life: A Chinese Literary Tradition	26
The Vital Breath, or *qi*, as Dominant Factor for Literature and as Exhaustible Resource	29
Foundational Observations: Acknowledging Human Predisposition	32
Literary History as a History of Growing Mental Exhaustion	35
Accepting Differences in Age and Talent: Shallow Prodigies versus Overthinking Elders and Ducks on Tiptoe versus Long-Legged Cranes	38
Writers Wearing Out Their Spirit: Cautionary Tales	42
An Internal Digression: Tortured Writing in "Spirit Thought"	45
External Digressions: Death by Candlelight and Other Warnings	53
Introducing the Idea of Deliberate Self-Harm	57
External Digressions, Continued: Book Mania in China and Europe	61
Dealing with Writer's Block and Other Obstacles	67
The Encomium: Summation and Exaltation	75
Literati Bodies Between Sanctioned Self-Harm and Self-Preservation	76

x *Contents*

PART II. WRITING THE SICK SELF: AUTOBIOGRAPHICAL ACCOUNTS OF HEALTH AND ILLNESS   79

Chapter 1. The Body in the Paratext: Five Authorial Prefaces and a Letter   83

Sima Qian: Writing the Damaged Self   85

Wang Chong: Innate Vigor and Aging   92

Cao Pi: Self-Portrait of the Crown Prince as an Athlete and Warrior   96

Ge Hong: Physical Defects as Emblems of Distinction   100

Xiao Yi: Coming to Terms with Illness and Impairment   106

Chapter 2. Corresponding Bodies: Health and Illness in Epistolary Genres   116

Omitted, Obscured, Edited Out: Health and Illness in Letter-Writing   118

The Ailing Doctor: Huangfu Mi's Memorial Declining the Summons to Office   126

Not a Digression: Pretending to Be Sick in Chinese Literature   133

Wang Xizhi's Notes: Self-portrait of the Artist as a Sick Man   136

Life-Changing Illness in Tao Qian's Letter to His Sons   145

Illness and Recovery as a Time to Grow: Yu He's Memorial about Calligraphy   152

Far From Reticence: Shen Yue's Epistolary Modes of Self-Revelation   156

Selfhood, Public Persona, and Health in Early Medieval Self-Narratives   167

PART III. TEACHING FROM THE SICKBED: NOTIONS OF HEALTH AND ILLNESS IN THE *VIMALAKĪRTI SUTRA* AND CHINESE POETRY   171

Chapter 3. Health and Illness in the *Vimalakīrti Sutra*   173

Content and Narrative Features of the *Vimalakīrti Sutra*   176

Digression: Sickbed Visits in Early Chinese Literature—Everyday Practice and Exceptional Opportunity   179

Vimalakīrti Teaching about Illness   186

Contents   xi

Chapter 4. Emulating Vimalakīrti in Early Medieval Chinese Poetry   194

Poems Written While Lying Sick: An Overview   194

Xie Lingyun: "Lying Sick with Much Happy Leisure"   197

Huijing: "Suffering Brought Me to a Halt"   207

Wang Zhou: "In the City of Vaiśālī Lived an Elder"   209

Looking Ahead: The Flourishing of Sickbed Poetry in the Tang   212

Afterword   219

Abbreviations   223

Bibliography   225

Index   251

ACKNOWLEDGMENTS

Talking about illness is hard, but not talking about it can turn out to be even harder. It took me years and witnessing the different illnesses of different people to fully understand this. One moment stands out in my memory: a December afternoon at the Institute of East Asian Studies in Munich in 1996. Wolfgang Bauer and the students in his seminar had gathered for the traditional Christmas event before the break, chatting and enjoying cookies and orange juice. At the beginning of that term, we had learned that Bauer was critically ill. He had known for two years but had kept it from students and most colleagues, perhaps hoping for recovery. By the fall of 1996, this hope was gone. When Bauer announced he would teach a seminar on Chinese ideas of death and immortality, we gasped—realizing this was how he wanted to go. His final decline was swift. The weekly sessions of his seminar, intense and inspiring on many levels, showed us a man who still took deep and joyful pleasure in intellectual pursuits but also a man whose body was dwindling away, session by session. By mid-December, six weeks into the semester, he was starkly diminished and clearly bore the mark of death.

Bauer was my doctoral advisor, and we had a few conversations about my dissertation that last semester, but none of us ever broached the subject of his illness or his impending death. Our final meeting at that Christmas party was no different. The look of silence I exchanged with him across the room that afternoon has been on my mind ever since. I still regret missing the opportunity to tell him how grateful I felt to have been his student and how sad I was that we would have to part ways so soon—although he would probably have laughed and shrugged it off. He saw his role, as he once said, as that of a "Milchzahn," a baby tooth, that his students would

xiv *Acknowledgments*

eventually lose to make room for teeth of their own. Despite my regret about this lost opportunity to connect, I have also learned to treasure this failure. It helped me become more courageous in future conversations about illness and death—adding one more facet to the gratefulness I feel toward Wolfgang Bauer. In the decades that have passed since that December afternoon, I have had many, too many, occasions to talk about illness with my family and with dear friends and colleagues. I would like to thank them all for their wisdom and trust and for helping me sharpen my sensibilities when it comes to understanding what it means to be ill.

My own health problems have helped as well, of course. To cite just one example: at a time when I felt that I was getting close to finishing this book, the line "For who when healthy can become a foot?" from W. H. Auden's sonnet "Surgical Ward" took on unexpected concreteness after I broke my ankle during a bike ride. The lengthy and complex process of moving from relatively whole to partly broken to more or less whole again not only grounded me in a variant of the experiences I was reading and writing about, but it also provided yet another impetus to bridge what has often been described as two starkly different worlds or "kingdoms," to borrow a term made famous by Susan Sontag's 1978 essay "Illness as Metaphor."

Where Auden, in his 1939 sonnet, highlights the impossibility of fully realizing what it means to be sick when healthy and vice versa, Sontag is more concerned with the "dual citizenship" that we all inevitably hold "in the kingdom of the well and in the kingdom of the sick." It is this aspect of the human condition—the countless border crossings we all undertake throughout our lives between these two kingdoms, whether grudgingly or eagerly—that has always fascinated me, both in real life and in literature. In English literature, powerful lines of tradition connect Sontag to John Donne, who in 1624 may have been the first to speak of a disease as establishing "a kingdom, an empire in me" in his *Devotions upon Emergent Occasions*. Another line leads from Auden to Oliver Sacks, whose 1984 memoir *A Leg to Stand On* resonated with me even more profoundly once I had shared the experience expressed in the title. Other "friends in antiquity" from English and German literary history have made their way into the epigraphs and notes of this book, creating other kinds of bridges between the literary worlds I grew up in and those of Chinese literature that I have pursued for more than half of my life.

Acknowledgments xv

I am indebted to colleagues and friends for their generous support and advice in the years since I began working on this book. It grew on me slowly, evolving from my work on Chinese letter writing, where illness plays a prominent role. In hindsight, I can trace the inception of this book to the term I spent at the Needham Research Institute in 2011. The inspiring atmosphere of the institute (I am thinking especially of Geoffrey Lloyd, John Moffet, and Susan Bennet) and of Cambridge more generally (shaped indelibly by Michael Loewe and the late Joe McDermott) allowed me to see that the original research plan that had brought me to the institute—a study of the illness narratives in the letters of the early medieval calligrapher Wang Xizhi—was part of a much larger project. Discovering the latent possibilities of this project and pursuing concepts and narratives of illness and healing through Chinese literature and scholarship have kept me engaged for the last several years.

During that time, I accumulated many more debts than I could possibly mention here. The largest of these debts I owe is to Charles "Chip" Chace, my friend and collaborator during my first eleven years in Boulder. Chip helped me unlock Wang Xizhi's letters on illness—work that we eventually published in *T'oung Pao*. That article was the outcome of a truly collaborative process, where I benefited enormously from Chip's extensive knowledge and practical experience in all matters concerning Chinese medicine. Thinking with him has shaped my process and sharpened my mind in countless ways. Chip died in 2018, far too soon, following a brief but unrelenting illness. Although he never saw this book take shape, I still find myself consulting his wisdom, grateful that his inspiration endures.

I have also benefited from many generous invitations to present and discuss my research. I am thinking especially of Valerie Lavoix's *Wenxin diaolong* panel in Paris in 2012, Paula Varsano's West Coast Workshop on Premodern Chinese Literature and Culture in Berkeley in 2016, Meow Hui Goh's invitation to present my work at the Plenary Session of the American Oriental Society (AOS) in 2017, the workshop on "Illness, Healing, & Ritual in Chinese Religion" organized by Michael Puett and Robert Weller at Harvard in 2017, and Luke Bender's and Anna Shields's invitations to speak at Yale and Princeton in 2019. That same year, I also introduced my research at the Annual Chinese Medieval Studies Workshop organized by Wendy Swartz at Rutgers—although my appreciation for

xvi   *Acknowledgments*

the unique community of scholars and friends created by Wendy's unceasing enthusiasm extends to well before and after that year.

I also thank the journal *T'oung Pao*, where a part of chapter 2 first appeared in 2017 in the article "The Trouble with Wang Xizhi: Illness and Healing in a Fourth-Century Chinese Correspondence," coauthored by Charles Chace and me. Parts of chapters 3 and 4 appeared in 2020 in an earlier form as "Teaching from the Sickbed: Ideas of Illness and Healing in the *Vimalakīrti-nirdeśa-sūtra* and Their Reception in Medieval Chinese Literature," in *Buddhism and Healing in China and Japan: Global and Local Perspectives*, edited by C. Pierce Salguero and Andrew Macomber, and are used here with permission from University of Hawai'i Press.

Special thanks are due to friends and colleagues who, throughout the years, read drafts of parts of this book and generously shared their feedback with me, often saving me from embarrassing errors through their supreme scholarship and always providing rich food for thought. Paul Kroll, my esteemed colleague and friend here in Colorado, whose profound knowledge of literature never fails to impress me, has supported and inspired my research since I came to Boulder. He has always been willing to share his vast expertise in medieval Chinese literature and beyond, and I am deeply grateful for the many occasions when I could count on him as a critical yet congenial reader. I also thank Xiaofei Tian for her friendship and brilliant advice time and again: as a sympathetic discussant on a panel at one of the meetings of the Association of Asian Studies (AAS) where I introduced part of my research for this book, as an eagle-eyed editor of the article that grew out of this talk for a publication in *Nanyang Journal of Chinese Literature and Culture*, and as a highly perceptive and dedicated reader of the whole manuscript of this book. I was also fortunate to receive crucial comments from other generous readers, including Jan Nattier, C. Pierce Salguero, Meow Hui Goh, and Pablo A. Blitstein. All remaining errors are, of course, my own.

I am grateful to many other friends, colleagues, and teachers. From my graduate student days in Munich, Ute Engelhardt's classes first introduced me to Chinese medical culture, and Klaas Ruitenbeeck's seminar on Buddhist painting opened my eyes to the reception of the *Vimalakīrti Sutra* in China. Others from that time whose friendship and advice I value deeply include Anja Zuncke, Christoph Zuncke, Thomas Jansen, Daniela Küster Yew, Annette Kieser, and Roland Winkler. Following my graduation in 1998, Gudula Link in Kiel decisively shaped my understanding of what it means to be a professional in academia without losing sight of everything else in the world. I have cherished her friendship and guidance ever since.

Becoming part of the academic community in Chinese studies in the United States has been tremendously rewarding, from my colleagues and graduate students in the department to the vibrant academic scene beyond Colorado. I am grateful to have found such an inspiring intellectual home here. I have learned a tremendous amount from *all* my students and colleagues, but I can only name a few who have played a special role in this project. Thank you to David Atherton, Camille Byrne, Graham Chamness, Luke Coffee, Fletcher Coleman, Jackie Coombs, Heng Du, Kay Duffy, Kangni Huang, Qian Jia, Li Sijia, Clara Luhn, Yiyi Luo, Zhujun Ma, Tom Mazanec, Xiaojing Miao, Asuka Morley, Rahul Parson, Xiao Rao, Ann Roddy, Huizhi Wang, Yunxiao Xiao, and Kun You (all at one time or still in Boulder). I am also grateful to Dore J. Levy, J. Michael Farmer, Andrew Schonebaum, and Lik Hang Tsui (who joined me for a panel at the AAS in 2016), Cynthia Chennault, Monique Nagel-Angermann, and S. J. Zanolini (AAS 2019), and to Donald Harper, Marta Hanson, Hilary Smith, and the late Nathan Sivin, who have generously offered their advice and criticism. Last but not least, I would like to express my thanks to my friends and colleagues at the Early Medieval China Group, the AOS, and particularly the AOS Western Branch for welcoming close to a dozen presentations over the years on matters related to this book and for providing invaluable feedback to each one of them.

I also owe deep thanks to the team at the Harvard University Asia Center. Kristen Wanner has been an expert guide throughout, from the review process—where I benefited from the insightful comments of two exceptionally astute readers—all the way to production.

My gratitude to Matthias is boundless. Wise and funny, he has been helping me think about illness and to put illness out of our minds since the day in Jena in 1984 when we first opened that bottle of Pálinka—probably the world's best cure for the common cold.

Antje Richter
Boulder, Colorado, March 2024

EDITORIAL CONVENTIONS

I use the Pinyin system for romanizing Chinese throughout. Chinese characters are added when necessary, usually at the first mention of a name, title, or term, and at most of my translations. All translations, unless otherwise stated, are my own. With the exception of well-known romanized titles (e.g., *Liezi*), English glosses are generally used throughout the running text for the titles of non-English works and do not necessarily imply that a published English translation exists (though where one does, this is acknowledged explicitly). Translations of official titles are usually based on Hucker's *Dictionary of Official Titles*.

For citations of early medieval sources, I generally use Lu Qinli's collection of poetry and Yan Kejun's collection of prose, occasionally followed by modern annotated editions. Citations of Lu Qinli's collection indicate page numbers (e.g., Lu Qinli, *Xian Qin Han Wei Jin Nanbeichao shi*, 1786), while those to Yan Kejun's collection consist of the volume title followed by scroll (*juan* 卷) and page numbers, omitting the name of the compiler (e.g., *Quan Hou Han wen* 66.2b). Citations of standard histories are based on the Zhonghua shuju editions and indicate scroll and page numbers without including authors or compilers (e.g., *Shi ji* 130.3295). Citations of Liu Xie's *The Literary Mind and the Carving of Dragons* are based on the 1958 annotated edition by Fan Wenlan, *Wenxin diaolong zhu*, while those of the *Master of the Golden Tower* are to the 2011 annotated edition by Xu Yimin, *Jinlouzi jiaojian*—both indicate chapter and page number (e.g., *Wenxin diaolong* 26.494) and both are occasionally complemented by references to other editions of the text.

When referring to specific passages in Chinese texts, I adhere to the following conventions:

xx Editorial Conventions

- a colon (:) separates a physical volume in a set from a page number in that volume (e.g., Seneca, *Epistles*, 1:6–7);
- a period (.) separates a chapter or scroll number from a page number (e.g., *Shi ji* 130.3295);
- lowercase letters following page numbers indicate recto (a) and verso (b) pages or (in the case of the *Taishō* canon) horizontal registers (a, b, or c) (e.g., *Fayuan zhulin* 17.53.409b).

Introduction

Why have humans written about health and illness since the invention of writing? Is it only because illness often spelled death, or did the inevitable failings of our bodies provoke more profound reflections on the human condition? Answers to these questions lie in early writings from various cultures across the world, including Sumerian clay tablets, Egyptian papyri, and Mayan codices.[1] Among them are the earliest texts from ancient China, inscribed on turtle plastrons and ox scapulae.

The oracle bone inscriptions produced at the court of the Shang dynasty in the late second millennium BCE document dozens of individual health complaints, from toothaches to injuries and insomnia, often hinting at stories of successful or failed healing. Whether they concern diagnosis, prognosis, treatment, or cure, these records firmly embed health and illness into the worldview of the Shang court. They reveal that most maladies afflicting the king or royal consorts were believed to be caused by ancestors. Identifying the responsible ancestor through divination and appeasing them with appropriate sacrifices—also determined through prognostication—were essential steps in the healing process. The notion of ancestral influence on the health of the living was also instrumental in the assumption that calendrical factors played a significant role in the development of illnesses.

Our understanding of Shang beliefs and values would be infinitely poorer if the diviners had only documented agricultural practices and warfare, omitting the troubles inflicted by "having a body," as the *Laozi* 老子 puts it.[2] Despite their brevity and lack of detail, the oracle bone inscrip-

---

1. Representative studies include Biggs, "Medicine, Surgery, and Public Health"; Nunn, *Ancient Egyptian Medicine*; Ortiz de Montellano, "Disease, Illness, and Curing."

2. "The reason for the great troubles I have is that I have a body. If I had no body, what trouble could I have?" (吾所以有大患, 為吾有身。及我无身, 吾有何患, *Laozi* 13.49).

2   *Introduction*

tions convey the suffering and trepidation felt by the ill and those around them. Thus, they have the power to forge a visceral connection across more than three thousand years between us and these distant men and women.[3] This connection is deepened by our acute awareness of the limited curative means available at the Shang court, a situation that mirrors the limits of modern medicine, reminding us that, despite our hubris, we often face similar challenges today. Exploring these ancient illness narratives thus becomes an exercise in shared humanity, bridging the gap between the past and present.

While the oracle bone inscriptions, due to their elite provenance and divinatory character, represent only a tiny fraction of Chinese Bronze Age ideas about health and illness, the scope broadens in the first millennium BCE. In the more diverse and extensive Zhou dynasty (ca. 1046–256 BCE) sources available to us, illness narratives begin to appear in historical records, poetry, and Masters literature (*zishu* 子書), serving different rhetorical functions depending on genre and context. The *Zuo Tradition* (*Zuozhuan* 左傳), dating to the Warring States period (453–221 BCE), a prestigious historical text later incorporated into the Confucian canon, includes "more than forty-five consultations or descriptions of diseases," as Joseph Needham observed in 1966, alongside an even larger number of illness narratives.[4]

This development continues into the early empire (ca. 200 BCE–200 CE) and intensifies in early medieval China (ca. 200–600 CE), the period under scrutiny in this book. During early medieval China, health and illness emerged as crucial elements in stories of loyalty and friendship, treachery and murder, and personal and authorial identity. They appeared in historical accounts, biographies, autobiographical prefaces, personal letters, memorials requesting resignation from office, sickbed poems, liter-

---

This well-known adage plays on the multiple meanings of *shen* 身, which can refer to the body as well as to one's self and social status. See Qian Zhongshu's analysis of this dictum in *Guanzhui bian*, 427–32; also Egan, *Limited Views*, 274–81.

3. On illness in oracle bone inscriptions, see Keightley, "The 'Science' of the Ancestors," esp. 150–68; Li Zong-kun, "Cong jiaguwen kan Shangdai"; Song Zhenhao, "Shangdai de jihuan yiliao"; Cook, *Medicine and Healing*, 10–13.

4. Needham, *Clerks and Craftsmen*, 264. One of the *Zuo Tradition*'s case histories is introduced in the first chapter of Miranda Brown's *Art of Medicine in Early China*, 21–40; another can be found in Jeffrey Riegel's "Curing the Incurable."

Introduction 3

ary criticism, and religious scriptures. Metaphors of illness and health were employed abundantly throughout nonmedical literary texts, transcending genre, topic, or register.

Few of these narratives and tropes have been studied, despite their profusion and despite offering unique insights into the individual and social concerns of the communities in which they arose. This great, unfulfilled potential—aptly described by Virginia Woolf (1882–1941) as an "unexploited mine"[5]—is at the heart of this book. By examining how accounts of health and illness evolved and are represented in the literature of this period, this book seeks to understand their role in the literary and intellectual world of early medieval China. In doing so, it aims to round out our knowledge of this pivotal period in Chinese history, which saw the emergence of intellectual, literary, artistic, and other cultural phenomena that were to shape the country for centuries to come, including up to the present day. Among these are the rise of calligraphy, the inception of literary and art criticism, and the transformative encounter with Buddhism.

The Rise of the Health Humanities

First conceptualized in the second half of the twentieth century, the medical or health humanities have become a vibrant academic and applied discipline in the twenty-first century.[6] Working in two distinct directions, they connect with the medical professions in clinical training and practice

5. Woolf's essay "On Being Ill," first published in the quarterly *New Criterion* in January 1926, was reprinted in the American journal *The Forum* in April that year with the title "Illness: An Unexploited Mine."

6. Influential studies include Arthur Kleinman's *Illness Narratives* (1988) and Rita Charon's *Narrative Medicine* (2006). A handful of lively journals cover various parts of the field, including *Literature and Medicine* (founded in 1982), *Medical Humanities* (founded in 2000), and *Ars Medica* (founded in 2004). The comprehensive Literature, Arts, & Medicine Database (LitMed, https://medhum.med.nyu.edu) was established in 1993 at the New York University School of Medicine. Bachelor and graduate programs in the health humanities have proliferated and thrive at many North American universities, on which see Berry et al., "Health Humanities." As early as 2000, Ann Hawkins and Marilyn McEntyre published the anthology *Teaching Literature and Medicine*. There have also been more specialized projects, such as the "Hippocrates Initiative for Poetry and Medicine" at the University of Warwick (https://www.hippocrates-poetry.org).

4   Introduction

to enhance public health and health care while also exploring a range of health-related issues in the arts and humanities. This exploration spans from literary and artistic representations of health and illness to sociohistorical, philosophical, and bioethical questions.

The flourishing of the health humanities and the study of illness narratives in the last several decades in the West, alongside a significant increase in autobiographical works about health and illness across various art forms, has profoundly altered individual and cultural perceptions of illness in Western societies. Many socially imposed taboos surrounding illness and certain bodily aspects of human life have softened, giving way to greater freedom in the literary and artistic expression of physical and medical matters. These topics are increasingly recognized as essential parts of the human condition.[7] This expansion in legitimacy not only has generated new voices and images to express the diverse experiences of our bodies, but also has heightened awareness of the shortcomings in contemporary medical care and inspired efforts to improve it. That the voices of ill people are increasingly being heard in medical and cultural contexts is both a cause and a consequence of this development.

Although the health humanities have produced countless books and articles on a multitude of subjects in many Western cultures, they remain an emerging field in Chinese studies. The few books and articles published so far, whether in English or Chinese, focus primarily on the early modern, modern, and contemporary periods. Interest in illness narratives within Chinese studies began in the 1970s, around the same time the field was established in the West.

While Wolfgang Bauer's penetrating essay about notions of health and illness in the Masters text *Liezi* 列子 has long remained something of an isolated case, Wilt L. Idema's early inquiry into "passages of medical interest" in six novels from late imperial China was further developed in the

---

7. Books that contributed to this development and helped introduce key issues in the health humanities to mainstream intellectual discourse in the second half of the twentieth century include Michel Foucault's *The Birth of the Clinic* (*Naissance de la clinique*, 1973), Ivan Illich's criticism of contemporary institutionalized medicine in *Medical Nemesis* (1976), and Susan Sontag's challenge to the popular understanding of certain illnesses in *Illness as Metaphor* (1978).

1990s by scholars like Laurence G. Thompson and Christopher Cullen, who both focused on *Jin Ping Mei* 金瓶梅, and Dore Levy, who worked on *The Story of the Stone* (*Shitou ji* 石頭記 or *Honglou meng* 紅樓夢).[8] Remarkably, Levy's article on Baoyu's "attention deficit disorder" remains one of only half a dozen articles dedicated to Chinese literature in the journal *Literature and Medicine* over its more than forty-year history, and it is still the only article concerned with premodern Chinese literature in this venue.

The early 2000s saw the publication of Grace Fong's work on representations of illness in late imperial women's autobiography and poetry, as well as Qianshen Bai's exploration of early Qing calligraphic inscriptions and colophons that document the artists' physical handicaps and health problems, revealing the potential for studying illness narratives in Chinese visual arts.[9] Scholars have also examined medieval religious texts from a medical perspective, including Chi-tim Lai's work on Celestial Masters Daoism and C. Pierce Salguero's studies on medieval Buddhist biographies.[10] Several other medieval Chinese texts have been analyzed for their representations of health and illness, such as Wang Xizhi's 王羲之 (303–361) letters or sickbed poetry during the Tang dynasty (618–907).[11] In

8. Idema, "Diseases and Doctors" (1977); Bauer, "Krankheit und Heilung bei Liehtzu" (1980); Thompson, "Medicine and Religion" (1990); Cullen, "Patients and Healers" (1993); Levy, "'Why Bao-yu Can't Concentrate'" (1994) and *Ideal and Actual in "The Story of the Stone"* (1999), esp. chap. 3. See also Chi-hung Yim's article "Deficiency of Yin," also about *The Story of the Stone*, and Daria Berg's *Perceptions of Lay Healers*, a study of the novel *Marriage Destinies to Awaken the World* (*Xingshi yinyuan zhuan* 醒世姻緣傳), both published in 2000. Andrew Schonebaum's 2016 book *Novel Medicine* explores illness and healing in a broad swath of early modern vernacular fiction.

9. Fong, "'Record of Past Karma' by Ji Xian" and "Writing and Illness"; Bai, "Illness, Disability, and Deformity." In the visual arts, Ari Larissa Heinrich's *The Afterlife of Images* deserves mention here, although it is mostly concerned with medical texts and discourses. See also Wagner, "Visual Translations."

10. Lai, "Ideas of Illness"; Salguero, "Flock of Ghosts" and *Translating Buddhist Medicine*; Liu, Lo, and Chiu, "Lidai sengzhuan jibing xushu," all published 2010 and later.

11. Richter and Chace, "Trouble with Wang Xizhi"; Hu-Sterk, "Maladie et poésie." For Fan Ka-wai's study of reflections of health and illness in Bai Juyi's 白居易 (772–846) work, see *Zhonggu shiqi*, esp. 200–222, 250–58, 288–97.

6 Introduction

the last decade, the topic of illness has also gained attention in the field of Chinese history, exemplified by studies on sick leave policies.[12]

While it is possible to summarize Western publications on illness narratives in premodern Chinese literature in a mere paragraph, the situation becomes more complex when addressing modern and contemporary China. Over the last decade, there has been not only a growing number of articles exploring Chinese literary and cultural representations of illness in the twentieth and twenty-first centuries but also an increase in disciplinary awareness. Where the works on late imperial China I just mentioned seem to exist independently of each other, scholars working on modern representations of illness are keenly aware of their place within a global field.

This awareness is evident in the seven essays featured in the 2011 special issue of *Modern Chinese Literature and Culture*, edited by Carlos Rojas, titled "Discourses of Disease," as well as in Howard Choy's 2016 edited volume of the same title. Both collections offer reflections on the field in their introductions. Rojas emphasizes "the ways medical concepts and assumptions have been appropriated within *cultural* texts" and the influence these cultural texts have on "the popular understanding and imagination of health and disease."[13] Choy, who collected nine essays by yet another set of authors in his *Discourses of Disease*, focuses on "the ways in which our knowledge about disease ... is produced through discourse," and he highlights that "these discourses of disease also reveal the 'diseases' of discourse," that is, the challenges of illness writing, particularly in a society where public discourse is strictly controlled.[14]

In China, interest in the medical humanities (*yixue renwen* 醫學人文), narrative medicine (*xushi yixue* 敘事醫學), and illness narratives (*jibing xushi* 疾病敘事) has largely emerged in the twenty-first century, marked by the establishment of academic institutions and journals dedicated to

---

12. See Li Jianmin, *Shengming shixue*, 129–48; He Bian, "Too Sick to Serve"; Farmer, "Calling in Sick."

13. Rojas, "Introduction," 5.

14. Choy, *Discourses of Disease*, 10–11. For scholarship on modern and contemporary illness narratives, see also Pritzker, "Thinking Hearts, Feeling Brains"; Knight, "Cancer's Revelations"; Dauncey, *Disability in Contemporary China*.

these fields.[15] In 2020, Guo Liping 郭莉萍, who translated Rita Char-on's groundbreaking *Narrative Medicine* into Chinese in 2015, became the director of the new Center for Narrative Medicine at the School of Health Humanities at Peking University.[16] Guo has referred to 2011 as the "year zero" of narrative medicine in China, and indeed, publications have nota-bly increased since the 2010s.[17]

In China, the focus also predominantly lies on the modern and contem-porary periods, with some attention to the early modern period.[18] Illness narratives from before the Ming dynasty (1368–1644) have received little attention in both Chinese and Western scholarship. Straddling the divide between the humanities and the sciences, these narratives have been over-looked by both literary and medical historians. Historians of Chinese medicine have traditionally concentrated on the abundance of medical texts, whether transmitted or archaeologically retrieved. When they have ventured into nonmedical literature, it has usually been with specific inter-ests in mind, such as the practices of legendary physicians or the iden-tification of medicinal substances. Consequently, this type of research is typically conducted and read by medical rather than literary scholars.[19]

15. Peking University, for example, has published several editions of the Chinese Medi-cal Humanities Review (Zhongguo yixue renwen pinglun 中國醫學人文評論) series since 2007, and in 2008, it founded the Institute of Medical Humanities (Beijing daxue yixue renwen yanjiuyuan 北京大學醫學人文研究院). The monthly journal *Chinese Medical Humanities* (Zhongguo yixue renwen 中國醫學人文) was established in 2015, and the bimonthly journal *Narrative Medicine* (Xushi yixue 敘事醫學) first appeared in 2018.

16. Beijing daxue yixue renwen xueyuan 北京大學醫學人文學院, https://shh.bjmu.edu.cn.

17. Guo, "Overview of Narrative Medicine," 205. See also Hanson, "Narrative Medicine in China."

18. See the following monographs and edited volumes: Ye Shuxian, *Wenxue yu zhiliao* (1999); Tan Guanghui, *Zhengzhuang de zhengzhuang* (2007); Deng Hanmei, *Zhongguo xiandangdai wenxue zhong* (2012); Yim Chi-hung, *Qian Qianyi "Bingta xiaohan zayong" lunshi* (2012); Lin Xiurong, *Zhong shen xian ying* (2013); Gong Ailing, *Shenmei de jiushu* (2014); Cheng Guiting, *Jibing dui Zhongguo xiandai zuojia chuangzuo* (2015).

19. For example, scholarly attention has been paid to the healing methods reported in biographies of figures such as Bian Que 扁鵲 (fourth/fifth century BCE) and Chunyu Yi 淳于意 (216–ca. 150 BCE) (*Shi ji* 105.2785–94). For a recent study on the latter, see Brown, *Art of Medicine*, 41–86. Scholars have also addressed drugs or other medically rele-vant information mentioned in texts such as the *Canon of Mountains and Seas* (*Shanhai jing*

8 Introduction

On the other hand, scholars of Chinese literature often prioritize biographical, historical, or philological matters over the ailments mentioned in the texts of the period. Given the extensive corpora of transmitted literature from early and medieval China, studies of illness narratives published to date barely scratch the surface. As such, there remains significant untapped potential for further research in this area, which could offer deeper insights into the cultural and historical contexts of health and illness in medieval China.

Concepts and Terminology

Health and Illness

Recent Western attempts at conceptualizing health and illness have sparked complex and controversial debates, generating a substantial body of literature, particularly in the fields of philosophy of medicine, anthropology, and sociology. These discussions often explore health and illness alongside questions of normality, variation, and adaptability. While there is broad acknowledgment of the difficulty in defining either health or illness, the positions taken in these debates typically fall into two categories: naturalist (also known as objectivist or descriptive) and constructionist (also known as normative).[20]

Naturalists view illness as an objectively definable malfunction of a bodily subsystem, whereas constructionists emphasize that culturally and historically specific value judgments determine whether a malfunction is considered an illness. Philosophers of medicine have also proposed approaches that avoid the dichotomy of health and illness, suggesting, based on Ludwig Wittgenstein's (1889–1951) notion of "family resemblances," that health and illness are concepts "with blurred edges."[21]

山海經), the *Family Instructions of the Yan Clan* (*Yanshi jiaxun* 顏氏家訓), and others. See Gao Hao, "*Shanhaijing* 'Zhongshanjing' jibing jizai yanjiu"; Chen Xiaolin, "Qiantan *Yanshi jiaxun* de yixue sixiang."

20. See, e.g., Owsei Temkin's overview in the *Dictionary of the History of Ideas*, "Health and Disease," 365.

21. Wittgenstein, *Philosophical Investigations*, secs. 65–71. See also Sedgewick, "Nietzsche, Illness," esp. 320. Much of the extensive and heterogeneous recent scholarship on defini-

Introduction 9

Two significant voices that aligned with the latter school of thought in their rejection of clear-cut distinctions between health and illness are the French philosopher and physician Georges Canguilhem (1904–1995) and the German philosopher Hans Georg Gadamer (1900–2002). In 1988, Canguilhem argued that "health is not a scientific concept; it is a crude concept . . . which is not to say that it is trivial or out of reach, but simply rough and inexact." He characterized bad health as the "restriction of margins of organic security, the limitation of the power to tolerate and compensate for the aggressions of the environment," considering a body's adaptability the key criterion of health.[22] In his view, the healthy state "is the state which allows transition to new norms," whereas the pathological state "expresses the reduction of the norms of life tolerated by the living being, the precariousness of the normal established by disease."[23] Canguilhem thus stands in the tradition of the physician-historian Rudolf Virchow (1821–1902), who suggested that "the body's well-known marvelous ability to adjust indicates the dividing line between health and illness," meaning that illness begins when the body's regulatory mechanisms fail.[24]

Gadamer's approach is more from the patient's perspective than the physician's perspective. In his article "On the Hiddenness of Health," he asserts that "health does not actually present itself to us," whereas illness "imposes itself on us as something threatening and disruptive which we seek to be rid of." Although he explicitly refers to physiological adaptability, he describes health in terms consistent with this approach, as "the rhythm of life, a permanent process in which equilibrium reestablishes itself."[25]

---

tions of health and illness is introduced in Carel and Cooper, *Health, Illness, and Disease.*

22. Canguilhem, "Health: Crude Concept," 469, 473. Referring to the impossibility of perfect health, the Bavarian comedian Karl Valentin (1882–1948) said, "Not being sick at all isn't healthy either." Valentin, *Gar ned krank is a ned g'sund.*

23. Canguilhem, *Normal and Pathological*, 228.

24. Virchow, "Über die heutige Stellung der Pathologie," 93. In his 1869 talk, Virchow lays out his understanding of illness as a physiological process, that is, in modern terminology, as functional rather than ontological.

25. Gadamer, "On the Enigmatic Character of Health," 107, 105, 114. The title of this essay in the published English translation does not accurately represent Gadamar's original title: "Über die Verborgenheit der Gesundheit."

10   *Introduction*

Texts and manuscripts from early and early medieval China reveal the coexistence of different approaches to health and illness without explicitly defining either concept.[26] The oldest and most enduring etiology, evident in the oracle bone inscriptions of the Shang dynasty and remaining relevant throughout Chinese history, attributes illness to ancestral spirits and other demonic entities that invade the body and need to be exorcised to restore health.

Starting in the late Warring States period, a different etiology began to develop, although it never fully displaced the demonological approach. Often described as naturalistic or correlative, this new approach viewed health as a state in which a person's vital breath or energies (*qi* 氣) were balanced, constantly and freely moving within the body, and harmoniously interacting with the *qi* of heaven and earth.[27] External pathogens, especially climatic excesses, and internal pathogenic factors, including inappropriate behaviors and mental states, could disrupt this microcosmic balance by disturbing the flow and level of a body's *qi*, leading to stagnation, obstruction, depletion, or repletion of vital energies. In this view, illness was the result of an energetic imbalance.[28]

Although demonic and correlative approaches to health and illness were partly in competition, they also continually interacted with each other. This interplay makes it difficult to neatly separate an ontological understanding of illness, which grants illnesses a quasi-independent existence, from a functional or physiological understanding, which assumes illness to be specific to the person suffering from it.[29]

In early and medieval China, healing was mostly in the hands of nonspecialists.[30] Advertising his book *Prescriptions from the Jade Case* (*Yuhan fang* 玉

---

26. Sivin, *Traditional Medicine*, 95; Ma Boying, *Zhongguo yixue wenhua shi*, 118.

27. Attempts at defining and translating this broad term abound. See, e.g., Sivin, *Traditional Medicine*, 46–53, and *Health Care in Eleventh-Century China*, 19, 73 (Sivin does not translate *qi* but uses a transliteration); Harper, *Early Chinese Medical Literature*, 77 ("vapor").

28. Overviews from different perspectives and with different emphases include Sivin, *Traditional Medicine*, 95–111; Harper, *Early Chinese Medical Literature*, 68–76; Salguero, *Translating Buddhist Medicine*, 23–29; Li, "They Shall Expel Demons."

29. Harper, "Conception of Illness," 210n2.

30. On the greater reliance on family treatments in early medieval China, see Li Jianmin, "Zhongguo yixue shi yanjiu," 215.

函方), Ge Hong 葛洪 (ca. 283–343) seems to have addressed such an audience when he promoted self-diagnosis and self-treatment based on his work as superior to relying on physicians. According to Ge, physicians were not only difficult to find but often also of questionable competence and driven by a thirst for glory and riches.[31] When self-therapy or family therapy failed, healers from a variety of backgrounds would be consulted. Ge Hong singled out scholar-physicians (*yi* 醫), who practiced different strands of classical, elite medicine, but there was also a variety of popular and elite religious healers, including shamans (*wu* 巫), ritual masters (*fangshi* 方士), and Daoist and Buddhist healers.[32] The historical account of the final illness of the poet Shen Yue 沈約 (441–513) illustrates the variety of healing expertise that could be summoned when a member of the elite fell ill: first, a shaman was called in; then, Shen sent for a Daoist priest to confess his sins and petition the celestial authorities; finally, the emperor sent his personal physician.[33]

Illness, Sickness, Disease

Despite the conceptual and terminological differences in contemporary Western discourse, many scholars writing in English distinguish between the terms "illness," "disease," and "sickness," while acknowledging that these terms may overlap in meaning. "Illness" refers to the subjective, individual experience of being unwell; "disease" pertains to a particular pathological process that can be objectively diagnosed by a medical expert; and "sickness" encompasses the social ramifications of an illness or disease. As Kenneth M. Boyd succinctly puts it, "Whether or not someone is ill, is something the person concerned ultimately must decide for him- or herself. But whether that person has a disease or is sick is something doctors and others may dispute."[34]

31. *Baopuzi neipian* 15.247. Ge Hong will be discussed in part II.

32. See C. Pierce Salguero's description of what he calls the "religiomedical marketplace" in *Translating Buddhist Medicine*, 60–66. Nathan Sivin's characterization of the diversity of healing in *Health Care in Eleventh-Century China* focuses on a later period in Chinese history, but many of his astute observations are relevant to early medieval China too.

33. *Liang shu* 13.243. For more on Shen Yue, see part III.

34. Boyd, "Disease, Illness," 11. See also two 2017 overviews of the wide range of approaches to these terms: Hofmann, "Disease, Illness, and Sickness," and Hausman, "Health and Well-Being."

12   *Introduction*

Analogous distinctions have been made between impairment, disability, and handicap.[35] While these differentiations hold significant sociological and political relevance today, their applicability to premodern discourses has been questioned. Andrew Cunningham, discussing how to identify diseases in history, noted that "at all times and places, in all societies, disease identity, and especially the cause dimension of it, is going to be an expression of how people in that society think the world functions."[36]

The medical historian Ma Boying, who translated "disease" as *jibing* 疾病, "illness" as *binghuan* 病患 or *bingtong* 病痛, and "sickness" as *huanbing* 患病, observed that Chinese medical sources and other early Chinese texts do not support a clear differentiation between these terms.[37] I have found the same to be true in my own translations and discussions of early and early medieval Chinese literature. Nevertheless, I use the English terms "illness" and "sickness," even if it is not always possible to differentiate between them. I generally avoid the term "disease," as it is closely associated with the currently dominant biomedical approach, which tends toward a descriptive understanding of disease as independent of cultural or historical context. To maintain awareness of the specificity of the texts under consideration, I will instead use the less loaded term "disorder" when an early or medieval Chinese text refers to specific kinds of ailments diagnosable by a medical authority.[38]

However, there are no easy rules for translation. Mediating between the numerous Classical Chinese and English terms that can denote health and well-being on the one hand and ill health and physical suffering on the other requires close attention to genre, register, and context to match the subtle differences in meaning found in early or early medieval Chinese texts. The familiar terms for health and illness in Classical Chinese exemplify the semantic challenges very well. Not only do words such as *bing* 病 and *ji* 疾, which commonly denote illness, possess extensive metaphorical potential, they can also refer to a wide range of issues beyond health,

35. See Mervyn Susser's "capsule history" of these terms in his "Editorial: Disease, Illness."

36. Cunningham, "Identifying Disease in the Past," 14.

37. Ma Boying, *Zhongguo yixue wenhua shi*, 118–19.

38. On these terminological difficulties, see also the chapter "Health and Disorder" in Sivin, *Traditional Medicine*, esp. 95–100, and Smith, *Forgotten Disease*, 31–35.

Introduction   13

including poverty, personal defects, stylistic faults, resentment, criticism, envy, and velocity.

When related specifically to health, *bing* and *ji* can describe various issues, from minor indispositions to serious general conditions and specific medical disorders.[39] Annotating a passage in the *Analects* (*Lunyu* 論語), the early medieval scholar He Yan 何晏 (190–249) cites the Han dynasty commentator Bao Xian 包咸 (6–65 BCE), who defined *bing* 病 as a "serious illness" (疾甚).[40] Early Chinese medical texts suggest that *bing* was used classificatorily to denote "a morbid condition which can be given a name."[41] In early medieval literary texts, it is often impossible to discern a semantic difference between *bing* and *ji*. Some texts may differentiate between them terminologically or stylistically, with *ji* sometimes preferred as a more elegant or euphemistic choice in elevated registers, though this is by no means a general rule.

Other terms for illness in general, such as *mo* 瘼 and *ke* 痾, and even those for specific health disorders, also possess significant metaphorical potential (even if not to the same degree as *ji* and *bing*). An example of this can be found in the *Outer Chapters* of Ge Hong's *The Master Who Embraces Simplicity* (*Baopuzi* 抱朴子). Ge Hong uses various terms for illness (*ji* 疾, *bing* 病) apparently interchangeably, alongside a specific disorder (*feng* 風, pathogenic wind), to create an extended analogy comparing the effects of drinking alcohol to a medical disorder caused by a climatic excess.[42]

A second semantic issue involves the figurative and often euphemistic use of nonspecific, inoffensive words to denote unpleasant and particularly graphic ailments.[43] For example, the term *xia* 下 (downward) is used to

39. Martha Chiu offers an excellent exposition of the semantic multivalence of the term *bing* and its implications on medical understanding in "Mind, Body, and Illness," 171–77. For early Chinese, see also the entries for *bing* and *ji* in the *Thesaurus Linguae Sericae*.

40. *Lunyu* 9.12; also see 7.35.

41. Harper, *Early Chinese Medical Literature*, 72–73.

42. *Baopuzi waipian* 24.579.

43. Early Chinese texts and commentaries offer various euphemisms to describe the illnesses of individuals from different social classes. He Xiu's 何休 (d. 175 CE) commentary to the *Gongyang Tradition* (*Gongyang zhuan* 公羊傳) explains the terminology used: the son of heaven is described as "indisposed" (*bu yu* 不豫), feudal lords as "burdened" (*fu zi* 負茲), and grandees as "[worn out] like dogs and horses" (*quan ma* 犬馬). This can be found in *Chunqiu Gongyang zhuan zhushu* 5.28 (Huan 16). A fragment from the *Comprehensive*

14 Introduction

refer to diarrhea. Words related to health follow a similar pattern, referring to an ideal state of microcosmic balance with terms like *ping* 平 (level, normal) and even less specific terms such as *ke* 可 (passable) and *jia* 佳 (fine).[44]

The language of health and illness in early and medieval Chinese literature is not only rich and metaphorically potent but also replete with explicit comparisons and analogies between the body, state, and cosmos.[45] Illness metaphors are used to describe societal ills; for example, a serious political threat to the state might be characterized as "an illness of the heart or abdomen" (心腹之病) rather than as a relatively harmless "skin disorder" (皮膚之疾).[46] Additionally, societal metaphors elucidate bodily functions, such as describing the heart as the ruler overseeing bodily processes.[47]

Health and illness are also conceptualized through semantic fields in catalogs of desirable and undesirable matters found in many texts, from the Confucian canon to Buddhist scriptures. These lists often associate illness with poverty and other evils, while health is linked with beauty, longevity, and other blessings. One notable example is the lists of "Five Happinesses" (*wu fu* 五福) and "Six Extremities" (*liu ji* 六極) in the chapter "The Great Plan" ("Hong fan" 洪範) of the *Book of Documents* (*Shangshu* 尚書), which encompass both good health and illness. In Buddhist scriptures, an extensive list of afflictions and difficulties befalls those who disparage the *Lotus Sutra* (*Saddharma puṇḍarīka sūtra*; *Miaofa lianhua jing* 妙法蓮華經).[48]

Notions of health and illness in early and early medieval Chinese liter-

---

Discussions in the White Tiger Hall (*Baihutong* 白虎通, ca. first century CE) presents slightly different wording; see *Baihutong shuzheng*, 599–600.

44. See Sivin, *Traditional Medicine*, 95–96; Richter and Chace, "Trouble with Wang Xizhi," 42. Sivin has also highlighted that the names of disorders that appear in historical writing were often those used by family members and may not have been the names a physician might have chosen. See *Health Care in Eleventh-Century China*, 45.

45. For extended analogies of the body politic in terms of illness and healing, see *Hanfeizi* 21.396–97; *Qian Hanji* 6.52; *Lunheng* 80.1107; *Baopuzi waipian* 14.331.

46. *Wu Yue chunqiu* 5.12.

47. *Huangdi neijing Suwen* 8.76. This is described in more detail for early China and the *Inner Canon* tradition in Lloyd and Sivin, *Way and the Word*, 214–26, and, for Buddhist medical metaphors, in Salguero, *Translating Buddhist Medicine*, chap. 3, esp. 67–83. See also Rothschild, "'Tumor-Rash Axiom.'"

48. *Shangshu* 12.81a; *Miaofa lianhua jing* 3.15c–16a.

Introduction 15

ature vary widely based on genre, register, and specific context. They rarely align clearly with any specific medical tradition, whether classical correlative approaches or religious ones. Consequently, reflections on concepts, terminology, metaphors, and translation will recur throughout this book. By examining individual literary texts, this approach aims to do justice to the diverse health-related notions preserved in many works, which have not yet been adequately explored.

Scope and Content of This Book

Exploring early medieval notions of health and illness in Chinese literary texts, this book seeks to answer a range of questions. How did writers of the period understand health and illness? In what ways did they integrate health into notions of self and social role? How did early medieval authors reflect on the personal experience of health and illness? On what occasions and in which genres was writing about physical matters considered appropriate? What could have been the appeal of fashioning oneself as sick? Were there literary conventions that governed writing about illness? What are the rhetorical and performative functions of these narratives? How is writing about health and illness related to reflections on the role of literature and its development in early medieval China?

An important initial finding of this inquiry has been the realization that illness accounts outside of medical literature and other specialized texts, such as biographies of healers, are relatively rare and restricted to certain contexts. If body parts or complaints are mentioned in a literary text, it is usually safe initially to assume that they are used as metaphors. For instance, Liu Xie 劉勰 (ca. 465–ca. 532) describes his work in literary criticism as "splitting muscles and dividing veins" (擘肌分理). A headache (*shouji* 首疾) might symbolize separation from a loved one in a song. Moreover, words for "illness" might be used metaphorically for all kinds of undesirable matters, as we mentioned earlier.[49] Actual illness is so rarely mentioned in high-register literary texts that one suspects the topic was

49. See *Wenxin diaolong* 50.727; *Mao shi* no. 62, "My Husband" ("Bo xi" 伯兮); Wang Sengru 王僧孺 (465–522), "Letter to He Jiong" ("Yu He Jiong shu" 與何炯書), in *Quan Liang wen* 51.4b.

16   *Introduction*

shunned. Xiaofei Tian has observed that in classical Chinese literature, "disease and death are rarely treated in great detail" but are "described in vague, general terms; except in medical works, the depiction of diseases is highly conventionalized."[50] Similar taboos were at work in other premodern literary cultures.[51]

In early and medieval China, a specific reason for the scarcity of illness accounts may have been the widespread association of illness with guilt and moral deficiency. When an illness or impairment could prevent an individual from participating in rituals, deny them access to an official career, or hinder their promotion, such circumstances were less likely to be documented in biographical or autobiographical accounts. This may also explain why health reports in China are seen more frequently in certain contexts, such as pleading illness to justify retirement. Other areas where it appears to have been permissible to write about illness include excessive dedication to study or mourning one's parents, both of which could be subsumed under the social value of filial duty. However scarce narratives of health and illness are in early and medieval Chinese literature, "mountains of reliable information survive upon which to build credible profiles of bodies in the past," as medical historian Roy Porter highlighted in his 2001 overview of the field.[52]

The literary landscape of early and medieval China was not divided by rigid generic boundaries—belles lettres here, technical literature there. Medical texts, though primarily addressed to scholar-physicians, were widely read in educated circles.[53] However, this book does not privilege Chinese medical texts, citing them only occasionally, nor does it adopt a medical perspective by attempting to diagnose or identify specific complaints or treatments in medical terms. It also avoids focusing on representations of medical encounters, which emphasize physicians, healers, and the medical arts.

Instead, this book centers on texts that represent lay perspectives on health and illness—the experiences of those who are ill and the people

50. Tian, *Beacon Fire and Shooting Star*, 180.
51. Cook, "Illness and Life Writing," 457.
52. Porter, "History of the Body Reconsidered," 235.
53. On the rise of medical texts, their audience, and related questions, see Harper, *Early Chinese Medical Literature*, 42–67.

Introduction 17

around them who were tasked with nursing them or were otherwise affected.[54] Illness is understood broadly, encompassing mild and critical illnesses, injuries, ailments of old age, temporary and chronic conditions, impairments, and disabilities, which often overlap and blend into each other. The main criterion for early and medieval Chinese texts to deem an illness noteworthy appears to have been the interruption of everyday life, where a condition was life-threatening, made participation in expected activities impossible, or had other social ramifications.

The most tangible analytical focus is autobiographical, reading narratives of health and illness as documents of their authors' struggle to make sense of and legitimize their physical conditions—an aspect of life largely avoided or marginalized in Chinese self-writing. The second, equally important analytical focus is rhetorical, uncovering the unspoken conventions of writing about illness and the changes these conventions underwent. Drawing attention to the foundation of literature in the lived experience of their creators' individual bodies, with their peculiar challenges, contributes to a fuller understanding of the conditions of literary production in early medieval China. Knowledge about the rhetorical functions of illness narratives, both within their surrounding texts and in their cultural contexts, sheds new light on historical, literary, and intellectual developments in early medieval China.

This book also pursues metacritical questions. The first concerns genre conventions, particularly the transmutability of narratives or motifs across different literary genres or registers. The second addresses the role of the literary imagination. Narratives about health and illness in early medieval Chinese literature are shaped by the genre and the social sphere in which they were created, performed, and received. Personal correspondence in free prose, literary treatises, official communications in ornate parallel prose, historical writing, Masters literature, classical poetry, and Buddhist scriptures each follow distinct conventions and employ specific stylistic registers, resulting in narratives of health and illness that differ in character. For instance, a poem written while lying sick might only allude to illness obliquely, whereas writers of personal letters could openly complain about digestive trouble. Exploring across genres is promising because authors

---

54. Porter made an early plea for this approach in his 1985 article "The Patient's View."

18 Introduction

rarely restricted themselves to a single genre, often engaging with multiple forms to suit different social contexts. Genre differences also highlight the role of literary imagination in creating narratives about health and illness. This becomes particularly evident in recurring narratives and motifs, such as sickbed visits or feigned illnesses, that appear in various texts.

The most general and ambitious goal of this book is to contribute to the establishment of early medieval Chinese literature as part of "world literature." Many of the urgent concerns driving literary production, reception, and discourse today are present in Chinese texts as well, making it worthwhile to include them, in all their historical and cultural specificity, within current dominant frameworks of understanding. Illness is particularly suited to this goal. It is a multifaceted topic in historical sources, allowing for discussion from diverse conceptual angles, intersecting with fields outside of literary studies proper and outside of Chinese studies. These fields include the history of medicine, anthropology, religion, philosophy, and ethics—each characterized by a profusion of competing approaches. Although this historical and disciplinary complexity is challenging, it also signifies the enormous potential for discourse across academic fields.

The three parts of this book trace reflections on health and illness across the diverse literary landscape of early medieval China. While the primary focus is on texts from the period of disunion (ca. 200–ca. 600 CE), texts from early China (ca. 800 BCE–ca. 200 CE) also play an important role. These earlier texts prefigure many early medieval ideas and persist in the web of allusions that permeates early medieval literature. Each part focuses on different genres—literary criticism, self-writing in the form of prefaces and correspondence, historical narratives, religious scriptures, and poetry—investigating various facets of health and illness as they emerge in these genres or individual texts.

Part 1, "Between Self-Care and Self-Harm: Health and Creativity in Liu Xie's 'Nurturing the Vital Breath,'" centers on the translation, annotation, close reading, and in-depth contextualization of the essay "Nurturing the Vital Breath" ("Yang qi" 養氣), chapter 42 of Liu Xie's compendium of literary thought and criticism, *The Literary Mind and the Carving of Dragons* (*Wenxin diaolong* 文心雕龍). Liu Xie's intricately composed essay is the first transmitted text to describe writing not only in terms of the intellectual effort required but also in terms of the physiological toll it can take on the writer. Since writing was a key part of the work and competency expected of the educated class in early medieval China, Liu Xie takes what we might call an occupational approach to the health of his fellow writers. Although "Nurturing the Vital Breath" ostensibly focuses on avoiding illness and ensuring a long and healthy productive life in the service of literature, the essay simultaneously evokes the destructive potential of writing and the harmful effects that mental exertion can have on a writer's health and well-being. Exploring the main ideas of Liu Xie's text, along with the wealth of historical figures and narratives associated with self-care and self-harm evoked throughout the essay, reveals a rich tapestry of Chinese elite attitudes toward health and illness.

Part II, "Writing the Sick Self: Autobiographical Accounts of Health and Illness," shifts to reflections on the individual experience of being in good or ill health. These experiences were expressed in various forms of literary self-expression that follow distinct genre-specific conventional patterns, including authorial postfaces, correspondence, and religious confessions. In autobiographically inspired authorial postfaces, reflections on illness and other physical challenges are usually incorporated into a self-narrative of strength and grandeur. Intimate letters about illness differ from official communications, where health reports often justify retirement. The instrumentalization of real or feigned illness as an accepted excuse to escape onerous official, social, or familial obligations is a powerful motif throughout early medieval literature. Examining the intertextual relations between these health reports alongside the historical development of the genres in which they appear reveals a change in literary conventions regarding first-person illness narratives, suggesting that health and illness were increasingly accepted as part of an author's public persona and as subjects of refined literature (wen 文).

Part III, "Teaching from the Sickbed: Notions of Health and Illness in the *Vimalakīrti Sutra* and Chinese Poetry," turns to sickbed visits as a prominent social aspect of ill health and a recurrent topic in early and early medieval Chinese literature. It describes patterns of this topic's use for different rhetorical purposes, with a focus on the *Vimalakīrti Sutra*, one of the most popular and influential Buddhist scriptures in medieval China. This sutra revolves around the householder Vimalakīrti, who famously manifested sickness to create an opportunity to engage those who gathered at his sickbed in discussions of Mahāyāna Buddhist teachings, ultimately guiding them toward enlightenment. The *Vimalakīrti Sutra* addresses illness both by taking a sickbed visit as its main setting and by offering explicit observations about the human body's propensity for illness and decay. This part explores Buddhist notions of health and illness expressed in this sutra and examines how Chinese writers engaged with the text from the fourth century onward. The *Vimalakīrti Sutra* enriched Chinese literature and culture in at least three significant ways: through its powerful poetic descriptions of illness, its nondualistic approach to health and illness, and its sickbed setting—all of which interacted with indigenous Chinese traditions and helped make health and illness more acceptable as poetic topics in China.

While the three parts of this book do not present a continuous narrative arc, their arrangement and internal composition are designed to help the reader navigate the extensive array of texts and authors discussed. Beginning with a translation and analysis of Liu Xie's "Nurturing the Vital Breath" offers an effective introduction to crucial ideas about health and illness in early and early medieval Chinese writing. Liu Xie's highly allusive parallel prose condenses many of these ideas, and unpacking his historical and textual references provides an overview of the semantic field, introducing the elite lens on health and illness that shapes the literary sources and our understanding of the period. Where part I revolves around an essay from the early sixth century, part II introduces a variety of autobiographical texts in different genres from the first century BCE to the sixth century CE. This part progresses roughly chronologically, presenting self-reflections on health and illness and examining how the chosen literary forms—mainly paratexts and correspondence—influence the physical self-representation in the texts. Part III considers the literary and cultural transformations prompted by the Chinese encounter with Buddhism, especially from the fifth century onward. This part expands the range of genres reflecting on health and illness to include Buddhist scripture and Chinese poetry. Unlike part I, which looks into the past to explore the literary background shaping Liu Xie's view on literati health and illness, part III looks ahead to gauge the impact of early medieval literary developments on subsequent centuries, including the establishment of a poetic space for personal expressions of health and illness during the Tang.

Health and the Art of Living presents a broad spectrum of reflections on health and illness in literary texts from early and early medieval China. These reflections integrate with and significantly complement our understanding of early medieval literary and intellectual history. The rise of illness narratives across genres indicates that ideas of selfhood and authorship evolved alongside notions of what constituted refined literature. While this book aims to represent a substantial portion of the literary landscape of early medieval China, it also highlights the vast number of extant texts still awaiting recognition and analysis for their narratives of health and illness. Given the richness of Chinese literature and the relevance of this topic at the intersection of literature and medicine, further discoveries are to be expected, particularly in historical writing, biography, and religious literature, both Daoist and Buddhist.

PART ONE

Between Self-Care and Self-Harm

Health and Creativity in Liu Xie's "Nurturing the Vital Breath"

> If we melt away our vital energies and cramp the harmonious flow of our vital breath, then holding the writing tablet will hasten our death, and moistening the brush will hack away at our life.
>
> —Liu Xie, *Literary Mind*

Ideas and practices of nurturing life (*yangsheng* 養生) have long been recognized as central to ancient Chinese thought. At one end of the spectrum, these practices revolve around the smooth regulation and prudent expenditure of one's vital breath to prevent illness, infirmity, and premature aging. At the other end, they go well beyond such modest goals and strive for extreme, if not infinite, longevity and the transcendence of mortal life. There is a rich tradition of describing these practices in various literary and artistic forms, and the core ideas they express are often, and rightly, cited as examples of enduring ancient Chinese wisdom.

The counterpart to this tradition of self-care is an equally solid, if less frequently emphasized, tradition of tolerating and even encouraging self-harm for a higher purpose, such as loyalty, filial duty, or scholarly learning. The most prominent early medieval text in which these strands are woven together is the essay "Nurturing the Vital Breath" ("Yang qi" 養氣), which forms chapter 42 of Liu Xie's monumental early sixth-century compendium

24   Part One

of literary thought, *The Literary Mind and the Carving of Dragons* (*Wenxin diaolong* 文心雕龍).

In "Nurturing the Vital Breath," Liu warns of the health risks associated with literary and scholarly writing—activities that were central to the intellectual work expected of scholar-officials in early medieval China. He proposes methods to mitigate these occupational hazards and thrive as creators of literature. Liu also integrates warnings about mental exhaustion and suggestions for a healthier approach to writing into broader critical concerns. Although "Nurturing the Vital Breath" is ostensibly dedicated to avoiding illness and ensuring a healthy, productive life in the service of literature, it also carries a strong undercurrent of cautionary tales about scholarly self-harm leading to illness, injury, and premature death.

This ambivalence, along with Liu's heavy reliance on literary and historical allusions, makes Liu Xie's essay an ideal starting point for our inquiry into reflections on health and illness in early medieval literature: not only does "Nurturing the Vital Breath" describe the literati concern with health and well-being as a struggle between self-care and self-harm, it also highlights the illness narratives that had become canonical in the course of the Han dynasty and continued to shape reflections on health and illness in literature of the early medieval period.

The first part of this book situates "Nurturing the Vital Breath" within Liu's *Literary Mind* and the broader Chinese literary tradition. It presents an annotated translation and close reading of Liu's essay, occasionally interrupted by "digressions" that extend the inquiry to related texts, including other chapters of *Literary Mind*, other works of Chinese Masters literature, and Western texts on scholarly health. This in-depth contextualization helps develop an understanding of early medieval literati approaches to health and well-being beyond *Literary Mind*, providing an entranceway into the illness narratives analyzed later in the book. Remarkably, much of the biographical material adduced in this first part is fragmentary and only transmitted in commentaries and commonplace books (*leishu* 類書, also known as encyclopedias). It is uncertain whether this is coincidental or if texts dealing with health and illness were less likely to be preserved in other works.

Since the ideas in "Nurturing the Vital Breath" are significant elements of Liu's theory of literary creativity, the chapter is often treated as a supplement to chapter 26, "Spirit Thought" ("Shen si" 神思) of the same work.[1] However, these chapters have been received quite differently. "Spirit Thought" has garnered extensive scholarly attention and may well be the most famous exposition in *Literary Mind*. In contrast, "Nurturing the Vital Breath" has received much less recognition, likely because it addresses the darker side of writing, including its destructive potential and the limitations writers face.[2]

This relative lack of attention is surprising, as "Nurturing the Vital Breath" is the first transmitted text to describe writing not only as an intellectual activity but also in terms of the physiological toll it takes on writers. While many ideas in "Spirit Thought" echo Lu Ji's 陸機 (261–303) "Rhapsody on Literature" ("Wen fu" 文賦), "Nurturing the Vital Breath" breaks new ground by conceptualizing literary creativity as rooted in the writer's physiology. "Spirit Thought" celebrates the lofty idea of the creative spirit "racing ahead with the wind and clouds" (與風雲而並驅),[3] representing something of the *yang* 陽 to the *yin* 陰 of "Nurturing the Vital Breath," which focuses on the physiological conditions of the writing process and acknowledges such mundanities or embarrassments as personal hygiene and writer's block.

Liu Xie claimed comprehensiveness for *Literary Mind*. In reviewing the efforts of his predecessors, such as Lu Ji and Cao Pi 曹丕 (187–226, Emperor Wen of the Wei dynasty 魏文帝, r. 220–226), Liu acknowledged their success in addressing individual issues, but he also criticized them for merely "illuminating nooks and gaps" instead of "keeping an eye on the main avenues" (各照隅隙, 鮮觀衢路).[4] Indeed, *Literary Mind* is the most extensive and systematic examination of literature transmitted from early

1. See, e.g., Huang Kan's judgment in his 1926 commentary, *Wenxin diaolong zhaji* 42.204. Scholars insisting on the autonomy of "Nurturing the Vital Breath" are rare, although eminent figures such as Wang Gengsheng are among them. See Wang, "Liu Xie *Wenxin diaolong*."

2. Qi Liangde's bibliography *Wenxin diaolong xue fenlei suoyin*, which covers the period from 1907 to 2005, lists 249 articles on "Spirit Thought," compared with only 31 articles on "Nurturing the Vital Breath." A search of the China Academic Journals Database at https://www.eastview.com/resources/journals/caj/ yields many more articles but a similar ratio.

3. *Wenxin diaolong* 26.494.

4. *Wenxin diaolong* 50.726.

26 *Part One*

or medieval China. Liu's work takes literature with utmost seriousness, encompassing a broader range of manifestations than acknowledged by earlier or contemporary authors and addressing the entire literary process from preparation and creation to reception and transmission. Liu Xie's reverence for literature is evident in his own mastery of the art he set out to explain: the deeper we delve into his text, the more we discover its brilliant construction. The literary shapedness of *Literary Mind* is truly striking, from its ornate parallel style and the concentration of allusions in every passage to the dense and intricate web of internal cross-references. This last feature—what could be called *Literary Mind*'s covert running commentary on itself—helps to keep the text of the compilation together as a whole beyond its obvious topical structure.

Writing about Nurturing Life: A Chinese Literary Tradition

In the light of the literary complexity of *Literary Mind*, Liu's warning cited at the beginning of this part that "holding the writing tablet will hasten our death, and moistening the brush will hack away at our life"[5] may have been based on his personal experience with the potential harm intellectual strain can cause. Liu employs this criterion right at the beginning of "Nurturing the Vital Breath," referencing not his own experience but that of Wang Chong 王充 (27–ca. 100), another writer driven by the desire to say it all:[6]

	昔王充著述	In the past, when Wang Chong wrote,
2	制養氣之篇	he also composed chapters on nurturing the vital breath.
	驗己而作	They were written based on his own experience—
4	豈虛造哉	how could they have been empty fabrication!

---

5. See ll. 55–58 in my translation below.

6. The text of the "Nurturing the Vital Breath" chapter quoted here follows *Wenxin diaolong* 42.646–50. I have also consulted *Wenxin diaolong yizheng*, compiled by Zhan Ying in 1989, among numerous other editions, as well as Vincent Yu-chung Shih's translation *The Literary Mind and the Carving of Dragons* published by the Chinese University Press in 1983. The line numbers (which exclude extrametrical words) are my addition.

Wang Chong's "chapters on nurturing the vital breath" have not survived and may have already been lost by Liu Xie's time four centuries later. However, we know about them from Wang's autobiographical "Records about Myself" ("Zi ji" 自紀), which survive as part of his encyclopedic work *Discourses Weighed in the Balance* (*Lunheng* 論衡). In "Records about Myself," Wang describes how the experience of aging, with its accompanying physical and mental decline, motivated him to "write the book *Nurturing Inborn Nature* in sixteen chapters" (作養性之書凡十六篇).[7]

The seemingly unremarkable beginning of Liu Xie's "Nurturing the Vital Breath" is rich in connotations and signals at least five distinct rhetorical goals to his intended audience. First, Liu affirms his authorial legitimacy by pointing out that Wang Chong wrote from personal experience, assuring readers that writing about scholarly self-care is part of a time-honored literary tradition. Second, this also suggests that Liu Xie himself writes from personal experience. By starting his essay with Wang, Liu achieves a third rhetorical goal by sending a clear signal where on the spectrum of approaches to nurturing life his essay was situated: not on the end dedicated to the pursuit of immortality and transcendence, which Wang scorned in *Discourses Weighed*, but rather on the pragmatic end dedicated to the prevention of illness and an untimely death. This is in line with Wang, who repeatedly mentioned a regular lifespan of one hundred years—a number consistent with other early Chinese texts and medical writings.[8] This clear demarcation of his subject must have been important

---

7. *Lunheng* 85.1209. See also the translation by Forke, *Lun-hêng*. In the quotation of this passage in *Imperial Reader of the Taiping Era* (*Taiping yulan* 太平御覽), the title of Wang Chong's book is given as *Nurturing Life* (*Yangsheng* 養生); see *Taiping yulan* 720.5b. No such book by Wang Chong is listed in the bibliographic chapter, "Monograph on Canonical and Other Books" ("Jingji zhi" 經籍志), of the *Book of Sui* (*Sui shu* 隋書). Wang's description of his failing health will be discussed in part II.

8. For Wang Chong's denial of the pursuit of immortality, see especially "Daoist Falsities" ("Dao xu" 道虛), in *Lunheng* 7.313–38. The regular lifespan of one hundred years is mentioned in "Vital Breath and Longevity" ("Qi shou" 氣壽), in *Lunheng* 4.29. See also *Huangdi neijing Suwen* 1.2; Sivin, *Traditional Medicine*, 98. Toward the end of the early medieval period, Yan Zhitui 顏之推 (531–ca. 591) wrote in a similar vein: in chapter 15, "Nurturing Life" ("Yangsheng" 養生), of the *Family Instructions of the Yan Clan*, he disparages the pursuit of immortality and transcendence while affirming the usefulness of select measures aimed at preventing a premature death, as Wang Chong had done four centuries earlier. See *Yanshi jiaxun* 15.356–64; Tian, *Family Instructions*, 276–83.

28   *Part One*

to Liu, as he reiterates it toward the end of the essay by explicitly distinguishing "Nurturing the Vital Breath" from esoteric techniques such as "embryonic breathing" (ll. 77–82). He also selects allusions that affirm his pragmatic approach, for example, by repeated references to the *Zhuangzi* 莊子 chapter "Fundamentals of Nurturing Life" ("Yangsheng zhu" 養生主), which advocates a pragmatic approach to nurturing life, aiming at "living out one's [allotted] years" (盡年).[9]

Liu Xie also harnessed the rhetorical power of absences, a strategy I have explored in previous work.[10] Although it remains difficult to assess which books Liu Xie knew if he does not mention them in his own work, we know he had better access to the transmitted literature of his time than most contemporary scholars, due to his positions near extensive libraries. One such position was at Dinglin Temple (定林寺) near Jiankang, where Liu assisted Sengyou 僧祐 (445–518) in compiling eminent Buddhist scholarly works. Another was at the residence of Xiao Tong 蕭統 (501–531), Crown Prince Zhaoming (Zhaoming taizi 昭明太子) of the Liang dynasty (502–557).[11] Given this access, if certain texts about nurturing life do not appear in *Literary Mind*, it is thus likely that Liu intentionally omitted them because they did not align with his understanding of "Nurturing the Vital Breath." A notable example is Xi Kang's 嵇康 (223–262) "Discourse about Nurturing Life" ("Yangsheng lun" 養生論), a text Liu certainly knew since it was included in Xiao Tong's *Selections of Refined Literature* (*Wen xuan* 文選).[12] Another conspicuous absence is Ge Hong's *Master Who Embraces Simplicity*. Liu likely omitted these texts because

9. *Zhuangzi* 3.115. Elsewhere in the *Zhuangzi*, certain techniques to achieve longevity by "nurturing the body" (養形) are rejected; see *Zhuangzi* 15.535 (the chapter titled "Constraining the Will," "Ke yi" 刻意); see also Watson's translation, *Complete Works of Zhuangzi*. In other chapters of the *Zhuangzi*, the idea of living out one's years is phrased as "finishing one's heaven-endowed years" (終其天年); see *Zhuangzi* 4.172–180, 6.224, 20.667–68.

10. Richter, "Empty Dreams."

11. On the difficulties of accessing books, and especially whole books, in a manuscript culture such as early medieval China, see Tian, "Tao Yuanming de shujia." Also see Nugent, "Literary Media."

12. Xi Kang's essays in general are mentioned in *Wenxin diaolong* 47.700. For an annotated translation of "Discourse about Nurturing Life" (in *Wen xuan* 53.2287–93), as well as the ensuing debate with Xiang Xiu 向秀, see Henricks, *Philosophy and Argumentation*, 21–70.

they emphasize the possibility and pursuit of extreme longevity and transcendence, diverging from his own more pragmatic approach.

Other early Chinese texts containing passages on nurturing life also do not appear in *Literary Mind*. These include *Guanzi* 管子, *Xunzi* 荀子, Han Ying's 韓嬰 (ca. 200–120 BCE) *Outer Tradition of the Odes According to Han* (*Hanshi waizhuan* 韓詩外傳), Xun Yue's 荀悅 (148–209) *Extended Reflections* (*Shenjian* 申鑒), and various medical texts. However, there is no clear reason to believe that Liu intentionally excluded them. The same applies to early medieval specialized works, such as Zhang Zhan's 張湛 fourth-century *Collection of Essentials about Nurturing Life* (*Yangsheng yaoji* 養生要集) and other books listed in the bibliographic monograph of the *History of the Sui Dynasty* (*Sui shu* 隋書).[13] While nurturing life is often perceived as a predominantly Daoist concern, the range of titles mentioned indicates its relevance to thinkers of various persuasions, including those typically labeled Confucians.[14]

The Vital Breath, or *qi*, as Dominant Factor for Literature and as Exhaustible Resource

Liu Xie's fourth rhetorical goal at the beginning of "Nurturing the Vital Breath" must have been to highlight his choice of title, a practice observable in other chapters of *Literary Mind*. Here, he contrasts Wang Chong's book title, *Nurturing Inborn Nature*, as described in Wang's autobiography, with

---

13. *Sui shu* 34.1043 and 1049–50. The bibliographic catalog in the *History of the Han Dynasty* does not contain a nurturing life section, but it is possible that some of the lost texts in the medical section (*Han shu* 30.1776–81) would have fit this category. For a study and translation of extant fragments of the *Collection of Essentials about Nurturing Life*, see Stein, *Zwischen Heil und Heilung*.

14. Vivienne Lo has remarked that the small number of Dunhuang manuscripts relating to self-cultivation "may be testimony to the marginalization of hygienic practice in the scholarly traditions"; see Lo, "Self-Cultivation," 208. For an overview of early and early medieval notions of nurturing life, see Harper, *Early Chinese Medical Literature*, 110–19; Stein, *Zwischen Heil und Heilung*, 9–98. Livia Kohn's *Source Book in Chinese Longevity* is an anthology of relevant texts, mostly from the Daoist canon. A survey of predominantly Confucian approaches to self-cultivation, including a literature review, can be found in Weingarten, "'Self-Cultivation.'"

30 Part One

his own chapter title, "Nurturing the Vital Breath." The phrase "nurturing the vital breath" forms the first element of Wang Chong's catalog of self-cultivation strategies and is the only element of that catalog to interest Liu Xie.

In the context of nurturing life, the words *xing* 性 and *qi* 氣 overlap semantically: *xing* denotes one's inborn nature or natural disposition, also conceptualized as primal *qi* (*yuan/tian qi* 元/天氣)—the original *qi* received in utero that determines much of one's life.[15] *Yuanqi* is a broader term than *xing*, as it can also refer to the cosmic *qi* of the universe, not to mention the broader semantic scope of the word *qi* alone. In Chinese philosophy and medicine, *qi* is a fundamental concept, understood as the vital breath or energy within the human body and throughout the universe. Everyone is born with a certain amount and type of *qi*, which moves within the body and interacts with the *qi* of heaven and earth.

By using the word *qi* in the title, Liu Xie links the chapter to earlier texts discussing *qi* in connection with literature.[16] Among those, the link to the third-century writer and ruler of the Wei dynasty Cao Pi must have been particularly important to him. In his "Discourse on Literature" ("Lun wen" 論文), Cao Pi presents *qi* as an inborn quality that necessarily shapes a writer's literary production: "Literature is dominated by vital breath. Its clarity or turbidity are of a certain embodiment and cannot be brought about forcibly" (文以氣為主, 氣之清濁有體, 不可力強而致).[17] Cao Pi extends this approach by emphasizing the unique individuality of every writer to include musical performance. Later writers reflecting on other art forms in China, particularly calligraphy, embraced this idea as well.

Liu Xie adopts Cao Pi's qualitative approach to the writer's vital breath throughout *Literary Mind*. Significantly, he first does so in connection with Confucius (Kongzi 孔子, trad. 551–479 BCE), whose "exquisite vital breath

---

15. See, e.g., *Lunheng* 7.59 and 62.875.

16. See Pollard, "Ch'i in Chinese Literary Theory"; Cutter, "To the Manner Born?" It is possible that Liu Xie was also alluding to Mengzi's "I am good at nurturing my flood-like *qi*" (我善養吾浩然之氣, *Mengzi* 2A2), a statement that neither Pollard nor Cutter discuss—but see Richter, "Must We All Have a Vast, Flowing *qi*?"

17. *Wen xuan* 52.2271. On Cao Pi's physically determined self-presentation, see also part II.

became literary coloration" (秀氣成采).[18] Liu explicitly refers to Cao Pi's understanding of *qi* and elaborates on it in "Wind and Bone" ("Feng gu" 風骨), where he notes that Cao Pi and others from his circle "shared an emphasis on the vital breath" (並重氣之旨).[19] In "Style and Inborn Nature" ("Ti xing" 體性), Liu Xie observes that talent "originates from one's vital energies, which charge the intentions, which in turn determine words. In the creation of literary beauty, there is nothing that does not arise from one's true nature" (肇自血氣, 氣以實志, 志以定言, 吐納英華, 莫非情性).[20] He uses the same phrase, "originates from one's vital energies," in his chapter on prosody ("Sheng lü" 聲律) to describe the characteristics of the human voice, extending the idea of literature as physiologically rooted by including lips and mouth to represent the speech organs.[21]

Several of Liu Xie's observations indicate that he conceived of vital breath as something that is transferred from a writer to a literary work. For instance, he demands that writers "hone their vital breath and make sure their brush tips stir up a storm" (砥礪其氣, 必使筆端振風) and asserts that a writer's vital breath "flow in the ink" (氣流墨中) and "manifests in words" (氣形於言矣).[22] This understanding leads to the notion of literary texts as imbued with a particular vital breath, such as when Liu describes the writings of Liezi as characterized by their "majestic vital energy and rare literary coloration" (氣偉而采奇).[23]

"Nurturing the Vital Breath" is the only part of *Literary Mind* that explores *qi* not only qualitatively, as the decisive factor that shapes one's distinctive personality and writing, but also quantitatively, as an exhaustible and diminishing resource whose depletion leads to illness, the decline of literary creativity, and eventually the untimely loss of life. To highlight

---

18. *Wenxin diaolong* 2.17.

19. *Wenxin diaolong* 28.513–14.

20. *Wenxin diaolong* 27.506. Since *xue* 血 (blood) was considered a form of *qi*, along with several other physiological constituents, the compound *xueqi* is best understood as consisting of two near-synonyms and translated as "vital energies." My translations aim to reflect the type of *qi* mentioned in the text. When more than one type is mentioned, as a compound or in an enumeration (as in *jingqi* 精氣 and *jingdan* 精膽), I generally use "vital energies" as an umbrella term.

21. *Wenxin diaolong* 33.552; see also 43.650.

22. *Wenxin diaolong* 23.422, 23.423, and 47.698.

23. *Wenxin diaolong* 17.309.

32   *Part One*

this aspect of *qi* must have been Liu's fifth rhetorical goal in beginning his chapter with a reference to Wang Chong. The only other time he mentions the Han thinker in *Literary Mind* is in "Spirit Thought," where he also discusses *qi* quantitatively, noting that "Wang Chong exhausted his vital breath by thinking too much" (王充氣竭於思慮).[24]

Foundational Observations: Acknowledging Human Predisposition

After opening the chapter with a reference to Wang Chong's lost book and implicitly delineating his understanding of "Nurturing the Vital Breath," Liu Xie continues his introduction with a statement about the general workings of the human disposition, further legitimizing the chapter by pointing out the universal relevance of its subject:

夫	We know that[25]
耳目鼻口, 生之役也	"ears and eyes, nose and mouth are in the service of life,"[26]
6 心慮言辭, 神之用也	mind and thought, words and literature are in the employ of the spirit.
率志委和	If we pursue our intentions in a "yielding and gentle" manner,[27]

24. *Wenxin diaolong* 26.494.

25. Rudolf G. Wagner has described the rhetorical heft of the initial particle *fu* 夫 in his "Building Block of Chinese Argumentation," 46–50. While I agree with Wagner's proposition to make the particular function of the word explicit in a translation, his suggestion to translate *fu* as "it is a general rule or principle that" does not fit Liu Xie's use of the word in this chapter. Nevertheless, Liu Xie does use *fu* to introduce sentences "of a higher validity than sentences not marked in this manner" and statements "that are supposed to be known to the reader," in line with Wagner's argument; see "Building Block," 46.

26. This is a verbatim quotation from the chapter titled "Valuing Life" ("Gui sheng" 貴生) in the *Annals of Lü Buwei* (*Lüshi chunqiu* 呂氏春秋). See *Lüshi chunqiu* 2.2.74 (i.e., page 74 in chapter 2 of part II), trans. Knoblock and Riegel, *Annals of Lü Buwei*, 80. The quotation incorporates a reference to the *Canon of the Way and Virtue* (*Daodejing* 道德經; see *Laozi* 50.24). I generally mark quotations or allusions in my translations with quotation marks.

27. The phrase "yielding and gentle" may allude to the *Zhuangzi*'s "Knowledge Wanders North" ("Zhi bei you" 知北遊), where it is used in the sense of "an entrusted harmony" in

8	則理融而情暢	our reason will be concordant, and our inner state can unfold.
	鑽礪過分	If we drill and grind excessively,
10	則神疲而氣衰	our spirit becomes worn out and our vital breath diminished.
	此性情之數也	These are the workings of our predisposition and inner state.

Liu Xie first characterizes two elements of the human disposition: the sense organs we share with nonhuman animals, which help us stay alive, and our specifically human, intellectual faculties. *Shen* 神, one of several significant terms in this passage, can describe different kinds of "spirits" outside the human body, including divine beings and ghosts, but here it is understood physiologically as "the finest part" of *qi* "responsible for consciousness and allied activities."[28] *Shen*, as "that element of the human mind or psyche that corresponds to the manifold divinities of the natural world," as Ronald Egan has observed, connects us, who all possess *shen*, to the numinous or daimonic.[29]

Jing 精 (vital essence), *qi*, and *shen* are usually regarded as a continuum of *qi*, ranging from the distinctly physical and material *jing* to *qi*, which is often considered dual in nature and occasionally described as matter-energy, to the immaterial *shen*. Another essential term in *Literary Mind*, not least because of its prominent position in the book's title, is *xin* 心, the mind or heart. It is generally conceptualized as the abode of *shen* but may also appear as a function of *shen* or even be identified with it.[30]

The term *zhi* 志 indicates one's intention, determination, aspiration, or, as Stephen Owen put it, what is "intently on the mind."[31] *Zhi* is connected to both *qi* and *shen* (*qizhi* 氣志, *shenzhi* 神志, consciousness) as well as

---

a context closely related to Liu Xie's discussion: the chapter brings up the notion that life and death are owed to the accumulation and dispersal of *qi* (*Zhuangzi* 22.733) and that we do not actually possess a body or life but that they are the form and harmony entrusted to us by the universe (*Zhuangzi* 22.739). See also Wang Yuanhua, "Shi 'Yang qi pian' shuai zhi wei he shuo."

28. Sivin, "Emotional Counter-Therapy," 1.

29. Egan, "Poet, Mind, and World," 102.

30. See, e.g., *Huangdi neijing Lingshu* 80.604 (心者神之舍也).

31. Owen, *Readings in Chinese Literary Thought*, 26.

34 *Part One*

to *qing* (*qingzhi* 情志, sentiment). Interestingly, Liu Xie does not mention any of the common terms for "body" in this chapter (that is, *shen* 身, *ti* 體, *xing* 形, *qu* 軀).[32]

After briefly characterizing the human disposition, Liu Xie articulates the main point of the chapter—a message he will repeat and develop throughout the text, corroborating it with references to previous literature. These references come in the form of historical sketches or by explicitly naming or implicitly alluding to historical figures. Liu's message is twofold: an encouragement and a warning. He encourages writers to pursue their intentions in a manner that is "yielding and gentle" (l. 7), usually interpreted as abiding by their inborn nature, and warns them to beware of "drilling and grinding excessively" (l. 9).

The idea that one's vital energies suffer when imprudently taxed appears to have been a common connection, one that was already made by Sima Tan 司馬談 (d. 110 BCE) in his description of Daoist beliefs, as quoted in the *Records of the Historian* (*Shi ji* 史記). Where Sima Tan remains rather general, though, stating that "the spirit, if greatly used will become exhausted and the body, if put under great strain will wear out" (神大用則竭, 形大勞則敝),[33] other writers have been more specific about the activities that are most harmful. For example, the late Han scholar Gao Biao 高彪 (d. ca. 184, *zi* Yifang 義方) states that "thinking too much harms our spirit" (思慮害我神).[34] Liu Xie zooms in even further, transferring this connection into the realm of literary creation. He acknowledges that writing requires the application of one's sensory and intellectual faculties, vital breath, and spirit, but he also suggests that the extent of this application depends on whether we write in accordance with our inborn nature.[35]

The early fourth-century scholar Ge Hong made a similar point, noting in a list of things detrimental to health that "we harm ourselves if our

32. For a brief characterization of these terms, see Sivin, *Health Care in Eleventh-Century China*, 17–18.

33. *Shi ji* 130.3292. See also Watson's translation in *Ssu-ma Ch'ien*, 47–48. This is the earliest received formulation of an idea that was expressed in similar form in many later texts; see, e.g., *Baopuzi neipian* 5.99.

34. *Yiwen leiju* 23.418; *Quan Hou Han wen* 66.2b.

35. Liu Xie expresses a similar idea in "Spirit Thought," where he suggests that it is not necessary to think torturedly (無務苦慮) or to weary one's emotions (不必勞情); *Wenxin diaolong* 26.494. See the discussion of this passage in Egan, "Poet, Mind, and World," 113.

talent does not measure up but we exhaust ourselves thinking something through," or "if our vigor is not strong enough but we force ourselves to undertake something" (才所不逮, 而困思之, 傷也; 力所不勝, 而強舉之, 傷也).[36] In the immediately following passage, Liu Xie elucidates this point by presenting the development of Chinese literature as a process that increasingly requires authors to waste their vital breath on irrelevant literary qualities.

Literary History as a History of Growing Mental Exhaustion

	夫	We know that
	三皇辭質, 心絕於道華	in the age of the Three Sovereigns, literature was unadorned, and minds were detached from extravagant language.
12	帝世始文, 言貴於敷奏	Under the [Five] Emperors, patterned literature emerged, and words were valued in the [oral] presentation of memorials.[37]
	三代春秋, 雖沿世彌縟	During the Three Dynasties and the Springs and Autumns,[38] literature became more elaborate following the [taste of the] times,
14	並適分胸臆	but it remained in accordance with the minds [of its authors]
	非牽課才外也	who did not have to overstretch their inborn talent.

36. *Baopuzi neipian* 13.223.

37. Neither the "Three Sovereigns" nor the "Five Emperors" are fixed groups, and Liu Xie does not specify their identity anywhere in *Literary Mind*. For a summary of interpretations, see the commentary in *Shi ji* 1.1. Liu Xie discusses the development of genres of official communication addressed to superiors in chapters 22 ("Declarations and Memorials," "Zhang biao" 章表) and 23 ("Presentations and Communications," "Zou qi" 奏啟) of *Literary Mind*. On the oral presentation of early memorials (敷奏以言), see *Wenxin diaolong* 22.406 and 23.421. See also part II of this book on Yu He's "Memorial Discussing Calligraphy."

38. The Three Dynasties period refers to the prehistoric Xia dynasty (traditionally dated to ca. 2070–ca. 1600 BCE), the Shang dynasty (ca. 1600–1046 BCE), and the Zhou dynasty (ca. 1046–256 BCE). The Springs and Autumns period spans ca. 770 to ca. 480 BCE.

36 *Part One*

16	戰代權詐, 攻奇飾說[39]	In the Warring States, as literature became deceitful, [writers] delved into the strange to embellish their persuasions.
	漢世迄今, 辭務日新	From the age of the Han down to the present time, literature has been striving for continual innovation.
18	爭光鬻采, 慮亦竭矣	Writers have competed in flaunting their literary coloration and thus exhausted their thoughts.
	故	Therefore,
	淳言以比澆辭	if we compare simple words to adulterated phrases,
20	文質懸乎千載	the patterned and the artless appear a thousand years apart;
	率志以方竭情	if we contrast pursuing our intentions with "exhausting our inner state,"[40]
22	勞逸差於萬里	the strained and the relaxed appear ten thousand miles apart.
	古人所以餘裕	The ancients were "at ease,"
24	後進所以莫遑也	later generations "never get any leisure."[41]

Liu Xie presents an argument familiar from elsewhere in *Literary Mind*: the evolution—or rather, the deterioration—of literature from a state of unadorned, wholesome substantiality to later stages burdened with extravagant embellishment. As Wai-yee Li succinctly puts it, "ancient simplicity is juxtaposed with modern artifice and the obsession with novelty and glamour."[42] Liu's historical overview starts with unadorned oral literature, such as early memorials, progresses through the deceitfulness of Warring States persuasions, and finally characterizes the literary scene since the Han dynasty as engrossed with innovation.

Liu's assessment of this process aligns perfectly with the theme of "Nurturing the Vital Breath." He describes the historical development

---

39. For the emendation of 枝 to 權, see *Wenxin diaolong jiaozhu shiyi buzheng*, 374.

40. This phrase recalls a passage in Lu Ji's "Rhapsody on Literature" describing the difficulties Lu Ji encounters when trying to compose; see *Wen xuan* 17.773.

41. On the allusions to *Mengzi* and the *Book of Odes* in these two lines, see below.

42. Li, "Between 'Literary Mind' and 'Carving Dragons,'" 206.

of literature in terms of the mental effort or vital energies required for its creation, proposing that composing unadorned literature is less taxing for writers because it accords with their inborn nature. In contrast, "delving into the strange to embellish their persuasions," "striving for continual innovation," and "flaunting their literary coloration" (ll. 16–18) exhaust both their "thoughts" or contemplative powers (*lü* 慮) and their "inner state" (*qing* 情).[43]

The concluding contrast between the ease of the ancients and the lack of leisure of later generations may initially seem bland and not particularly indicative of a serious health risk. However, considering the literary background of Liu's choice of phrases, the last couplet markedly gains in insalubrious force. The term *yuyu* 餘裕 ("at ease"), which literally means "having a surplus of abundance," recalls a passage from *Mengzi* 孟子 where the phrase describes a situation in which one not bound by office is free to act on his own accord. This latitude, or "root-room," is a crucial condition for creativity but is lacking in the lives of later writers.[44]

Their plight is cast in terms familiar from the *Book of Odes* (*Shijing* 詩經), where the phrase "to get no leisure" (*bu huang* 不遑) appears in several odes to describe great personal sacrifices in service to one's state or lord, usually implying utter exhaustion.[45] By using the distributive *mo* 莫 (in no case, no one) instead of the simple negative *bu* 不, Liu effectively aggravates the phrase, making the lack of leisure for writers of later generations, including himself and his contemporaries, appear even more critical. Highlighting the intense demands of the literary environment of his day, Liu exposes the challenging working conditions faced by himself and his

---

43. That innovation can drain the vital breath is also mentioned in "Continuity and Change" ("Tong bian" 通變); see *Wenxin diaolong* 29.520.

44. *Mengzi* 2B5. *Hanyu da cidian* (s.v. 餘裕) quotes Guo Moruo 郭沫若 (1892–1972), who used the word in connection with literary creativity, maintaining that the author of a long and exceptional piece such as the poem "Encountering Sorrow" ("Li sao" 離騷) in the *Songs of Chu* (*Chu ci* 楚辭) must have had a certain psychological and physical latitude to create it. In Gerard Manley Hopkins's (1844–1889) poem "My Own Heart Let Me More Have Pity On" (1885), "root-room" is a mental space necessary to develop self-acceptance.

45. See, e.g., *Mao shi* nos. 19, "Deep Rolls the Thunder" ("Yin qi lei" 殷其雷), 162 "Four Steeds" ("Si mu" 四牡), 167 "Plucking Bracken" ("Cai wei" 采薇), 168 "Bring Out the Carriages" ("Chu che" 出車), 169 "Russet Pear" ("Di du" 杕杜), 197 "Small Wings" ("Xiao bian" 小弁), and 305 "Warriors of Yin" ("Yin wu" 殷武).

38   *Part One*

fellow literati, while simultaneously drawing attention to his own ability to cope with these demands.

Accepting Differences in Age and Talent: Shallow Prodigies versus Overthinking Elders and Ducks on Tiptoe versus Long-Legged Cranes

Having offered his view on the historical development of literature—which effectively amounts to a "naturalization" of the pre–Warring States period style and a "denaturalization" of later styles—Liu Xie begins to address the individual situation of authors in more detail. He begins with an observation about the specific strengths and weaknesses of young and old writers, once more situating literary creation in the writer's body, and advises one to accept the situation of one's particular body:

	凡	Usually,
	童少鑒淺而志盛	the young are of shallow understanding but full of ambition, and
26	長艾識堅而氣衰	the old have firm knowledge but their vital breath is diminished.
	志盛者思銳以勝勞	Those who are full of ambition are acute in thought and thus able to withstand strain,
28	氣衰者慮密以傷神	those whose vital breath is diminished ruminate scrupulously and thus harm their spirit.
	斯實	This truly is
	中人之常資	the regular constitution of ordinary people and
30	歲時之大較也	the general outline of their [situation at different] ages.

Liu assumes that aging diminishes one's vital breath. Although older writers are not impaired in knowledge or the general ability to think,[46] he

---

46. The *Annals of Lü Buwei* expresses the same idea—"in old age, one's body keeps diminishing while one's wisdom becomes ever more abundant" (人之老也, 形益衰, 而智

believes they are inclined to think too thoroughly or scrupulously, which harms their spirit and contributes to a further decline in their vital breath. According to Liu, the young are better off than the old: he characterizes them as sharp thinkers who do not mind hard work. Although this is not expressed explicitly, the young probably even benefit from their "shallow understanding" (l. 25), as it spares them the scruples and qualms that often lead to the perilous "drilling and grinding" (l. 9). Here and elsewhere, Liu does not differentiate much between the act of writing and the reflection that precedes and accompanies it.

The early Tang calligrapher Sun Qianli 孫虔禮 (ca. 648–702, *zi* Guoting 過庭) has depicted the strengths and weaknesses of the young and old in comparable terms. In his *Manual of Calligraphy* (*Shupu* 書譜, 687) he suggests that in "thinking through basic ideas and principles, the young are inferior to the old; but for mastering technique, the old are inferior to the young. With regard to thinking, the older one grows the more marvelous it is; with regard to technique, the young are better able to exert themselves" (若思通楷則, 少不如老; 學成規矩, 老不如少。思則老而愈妙, 學乃少而可勉).[47] Although Sun does not mention the vital energies, he operates from a similar understanding of aging: throughout their lives, calligraphers will gain a better understanding of their art, but they will also suffer a loss in exactitude and stamina in the execution of calligraphy, an art that is even more obviously physiological than literary composition.

Sun's characterization of the young as strong learners mirrors similar statements found elsewhere. Cao Pi, in his authorial preface ("Zi xu" 自敘) to the *Classical Discourses* (*Dianlun* 典論), quotes his father, Cao Cao 曹操 (155–220), as "often saying that the young are fond of learning and can think in a focused way, but once people grow up they tend to become forgetful" (常言人少好學則思專, 長則善忘). Unsurprisingly, this observation serves as an introduction to Cao Cao's declaration of his own exceptionality as someone who can still expand his learning as an adult.[48]

About a century later, Ge Hong connected the ability to remember, so

---

益盛, *Lüshi chunqiu* 16.7.103)—but presents it as an ideal that not everybody lives up to. See also the translation in Knoblock and Riegel, *Annals of Lü Buwei*, 398.

47. *Shupu* 5; Chang and Frankel, *Two Chinese Treatises on Calligraphy*, 11, with minor modifications.

48. *Sanguo zhi* 2.89.

40   Part One

important for success in study, with vital energies, remarking that "when we are young our intentions are focused, so we hardly forget anything, but when we get older the spirit becomes unrestrained and it is easy to lose track of things" (蓋少則志一而難忘, 長則神放而易失).[49] Writing toward the end of the sixth century, Yan Zhitui 顏之推 (531–ca. 591) expresses a similar idea: "When people are young, their spirit is focused and sharp, but once we have grown up, our thinking becomes scattered and unconfined—that's why we need to be taught early so as not to miss the opportune moment" (人生小幼, 精神專利, 長成已後, 思慮散逸, 固須早教, 勿失機也).[50]

Liu Xie complements his consideration of differences in age with a reflection on differences in talent, presenting talent as something as clearly determined by our physiology—specifically, our vital breath—as our age. This leads to a meditation on our propensity to compare ourselves unfavorably to others and on the inappropriate measures we take to make up for a perceived lack of genius. Liu starts by evoking one of the most famous maxims from the *Zhuangzi*: "My life flows between confines, but knowledge has no confines. If we use the confined to follow after the unconfined, there is danger that the flow will cease" (吾生也有涯, 而知也无涯。以有涯隨无涯, 殆已).[51] Liu's allusion presents this sobering remark, which introduces the *Zhuangzi*'s "Fundamentals of Nurturing Life," with a twist, a technique he often applies to allusions and references in *Literary Mind*:

	若夫	Since
	器分有限	capability and talent are limited,
32	智用無涯	but there are "no confines" to employing one's intelligence,
	或	some,
	慚鳧企鶴	ashamed of being a duck stand on tiptoe to become a crane,[52]
34	瀝辭鐫思	sifting words and chiseling thoughts.

49. *Baopuzi waipian* 3.132.
50. *Yanshi jiaxun* 8.172; see also the translation by Tian, *Family Instructions*, 135.
51. *Zhuangzi* 3.115, here following the translation by Graham in *Chuang-tzu*, 62.
52. *Zhuangzi* 8.317.

	於是	As a consequence,
	精氣內銷	their vital energies will melt away within,
36	有似尾閭之波	similar to the waves [draining off] into Tail Gate,[53] and
	神志外傷	their spirit and intention will suffer harm from outside,
38	同乎牛山之木	just as the trees [chopped down] on Bull Mountain.[54]
	怛惕之盛疾亦可推矣	That anxiety will cause illness may indeed be deduced.[55]

That talents differ must have been important to Liu Xie, as iterations of this idea appear throughout *Literary Mind*.[56] Here, he is less concerned with the differences themselves and more with how some writers respond to what they perceive as the short legs of a duck rather than the long legs of a crane. In the *Zhuangzi* passage Liu alludes to, stretching a duck's naturally short legs and trimming a crane's naturally long legs are described as harmful because they violate these creatures' inborn nature. Liu's argument follows the same pattern as in his discussion of differences in age: the problem is not an apparent lack of talent (or advanced age) but the attempt to work against one's natural endowment (or current age). "Sifting words and chiseling thoughts" (l. 34), or overthinking, harms the vital energies, just as the earlier mentioned "drilling and grinding" do.

Again, we can find parallels to Liu's argument in other contexts. For instance, Sun Qianli, in his *Manual of Calligraphy*, creates a narrative of calligraphic decline that began with Wang Xianzhi 王獻之 (344–386/388), son of the renowned calligrapher Wang Xizhi. Sun declares, "From Wang Xianzhi on, calligraphers have strained too hard and used affectations to form a personal style" (子敬已下, 莫不鼓努為力, 標置成體),[57] In the

53. *Zhuangzi* 17.563.

54. *Mengzi* 6A8.

55. The word I translated as "anxiety," *dati* 怛惕, is rarely used, but it usually implies incessant worry, agitation, and restlessness. See, e.g., *Shi ji* 10.431.

56. Liu Xie elaborates on the topic in "Style and Inborn Nature." He also mentions it in the chapters on "Allusion and Reference" ("Shi lei" 事類) and "Fluency and Coherence" ("Fu hui" 附會). See *Wenxin diaolong* 27.505–6, 38.615, and 43.651, respectively.

57. *Shupu* 5; Chang and Frankel, *Two Chinese Treatises on Calligraphy*, 12.

42   *Part One*

context of Liu Xie's arguments against "artificial" developments in literature, Sun Qianli may well have implied that these calligraphers were working against their inborn nature.

Writers Wearing Out Their Spirit: Cautionary Tales

To provide narrative relief and support his admonition, Liu Xie asks his readers to consider the experiences of four well-known writers active between the Eastern Han (25–220) and the Western Jin (266–316). His choice of historical references is inclusive, reflecting the broad scope of *Literary Mind*, which considers both refined or "high-register" literature (*wen* 文), especially poetry, and utilitarian documents (*bi* 筆). Since the latter type of writing would have comprised the bulk of an official's responsibilities, Liu again signals his main audience: scholar-officials and other writers. The first two cases he cites describe scholars who worked incessantly, while the latter two cases portray poets who worried about the energy they expended on their compositions:

	至如	As for
40	仲任置硯以綜述	Wang Chong who placed ink stones [all over his house] when he composed his work, and
	叔通懷筆以專業	Cao Bao who [slept] clutching a brush whenever he was absorbed in a project,
42	既暄之以歲序	they were on fire year in and year out,
	又煎之以日時	and burning day after day.
	是以	This is why
44	曹公懼為文之傷命	Lord Cao who was afraid that composing literature would shorten his life, and
	陸雲歎用思之困神	Lu Yun who lamented that "thinking wears out the spirit,"
46	非虛談也	were not just making empty words.

Liu Xie's first cautionary tale revisits Wang Chong, referred to here in the original Chinese by his courtesy name, Zhongren, who is said to have placed writing materials throughout his house while working on his *Discourses*

Weighed in the Balance. Depending on the biographical record, these were either "brushes and inkstones" (筆硯) or "knives and brushes" (刀筆).[58] This habit may seem harmless if a little odd, but only when we overlook Wang's physical decline, as related in his own autobiography (discussed in part II) and as evoked in Liu Xie's "Spirit Thought" (discussed below).

If Wang's incessant and obsessive focus on writing is described in spatial terms, being prepared to write everywhere, Liu's next example provides a temporal complement, being prepared to write at all times. The rites specialist Cao Bao 曹褒 (d. ca. 102, *zi* Shutong 叔通), according to the *History of the Later Han Dynasty* (*Hou Han shu* 後漢書), "studied intensely day and night, immersed in reflection and absorbed in thought. He slept clutching brush and tablet and he walked chanting texts, often thinking about them so intensely that he forgot where he was going" (晝夜研精, 沈吟專思, 寢則懷抱筆札, 行則誦習文書, 當其念至, 忘所之適).[59] Although we are firmly in the territory of historiographical motifs here, the lack of balance between activity and rest is evident in both cases.[60] When Liu Xie describes the negative effects of overwork on these scholars' health in terms of heat, he echoes other texts that make this connection. For example, in the *Zhuangzi*, Zigao, Lord of She (葉公子高), responds to a challenging order from his king by developing inner heat and drinking ice water.[61]

58. These details are recorded in Xie Zheng's 謝承 third-century fragmentarily received *History of the Later Han Dynasty* (see *Beitang shuchao* 99.17.1a) and in Fan Ye's 范曄 (398–446) *History of the Later Han Dynasty* (see *Hou Han shu* 49.1629). For other aspects of Wang Chong's biography, see *Yiwen leiju* 35.627, 55.990.

59. *Hou Han shu* 35.1201–2. Two interesting variants of this biography have survived in the *Records of the Han from the Eastern Lodge* (*Dongguan Hanji* 東觀漢記) and the *Collection of Literature Arranged by Categories* (*Yiwen leiju* 藝文類聚). Both show Cao Bao "going to bed clutching a lead pen" (寢則懷鉛筆). Moreover, *Collection of Literature Arranged by Categories* describes him as "chanting the *Odes* and the *Documents* while he was walking" (行則誦詩書); see *Dongguan Hanji* 15.606; *Yiwen leiju* 55.990.

60. The chapter "Study" ("Du shu" 讀書) in *Collection of Literature Arranged by Categories* provides an overview of these and related motifs in the semantic field of devotion to study. See *Yiwen leiju* 55.990–92.

61. *Zhuangzi* 4.153. While I could not find the connection between (mental) overwork and heat discussed in medical texts, it does appear in the *Inner Chapters of The Master Who Embraces Simplicity*, when Ge Hong, in chapter 9, "The Meaning of *Dao*" ("Dao yi" 道意), describes the physical and mental state of the "common man" (俗人) who lacks

44 Part One

Liu Xie's second pair of historical examples shifts focus to the self-perception of writing as an explicit health risk. "Lord Cao who was afraid that composing literature would shorten his life" (l. 44) likely refers to Cao Zhi 曹植 (192–232). A biographical record, again only fragmentarily received, suggests that writing took a physical toll on Cao Zhi because he "was so intensely focused on writing that he reduced his eating and drinking and as a result developed a stomach disorder" (陳思王精意著作, 食飲損減, 得反胃病也).[62]

The identity of Lu Yun 陸雲 (262–303), younger brother of the more famous poet Lu Ji, is unambiguous. The surviving correspondence between the brothers indeed proves that they also communicated about these very issues. In one of his "Letters to his Elder Brother Lu Ji" ("Yu xiong Pingyuan shu" 與兄平原書), Lu Yun complains that "thinking wears one out" (用思困人) and can lead one to "strain and labor oneself" (自勞役),[63] a sentiment echoed by Liu Xie. Other letters from Lu Yun to his brother mention illness linked to intense writing. Lu Yun confesses multiple times that he is not well enough to think clearly or write effectively.[64] He also seems to have struggled with the question of why reading and composing literature could bring him so much joy and be so exhausting at the same time. In one letter, he admires his brother's rhapsodies, saying they "dispelled his sadness and made him forget his troubles" (文章既自可美。且解愁忘憂), but he then follows this with a remark that he himself "was not skilled

---

awareness of the *dao* in terms of heat: "He constrains his spirit by worries, dissipates his vital energies by labor, tortures [lit. "fires and boils"] his body, exploits [lit. "carves and cuts"] his primal *qi*, is intemperate in toil and rest, smashing his head to pieces begging to be employed" (若乃精靈困於煩擾, 榮衞消於役用, 煎熬形氣, 刻削天和, 勞逸過度, 而碎首以請命, *Baopuzi neipian* 9.156).

62. Transmitted in fragmentary form, as a quotation from Yu Huan's 魚豢 third-century *Brief History of the Wei* (*Wei lüe* 魏略), in *Taiping yulan* 376.10b. It is uncertain if *fanwei* 反胃 just referred to an upset stomach or to the more specific disorder, stomach reflux. For the latter, see, e.g., *Jingui yaolüe* 17.845.

63. "Yu xiong Pingyuan shu" no. 3, in *Quan Jin wen* 102.1b–2a.

64. See "Yu xiong Pingyuan shu" nos. 3, 21, 32, and 35, in *Quan Jin wen* 102.1b, 2b, 7a–b, 10b, respectively. Comprising forty-four letters or letter fragments, the surviving correspondence between Lu Ji and Lu Yun is among the largest transmitted epistolary corpora of the period. For more on health and illness in letter-writing, and on Lu Yun in particular, see part II. See also Wu, "Clarity, Brevity and Naturalness," 212–16.

at composition and finds writing both bothersome and exhausting" (但作之不工。煩勞而棄力). He adds, "A little thinking and I am worn out greatly—I don't know why that is" (小思慮便大頓極。不知何以乃爾). He continues describing how he tortured himself composing a rhapsody and that "the effort left him unwell for days" (羸瘵累日).[65] We know from a surviving letter fragment that Lu Ji shared this sentiment, noting that "tortured thinking brings about illness" (思苦生疾).[66]

Both Cao Zhi and Lu Yun worry that composing literature drains their energies. In Liu Xie's view, this would not only be an indication that they are overtaxing themselves but also that they are making matters worse by further exhausting their vital energies through worry. Two other, partially overlapping lists of writers who suffered physically from their work, found in the "Spirit Thought" chapter of *Literary Mind* and in the slightly later *Master of the Golden Tower* (*Jinlouzi* 金樓子) by Xiao Yi 蕭繹 (508–555), demonstrate the pervasiveness of the idea that writing could take a severe toll on one's health. These lists broaden our understanding of illness narratives and scholarly self-harm in Chinese literature.

An Internal Digression: Tortured Writing in "Spirit Thought"

In "Spirit Thought," Liu Xie juxtaposes writers with varying speeds of composition who nonetheless produce outstanding works. He first lists six writers known for their slow and painstaking methods: Sima Xiangru 司馬相如 (179–117 BCE), Yang Xiong 揚雄 (53 BCE–18 CE), Huan Tan 桓譚 (ca. 23 BCE–56 CE), Wang Chong, Zhang Heng 張衡 (78–139), and Zuo Si 左思 (ca. 250–ca. 305). This is followed by a catalog of six writers famous for their speed.[67] A closer look at the slow writers reveals that not everyone in this catalog is associated with harmful overexertion, probably because Liu Xie's main focus in "Spirit Thought" is on differences in natural endowment rather than on writers who worked against their inborn nature:

---

65. These quotations are from "Yu xiong Pingyuan shu" no. 15, in *Quan Jin wen* 102.5a. On this letter, also see Tian, *Halberd at Red Cliff*, 179.

66. This fragment is preserved in a commentary to Lu Ji's "Rhapsody on Literature"; see *Wen xuan* 17.773.

67. The fast writers are Liu An 劉安 (179–122 BCE), Mei Gao 枚皋 (fl. ca. 140 BCE), Cao Zhi, Wang Can 王粲 (177–217), Ruan Yu 阮瑀 (d. 212), and Mi Heng 禰衡 (ca. 173–198).

46 Part One

Sima Xiangru ruined his brushes by holding them in his mouth, Yang Xiong had an alarming dream when he put his brush aside, Huan Tan became ill from tortured thinking, Wang Chong exhausted his vital breath by thinking too much, Zhang Heng pored over his "Capitals" for ten years, and Zuo Si refined his "Metropolises" for a decade. Granted that they have gigantic works of literature to their name, they are still deliberate thinkers.

相如含筆而腐毫, 揚雄輟翰而驚夢, 桓譚疾感於苦思, 王充氣竭於思慮, 張衡研京以十年, 左思練都以一紀。雖有巨文亦思之緩也。[68]

The slowness of Sima Xiangru and Zhang Heng is depicted positively and not framed as a health risk. Sima Xiangru's small output is usually correlated with the excellence of his literary works, and neither his stutter (kou chi 口吃) nor his early death from illness is traditionally associated with his painstaking way of writing.[69] Similarly, Zhang Heng is not described as overstretching himself, even though it took him a decade to finish his rhapsodies on the two capitals of the Han dynasty.[70] The positive evaluation of these writers also rests on the genre they were working in. As Stephen Owen has observed, the "expenditure of time and effort was an unambiguously positive value in longer and more learned genres such as fu 賦 in the pre-Tang period."[71]

Elsewhere in *Literary Mind*, Liu Xie praises another writer, not included in the list above, for his deliberation. In the chapter "Survey of Talent" ("Cai lüe" 才略), he compares Cao Pi and Cao Zhi, contrasting Cao Zhi's "quick thinking and extraordinary talent" unfavorably with his elder brother, whom he praises for "thinking carefully and employing his vigor in a deliberate way"—even if Cao Zhi, who made it into Liu Xie's list of fast writers, would always be "the first to crow" (子建思捷而才儁 ... 子桓慮詳而力緩, 故不競於先鳴).[72]

---

68. *Wenxin diaolong* 26.494.

69. See, e.g. ,*Han shu* 51.2367. Sima Xiangru's ill health and stutter are mentioned in his biography in *Han shu* 57A.2529–30, 57B.2589, and 57B.2600.

70. For this detail, see *Hou Han shu* 59.1897. Zhang Heng's "Rhapsody on the Western Capital" ("Xi jing fu" 西京賦) and "Rhapsody on the Eastern Capital" ("Dong jing fu" 東京賦) are transmitted in *Wen xuan* 2.47–3.148.

71. Owen, "Spending Time on Poetry," 161.

72. *Wenxin diaolong* 47.700.

Interestingly, Sima Xiangru was not the only stutterer on Liu Xie's list. Yang Xiong and Zuo Si also suffered from speech impediments, as their biographies in the standard histories indicate.[73] Although Lie Xie never foregrounds this commonality, it is remarkable that half of his "tortured writers" are described as being halting of speech as well. Given the positive connotations of halting speech since the *Analects*, it is difficult to discern whether this is a historiographical motif or an actual idiosyncrasy.[74]

Liu Xie's tolerance of slow, deliberate writing and his reluctance to praise speed in composition per se can be read as an indirect criticism of the contemporary literary world, where the appreciation of facility and dexterity in writing was widespread at court and beyond.[75] At the same time, Liu may also have been covertly defending his own method of composition—although *Literary Mind* is difficult to date, we know it was written over an extended period, perhaps decades. If Liu's earlier criticism that "later generations never get any leisure" (l. 24) carried a subtext of self-assertion, he seems more subdued here, perhaps because he was acutely aware of a weakness (his very own "duck's legs") that he only grudgingly accepted.

The record for the remaining four slow writers in "Spirit Thought" is less favorable: they are all characterized as having drained their vital energies at the expense of their health in one form or another. The cases of Yang Xiong and Huan Tan, closely associated in life through their positions at the Han court, are connected in a fragmentarily received passage of the latter's *New Discourses* (*Xin lun* 新論). In Yan Kejun's 嚴可均 (1762–1843) reconstruction, this passage reads as follows:

---

73. *Han shu* 87.57.3514 (*kou chi* 口吃); *Jin shu* 92.2376 (*kou ne* 口訥).

74. See *Lunyu* 4.24, "The master said: 'The gentleman strives to be slow of speech but swift in action'" (子曰：君子欲訥於言, 而敏於行). See also D. C. Lau's translation in *Confucius: The Analects*. Other writers characterized as halting of speech are mentioned in parts 2 and 3 of this book, among them Ge Hong and Wang Xizhi. Also see Pitner, "Stuttered Speech and Moral Intent."

75. On the importance attached to the speed and efficiency of writing in the Qi and Liang periods, see Blitstein, *Les fleurs du royaume*, 197–99. For examples of imperially ordered speed writing contests, see chapter 5 of Kay Duffy's unpublished PhD thesis, "The Third Day of the Third Month in Early Medieval China."

48   *Part One*

When I saw, as a young man, how beautiful Yang Xiong's writing was and how lofty his discourses, I was so bold to desire, notwithstanding my young age and inexperience, that I would one day become just as good as him. There was one time when I became excited by something and composed a small rhapsody. I was thinking intensely and with great agitation, which promptly made me fall ill. It took me a whole day before I recovered.

Yang Xiong also said that once, during the reign of Emperor Cheng [r. 33–7 BCE], at the time when the Lady of Bright Deportment Zhao had just become the emperor's favorite and always accompanied him to Sweet Springs, the emperor ordered him to write a rhapsody about that palace.[76] Yang Xiong worked on it in haste and with great vehemence, thinking intensely and torturing himself. When the rhapsody was finished, he was tired and took a nap. He dreamed that his Five Viscera had spilled to the ground and that he shoved them back in again with his own hands. When he awoke, he felt ill. He was panting and palpitating and very short of breath. He was sick for a whole year.

余少時見揚子雲之麗文高論。不自量年少新進。而猥欲逮及。嘗激一事而作小賦。用精思太劇。而立感動發病。彌日瘳。子雲亦言。成帝時。趙昭儀方大幸。每上甘泉。詔令作賦。為之卒暴。思精苦。賦成。遂困倦小臥。夢其五藏出在地。以手收而內之。及覺。病喘悸大少氣。病一歲。[77]

Yang Xiong's gory dream of nearly losing his Five Viscera (*wu zang* 五藏/臟)—the heart, liver, spleen, lungs, and kidney—after feverishly completing an imperial writing assignment vividly illustrates the dangers of excessive intellectual activity, since these organs are conceptualized as depositories of different types of vital energy.[78] When Yang Xiong awakens from what must have been a deeply disturbing dream, he finds himself "very short of breath"—literally, "with very little *qi*"—which reads like a piece of medical dream interpretation, hinting at the severe depletion of vital energies he suffered as a result of intense mental exertion.

Yang Xiong's dream evokes a set of accounts involving the therapeutic

---

76. Yang Xiong's "Rhapsody on the Sweet Springs Palace" is transmitted in *Han shu* 87A.3522–34 (see also Knechtges, *Yang Xiong*, 17–25) and *Wen xuan* 7.321–37.

77. *Quan Hou Han wen* 14.6a. See also the collection and translation of related fragments in Pokora, *Hsin-lun*, 72–73.

78. See, e.g., *Huangdi neijing Suwen* 23.210; *Huangdi neijing Lingshu* 8.84.

rinsing of internal organs outside of the body. This technique is associated with eminent doctors who were also surgeons. In the biography of Bian Que (fourth/fifth century BCE), it is attributed to the legendary healer Yu Fu 俞跗, who is said to have "cleansed the intestines and the stomach and rinsed the Five Viscera" (湔浣腸胃, 漱滌五藏).[79] Hua Tuo's 華佗 (d. ca. 208) biography reports that he cured patients with bowel issues by "opening [their bellies], washing the intestines, and applying a salve after suturing the wound again" (病若在腸中, 便斷腸湔洗, 縫腹膏摩).[80] The motif also appears in Buddhist miracle tales. The famous healer and thaumaturge Fotudeng 佛圖澄 (d. 349) is said to have regularly cleansed his internal organs, pulling them out through a hole at the side of his abdomen—a hole through which his insides emitted a light so strong that it allowed him to read at night.[81] Similarly, the monk Zhu Fayi 竺法義 (d. 382), known for his "fondness for learning" (好學) and extreme dedication to the *Lotus Sutra* (*Saddharma puṇḍarīka sūtra*; *Fahua jing* 法華經), "suddenly started suffering from a heart *qi* disorder" (忽感心氣疾病).[82] His illness seemed intractable until he sought refuge with the bodhisattva Avalokiteśvara (Guanyin 觀音). Appearing to him in a dream as a monk, Guanyin healed him by "cutting open his belly and cleansing his internal organs" (刳出腸胃湔洗腑藏).[83] C. Pierce Salguero has suggested that this motif originated in India but was widely received and adapted in China. Salguero notes that "plotlines and individualized details about idealized medical procedures were appropriated, shared and emulated among religious and medical hagiographers."[84]

79. *Shi ji* 105.2788.

80. *Sanguo zhi* 29.799.

81. *Xinji Soushen houji* 2.18.

82. The connection between mental overexertion and "heart *qi*" is further explored in part II in connection with Xiao Yi's self-account.

83. Zhu Fayi's story appears in several early medieval sources; my citations follow two entries in the Buddhist commonplace book *Grove of Jewels in the Garden of the Dharma* (*Fayuan zhulin* 法苑珠林 17.53.409b and 95.53.988b). Robert F. Campany renders the phrase as "he suddenly felt a strange sensation in his heart"; see his translation of the late fifth-century collection *Mingxiang ji* 冥祥記, compiled by Wang Yan 王琰: *Signs from the Unseen Realm*, 132. A tale about a Buddhist nun from Liu Yiqing's 劉義慶 (403–444) *Records of the Invisible and Visible World* (*Youming lu* 幽明錄) combines washing her intestines with other physical manipulations of her body. See *Taiping yulan* 395.1955.

84. Salguero, *Translating Buddhist Medicine*, 132.

50   *Part One*

Yang Xiong's dream is not the only intriguing aspect of the passage from the *New Discourses* previously cited. In the context of scholarly self-harm, Huan Tan's attitude toward the breakdown of his older friend suggested in the incipit to the dream anecdote is equally fascinating. Far from being alarmed by the damage Yang Xiong inflicted on his health in his efforts to please and impress the emperor, Huan Tan presents this self-sacrifice as appropriate in the pursuit of literary greatness and official perfection. In his view, health counts for little when weighed against imperial power or the promise of literary immortality. Read in this light, Huan Tan's own experience of falling ill after a spell of intensive writing comes across almost as a boast. He parades his indisposition triumphantly, seeing it as a validation of his literary efforts and a predictor of future success, insinuating that it might elevate him to the same stature as Yang Xiong.

Yan Kejun's reconstruction of the text concludes with a year of illness, but other versions of the story are more dramatic, maintaining that Yang Xiong died from his exertions either within a year or even within a day. Although these versions can be dismissed as historically inaccurate—since the "Rhapsody on the Sweet Springs Palace" ("Ganquan fu" 甘泉賦) was written around 11 CE, long before Yang's death in 18 CE—they reflect different perspectives on the dangers of overexertion.

These differing views are also evident in the arrangement of fragments from the *New Discourses*. The early seventh-century commonplace book *Collection of Literature Arranged by Categories* (*Yiwen leiju* 藝文類聚) cites the Yang Xiong anecdote in Huan Tan's telling twice. In the chapter on illness, Yang Xiong "became ill and died after a year" (疾一歲而亡). In the chapter on rhapsodies, he does not; rather, the fragment continues with Huan Tan saying, "I have always loved literature, and seeing Yang Xiong's skill at rhapsodies, it was my desire to learn from him" (余素好文, 見子雲工為賦, 欲從之學).[85] This explanation closes the narrative frame and further amplifies Huan Tan's endorsement of self-harm in the pursuit of literary excellence.[86]

---

85. These two quotations are from *Yiwen leiju* 75.1289 and 56.1013, respectively.

86. Although it is a different project altogether, it would be interesting to explore whether the *Collection of Literature Arranged by Categories* generally adapts its stories according to the lemma under which they appear. In this case, it seems as if different stories are presented: one that seeks to avoid discouraging young rhapsodists from giving their

Yan Kejun's reconstruction of the *New Discourses*, however, conveys disapproval of mental overexertion. Although he explicitly dismisses the hyperbolic account of Yang Xiong's death following the episode and settles on the historically more plausible long illness, he adds a cautionary conclusion by Huan Tan that casts Yang's overexertion in a less favorable light: "Based on this, we can say that exhaustive thinking harms the spirit" (由此言之, 盡思慮, 傷精神也). This reading is supported by the context in which Yan Kejun places the anecdote: following a discussion of the theory that Yan Hui, who will be discussed shortly, died prematurely because he tried to emulate Confucius.[87]

The fragmentarily received *Miscellaneous Records from the Western Capital* (*Xijing zaji* 西京雜記) presents another dream anecdote about Yang Xiong. Unlike the gruesome imagery and cautionary message of the previous dream, this one is more prophetic and less foreboding, though it still touches on Yang's tendency to overwork himself. This story would have served well as an allusion in Liu's "Nurturing the Vital Breath" since it discourages self-mortification and advocates working from "a surplus of abundance," as mentioned earlier (l. 23, "at ease" in my translation):

> Yang Xiong was studying when someone said to him, "Don't torture yourself. The mysterious is certainly difficult to transmit." Suddenly, this person was no longer to be seen. When Yang Xiong wrote the *Canon of the Great Mysterious* (*Taixuan jing* 太玄經), he dreamed that he spat out a white phoenix that perched on [his manuscript] and then vanished again.
>
> 揚雄讀書。有人語云。無為自苦。玄故難傳。忽然不見。雄著玄。夢吐白鳳皇集上。頃之而滅。[88]

Instead of focusing on Yang Xiong's self-mortification, this anecdote highlights literary creation as an effortless process in harmony with the universe,

---

all, and another that relishes telling tall tales of untimely demise. Yang Xiong's dream is mentioned twice and in different forms in the commentary on the *Selections of Refined Literature* by Xiao Tong. One account suggests that the dream led to his death, while the other indicates it resulted "merely" in illness. See *Wen xuan* 7.321 and 17.773.

87. *Quan Hou Han wen* 14.5b.

88. *Taiping guangji* 161.1156. See also the slightly different version in *Taiping yulan* 915.8b and the translation by Nylan in *Yang Xiong and the Pleasures of Reading*, 30.

52   *Part One*

as manifested by the otherworldly messenger and the auspicious legendary bird that the author "spat out"—a figure of creativity—that lands on his manuscript. The appearance of a phoenix is usually associated with Confucius, who in the *Analects* laments its absence.[89] The motif of divine encouragement or literary inspiration in a dream is well established in Chinese literature, from Dong Zhongshu 董仲舒 (ca. 179–ca. 104 BCE) to Xie Lingyun 謝靈運 (385–433).[90] However, Liu Xie may have chosen not to mention these anecdotes to singularize a dream of his own that is used in exactly that way in the preface to *Literary Mind*. In this dream, which Liu had as a young boy, he saw clouds colorful as brocade, which he then ascended and eventually plucked (乃夢彩雲若錦, 則攀而採之).[91]

Dreams also portend the opposite—the loss of literary creativity—as illustrated by an anecdote about Jiang Yan 江淹 (444–505). According to Zhong Rong's 鐘嶸 (467?–518) *Poetry Gradings* (*Shi pin* 詩品), Jiang once dreamed that a handsome man, calling himself Guo Pu 郭璞 (276–324), asked for the return of a brush he had lent Jiang many years before. Jiang complied, only to find himself no longer able to compose poetry.[92] This dream anecdote exemplifies the anxiety associated with one's creative potential: since the reasons for being endowed with creativity are obscure, it is only natural to distrust its constancy.

According to his autobiography, Wang Chong, number four on Liu Xie's list of slow writers, managed to learn from his physical decline due to overworking and even succeeded in reversing it.[93] Wang's curious habit of placing writing materials throughout his house reappears in magnified form in the biography of Liu's sixth slow writer, Zuo Si. Famous for his rhapsodies on the metropolises Chengdu, Jiankang, and Ye—the three capitals of the Three Kingdoms period (220–280)—Zuo Si "planned and thought for ten years. He placed brushes and paper everywhere, even in the courtyard and the privy, so that whenever he would happen upon a line he could write it down right away" (遂構思十年, 門庭藩溷皆著筆紙,

---

89. *Lunyu* 9.9.

90. Dong Zhongshu's dream is recorded in *Miscellaneous Records from the Western Capital*; see *Taiping yulan* 602.1b. For Xie Lingyun's dream, see *Shi pin* 1.48.

91. See Richter, "Empty Dreams," 87, 93–95.

92. *Shi pin* 2.72; also see Kroll, "On Political and Personal Fate," 390.

93. Wang Chong's autobiography is discussed in part II.

過得一句, 即便疏之).[94] Although there are no records about Zuo Si's health, he is "tainted by association" with Wang Chong, making it likely that his constitution suffered from his exacting writing habits.[95]

Unlike the apparently strictly indoor writer Wang Chong, Zuo Si's desire to be prepared for writing whenever inspiration hit extends well beyond the house, into the courtyard and even the privy. This commitment to readiness is further escalated in the biographical imagination with the mid-Tang poet Li He 李賀 (ca. 790–ca. 816). Li is said to have written lines of poetry even while riding a donkey, accepting major inconvenience—at least if he was using brush and ink—to counteract his anxiety about missing a precious line.[96] Liu Xie would probably not have been surprised to learn that Li He died rather young.

External Digressions: Death by Candlelight and Other Warnings

Another brief catalog of writers who paid for their intense intellectual work with illness or even death can be found in the *Master of the Golden Tower* by Xiao Yi, who briefly reigned as Emperor Yuan of the Liang dynasty (梁元帝, r. 552–555). The catalog, part of the chapter "Establishing Words" ("Li yan" 立言), adds two new names to the repertoire of scholars who harmed their health in pursuit of learning:

> Yan Hui endeavored to become a second Sage and thus suffered an early death. Jia Yi was fond of learning and therefore hastened his own demise. There is talk that Yang Xiong had a dream about his intestines when he wrote a rhapsody, and some say that Cao Zhi suffered from an upset stomach when he wrote literature. "Life flows between confines, knowledge has no confines. Using confined life to follow after unconfined wisdom" [might cause the flow to cease. To escape that danger] I will rather nurture my

---

94. *Jin shu* 92.2376. The rhapsodies are collected in *Wen xuan* 4.172–6.320.

95. Later commentators, like Huang Kan, likely felt compelled to defend Zuo Si due to the common association of slowness in composition with slow-wittedness. They attributed his pace to the complexity of his material. See *Wenxin diaolong zhaji* 26.92; *Wenxin diaolong yizheng* 26.999.

96. Li Shangyin 李商隱 (ca. 813–ca. 858), "Short Biography of Li He" ("Li He xiao-zhuan" 李賀小傳), in *Quan Tang wen* 780.8149. See also Owen, *End of the Chinese "Middle Ages,"* 110–14.

54 *Part One*

inborn nature and my spirit so that I may "capture the unicorn"[97] by completing *The Golden Tower*.

顏回希聖所以早亡[98]。賈誼好學遂令速殞。揚雄作賦有夢腸之談。曹植為文有反胃之論。生也有涯。智也無涯。以有涯之生逐無涯之智, 余將養性養神, 獲麟於金樓之制也。[99]

Xiao Yi goes farther back in time for his first case, to Confucius's favorite disciple, Yan Hui 顏回 (trad. 521–481 BCE, *zi* Ziyuan 子淵). The *Analects* repeatedly emphasize the connection between Yan Hui's exceptional devotion to learning and his early death and underline Confucius's profound grief upon the loss of his disciple.[100] Other texts elaborate on Yan Hui's physical decline, mentioning, for instance, that "at twenty-nine, Hui's hair had turned completely white" (回年二十九, 髮盡白).[101]

Wang Chong is even more graphic and detailed in his description of Yan Hui's premature aging, possibly drawing on historical sources that have not survived or embellishing an originally bland historical record for dramatic effect. In the chapter "An Examination of Vigor" ("Xiao li" 效力) in *Discourses Weighed in the Balance*,[102] Wang examines what he calls "innate vigor" (才力), the forceful and abundant energy that distinguishes the select few, including sages and worthies of the past as well as competent administrators and erudite scholars of his present. He regards the ability to study literature as proof of that energy (能學文有力之驗也) and compares the stamina of outstanding scholars to legendary strongmen—an elite group among whom he clearly counts himself. To support his argument, Wang also cites failures:

At the time of Wang Mang [王莽, 45 BCE–23 CE, r. 9–23 CE], the paragraphs and lines of the Five Canonical works, amounting to two hundred

97. An allusion to *Zuozhuan* Ai 14; Durrant, Li, and Schaberg, *Zuo Tradition*, 1919–21.

98. For the emendation of 舜 to 聖, see *Jinlouzi shuzheng jiaozhu* 9A.664–65.

99. *Jinlouzi* 9A.857. See also Tian, "Twilight of the Masters," 485.

100. *Lunyu* 6.3, 11.7, 11.9, and 11.10. On Yan Hui's death, see also Csikszentmihalyi, "Allotment and Death in Early China," 180–85; Ivanhoe, "Death and Dying in the *Analects*," 139–42.

101. *Shi ji* 67.2188.

102. *Lunheng* 37.579–89.

Between Self-Care and Self-Harm   55

thousand, were checked. Guo Lu, a disciple of one of the Erudites, was settling old disputes at night when he expired under his candle. He simply could not cope with the intense thinking. His pulse stopped and his vital breath was extinguished.

The son of the Yan family was already on his way to overtake Confucius when he became weak, worn out, and extremely fatigued. His hair turned white, and his teeth fell out. Although his gifts almost reached [those of Confucius], he suffered the misfortune of a breakdown. Confucius's vigor was copious, Yan Hui could not bear [the same burden].

If someone's talent and vigor are not as strong as those of others, then his knowledge and thought will not reach their level either. Those who exert themselves to make it to the top will vomit blood into their washbasins and suffer from anxiety and confusion before they finally perish. Writing documents in five lines on wooden tablets or dozens of memorials—those with inferior talents for whom wielding brush and ink is particularly difficult, how could they correctly join paragraphs and lines in dozens or hundreds of chapters? Only those who have abundant vigor can do that.

王莽之時, 省五經章句, 皆為二十萬, 博士弟子郭路夜定舊說, 死於燭下, 精思不任, 絕脉氣滅也。顏氏之子, 已曾馳過孔子於塗矣, 劣倦罷極, 髮白齒落。夫以庶幾之材, 猶有仆頓之禍, 孔子力優, 顏淵不任也。才力不相如, 則其知思不相及也。勉自什伯, 嘔中嘔血, 失魂狂亂, 遂至氣絕。書五行之牘, 書十奏之記, 其才劣者, 筆墨之力尤難, 況乃連句結章, 篇至十百哉。力獨多矣。[103]

Although Wang focuses on vigor and stamina rather than the vital energies, he pursues a similar argument as Liu Xie, claiming that one must not overtax one's natural endowment. He clearly regards Yan Hui's early death as self-inflicted and a consequence of excessive intellectual strain, even repeating this point elsewhere in *Discourses Weighed in the Balance*. In a chapter exposing "Falsities in Books" ("Shu xu" 書虛), he mentions the theory that Yan Hui's premature decline was due to straining his eyes while hiking with Confucius on Mount Tai. Rejecting this interpretation, Wang writes that "someone's hair can turn white and their teeth fall out if they use up their vital energies in study and exert themselves devotedly without rest" (髮白齒落, 用精於學, 勤力不休), adding that "completely

---

103. *Lunheng* 37.583. On the assumption that people differ in their constitutions, intellectual and otherwise, see also Richter, "Must We All Have a Vast, Flowing *qi*?," 32–38.

56 *Part One*

exhausting one's vital energies will cause death" (氣力竭盡, 故至於死).[104] In the chapter "Written in Reply" ("Dui zuo" 對作), Wang brings up Yan Hui again, declaring that there is only one misfortune graver than Yan Hui's ambition and that is being sorrowful and dejected: a disposition that "reduces one's longevity and has no benefits for one's inborn nature" (賊年損壽, 無益於性).[105]

Jia Yi 賈誼 (ca. 200–168 BCE), the second case on Xiao Yi's list of writers who failed to balance their intellectual endeavors with their capacities, is also said to have died young, while still in his early thirties. However, the scant biographical information we have does not point to an early death due to his devotion to learning, as Xiao Yi implies, but rather to excessive grief and possibly feelings of guilt after the untimely death of his lord and tutee, Liu Yi 劉揖 (d. 169 BCE, Prince Huai of Liang 梁懷王, r. 178–169 BCE). It has been suggested that Liu Yi died after a riding accident, for which Jia Yi might have blamed himself.[106] Despite the absence of evidence in the transmitted literature, it is possible that Xiao Yi believed Jia Yi, known for his precocity, harmed his vitality through excessive study and was thus unable to cope with the additional stress of grieving.

Xiao Yi's characterization of Yang Xiong and Cao Zhi has already been mentioned. Xiao Yi concludes his catalog of these four men, who harmed themselves while striving for scholarly or literary greatness, with a familiar reference to the beginning of the *Zhuangzi*'s "Fundamentals of Nurturing Life," an allusion we also see in Liu Xie's "Nurturing the Vital Breath" (ll. 31–32). Xiao Yi presents the *Zhuangzi*'s maxim straightforwardly, assuring his readers that he will avoid the dangers of "using confined life to follow after unconfined wisdom" and instead nurture his inborn nature and spirit to complete his *Golden Tower*. It is likely that Xiao Yi emphasized the importance of self-care so clearly because he had been in poor health since childhood, a topic we will explore further.[107]

---

104. *Lunheng* 16.171.

105. *Lunheng* 29.1179.

106. *Shi ji* 84.2503. For a biographical sketch of Jia Yi, see Sanft, "Study of Jia Yi's *Xin shu*," 13–27.

107. For illness narratives in Xiao Yi's autobiographical preface to the *Master of the Golden Tower*, see part II.

Introducing the Idea of Deliberate Self-Harm

Returning to "Nurturing the Vital Breath" after these internal and external digressions, we notice that at this point in his chapter Liu Xie intensifies his admonitions by alluding to two historical figures who took extreme measures for the sake of their studies: they deliberately caused themselves physical injury or discomfort to stay awake at night and remain diligent in their scholarly pursuits:

	夫	We know that
	學業在勤	learning depends on devotion and
48	功庸弗怠	achievement does not allow for idleness.
	故有	Hence there was
	錐股自屬	he who pricked his leg with an awl to hurt himself and
50	和熊以苦之人	he who prepared bear[-gall pills] to torture himself.

Liu Xie introduces two methods to counteract sleepiness, often characterized as the student's enemy: inflicting pain and tasting something revolting. The first historical example is clear (and we will return to it directly), while the second is more obscure. Evidence of the second behavior appears as late as the ninth century, when the mother of the scholar-official Liu Zhongying 柳仲郢 (d. 864) is said to have "prepared bear-gall pills" (嘗和熊膽丸) for her son to chew on at night to stay awake.[108] Although the text of *Literary Mind* may simply be corrupt here, as some suggest,[109] it is also possible that earlier instances of such behavior existed but did not survive in the received literature. An early use of bile for staying uncomfortable and possibly awake is attributed to King Goujian of Yue (越王句踐, r. 496–465 BCE) after his defeat by King Fuchai of Wu (吳王夫差,

---

108. *Xin Tang shu* 163.5023. It is uncertain whether Liu Zhongying's mother prepared these pills for her son because of their revolting taste or because of their medicinal properties. Bear gall or bile, typically administered in pill form, was a recognized materia medica used to improve vision and treat various other disorders. See *Zhonghua bencao* 9.8745.

109. Scholars disagree whether lines 48–50 are part of this chapter or an interpolation. See, e.g., Fan Wenlan's commentary in *Wenxin diaolong* 42.647 and *Wenxin diaolong jiaozhu shiyi buzheng*, 377.

58   *Part One*

r. 495–477 BCE). According to legend, Goujian was so intent on keeping the spirit of revenge alive within himself that he adopted a strict regime of self-mortification, which included "tasting gall whenever he ate or drank" (飲食亦嘗膽也).[110]

Liu Xie's first historical example is the politician Su Qin 蘇秦 (d. ca. 320 BCE), who became known as "Sir Stabs-His-Thigh" (Cigu xiansheng 刺股先生).[111] The *Stratagems of the Warring States* (*Zhanguo ce* 戰國策), a collection of anecdotes about the political alliances and rivalries among Chinese states between the fifth and third centuries BCE, dedicates many pages to Su Qin's rise from itinerant political advisor to one of the most prominent and influential politicians of his time. Su Qin remains most famous today for his determination to persevere in the face of adversity. One anecdote in the *Stratagems of the Warring States* describes him as studying day and night to improve his strategic knowledge and persuasive powers, adding that "whenever he was afraid of falling asleep while studying, he pulled out an awl and stabbed his thigh until blood ran down to his foot" (讀書欲睡, 引錐自刺其股, 血流至足).[112] The anecdote continues to describe how Su Qin's extreme dedication to his studies was ultimately successful, leading to his subsequent rise to power and wealth.

For his assiduous study and self-disciplined defiance of physical weaknesses, Su Qin was also included in the late medieval *Three Character Canon* (*San zi jing* 三字經), an anonymous text likely from the thirteenth century that became one of the most widely used primers in late imperial China. It survives in countless editions, often illustrated with commentaries. Consisting of little more than a thousand words arranged in three-word verses, the *Three Character Canon* introduces the most basic facts of the natural world, the key values of Confucianism, and an overview of Chinese history. Large portions of the text, especially the beginning and the last third, praise education through allusions to historical exemplars of studying under adversity. The only two stories that involve self-mortification are those of Su Qin and Sun Jing, encapsulated by the phrase "head suspended from a beam, awl stabbing the thighs" (頭懸梁, 錐刺股).[113]

---

110. *Shi ji* 41.1742. On King Goujian's ascetic regime, see Richter, *Bild des Schlafes*, 136–38.
111. *Beitang shuchao* 97.11.4a.
112. *Zhanguo ce* 3.85. On Su Qin, see also *Shi ji* 69.2241–68.
113. *Xinyi San zi jing*, 200.

Sun Jing 孫敬 was a late Han dynasty scholar who is said to have practiced a much milder form of self-mortification than this citation from the *Three Character Canon* suggests. When he became tired, he bound his hair to a beam, hoping that the pain from nodding off would keep him awake. The little we know about him comes from fragments transmitted in commonplace books and commentaries. These sources depict Sun Jing as more of a paragon of Confucian virtue than "Sir Stabs-His-Thigh." Heavily laden with conventional biographical motifs, these fragments tell us that Sun Jing was fond of learning but showed his filial duty by prioritizing his mother's needs and that he was poor but compensated by finding a small house for his mother and even making his own copies of the canonical books. By staying behind closed doors, we may assume, he avoided the costly joys of company and demonstrated his dedication to study, earning him the epithet "Sir Shuts-His-Door" (Bihu xiansheng 閉戶先生).[114] The historical record also presents Sun Jing as uninterested in personal profit, declining a position that might have brought him riches.[115] Unlike Su Qin, Sun Jing's method of staying awake at night did not involve blood and physical injury and is thus better aligned with the Confucian injunction against harming the body entrusted to us by our parents.

It is remarkable that Su Qin and Sun Jing found their way into a condensed text such as the *Three Character Canon* at all, thereby becoming immortalized in the minds of millions of young Chinese for centuries to come. Should we interpret these men's unusual dedication as excessive, especially in the case of Su Qin, whose self-inflicted injuries could easily have led to infection and premature death? Or did these men merely do what was necessary to be successful? The inclusion of Su Qin and Sun Jing in the *Three Character Canon*'s catalog of paragons was clearly meant to encourage diligent study. Even if we explain away the self-harm as narrative hyperbole, the anecdotal and historical sources report only reward, not punishment, for these men's methods of "exacting study" (*ku xue* 苦學) and their efforts in self-discipline and defiance of physical weaknesses.[116]

---

114. *Yiwen leiju* 55.991.

115. See "Wei xue ri yi zhang" 為學日益章, in *Daode zhenjing yanyi shouchao*; *Wen xuan* 36.1661 and 38.1745; *Taiping yulan* 363.7a and 606.1b.

116. The phrase *ku xue* does not appear in records before the Tang dynasty and only became common during the Song dynasty (960–1279). However, its frequent use in *fanqie*

60   *Part One*

In Liu Xie's "Nurturing the Vital Breath," self-mortification occupies an uneasy place, which may be one of the reasons why the authenticity of this passage has been questioned. We cannot rule out the possibility that Liu did indeed approve of a certain degree of self-harm for students—perhaps because the young were "able to withstand strain" (l. 27). However, he certainly did not emphasize this point here or anywhere else in *Literary Mind*, and he appears to mention this aspect almost reluctantly. Although Liu identifies profound learning as a prerequisite for writing in several chapters of the book, he clearly ranked learning behind talent.[117] Another reason why "exacting study" plays a minor role in *Literary Mind* could be Liu Xie's ubiquitous veneration of Confucius. The master's fondness for learning, famously highlighted throughout the *Analects*, is entirely incompatible with the idea that one would have to force oneself to study by such crude means.[118] Ideally, learning should not even be tainted by ulterior motives—such as escaping a hard life—but pursued for the sake of acquiring knowledge.[119]

While this is the dominant narrative, Confucius and his disciples are also associated with exhaustion and weariness from study that could have necessitated "exacting study." In the *Analects*, the master himself finds it necessary to claim that "he does not grow tired of learning" (學而不厭).[120] In the *Liezi*, Confucius's disciple Zigong 子貢 (Duanmu Ci 端木賜, trad. 520–456 BCE), grown weary of study, expresses a desire for rest, whereupon Confucius responds dryly, "There is no rest for the living" (生无所息), pointing to a nearby graveyard.[121] The *Xunzi* cites another disciple, Youzi 有子 (You Ruo 有若, trad. 508–457 BCE), who singed the palms of his hands to stay awake. Although the text recognizes Youzi's willpower, it criticizes him for lacking a decisive quality: real devotion to study.[122]

反切 indications may not be coincidental. On self-inflicted violence, see also Ter Haar, *Religious Culture and Violence*, 55–59.

117. See, e.g., *Wenxin diaolong* 26.493, 38.615.

118. See, e.g., *Lunyu* 1.14, 5.15, 5.28, 6.3 (11.17), 8.13, 17.8.

119. *Lunyu* 16.9.

120. *Lunyu* 7.2; see also 7.34.

121. *Liezi* 1.26.

122. *Xunzi* 21.403; see also Knoblock's translation in *Xunzi*, 108, and more information on Youzi, 94–95. While extreme self-mortification is rare in early Chinese texts, such exam-

Between Self-Care and Self-Harm 61

External Digressions, Continued: Book Mania in China and Europe

Huangfu Mi 皇甫謐 (215–282) may have been the first scholar to be called a "book maniac" (*shuyin* 書淫).[123] His official biography reports that he earned this epithet because he became so immersed in his pleasure of books that he would forget to sleep or eat. The biography also introduces someone who cautioned that such excessive devotion to learning would damage his vital energies, only to reveal Huangfu Mi as something of a stoic. He serenely waved away the health risks of his book mania with a quotation from the *Analects*: "If you have heard of the Way in the morning, you may die in the evening" (朝聞道, 夕死可矣), adding that "The length of one's life is fixed by heaven anyway" (況命之修短分定懸天乎).[124] Huangfu Mi left a large and varied oeuvre, consisting of works about history, biography, and medicine, making it only too plausible that he lived a life absorbed in reading and was often sick.[125]

A contemporary of Huangfu Mi, the historian Du Yu 杜預 (222–285), reportedly used a similar term to describe himself. His biography tells us that Du was in the habit of calling certain friends who were too fond of horses or money "addicts" (*pi* 癖), which provoked Emperor Wu of the Jin dynasty (晉武帝, r. 266–290) to ask about Du Yu's own addiction. Du virtuously admitted to "having an addiction to the *Zuo Tradition*" (臣有左傳癖).[126] Although the focus on a single work may at first appear less impressive, anyone familiar with this canonical text will easily believe it is possible to spend one's life studying it. Du Yu obviously did so, as his received commentarial work on the *Zuo Tradition* demonstrates.

Two centuries later, book mania figures prominently in the biography of Liu Jun 劉峻 (*zi* Xiaobiao 孝標, 462–521). After describing his difficult childhood following the Xianbei invasion in 469, which led him to Sang-

---

ples become more frequent in later Buddhist contexts. Bodhidharma 菩提達磨, the alleged sixth-century founder of the Chan 禪 school in China, is said to have been so disturbed by the interruption of his meditation by sleep that he cut off his own eyelids.

123. See Wai-yee Li's study "Genealogies of Obsession in Chinese Literature."

124. *Jin shu* 51.1410. See also the translations by Declercq, *Writing Against the State*, 168, and Nagel-Angermann, "Diwang shiji," 18. For the quotation from the *Analects*, see *Lunyu* 4.8.

125. Huangfu Mi's autobiographical illness reports are discussed in part II.

126. *Jin shu* 34.1032.

62   Part One

gan (in present-day Shanxi), the biography turns to his intellectual life in terms reminiscent of Wang Chong, emphasizing Liu Jun's self-directed study and impressive vigor:

> Liu Jun was fond of learning. Because his family was poor, he stayed as a lodger at other people's houses. He studied by himself, often all through the night by the light of a hemp torch. Sometimes when he nodded off, the flame would singe his hair so that he would wake up and continue to read. He did not sleep all night; his assiduousness was like that. When he managed to return [to Jiankang] from Sanggan in the middle of the Yongming era [483–493] of the Qi dynasty [479–502], he felt that his reading had not been comprehensive enough. He searched for rare books, and whenever he heard of such a book in the capital, he went there to request that it be lent to him. Cui Weizu [d. 499] of the Qinghe Cui clan called him a "book maniac."
>
> 峻好學, 家貧, 寄人廡下, 自課讀書, 常燎麻炬, 從夕達旦, 時或昏睡, 爇其髮, 既覺復讀, 終夜不寐, 其精力如此。 齊永明中, 從桑乾得還, 自謂所見不博, 更求異書, 聞京師有者, 必往祈借, 清河崔慰祖謂之書淫。[127]

The great number of texts that Liu Jun cites in his extant commentary to *Traditional Tales and Recent Accounts* (*Shishuo xinyu* 世說新語) and his comprehensive, though largely lost, commonplace book *Garden of Categories* (*Lei yuan* 類苑) attest to his exceptionally wide reading.

A scholar and historian who may also have been something of a book maniac himself, though not labeled as such, is Fan Ning 范甯 (ca. 339–401). According to his biography, Fan once sought a prescription for his eye complaint from Zhang Zhan, whom we have mentioned as the author of the compendium *Collection of Essentials about Nurturing Life*. The teasing prescription Zhang wrote for him is preserved in Fan Ning's official biography:

> An old prescription: Master Yangli from Song obtained this art when he was young. He passed it on to Sire Dongmen from Lu, who passed it on to Zuo Qiuming. Afterward, it was transmitted from generation to generation. Du Qin and Zheng Xuan of the Han dynasty, Gaotang Long of the Wei dynasty,

---

127. *Liang shu* 50.701.

Between Self-Care and Self-Harm   63

and Zuo Si of the Jin dynasty, all of whom suffered from ophthalmological complaints, obtained the following prescription: first, cut back on reading; second, reduce thinking; third, focus on inward vision; fourth, ignore
outward vision; fifth, get up late in the morning; sixth, go to sleep early at
night. Stew these six together over the fire of the spirit and pass them down
through the sieve of vital breath. Store them in your breast for seven days
and then receive them into your heart. Practice this for a short time, and you
can count someone's eyelashes close up, and in the distance see what remains
of a "foot-long stick" [when it has been broken in half over and over again].[128]
Taken continuously over a longer period of time, you will see through walls.
Not only will your eyes become clear, but you will also prolong your life.

古方, 宋陽里子少得其術, 以授魯東門伯, 魯東門伯以授左丘明, 遂世
世相傳。及漢杜子夏鄭康成、魏高堂隆、晉左太沖, 凡此諸賢, 並
有目疾, 得此方云: 用損讀書一, 減思慮二, 專內視三, 簡外觀四, 旦
晚起五, 夜早眠六。凡六物熬以神火, 下以氣篩, 蘊於胸中七日, 然後
納諸方寸。修之一時, 近能數其目睫, 遠視尺捶之餘。長服不已, 洞
見牆壁之外。非但明目, 乃亦延年。」[129]

Much of the humor derives from the long lineage of fellow sufferers introduced in the pseudohistorical prelude to the prescription—a feature likely
inspired by the writings of Sima Qian 司馬遷 (ca. 145–ca. 87 BCE), as we
will see in part II. Many of Zhang Zhan's exemplars are blind, while others
are known for their excessive learning. Zuo Qiuming 左丘明 (trad. 556–451
BCE), the alleged author of the Zuo Tradition, was blind. The high-ranking
official Du Qin 杜欽 (zi Zixia, fl. 33–22 BCE) was called "blind Du Zixia"
(盲杜子夏), though only one of his eyes was unsighted.[130] The great scholar
and commentator Zheng Xuan 鄭玄 (zi Kangcheng, 127–200) is included
perhaps because, according to a later anecdote, he was "blind" to female beauty
during his time as a student of Ma Rong 馬融 (79–166).[131] No information
has been transmitted about ophthalmological complaints of the high official
and astrologer Gaotang Long 高堂隆 (d. 237) or of Zuo Si, whom we have
already encountered as one of Liu Xie's slow and painstaking writers.

128. The increasingly smaller parts of a stick that is repeatedly broken in half are
mentioned in Zhuangzi 33.1106.

129. Jin shu 75.1988–89. See also Stein, Zwischen Heil und Heilung, 101.

130. Shi ji 130.3300; Han shu 60.2667.

131. Hou Han shu 60A.1972.

64   *Part One*

In the European tradition, where "bibliomania" is a well-recognized literary motif, particularly in early modern Europe, book maniacs differ significantly from the Chinese scholars described as *shuyin* or *shupi* in early medieval China. Prototypical European bibliomaniacs are famously more interested in acquiring and possessing books than in reading them.[132] Examples include the fanatic bookseller Giacomo in Gustave Flaubert's novella *Bibliomania* (1836) and the wretched sinologist Peter Kien in Elias Canetti's novel *Auto-da-Fé* (*Die Blendung*, 1935).

While Huangfu Mi's love of books is certainly described in strong terms and with a hint of sensuality, it is clear that he, Du Yu, and Liu Jun were ardent and voracious readers. Du Yu's fixation on one book and Huangfu Mi's portrayal as "immersed in the pleasure of books" (耽翫/玩) resonate with another, more famous reader's obsessive relationship with a particular text: the aged Confucius's partiality to the *Changes of Zhou* (*Zhou yi* 周易).[133] Sima Qian portrays the relationship between this man and this book through an image of wear and tear, noting that "reading the *Changes*, he thrice broke the book's leather bindings" (讀易韋編三絕).[134] Yan Shigu's 顏師古 (581–645) commentary on the parallel account in the *History of the Han Dynasty* (*Han shu* 漢書) clarifies this, explaining that "this is to say that Confucius cherished the *Changes* very much" (言愛玩之甚), using the term *ai wan* 愛玩, which carries sensory and specifically tactile connotations.[135] It is likely no coincidence that this image of Confucius indulging in a book was created during the Han dynasty, a period marked by an increase in written texts that many may have found concerning.

Reading and reciting too much, studying too hard, brooding too long over texts—these topics connect the inquiry into excessive intellectual work in the Chinese tradition with a very different set of Western ideas and literary traditions. One of these is a branch of occupational medicine

132. See Metz, "Bibliomania and the Folly of Reading."

133. A similarly intense relationship with a single book is described in the biography of Shi Xie 士燮 (137–226), who is characterized as "immersed in the pleasure of the *Springs and Autumns Annals*, for which he also wrote a commentary" (耽玩春秋, 為之注解, *Sanguo zhi* 49.1191).

134. *Shi ji* 47.1937.

135. *Han shu* 88.3589–91. Also see Wai-yee Li, "Genealogies of Obsession in Chinese Literature," 217.

Between Self-Care and Self-Harm   65

dedicated to the dangers of being an intellectual or "brainworker." This tradition dates back to the first century, when the Roman scholar Aulus Cornelius Celsus (25 BCE–50 CE) remarked in the preface to his *Of Medicine* (*De medicina*) that learning, "pursued with greater application," although "most necessary to the mind . . . is no less hurtful for the body," noting that those "who had impaired their bodies by anxious thought, and nightly watchings, stood most in need of . . . assistance."[136]

Where Celsus points out the dangers of excessive learning, Seneca (ca. 4 BCE–65 CE), around the same time, focuses on the perils of too much and too random reading. He writes in the second letter to his young friend Lucilius:

> The primary indication . . . of a well-ordered mind is a man's ability to remain in one place and linger in his own company. Be careful, however, lest this reading of many authors and books of every sort may tend to make you discursive and unsteady. You must linger among a limited number of master-thinkers, and digest their works, if you would derive ideas which shall win firm hold in your mind.[137]

More than a millennium later, Francesco Petrarca (1304–1374), in his *Remedies for Fortune Fair and Foul* (*De remediis utriusque fortunae*), repeats and intensifies this warning:

> Books have led some to learning, and others to madness,[138] when they swallow more than they can digest. In the mind, as in the body, indigestion does

136. Celsus, *Of Medicine*, 2–3; as translated by James Greive. On Celsus and his reception in Europe, see Kümmel, "Homo litteratus." See also Ann Blair's comprehensive study, *Too Much to Know*.

137. Seneca, *Epistles*, 6–7; as translated by Richard M. Gummere. In early modern China, Zhu Xi's 朱熹 (1130–1200) advice not to strive for quantity in reading but to become intimately familiar with one's readings became similarly popular. See translations of Zhu Xi's "How to Read Books" ("Du shu fa" 讀書法) in Gardner, *Learning to Be a Sage*, 43–45, 132–36.

138. In the West, madness resulting from overexerting one's mental faculties is a common topos. Writing about the exhaustibility of the intellect, Arthur Schopenhauer (1788–1860), in chapter 19, "On the Primacy of the Will in Self-Consciousness," of his *The World as Will and Representation*, remarks that "all continuous mental work requires pauses and rest,

66   Part One

more harm than hunger; food and books alike must be used according to the constitution, and what is little enough for one is too much for another.[139]

Starting from the fifteenth century, and especially following Marsilio Ficino's (1433–1499) *Three Books on Life* (*De triplici vita*, 1489), whole books dedicated to the particular health issues of scholars began to emerge.[140] An interesting case is the sixteenth-century *Simple and Healthy Nourishment for Poor Students* (*Victus ratio, scholasticis pauperibus paratu facilis & salubris*) by Jacques Dubois (ca. 1478–1555), which lays out a comprehensive "regimen for poor scholars." Dubois acknowledges that "books are read with great sacrifice of the eyes and the seated body, especially those in Greek and even more so those in Hebrew," and he recommends reading silently to avoid wearying oneself and others.[141]

The most influential work of this genre was Samuel Tissot's (1728–1797) *On the Health of Writers* (*De la santé des gens de lettres*, 1766). The Swiss physician reiterates Celsus's warning of "anxious thought, and nightly watchings" and adds another concern: the scholar's "constant inaction of the body."[142] This even makes it into the title of this book's English translation, *An Essay on Diseases Incident to Literary and Sedentary Persons*. Interestingly, Tissot assumes that while "trifling books" merely cost us time, "those which by the strength and concatenation of ideas seem to raise the

---

otherwise stupidity and incapacity are the result." He attributes mental weaknesses typically ascribed to "old age in and by itself" to the "long-continued tyrannical overstraining of the intellect or the brain," citing writers who experienced mental decline due to overwork and others who remained clear-headed to the end. Schopenhauer concludes that "all this proves how very secondary and physical the intellect is," requiring "for almost a third of its life, the entire suspension of its activity in sleep" (Schopenhauer, *World as Will*, 213–14, as translated by E. F. J. Payne). This topos also appears humorously in Mark Twain's (1835–1910) *Tom Sawyer* (1876), where, in chapter 4, a "boy of German parentage . . . once recited three thousand [biblical] verses without stopping; but the strain upon his mental faculties was too great, and he was little better than an idiot from that day forth." See also part II, in connection with Xiao Yi's autobiography.

139. *Petrarch's Remedies*, 43, as translated by Conrad H. Rawski.

140. Ficino, *Three Books on Life*, as translated by Carol V. Kaske and John R. Clark.

141. O'Malley, "Jacobus Sylvius' Advice," 144–45.

142. Tissot, *Essay on Diseases*, 13, as translated by James Kirkpatrick.

soul as it were above itself, and compel it to meditate, wear out the mind, and exhaust the body." He cites numerous historical and contemporary examples, including one reminiscent of Yang Xiong's mental exhaustion following the composition of his "Rhapsody on the Sweet Springs Palace." In another parallel to Liu Xie, Tissot observes that the "erudites," arising "at the time that literature was in its decline," often "mortify themselves ... without adducing the slightest advantage to society from their voluntary sufferings," destroying "themselves with books, manuscripts, medals, antique inscriptions, and inexplicable characters."[143]

In Chinese medical or nurturing life literature, we find similar lineages of caution and warning about excessive intellectual labor. From the early Tang *Essential Prescriptions for Every Emergency Worth a Thousand in Gold* (*Beiji qianjin yaofang* 備急千金要方, 652) by Sun Simiao 孫思邈 to the late Ming *Eight Notes on Pursuing [the Right Path of] Life* (*Zunsheng bajian* 遵生八牋) by Gao Lian 高濂,[144] these texts often implicitly address scholar-officials. It is more likely that the portly men stretching and bending in the *Tableau of Guiding and Pulling* (*Daoyin tu* 導引圖) found in Mawangdui are scholars or administrators rather than farmers or craftsmen, and the same applies to the illustrations in later manuals of nurturing life.[145] In "Nurturing the Vital Breath," it is evident that Liu Xie writes for other writers.

Dealing with Writer's Block and Other Obstacles

Returning to *Literary Mind* and its chapter "Nurturing the Vital Breath" after our digression into Chinese and Western ideas of book mania, we find Liu Xie reiterating (from line 7) an important principle that every writer should observe:

至於文也[146]	As for literature,
52　則申寫鬱滯	it divulges and expresses that which is pent up inside.

143. Tissot, *Essay on Diseases*, 17, 33, 46–47.
144. See Despeux, *Prescriptions d'acuponcture*; Chen Hsiu-fen, "Nourishing Life."
145. On *Daoyin tu*, see Harper, *Early Chinese Medical Literature*, esp. 310–27.
146. For the emendation of 志 to 至, see *Wenxin diaolong jiaozhu shiyi buzheng*, 377.

68 Part One

	故宜	That is why we ought to
	從容率情	be leisurely and act in accordance with our inner state,
54	優柔適會	be gentle and in accordance with the moment.

This positive formulation is complemented by a harsher tone in the subsequent lines, where Liu emphasizes his basic message with a pair of evocative death threats:

	若	If we
	銷鑠精膽	melt away our vital energies and
56	蹙迫和氣	cramp the harmonious flow of our vital energies,
	秉牘以驅齡	then holding the writing tablet will hasten our death,
58	灑翰以伐性	and moistening the brush will hack away at our life.
	豈	How could this be
	聖賢之素心	the genuine intent of the sages and worthies
60	會文之直理哉	or the correct way of composing literature?

In this passage, Liu not only argues in terms of physiology but also evokes the "sages and worthies" of the golden past, when literary works were created in accordance with the natural capacity of their authors, which he had described in lines 11 to 15. Wang Chong's "An Examination of Vigor," mentioned previously in connection with Yan Hui's early death due to overexertion, might have been the first to explain the productivity of the ancients in terms of their natural endowment, emphasizing that the worthies possessed an "abundance of vigor" (多力), which also showed in their ability "to spit out ten thousand writing tablets of literature and more" (吐文萬牒以上).[147]

The harshness of this warning against "hastening death" and "hacking away at life" is momentarily relieved in the next passage, which addresses the everyday routine that makes up life for every writer. Liu takes the quotidian seriously in its influence on writing and encourages writers to do the same. His key example is taken from the canonical *Zuo Tradition*, but the incident it touches on is mundane enough to allow every reader to identify with: someone who has just washed his hair (and is thus immersed in daily life in a quite tangible way) may have good reason to turn away a visitor:

---

147. *Lunheng* 37.582.

	且夫	Furthermore,
	思有利鈍	"thinking, we have sharp and dull moments," and
62	時有通塞	"there are times of smooth running and of blockage."
	沐則心覆	"When one washes one's hair, the heart is upside down,"
64	且或反常	which may even overturn our normal [way of thinking].[148]
	神之方昏	If it so happens that our spirit has become dim-witted,
66	再三愈黷	to keep on trying will only make it grow dimmer.

Liu Xie's acknowledgment of the inevitable dull moments in a writer's life, coupled with his advice not to persist during temporary blocks, demonstrates both psychological acuity and a sense of reality. He validates his perspective by a reference to the lowly sphere of personal hygiene, which usually remains outside the purview of literary criticism but is here elevated by virtue of its canonical source. Rather than chastising his readers for experiencing writer's block or other obstacles during composition, Liu reassures them that such complications are a normal part of life, as unembarrassing as washing one's hair. However, he also implies that moments of blockage need to be recognized as potentially dangerous to a writer's health and should be addressed appropriately.

The other two references Liu makes are to the Lu brothers. The phrase "thinking, we have sharp and dull moments" (l. 61) is a direct quotation from a letter Lu Yun wrote to his brother Lu Ji.[149] The notion of "times of smooth running and of blockage" (l. 62) recalls the "Rhapsody on Literature," where Lu Ji dedicates extensive passages to the difficulties of composition. This line also evokes waterways, an image revisited in the subsequent chapter of *Literary Mind*.[150]

---

148. *Zuozhuan* Xi 24; Durrant, Li, and Schaberg, *Zuo Tradition*, 377.

149. Lu Yun, "Yu xiong Pingyuan shu" no. 7, in *Quan Jin wen* 102.3a. Yan Zhitui, writing more than half a century after Liu Xie, uses "sharp and dull" to describe different intellectual abilities rather than moments in our lives: "In scholarship, some are sharp and some are dull; in literary composition, some are skillful and some are clumsy" (學問有利鈍, 文章有巧拙). Yan declares that while dull scholars may flourish through persistence, clumsy writers will never succeed even if they try hard. See *Yanshi jiaxun* 9.254; Tian, *Family Instructions*, 191.

150. *Wen xuan* 17.764 and 17.772–73. See also Stephen Owen's translation and commentary

70 *Part One*

A similar point is made in a passage of the "Discourse on Styles" ("Lun ti" 論體), dated to the Sui (581–618) or early Tang periods, where an argument is made that also overlaps with other ideas that Liu expresses in this chapter. Since this essay, transmitted in Japan in Kūkai's 空海 (774–835) *Secret Repository of Discourses on the Mirror of Literature* (*Bunkyō hifuron* 文鏡祕府論), lacks information about an author or a secure date, it is unclear whether it was influenced by Lu Ji and Liu Xie, or if the ideas it expresses were more widespread in early medieval literature than current sources indicate:

> Yet the mind may be obstructed or running smoothly, and thinking may sometimes be dull and sometimes sharp. When [a thought] arrives it must not be suppressed; when it departs, it must not be kept back.[151] Then again, if you are troubled and wearied inside and work without inspiration, but you force yourself to press on, this will only result in torturing yourself. It is better to sheathe your brush and put it out of your sight for a while until later ideas [arise]. Wait for your mind and thought to become clear again and only then continue before you go on with your work. Not only is this the highest art of writing, but it is also a great method for nurturing life.
>
> 然心或蔽通, 思時鈍利, 來不可遏, 去不可留。若又情性煩勞, 事由寂寞, 強自催逼, 徒成辛苦。不若韜翰屏筆, 以須後圖, 待心慮更澄, 方事連緝。非止作文之至術, 抑亦養生之大方耳。[152]

The explicit connection between writing and nurturing life in this text may well demonstrate the mainstreaming of ideas of nurturing life in early medieval China.

After this moment of narrative and almost comic relief in introducing an element of personal hygiene into his deliberations, Liu Xie further elab-

---

in *Readings in Chinese Literary Thought*, ll. 43–44, 57–58, 235–46. In the *Commentary to the Canon of Waterways* (*Shuijing zhu* 水經注) by Liu Xie's contemporary Li Daoyuan 酈道元 (d. 527), the phrase "there are times of smooth running and of blockage" (時有通塞, *Shuijing zhu* 7.124) describes the situation of rivers.

151. In Lu Ji's "Rhapsody on Literature" we read, "when it arrives it must not be held back; when it departs, it must not be stopped" (來不可遏, 去不可止, *Wen xuan* 17.772).

152. *Wenjing mifulun*, 398–99. See also the translation by Bodman in "Poetics and Prosody," 435–36.

orates on his main point—that writers should stop when things are not going smoothly. He supports his case with evidence from a wide range of literary sources:

	是以	This is why,
	吐納文藝	in the creation of literary art, we should
68	務在節宣	strive to "release [our vital energies] in regulated fashion,"[153] and
	清和其心	clear and harmonize our minds,
70	調暢其氣	so that our vital energies are well adjusted and running smoothly.[154]
	煩而即捨	"If something becomes overly complicated, one gives it up" at once,[155]
72	勿使壅滯	so as not to cause stagnation.
	意得則舒懷以命筆	If we have obtained a meaning, we should follow our heart and command the brush, but
74	理伏則投筆以卷懷	if reason eludes us, we should discard the brush and withdraw our heart.[156]
	逍遙以針勞	"Free and easy" wandering can serve as acupuncture if we are weary,
76	談笑以藥勮	conversation and laughter as medicine if we are worn out.

The diverse terminology in this passage reveals a blend of Confucian ideas,

---

153. *Zuozhuan* Zhao 1; Durrant, Li, and Schaberg, *Zuo Tradition*, 1327.

154. When Liu Xie characterizes epistolary writings, he expresses a similar idea, suggesting that "words are meant to dispel pent-up emotions and to carry feeling and coloration, and should therefore be smooth in order to convey the thrust [lit. "to carry the *qi*"] and gentle in order to delight the heart" (言以散鬱陶, 託風采, 故宜條暢以任氣, 優柔以懌懷, *Wenxin diaolong* 25.456).

155. The *Zuo Tradition* continues, following the quoted phrase, "lest one fall ill because of it" (至於煩乃舍也已無以生疾, *Zuozhuan* Zhao 1; Durrant, Li, and Schaberg, *Zuo Tradition*, 1331). See also a similar passage in the "Discourses on Literature and Meaning" ("Lun wen yi" 論文意) chapter of Kūkai's *Mirror of Literature*, in *Wenjing mifulun*, 360–61. Zhu Xi's "How to Read Books" similarly recommends varying exertion with rest; see also Gardner, *Learning to Be a Sage*, 147

156. Alluding to *Lunyu* 15.7.

72 Part One

Daoist notions, and medical concepts—intellectual strands that are impossible to disentangle. Liu first uses *tuna* 吐納 (lit."to spit out and draw in") in the sense of creating literature, whether orally or in writing—a usage that may only have become common during his time. In the context of Daoist ideas of nurturing life, "to spit out the old breath and draw in the new" (吐故納新), as we find it in a list of practices to nurture one's body in the *Zhuangzi* and many other texts, describes a technique to manipulate one's vital breath.[157] While the term *tuna* appears throughout *Literary Mind* to indicate writing, it seems particularly apt in this chapter focused on vital breath.

The phrase *jiexuan* 節宣 (lit. "to moderate and disperse") recalls an important historical and literary example of health advice found in the canonical *Zuo Tradition*. The term is used by Zichan 子產 (Gongsun Qiao 公孫僑, trad. d. 522 BCE), a minister under Lord Ping of Jin 晉平公 (r. 557–532 BCE), in a speech where he explains the reasons for his master's indisposition. Embarking on a long admonition, Zichan rejects the notion that Lord Ping's present illness is caused by spirits and instead identifies the lord's dissolute way of life as the culprit:

> As for the body of the ruler, that is a matter of his behavior while abroad and while at home, his drinking and eating, and his sorrows and delights. What do the spirits of the mountains and rivers or stars and constellations have to do with it? I have heard that for the noble man there are four periods to the day: in the early morning he hears administrative business, during the daylight hours he consults, in the evening he crafts his commands, and at night he rests his body. In this way he releases his life force in regulated fashion, not allowing any blockage or stagnation to weaken his constitution, lest his heart be muddied and all the standards of order be thrown into confusion. But now he has collapsed all four periods into one, has he not? And he has in consequence fallen ill.
>
> 若君身，則亦出入飲食哀樂之事也，山川星辰之神又何為焉？僑聞之。君子有四時。朝以聽政。晝以訪問。夕以脩令。夜以安身。於是乎節宣其氣。勿使有所壅閉湫底。以露其體。茲心不爽。而昏亂百度。今無乃壹之。則生疾矣。[158]

157. *Zhuangzi* 15.535.

158. *Zuozhuan* Zhao 1; Durrant, Li, and Schaberg, *Zuo Tradition*, 1327. Several years later, we see Zichan take a different approach to diagnosing an illness of the same ruler.

Unsurprisingly, Zichan's words were frequently quoted in literary texts from the Han dynasty onward, such as by Xun Yue in his *Extended Reflections*, which includes several discussions on "nurturing inborn nature" (養性).[159]

In an ingenious move, Liu Xie emphasizes his message through medical metaphors, recommending sweeter and more agreeable substitutes for the possibly painful and bitter treatments that acupuncture and medicine offer.[160] The phrase "free and easy wandering" brings to mind the *Zhuangzi*, especially its first eponymous chapter ("Xiaoyao you" 逍遙遊), as well as other Zhuangzian images of effortless creativity and existence.[161] The second pair of remedies, "conversation and laughter," gains an additional facet of meaning when we recall that the only other time Liu Xie uses this phrase in *Literary Mind* is to evoke the exuberant creative atmosphere in poetic circles during the late Jian'an period (196–220), when writers "moistened their brushes to create elated songs and mixed ink to raise talk and laughter" (灑筆以成酣歌, 和墨以藉談笑).[162]

Liu Xie continues by intertwining references to the *Zuo Tradition* and the *Zhuangzi* with medical metaphors:

常弄閑於才鋒	If we always act comfortably from within the edges of our innate talent and
78 貫餘於文勇	"buy from a surplus" of literary valor,[163]

On that occasion, he suggests, based on his interpretation of a dream the ruler reported, that the ruler was ill because he had neglected a ritual (*Zuozhuan* Zhao 7; Durrant, Li, and Schaberg, *Zuo Tradition*, 1423). On Lord Ping's indispositions and other "elite illnesses" in early Chinese literature, see also Riegel's "Curing the Incurable."

159. *Shenjian* 3.17. See also Ch'i-yün Ch'en, *Hsün Yüeh and the Mind of Late Han China*, 157–58. Overindulgence as the root of illness is also at the center of Mei Cheng's 枚乘 (d. 140 BCE) "Seven Stimuli" ("Qi fa" 七發), in *Quan Han wen* 20.4a–8a; see Knechtges and Swanson, "Seven Stimuli for the Prince."

160. Liu Xie uses images of health, illness, and healing elsewhere in *Literary Mind*, in line with much else in Chinese prose. Defining the genre of admonition (*zhen* 箴, lit. "needle"), for instance, he writes that "admonitions attack illnesses and guard against afflictions; they resemble acupuncture needles" (箴者所以攻疾防患, 喻鍼石也, *Wenxin diaolong zhu* 11.194).

161. See, e.g., *Zhuangzi* 14.519; also 28.966.

162. *Wenxin diaolong* 45.673.

163. The strongman Gao Gu 高固 (fl. 604–588 BCE) supposedly once proposed, full

	使刀發如新	we will keep our "blade like new" and
80	腠理無滯[164]	foramina and veins free from stagnation.[165]
	雖非胎息之萬術[166]	Although this may not be among the ten thousand techniques of "embryonic breathing,"
82	斯亦衛氣之一方也	it is still a method of protecting our vital energies.

The beginning of this passage resumes the idea of surplus that Liu first mentioned when he characterized the conditions under which the ancients wrote before the Warring States period (l. 23, "The ancients were 'at ease'").[167] The blade that remains sharp despite years of constant use evokes the virtuoso Cook Ding 庖丁, a key protagonist in the *Zhuangzi's* "Fundamentals of Nurturing Life," an allusion that also serves to prepare the encomium.[168] By operating with medical terms, the line on keeping "the foramina and veins free from stagnation" returns to the movement of the vital energies within the body. Liu describes their ideal state as "harmonious flow" (和氣, l. 56) and "well-adjusted and running smoothly" (調暢其氣, l. 70), while warning of "blockage" (塞, l. 62) and "stagnation" (壅滯, l. 72). He develops these ideas further in the chapter immediately following "Nurturing the Vital Breath." Also using metaphors of the body and waterways, chapter 43, "Fluency and Coherence" ("Fu hui" 附會), transposes the unobstructed flow of vital energies from the human body to the body of the text.[169]

---

of swagger, that "those who want valor can buy my surplus" (欲勇者賈余餘勇, *Zuozhuan* Cheng 2; Durrant, Li, and Schaberg, *Zuo Tradition*, 715).

164. For the emendation of 湊 to 腠, see *Wenxin diaolong jiaozhu shiyi buzheng*, 379.

165. Although transmitted medical texts do not discuss the foramina and veins (*couli*) in terms of stagnation (*zhi*), philosophical texts do; see, e.g., *Lüshi chunqiu* 3.3.144.

166. For the emendation of 邁 to 萬, see *Wenxin diaolong jiaozhu shiyi buzheng*, 379.

167. With regard to reading, this idea was also expressed in Zhu Xi's "How to Read Books," together with the warning of reading too much mentioned earlier. See Gardner, *Learning to Be a Sage*, 133.

168. *Zhuangzi* 3.119. In the chapter "Mastering Life" ("Da sheng" 達生), two other craftsmen, Carpenter Qing 梓慶 and Artisan Chui 工倕, are characterized similarly. Carpenter Qing, for example, describes how he prepares for his work, starts with the words, "I would never let it wear out my vital breath" (未嘗敢以耗氣也, *Zhuangzi* 19.658).

169. *Wenxin diaolong* 43.6651.

Between Self-Care and Self-Harm   75

"Embryonic breathing" is a Daoist longevity technique described in several texts since the late Han dynasty.[170] Liu Xie uses the term metonymically to refer to the more esoteric methods of nurturing life that he does not discuss in this chapter. The reference toward the close of the chapter operates similarly to the initial reference to Wang Chong, clearly demarcating his take on "Nurturing the Vital Breath." By this point, the reader knows that Liu Xie does not dwell on practices typically found in nurturing life literature. There is no advice on breathing exercises, dietary restrictions, meditation, sexual cultivation, drugs, or therapeutic gymnastics—all elements in Wang Chong's lost *Nurturing Inborn Nature*. Nor does he give advice on sleep or other aspects of physical hygiene. Liu does not even concern himself with staving off old age; rather, as we have seen, he suggests working within the limitations it brings. "Nurturing the Vital Breath" is solely concerned with health in respect to literary creativity.

The Encomium: Summation and Exaltation

Each chapter of *Literary Mind* concludes with an encomium or appraisal (*zan* 贊) in the form of a tetrasyllabic poem. Liu Xie's encomia not only provide a succinct summary of the main ideas of each chapter, but they do so in an even higher register. The encomium to "Nurturing the Vital Breath" reads as follows:

	贊曰	The encomium says:
	紛哉萬象	Many and various, indeed, are the ten thousand phenomena,
84	勞矣千想	weary we have become from envisioning them a thousand-fold.
	玄神宜寶	The mysterious spirit should be treasured,
86	素氣資養	the original vital breath be preserved and nurtured.
	水停以鑒	Waters that are still serve as mirrors,[171]

---

170. See, e.g., *Baopuzi neipian* 8.136. See also the entry on *taixi* 胎息 by Catherine Despeux in Pregadio, *Encyclopedia of Taoism*, 953–54.

171. This image is used in *Zhuangzi* 5.193 and 5.214 and other early texts. See also *Shishuo xinyu* 2.90.

76 Part One

88	火靜而朗	fires that are calm burn bright.
	無擾文慮	Do not upset your literary contemplations,
90	鬱此精爽	and your spirit will remain effervescent.[172]

Liu acknowledges the infinite complexity of the world and the strain this places on human minds as they try to comprehend even a fraction of it. The difference in numerals—"ten thousand" and "one thousand"—though dictated by the parallel style and often simply indicating large numbers, may actually be meaningful here. The beginning of the encomium is a variation on the Zhuangzian theme, "My life flows between confines, but knowledge has no confines," an idea so vital to Liu that he explicitly mentions it several times throughout *Literary Mind*, including in "Nurturing the Vital Breath," and most prominently in the encomium of the book's final chapter to round off the entire compilation.[173]

Literati Bodies Between Sanctioned Self-Harm and Self-Preservation

Reviewing the main ideas and general thrust of Liu Xie's chapter on "Nurturing the Vital Breath," along with the historical figures and narratives he evokes, reveals a rich tapestry of literati attitudes to health and illness. Their most impressive feature is the awareness of the health risks inherent in intellectual work and the realization that avoiding these risks is difficult for any writer operating in a competitive and often violent public and official sphere. "Nurturing the Vital Breath" was clearly written in response to the conditions under which Liu Xie and contemporary writers had to work. Whether driven by the need to study countless books as part of the required curriculum or compelled by a superior's orders to compose specific texts, Chinese writers were acutely aware of the warning signs their bodies might send. The delicate balance between these conflicting demands is at the heart of several narratives, most pointedly in Huan Tan's apparently paradoxical embrace of illness as a

172. On the term *jingshuang* 精爽, rendered here "effervescent," see *Zuozhuan* Zhao 7; Durrant, Li, and Schaberg, *Zuo Tradition*, 1427.

173. *Wenxin diaolong* 50.728.

badge of honor in response to Yang Xiong's harrowing dream and ensuing sickness.

In "Nurturing the Vital Breath," good health is presented as the ability to fulfill one's official and scholarly duties, particularly the production of fine literary texts as part of these duties. Conversely, ill health is not depicted merely as an obstacle to literary productivity and excellence but rather as a consequence of an incorrect approach to learning and writing. Specifically, it results from excessive dedication to learning that disregards one's natural endowment and from "unnatural," strained writing. In this respect, Liu Xie is clearly indebted to Wang Chong and Cao Pi. These early medieval thinkers, writing in the first two centuries CE, proposed the connection between a writer's vital breath and their ability to create literature—a connection we will explore further in part II.

Modern readers of early and early medieval Chinese literature often emphasize the principles of moderation and the Golden Mean extolled in many normative texts. However, there were also spheres where excess was sanctioned and encouraged by the dominant value system, with learning being a prominent example. Moderation took a back seat too when it came to narratives of filial duty, propriety, loyalty, and, increasingly, religious fervor.[174] At the heart of the literati acceptance of certain forms of self-mortification is the difficult truth that for most men in early and early medieval China, substantial self-sacrifice, including the sacrifice of one's health, was the only way to become or remain part of the elite. Despite prescriptive ideals about preserving one's body, scholarly self-harm was not only common but also often expected. Liu Xie's advice against such methods likely stems from the fact that *Literary Mind* does not address young people who still need encouragement to study but rather targets a well-educated adult elite who, after years of grueling study, need a reminder to "be leisurely and act in accordance with our inner state" to preserve their creativity and productivity.

---

174. Jimmy Yu has written about this regarding late Ming (1368–1644) and early Qing (1644–1911) China in *Sanctity and Self-Inflicted Violence*. An early medieval example of filial duty leading to bodily harm, though unintentionally, would be Yin Zhongkan 殷仲堪 (d. 399/400), who is said to have caused one of his eyes to go blind by wiping away his tears with the hand that had been holding medicine for his sick father, Yin Shi 殷師; see *Jin shu* 84.2194. On Yin Zhongkan, see also part II.

78   *Part One*

Nevertheless, how many knives did Cook Ding ruin before he achieved expertise in the art of cutting up oxen? How could anyone write parallel prose in a "leisurely" way? A passage from the Tang dynasty "Discourses on Literature and Meaning" ("Lun wen yi" 論文意), transmitted in Kūkai's *Mirror of Literature*, highlights the writer's dilemma in a less visceral, though no less paradoxical, way than Huan Tan's story. The essay first declares that "Generally, literary writings should always read as neither difficult nor tortured" (凡文章皆不難又不辛苦), but then advises writers to "torture their mind and exhaust their knowledge" (苦心竭智), all while "making sure to forget themselves and loosen up" (必須忘身, 不可拘束).[175] This apparent dilemma, while not directly addressed in "Nurturing the Vital Breath," is explored in other chapters of *Literary Mind*, which emphasize that effortless creation requires the stage to be well prepared. In "Spirit Thought," Liu Xie asserts that there is no need for tortured thinking if one has prepared one's mind and nurtured one's art to a degree of full authority: "If we carry the seal and wield the tally, there is no need to strain our inner state" (含章司契, 不必勞情也).[176] Another chapter that highlights the value of preparation is the "Art of Gathering Up" ("Zong shu" 總術), where Liu compares the good writer to an accomplished chess player in full command of the game.[177]

If we are to trust Liu Xie, he managed to achieve the literary complexity and intricacy of *Literary Mind* not only through talent and years of arduous study but also by keeping his blade like new, acting leisurely, and in accordance with his disposition.

---

175. *Wenjing mifulun*, 334–35. The essay is often attributed to Wang Changling 王昌齡 (ca. 698–757). See also Bodman, "Poetics and Prosody," 381.

176. *Wenxin diaolong* 26.494.

177. *Wenxin diaolong* 44.656. The same argument is used in "Casting and Tailoring" ("Rong zai" 鎔裁), in *Wenxin diaolong* 32.543.

PART TWO

Writing the Sick Self

Autobiographical Accounts of Health and Illness

Variable, and therfore miserable condition of Man; this minute I was well, and am ill, this minute. I am surpriz'd with a sodain change, and alteration to worse, and can impute it to no cause, nor call it by any name. We study Health, and we deliberate upon our meats, and drink, and ayre, and exercises, and we hew, and wee polish every stone, that goes to that building; and so our Health is a long and a regular work; But in a minute a Canon batters all, overthrowes all, demolishes all; a Sicknes unprevented for all our diligence, unsuspected for all our curiositie; nay, undeserved, if we consider only disorder, summons us, seizes us, possesses us, destroyes us in an instant. O miserable condition of Man!

—John Donne, *Devotions upon Emergent Occasions*[1]

Where part I of our investigation focused on universal notions of health and illness relevant to the literati profession in early medieval China, part II turns to first-person accounts of being in good or ill

---

1. First published in 1624. The literature on John Donne (1572–1631) is extensive. For how Donne transforms the body into language, see Scarry, "Yet the Body Is His Booke," xv, 77–78. Also see Targoff, *John Donne, Body and Soul.*

80 Part Two

health. These individual experiences are articulated in a range of distinct forms of literary self-expression, from authorial prefaces to letters, confessional writings, and poems. Situated in different literary genres that played various social roles, early Chinese self-writings follow specific conventions that shaped their production in distinct ways, including diverse modes of depicting health and illness.[2]

In these early and early medieval Chinese texts, we do not find fully fledged illness memoirs like those burgeoning worldwide, alongside other types of autobiographical writing, with the rise of modernity. As early as 1990, Pei-Yi Wu described the general increase in self-writing as "torrential," and ten years later, Jeffrey K. Aronson spoke of a "deluge" of autopathography—both pluvial hyperbolae that nevertheless now seem understated in light of the exponential rise in autobiography and autopathography in the twenty-first century.[3] In our time, new biomedical technologies have blurred the boundaries of the individual, the human body, and life itself, leading to intense reflections on the relationship between human corporeality and personal identity. The easy availability of digital media for the publication of self-writings has also contributed to the growth of pathography.[4] Where G. Thomas Couser in the late twentieth century lamented the marginalization of illness in autobiography, contemporary culture has certainly moved on, giving full "cultural authorization" to self-narratives of illness.[5] Patients' stories about struggles with various conditions that used

2. Since the 1980s, there has been a growing interest in the study of autobiographical literature in China. Early articles demonstrating the range of approaches include Stephen W. Durrant's "Self as the Intersection of Traditions" (1986) and Stephen Owen's "The Self's Perfect Mirror" (1986). Two comprehensive explorations of autobiographical literature were published in 1990: Pei-Yi Wu's *The Confucian's Progress* and Wolfgang Bauer's extensive tome *Das Antlitz Chinas*.

3. Wu, *Confucian's Progress*, xii; Aronson, "Autopathography," 1600. Sarah Dauncey has similarly noted that "the popularity of auto(biographical) narratives of disability and illness" has been so great that "seemingly no element of the body or its functions has escaped scrutiny." See Dauncey, *Disability in Contemporary China*, 164.

4. Useful overviews of this development are provided in Jurecic, *Illness as Narrative*, 4–17, and Emeney, *Autobiographical Medical Poetry*, 11–46. On autobiographical illness narratives, see also Frank, *The Wounded Storyteller*; Avrahami, *The Invading Body*.

5. Couser, "Embodied Self," 1–2 (see also his *Recovering Bodies*). Couser is credited with

Writing the Sick Self 81

to be concealed have come to form an aspect of the "confessional society" described by Zygmunt Bauman in 2007.[6] As Andrew Solomon wrote in a 2022 review of Meghan O'Rourke's illness memoir *The Invisible Kingdom*, "Self-reflection on maladies has become such a commonplace that it is almost impossible to bring freshness to the project."[7]

Turning to early and early medieval China, we must be content with more fragmented and dispersed self-representations of illness than those published nowadays. In this respect, autobiography in early and early medieval China aligns with other premodern cultures, where historical attitudes about public life and decorousness often prevented illness or impairment from becoming part of self-presentations.[8] Despite their relative scarcity, Chinese self-accounts of health and illness from this period are highly symptomatic. They not only point to an understanding of authorship as deeply rooted in the somatic but also reveal the acceptance of illness as an element of an author's public persona and as a subject of refined literature. These two aspects will guide our readings of autobiographical texts in this part of the book.

The two chapters of part II focus on two main genres: authorial prefaces and correspondence. The first chapter examines openly public self-accounts in the form of prefaces, exploring how remarks about illness and other physical challenges that made it into these texts contributed to self-narratives of strength and grandeur. The second chapter delves into epistolary writings, which are, at least ostensibly, addressed to a more limited audience, typically a single individual. In analyzing letters about illness and impairment, we will explore how the epistolary genre—whether informal notes, formal letters, or official communications—influences the narrative. We will also examine how the "epistolary pact" inherent in correspondence

---

having introduced the term "autopathography" into the discussion in 1991; see his "Autopathography," 66 (published nine years later in the *British Medical Journal*).

6. Bauman, *Consuming Life*, 3.

7. Solomon, "Mystery Illness."

8. Commenting on the scarcity of illness narratives in the West before the nineteenth and twentieth centuries, Kay Cook suggests that "illness would not be considered relevant or proper to the writer interested in recounting the main stages in his or her life." See Cook, "Illness and Life Writing," 457.

82   *Part Two*

intersects with the notion of the "autobiographical pact." The fact that several authors discussed have left autobiographical writings that touch upon health and illness in multiple genres will further help to throw different modes of self-writing into sharper relief.

CHAPTER ONE

The Body in the Paratext

Five Authorial Prefaces and a Letter

One of the main sources of autobiographical writing in early and early medieval China is the "self-account" (*zi xu* 自序, *zi ji* 自記, or similar terms) that authors appended to their writings. While not all self-accounts include autobiographical information, and many remain silent about the author's health, significant self-accounts from this period do mention (explicitly or obliquely) their author's physical condition. Among these are authorial prefaces or postfaces by Sima Qian, Wang Chong, Cao Pi, Ge Hong, and Xiao Yi, written between the first century BCE and the sixth century CE. These fragmentary health reports are not mere revelations of the physical self but support the overall rhetorical strategy of the preface, which is closely connected to the book of Masters literature it accompanies.

As Xiaofei Tian observes, "The larger work and the final self-account must be received as *one* package of the author's 'self,' as they are both essential for his sense of 'self' and for his self-representation."[1] Tian's assessment aligns with Gérard Genette's characterization of the authorial preface as "one of the instruments of authorial control," whose "most important function . . . is to provide the author's interpretation of the text or, if you prefer, his statement of intent."[2] Genette also suggests that the postface be included under the category of the preface, as both preludial and postludial introductory texts pursue similar rhetorical goals.[3]

---

1. Tian, "Twilight of the Masters," 470.
2. Genette, *Paratexts*, 221–22.
3. Genette, *Paratexts*, 161.

84   *Chapter One*

Early medieval Chinese characterizations of the preface (*xu* 序) as a literary genre are brief. In *The Literary Mind and the Carving of Dragons*, prefaces are not accorded a separate genre chapter but are treated in connection with other subjects. Although Liu Xie added his own self-account as chapter 50 of *Literary Mind*, he did not mention other self-accounts in his work at all.[4] Xiao Tong's preface to his *Selections of Refined Literature* also omits self-accounts and does not include an example of the genre in the anthology's chapters that collect prefaces.[5] The first Chinese author to treat the self-account in some detail was Liu Zhiji 劉知幾 (661–721), almost two centuries after Liu Xie and Xiao Tong, in his historiographical work *History Understood Thoroughly* (*Shitong* 史通). Liu Zhiji evaluates past self-accounts mainly by their authors' descriptions of their ancestry, which he understands as expressions of filial duty. He also praises authors who recount events of their life from youth to adulthood but advises against full disclosure and recommends the creative omission of personal weaknesses and unfavorable matters in one's family background:

> In an authorial preface, it is appropriate to conceal one's shortcomings and to extol one's strengths. So long as something is not fallacious, it can be taken as a factual record.... When speaking about one's family history in an authorial preface, the most important thing is to illuminate the reputation of one's parents. If there is no one [to praise in one's family], one may omit this part.
>
> 然自敘之為義也, 苟能隱己之短, 稱其所長, 斯言不謬, 即為實錄。...
> 夫自敘而言家世, 固當以揚名顯親為主, 苟無其人, 闕之可也。[6]

Liu Zhiji's advice highlights the inherent ambivalence in autobiographical narration: while it purports to offer factual (and often exclusive) insights into the life and work of its author, it simultaneously casts doubt on its own credibility because it relies solely on the author as the source of authentication. This ambivalence is compounded by what Stephen Owen describes

---

4. On Liu Xie's "Statement of Intent" ("Xu zhi" 序志), see Richter, "Empty Dreams," esp. 106–7.

5. *Wen xuan* 45.2019–46.2088.

6. *Shitong* 32.6b. See translations in Xiong, *Thorough Exploration in Historiography*, 128–30; Bauer, *Antlitz Chinas*, 239–42. See also Wells, *To Die and Not Decay*, 135–38.

as "the suspicion of self-interest that surrounds the act of autobiography."[7] Rather than deterring readers, these ambivalences and suspicions are key elements of the enduring fascination with self-narratives. To address questions about the truthfulness of self-writing, Philippe Lejeune proposed the notion of an "autobiographical pact" between writers and readers. First articulated in the early 1970s, Lejeune suggested that texts that posit the threefold identity—especially in name—of author, narrator, and protagonist offer readers a contract to read the text as autobiographical, that is, as truth rather than fiction. In Lejeune's words:

> An autobiography is not a text in which one speaks the truth about oneself, but a text in which a real person says that he or she is speaking the truth about himself or herself. And this commitment has specific effects on how the text is received. You don't read a text the same way if you believe it to be an autobiography as you do if you believe it to be a work of fiction.[8]

Over the last half-century, Lejeune and other scholars have further developed this approach, moving beyond the earlier concern with genre differentiation to recognize autobiography as a personal and social practice. The term "autobiography" continues to elude easy definition, especially given the many forms in which autobiography overlaps with autofiction.[9]

Sima Qian: Writing the Damaged Self

The first surviving authorial preface is Sima Qian's "Self-account of the Director of Archives" ("Taishigong zi xu" 太史公自序), transmitted as the final (130th) chapter of the *Records of the Historian*, likely dating to the early first century BCE.[10] Much of Sima Qian's self-account is devoted to

---

7. Owen "The Self's Perfect Mirror," 74. On the inherent ambivalence of autodiegetic narration, also see Glauch and Philipowski, "Vorarbeiten zur Literaturgeschichte," 50–51.

8. Lejeune, "From Autobiography to Life-Writing."

9. For early works on the topic, see the essays in Lejeune, *On Autobiography*, esp. "The Autobiographical Pact (bis)," 119–37. For recent developments in Lejeune's work, see Allamand, "The Autobiographical Pact, Forty-Five Years Later."

10. *Shi ji* 130.3285–3322; Watson, *Ssu-ma Ch'ien*, 42–57. See also Durrant, "Self as the Intersection of Traditions."

86   Chapter One

his ancestors, particularly his father, Sima Tan. He quotes his father's treatise on what has been traditionally called the Six Schools (*liu jia* 六家)[11] and foregrounds his dedication to the historical work his father could not complete. Central to Sima Qian's self-account is his father's deathbed instruction, which recalls the *Canon of Filial Duty* (*Xiaojing* 孝經), urging him to continue the work: "Filial duty starts with serving one's parents, its middle is serving one's lord, and its end is to establish oneself; making one's name known to posterity in order to call attention to one's parents is the greatest act of filial duty" (孝始於事親, 中於事君, 終於立身。揚名於後世, 以顯父母, 此孝之大者).[12] Sima Qian further underscores his own contribution to the family vocation with extensive remarks on his understanding of the historian's craft, especially toward the end of the preface. Additionally, he dedicates more than half of the preface to a brief introduction of the *Records of the Historian*'s contents.

Within the "Self-account of the Director of Archives," there are only glimpses of what we might today call autobiographical information, let alone a full-blown pathography. Despite this, we know that the text was authored by someone who survived punitive emasculation, a drastic form of physical mutilation also known as "palace punishment" (*gongxing* 宮刑), among other names for the procedure.[13] In his self-account, Sima Qian mentions the reason for this punishment only obliquely, writing that "the Director of Archives encountered the Li Ling calamity" (太史公遭李陵之禍).[14] Li Ling 李陵 (d. 74 BCE) was a Han general who, with his small troop of soldiers, was forced to surrender to the enemy on a military mission into northern territory in 99 BCE. When Sima Qian defended Li Ling, he provoked the anger of Emperor Wu (Han Wudi 漢武帝, r. 141–87 BCE) and was sentenced to death for supposed *lèse-majesté*. The

---

11. More recent scholarly discussions have pointed out that the understanding as "schools" is misleading and that the term *jia* refers to areas of expertise that are not necessarily identical with consistent teaching traditions. See Peterson, "Ssu-ma Ch'ien as Cultural Historian"; Smith, "Sima Tan and the Invention of Daoism"; Csikszentmihalyi and Nylan, "Constructing Lineages."

12. *Shi ji* 130.3295.

13. On punitive emasculation in preimperial and Han China, see Hoeckelmann, "To Rot and Not to Die," esp. 1–20.

14. *Shi ji* 130.3300.

capital punishment was eventually reduced to emasculation, which Sima Qian suffered in 98 BCE.[15]

We can safely assume—but we surprisingly rarely do—that the physical injury inflicted during this punishment left him suffering from pain and discomfort for the rest of his life, profoundly shaping his outlook. None of this, however, rises to the surface in his authorial preface to the *Records of the Historian*. Instead of detailing his physical suffering, Sima Qian relies on his readers' knowledge of his fate to grasp the underlying subtext.

The harshest, if still rather vague, term he uses in his self-account to describe the ills that befell him is *hui* 毀, "damaged" or "broken." Referring to himself, he uses the word *shen* 身, which can denote the physical body, one's sense of self, and even social status—his father had used the same word when reminding him that the ultimate filial duty is to "establish oneself" (*li shen* 立身). When Sima Qian proclaims that his *shen* is damaged, he implies that the corporal punishment harmed all three aspects: his physical body, his sense of self, and his social status, rendering him "no longer of use" or unfit for office (身毀不用矣). This statement is further amplified by his subsequent reference to other historical figures who suffered misfortunes, suggesting a broad spectrum of adversity and evoking physical impairments such as blindness and amputated feet.

By listing these fellow sufferers, Sima Qian inserts himself into a nonfamilial lineage of historical exemplars who, despite their suffering—or perhaps because of it—left indelible marks on the Chinese intellectual landscape. This lineage includes King Wen of the Zhou dynasty 周文王 (fl. eleventh century BCE), Zuo Qiuming (trad. 556–451 BCE), Confucius (trad. 551–479 BCE), Sunzi 孫子 (trad. 544–496 BCE), Qu Yuan 屈原 (trad. 340–278 BCE), Lü Buwei 呂不韋 (trad. 291–235 BCE), Hanfeizi 韓非子 (ca. 280–233 BCE), and the creators of the *Odes*. Although he withholds the details of his physical ordeal from the readers of his self-account, Sima Qian ensures they remember his suffering as the price he paid to complete the work entrusted to him by his father. In Genette's terms, this powerful strategy of authorial control serves to affirm the momentousness of his work and the significance of Sima Qian's familial legacy.

---

15. For a concise summary of these events, see Durrant, *Cloudy Mirror*, 8–10.

88 Chapter One

Sima Qian's letter in reply to Ren An 任安 (d. ca. 91 BCE), first transmitted in the *History of the Han Dynasty*, appears to serve a similar purpose.[16] Focused on the Li Ling affair that led to his prosecution and punishment, the letter provides crucial background information that complements the "Self-account of the Director of Archives." The letter clarifies what Sima Qian did not express explicitly in his preface: that he chose to endure the disgrace of emasculation rather than commit suicide, the more honorable way out, in order to fulfill his father's wish to complete the *Records of the Historian*. Balancing two types of filial offense—rendering his physical body incomplete versus leaving his family's body of work incomplete—Sima Qian chose personal over familial humiliation. Paradoxically, this choice allowed him to associate his damaged body with the fundamental value of filial duty.

This is no mean feat if we remember that filial children were expected to preserve their bodies intact, returning them unscathed at the end of their lives as received from their ancestors. This expectation is articulated in several canonical texts from early China, although the words spoken by Confucius in the *Canon of Filial Duty* are the most familiar. Matching Sima Qian's dilemma very well, the first chapter states:

> Our body (*shen*), limbs, hair, and skin are all received from our parents. Not daring to damage (*hui*) or harm them is the beginning of filial duty. Establishing ourselves (*shen*) and practicing the Way, and making our name known to posterity in order to glorify our parents is the end of filial duty.
>
> 身體髮膚, 受之父母, 不敢毀傷, 孝之始也。立身行道, 揚名於後世, 以顯父母, 孝之終也。[17]

---

16. "Bao Ren Shaoqing shu" 報任少卿書, in *Han shu* 62.2725–36; *Wen xuan* 41.1854–69; Watson, *Ssu-ma Ch'ien*, 57–67; Owen, *Anthology of Chinese Literature*, 136–42. The letter has been widely discussed and translated. See the references in Fuehrer, "Court Scribe's *Eikon Psyches*," 175n29; Knechtges, "'Key Words,'" 75n1. See also Durrant et al., *Letter to Ren An*. On the incorporation of letters into standard histories, see Luhn, *Von Briefen und Kompilatoren*, 7–98.

17. *Xiaojing* 1.7b. Similar ideas are expressed in ritual texts; see, e.g., *Da Dai liji* 52.186. See also Galvany and Graziani, "Legal Mutilation and Moral Exclusion," 12–18. The expectation to preserve the integrity of the body throughout one's life will also be discussed in connection with sickbed visits in part III of this book.

Remarkably, Sima Qian omits the *Canon of Filial Duty*'s explicit precept about preserving "body, limbs, hair, and skin" when recounting his father's deathbed admonitions in his preface to the *Records of the Historian*. By only alluding to them through the term "damage" (*hui*), he avoids directly referring to the corporal punishment he endured.

Choosing the format of the letter of reply—whether factual or literary conceit—was an ingenious move by Sima Qian. Writing a response allowed him to present selected aspects of his life experience in reaction to Ren An's presumed prompts, without having to frame his narrative as a consistent life story.[18] This approach enabled him to create a stronger subtext of physical injury and suffering. Not only does the list of suffering writers from his preface reappear in the letter, but Sima Qian also introduces a second group of historical figures who endured various legal punishments, including mutilation, and emphasizes that none of these writers committed suicide. Addressing Ren An, he describes himself as "mutilated and dwelling in impurity" (身殘處穢) and "a remnant of knife and saw" (刀鋸之餘) whose "body is now missing a part" (大質已虧缺).[19] He refrains from detailing the physical consequences of his punishment but frequently evokes the mental anguish it causes him. The closest he comes to describing his physical condition is through the manifestations of his shame:

> It makes my gut churn all day long. At home, I feel confused, as if something is slipping away from me; when I go out, I don't know where to turn. Whenever I remember this shame, my back breaks into a sweat that soaks my clothes.
>
> 是以腸一日而九回, 居則忽忽若有所亡, 出則不知所如往。每念斯恥, 汗未嘗不發背霑衣也。[20]

Sima Qian's authorial voice, while not explicit about his physical suffering, is firmly rooted in his physical experience, ensuring his readers do not forget this aspect. In light of this, even the brief account of his youthful travels in his preface gains a physical dimension that is easily overlooked

---

18. For a discussion of the particular rhetorical potential of letters of response, see Richter, "Literary Criticism in the Epistolary Mode," 20–21.

19. *Han shu* 62.2725, 2727.

20. *Han shu* 62.2736.

90   *Chapter One*

but functions as a powerful foil of intact health: we see him scrambling up mountains, crawling into caves, wading through rivers, and handling bow and arrow.[21]

Two aspects stand out in this initial example of writing the ailing self: first, this is not a simple case of illness, and second, different genres yield different kinds of autobiographical information. Let us approach the first aspect by considering how to describe Sima Qian's physical condition. The writer of the self-account in the *Records of the Historian* and the letter to Ren An had in the past suffered a severe physical injury, arguably lawfully inflicted, that left him, after a period of recovery, with permanent physical impairments and possibly ongoing pain and discomfort. Since early and early medieval Chinese historical or medical sources on the aftereffects of surviving emasculation are lacking, we must rely on medical and anthropological observations from the late nineteenth and early twentieth centuries when Qing court eunuchs consulted foreign physicians. Although these reports have been shown to be problematic due to their orientalist approach, it is reasonable to assume that most men who underwent emasculation, which in late imperial China was often a voluntary step to becoming a court eunuch, struggled with health issues originating from the procedure, especially urinary conditions.[22]

Depending on how well Sima Qian adapted to his new situation, he might not have felt ill at all times and might to the eyes of others have passed as healthy. He assures Ren An that he has resumed demanding intellectual work and writing, and his letter suggests he is apparently able to travel without difficulties with Emperor Wu as a member of his entourage. Nevertheless, it is likely that he suffered from chronic health conditions and felt at least partially disabled. His writings demonstrate a painful awareness of being perceived socially as an "invalid," causing him additional physical and psychological suffering. The complex relationship between physical and social identity in Sima Qian's case exemplifies the fundamental difficulties of conceptualizing health and illness discussed earlier in this book, highlighting how intertwined temporary illness and long-term impairment or disability can be.

21. *Shi ji* 130.3293; see also Watson, *Ssu-ma Ch'ien*, 48.

22. See Howard Chiang's analysis of these reports in *After Eunuchs*, 15–70. On medical problems following emasculation, see esp. p. 40.

The second aspect, concerning the generic differences between Sima Qian's self-account and his autobiographical letter, leads us to notions of genre in the Chinese tradition and particularly to the importance of Sima Qian for later compositions of both self-accounts and personal letters, as well as for the traditional understanding of these genres as described in the writings of Liu Xie and Liu Zhiji. Liu Zhiji describes Sima Qian's self-account in the *Records of the Historian* as the ideal combination of two approaches: Qu Yuan's focus on his ancestors in the poem "Encountering Sorrow" and Sima Xiangru's focus on his own life in a self-account that has unfortunately not survived. Liu Zhiji praises Sima Xiangru for recounting his life from youth to adulthood but criticizes him for writing with too little restraint. In Liu Zhiji's view, authors should, as Sima Qian did, suppress depictions of morally questionable matters and the flaws of oneself and one's ancestors.[23]

The first detailed description of the historical development and literary capacity of letters is found in chapter 25 of Liu Xie's *Literary Mind*. Although Liu Xie mentions Sima Qian's letter to Ren An only once—praising it for its expansive intent, thrust, and distinct hue—the letter appears to have played a key role in Liu Xie's general assessment of the genre. Liu writes that "the epistolary genre, both in detail and in general, is rooted in the full expression of words, words that are meant to dispel pent-up emotions and to carry feeling and coloration" (詳總書體, 本在盡言, 言以散鬱陶, 託風采).[24] Liu's "full expression of words" (*jin yan* 盡言) connotes the "full expression of meaning" (*jin yi* 盡意) evoked (and denied) in the closing of Sima Qian's letter, where he writes that "writing cannot fully express my meaning" (書不能盡意).[25] Liu's characterization of correspondence as a means to release pent-up emotions further recalls two moments in Sima Qian's letter inspired by Qu Yuan: the lament that he feels "depressed and stifled with no one to talk to" (抑鬱而無誰語) and the description of his fellow sufferers as men who "all had something that was pent up in their minds" (皆意有所鬱結).[26] Ban Gu 班固 (32–92),

23. *Shitong* 32.257.
24. *Wenxin diaolong* 25.446. For an analysis of chapter 25 of *Wenxin diaolong*, see Richter, *Letters and Epistolary Culture*, 49–62.
25. *Han shu* 62.2736.
26. *Han shu* 62.2725, 2735.

92   Chapter One

who quotes the letter to Ren An in his biography of Sima Qian in the *History of the Han Dynasty*, intensifies this connection by extending the allusion to Qu Yuan and concluding that Sima Qian's letter is trustworthy because he "vented his grievances from the dark" (幽而發憤, 書亦信矣).[27] The resulting genre paradigm of the decorous and restrained preface versus the more expressive and authentic letter has not always facilitated a deeper understanding of Chinese epistolary literature.[28]

Sima Qian's role in Chinese literature has often been described in foundational terms as the father of Chinese historiography, autobiography, and epistolary literature and as "the central figure in the formation of authorship in China."[29] Recognizing that, moreover, he made it socially acceptable to write about the damaged body in historical and epistolary genres by likening himself to historical exemplars and emphasizing his filial duty, we must also credit Sima Qian with establishing a mode of self-writing that allows an author to emerge as a decidedly embodied and even physically damaged being.

Wang Chong: Innate Vigor and Aging

About two centuries after Sima Qian, another author, who we met in part I, included his physical self in his autobiography: Wang Chong in "Records about Myself," part of his extensive collection of essays, *Discourses Weighed in the Balance*.[30] Wang's self-account mirrors Sima Qian's focus on the intellectual and moral life in relation to his main work. However, Wang takes a radically different approach to his ancestry, which would eventually earn him Liu Zhiji's disapproval. He also incorporates more elements of what we now consider life-writing, including the first somewhat detailed report of a childhood in Chinese literature.[31]

---

27. *Han shu* 62.2738.

28. On the assumption that letters are just veracious expressions of their authors' minds, see also the second chapter of part II.

29. Owen, *Making of Early Chinese Classical Poetry*, 214. On authorship in early China, also see Du, "The Author's Two Bodies."

30. *Lunheng* 85.1187–1210; Forke, *Lun-hêng*, 1:64–82.

31. See Bauer, *Antlitz Chinas*, 113.

In another departure from Sima Qian's precedent, Wang portrays himself as an outstanding scholar and individual throughout the chapter, using numerous inventive comparisons in an openly self-congratulatory manner. Fittingly, he omits any mention of illnesses or complaints during his adolescence and adulthood. His physical body only appears toward the end of the self-account, where he discusses his old age—a time when physical decline would have been expected and excused. Interestingly, this is the only part of his self-account where he uses the humble self-designation *yu* 愚 ("this ignorant, untaught person"):

> In the third year of the Zhanghe era [89 CE], I resigned from my provincial [office in Yangzhou] to stay at home. Since I was approaching seventy, it was time to go into retirement. My official career had come to an end, and my resolve was spent as never before. I experienced adversity in my affairs, and my health declined. My hair turned white, my teeth fell out, and I became older every day. Friends of my generation became ever scarcer, and there were few people on whom I could rely. I was poor without the means to support myself properly, and I was unhappy in my mind. Time gently went by, and I approached the period of *geng* and *xin*.[32] Although I had feared that my end was near, I found myself still brimming [with energy]. Thus, I wrote the book *Nurturing Inborn Nature* in sixteen chapters, [covering practices such as] nurturing the vital breath to safeguard oneself, adjusting one's food and drink, closing one's eyes and ears, using one's vital essence sparingly to preserve oneself, and, if suitable, supporting oneself with medicine and physical exercises.[33] I hoped that these practices would prolong life and postpone

32. The interpretation of the phrase "*geng* and *xin*" is uncertain. It could refer to calendrical years and thus provide a *terminus post quem* for Wang Chong's death, but neither the *geng* and *xin* years 90–91 nor 100–101 fit, since Wang Chong's biography in *History of the Later Han Dynasty* states that he "died of illness at home during the Yongyuan era [89–104 CE]" (永元中, 病卒于家, *Hou Han shu* 49.1630). Understanding the phrase figuratively to refer to the years of impending death seems more convincing: Wang Chong, who believed his end to be near, unexpectedly recovered and found himself well enough to write yet another book. In the chapter "Evaluation of Ghosts" ("Ding gui" 訂鬼) of *Discourses Weighed in the Balance*, Wang Chong uses the phrase "the spirit of *geng* and *xin*" (庚辛之神) in the sense of "the spirit of death" (*Lunheng* 22.936).

33. Readers have interpreted the passage following "養氣自守" in various ways: some view it as a description of the book's contents, as reflected in my translation, while others see it as a catalog of Wang's personal longevity practices, as in Alfred Forke's translation

94   Chapter One

age for a while. But once our time is up, there is no way back, and only our books are left to instruct posterity [about ourselves]. Truly, human life is of a certain length, and there is a time to live and a time to die for humans, just as for animals.

章和三年, 罷州家居。年漸七十, 時可懸輿。仕路隔絕, 志窮無如。事有否然, 身有利害。髮白齒落, 日月踰邁。儔倫彌索, 鮮所恃賴。貧無供養, 志不娛快。曆數冉冉, 庚辛域際, 雖懼終徂, 愚猶沛沛, 乃作養性之書凡十六篇。養氣自守, 適食則酒, 閉明塞聰, 愛精自保, 適輔服藥引導, 庶冀性命可延, 斯須不老。既晚無還, 垂書示後。惟人性命, 長短有期, 人亦蟲物, 生死一時。[34]

Wang Chong describes the effects of old age on his body in forthright if disappointingly formulaic terms. It is possible that he was not so much driven by the wish to represent his physical decline truthfully but rather by rhetorical motives. Given that personal experience is a central theme throughout *Discourses Weighed in the Balance*, his failing health and remarkable recovery in old age may have helped establish his credibility as the author of a book on nurturing vitality. Additionally, Wang might have vividly evoked his decline to set a striking backdrop for yet another outburst of his scholarly creativity and intellectual vigor—qualities essential to his authorial identity in *Discourses* as a whole.

Regardless of Wang's rhetorical intentions, closing an autobiographical account not merely with a perfunctory nod to the transitoriness of life but with an evocation of one's inevitable physical decline as a human animal is a powerful move.[35] As we noted in part 1, Wang Chong clearly rejected the notion that striving for exceptional longevity and transcendence was a realistic pursuit.

Lun-hêng, 1:82. There may be no actual contradiction between these interpretations, since Wang likely wrote about practices he personally engaged in.

34. *Lunheng* 85.1208–10.

35. Wang Chong also highlights the similarities between humans and animals in a chapter dedicated to insects ("Shang/Shi chong" 商/適蟲) in *Discourses Weighed in the Balance* (see *Lunheng* 49.716). This idea has parallels in a wide range of non-Chinese traditions. For example, Ecclesiastes 3:19 in the King James Bible states, "For that which befalleth the sons of men befalleth beasts; ... as the one dieth, so dieth the other; yea, they have all one breath; so that a man hath no preeminence above a beast: for all is vanity."

Among the writers who have left self-accounts mentioning their physical bodies, Wang Chong was unique in addressing his advanced age and providing readers a sense of an ending, possibly because he is the oldest writer of a surviving authorial preface. For Sima Qian, we lack sufficient biographical information to determine when his "Self-account of the Director of Archives" was written, but it is unlikely that he lived beyond sixty years of age, the same as Ge Hong. Cao Pi and Xiao Yi died even younger, in their late thirties and forties, respectively. Although we cannot compare different autobiographical representations of old age in authorial prefaces, we know that Wang Chong was by no means explicit when he cited graying hair and tooth loss in a conventional *pars pro toto* reference to his declining body. In contrast, descriptions of old age elsewhere in early medieval literature, whether of the author himself or someone else, can be considerably more specific. Ge Hong, for example, described an old man of his acquaintance in drastic terms: not only gray and toothless but also withered, coughing, dim-sighted, hard of hearing, and demented. This description is rhetorically motivated as well, as Ge sought to expose the man as a charlatan who falsely claimed mastery of longevity techniques.[36] As Robert Campany has noted, "In a culture in which visual bodily and facial details were assumed to indicate otherwise hidden, inward truths about individuals ... the adept's appearance was the set of indicators read by other people to ascertain the authenticity of an adept's claims and the power of his methods."[37]

Where Sima Qian's mutilated body emerges from the subtext of his preface to emphasize the grandeur of the *Records of the Historian* and the worthiness of the Sima family—implying that these are worth any personal sacrifice—Wang Chong's aging body, though subject to "nature's changing course," is beholden only to himself. Wang declares his independence from his family early in his self-account, likening himself to "the bird without a pedigree: the phoenix; or the beast without a species: the unicorn; or the man without an ancestry: the Sage; or the object without a counterpart: the treasure" (鳥無世鳳皇, 獸無種麒麟, 人無祖聖賢, 物無常嘉珍). He concludes this argument for his own singularity by asserting that

36. *Baopuzi neipian* 9.159. See also Shen Yue's epistolary description of his own aged body, discussed in the penultimate section of chapter 2.

37. Campany, *Making Transcendents*, 132.

96   Chapter One

ancestry is no guarantee of scholarly success and that only those who "have been bestowed with a surplus of original vital energy can write literature" (更稟於元, 故能著文).[38]

We previously encountered this argument in part 1, where we introduced Wang Chong's explanation of Yan Hui's early death. According to Wang, Yan Hui, who initially suffered from a lack of "innate vigor," accelerated his decline by overtaxing his supposedly meager natural endowment in an attempt to pursue learning on par with his inimitable master, Confucius. Wang described the prematurely aged Yan Hui in the same terms he used to characterize his own advanced age: turning gray and losing his teeth. While Yan Hui perished in his thirties, Wang Chong, who presents himself as blessed with exceptional innate vigor, lived into his seventies and remained productive well into old age. Ironically, this has not prevented later readers from interpreting Wang's physical decline as a consequence of excessive study, as discussed in part 1.

It is not a coincidence that Wang Chong, who so clearly conceives of himself as a singular individual, also confidently writes about himself as a physical being and views writing as intellectual work rooted in one's individual vital energy.[39]

Cao Pi: Self-Portrait of the Crown Prince as an Athlete and Warrior

Cao Pi, who ruled as Emperor Wen of the Wei dynasty from 220 to 226, would certainly have agreed with Wang Chong on the importance of vital energy in literature. In his "Discourse on Literature," part of his Classical Discourses, Cao Pi asserts that "literature is dominated by the vital breath" (文以氣為主).[40] Unfortunately, only excerpts of the Classical Discourses have been preserved, and the "self-account" attached to these essays has not

38. The two quotations are from Lunheng 85.1206–7.

39. Wang Chong anticipates arguments presented by Cao Pi in his "Discourse on Literature" in favor of the individuality of writers; see e.g. Lunheng 85.120.

40. Wen xuan 52.2271. Paul W. Kroll has noted the connection between Wang Chong and Cao Pi, observing "curious echoes . . . of certain passages from Wang's Lunheng" in Cao Pi's "Discourse on Literature." See Kroll, "Literary Criticism and Personal Character," 533.

survived in its entirety. Given its fragmentary nature, it is challenging to determine whether the extant parts of this authorial preface are representative of the whole text or provide a skewed impression. The best we can do is to keep its incomplete nature in mind.[41]

In the surviving fragments of his self-account, Cao Pi reports no illnesses whatsoever; on the contrary, he extensively details his excellent health and numerous physical accomplishments. His athletic abilities clearly overshadow his literary achievements. He describes how, as a young boy just ten years old, he learned riding and archery and escaped on horseback during a military operation.[42] He insists that he still possesses the riding and archery skills he acquired in childhood and claims that he is becoming physically stronger all the time without ever tiring of these activities (少好 弓馬, 于今不衰。... 日多體健, 心每不厭).

The self-account includes a series of situations showcasing Cao Pi in conversation and competition with highly skilled opponents, none of whom prove to be his match. In these vividly told anecdotes, Cao Pi openly boasts of his physical superiority and daring, and he even incorporates the applause he received from admiring bystanders into his narrative. When Xun Yu 荀彧 (163–212), one of his father's senior military advisors, politely compliments Cao Pi on his reputation as an archer, the young man in his early twenties does not respond by expressing thanks for a senior's good opinion of him. Instead, he seizes the opportunity to paint an even more impressive picture of his archery skills.

At one point, Cao Pi almost surprises us by stating that one should not present oneself as preeminent in anything (夫事不可自謂己長), as he might have done before meeting his esteemed martial arts teacher, Yuan Min 袁敏. However, true to the persona he creates in this text, Cao Pi credits Yuan Min for helping him become the virtuoso he is now. This

---

41. Cao Pi's self-account is preserved in Pei Songzhi's (372–451) commentary to *Sanguo zhi* 2.89 and, in a slightly longer version, in *Taiping yulan* 93.8b–9a; see also the translation by Wells, *To Die and Not Decay*, 129–33. My quotations from Cao Pi's self-account are based on the version in Pei Songzhi's commentary.

42. In our terms, "ten *sui*" (十歲) would indicate that Cao Pi was nine, possibly eight years old, since reckoning a person's age in terms of *sui* would have started from the time of conception, with one year added at the beginning of the lunar year. Since the exact age is rarely important, I preserve in my translations the number given in the text.

98   *Chapter One*

passage mainly serves the rhetorical function of transitioning from one type of athletic feat to the next.

Liu Zhiji criticizes self-aggrandizement in self-accounts, quoting a memorial by Cao Pi's younger brother and rival, Cao Zhi, who wrote that "it is shameful for a man to flaunt himself and for a woman to act as her own matchmaker" (夫自衒自媒者, 士女之醜行也).[43] This choice of allusion may not be a coincidence because Cao Pi leads the list of writers Liu Zhiji identifies as guilty of self-praise. Although Liu's criticism of writers who meticulously analyze their own virtues or detail their slightest skills fits Cao Pi's approach, the latter's lively and colorful account significantly enhances our understanding of physical exercise and competition in early medieval China.

As mentioned, Cao Pi's self-account may be incomplete—at approximately one thousand characters, the transmitted text is less than a quarter of the length of the autobiographical prefaces by Wang Chong and Ge Hong. In its current form, it harmonizes with the emphasis on the physical found in Cao Pi's "Discourse on Literature," where he asserts that an author's vital breath determines his literary production and underscores the perishability of the physical body.[44] Surprisingly, literature as a topic plays only a marginal role in his self-account. Cao Pi brings up his own literary work almost as an aside, singling out his enjoyment and skill at pellet chess and mentioning that he wrote a rhapsody about the game in his youth.

Only the last tenth of the extant text of the self-account deals with literary matters, and half of that is dedicated to the learnedness of Cao Pi's father, Cao Cao. Cao Pi emphasizes that his father continued to read as an adult and "would always be found with a book in his hand, even when he was with the troops" (雖在軍旅手不釋卷). He also notes that his father viewed this as a personal distinction, setting him apart from those whose ability to learn declined with age.[45] Although Cao Pi also refers to other relatives, he avoids discussing his ancestry, perhaps to sidestep the topic of his grandfather's background as the adopted son of a eunuch. This omis-

---

43. *Shitong* 32.6b. For the text of Cao Zhi's "Memorial Seeking to Prove Myself" ("Qiu zi shi biao" 求自試表), see *Wen xuan* 37.1675–84.

44. *Wen xuan* 52.2271–72.

45. Differences in intellectual strength between the young and old are also discussed in part I.

sion might have inspired Liu Zhiji's recommendation to overlook one's forebears in a self-account if there is no one praiseworthy in one's family.

Cao Pi is clearly concerned with balancing *wen* 文, associated with activities of the mind, and *wu* 武, which has a strong physical aspect. He explicitly states this early in his self-account, asserting that the civil or literary way and the martial way each have their time (夫文武之道, 各隨時而用). Rhetorically, Cao Pi's emphasis on his health and physical fitness may have been intended to prove himself as fully "martial" and thus prepared for the throne. That he showcases this in a celebrated piece of literature adds to its appeal.

We do not know precisely when Cao Pi completed his *Classical Discourses* or when he wrote the preface, but the nature of his self-praise and the way he extols Cao Cao as his teacher and model throughout the text suggest that his self-account might have been written to impress his living father, who may still have been undecided about whom to name as his successor—Cao Pi or Cao Zhi (whose name does not come up once in the extant version of Cao Pi's self-account). Presenting his father with this text, which on the surface was all about the son's martial distinctions while at the same time sparkling with narrative exuberance and poetic facility, would have been a shrewd move. The following passage exemplifies how effectively Cao Pi merges these rhetorical goals:

> In the tenth year of the Jian'an period [205 CE], Jizhou [in modern-day Hebei Province] was first pacified. The Wei and Mo [in the northeast] offered fine bows as tribute, while the Yan and Dai [in the west] presented famous horses. In that year, at the dusk of spring, in the season watched over by Goumang [the god of spring], warm winds fanned the earth. With eager bows and nimble hands, when the grass was short and the animals were fat, I went hunting with my cousin Zidan [Cao Zhen 曹真, d. 231] west of Ye. At the end of the day, I alone had got nine river deer and thirty pheasants and rabbits.
>
> 建安十年, 始定冀州, 濊貊貢良弓, 燕代獻名馬。時歲之暮春, 勾芒司節, 和風扇物, 弓燥手柔, 草淺獸肥, 與族兄子丹獵于鄴西, 終日手獲麏鹿九, 雉兔三十。

Cao Pi died of what appears to have been an acute illness before he was forty—only a little older than Yan Hui when he passed away, but probably

100   *Chapter One*

in much better physical shape than Confucius's disciple. Regrettably, Cao Pi did not leave any compositions about his last illness, nor do historical sources provide details about his early death. His official biography merely mentions a "serious illness" (疾篤).[46]

Ge Hong: Physical Defects as Emblems of Distinction

For different reasons, none of the writers we have discussed so far describes himself as ill in the narrow sense of the word: Sima Qian acknowledges his impairment but writes from a position of someone who successfully adapted to his altered physical condition; Wang Chong admits to declining health in old age but emphasizes that his scholarly creativity is still going strong; Cao Pi characterizes himself as exceptionally athletic and, we are to imply, bursting with health, without suffering from illness or any other physical weaknesses. The first writer of a self-account who presents himself as ill and ill-favored is Ge Hong (ca. 283–343). He does so in two different texts included in *The Master Who Embraces Simplicity* (*Baopuzi* 抱朴子): mostly in the long autobiographical "Self-account" ("Zi xu" 自敘) attached to the forty-nine *Outer Chapters* (*Waipian* 外篇), but also in the brief "Preface" ("Xu" 序) to the twenty *Inner Chapters* (*Neipian* 內篇), which at not quite 500 characters is only a tenth as long as the "Self-account."[47]

The *Outer Chapters* discuss governance and morality and, according to Ge Hong's own words, "belong to the Confucian tradition" (屬儒家). They have received less attention than the *Inner Chapters*, which "belong to the Daoist tradition" (屬道家) and focus on defending the reality of transcendence or immortality (*xian* 仙) and promoting methods to achieve this state.[48] What limited information there is about Ge Hong's life suggests that he was a prolific writer with broad scholarly interests and substantial political experience in military and minor civil posts across southern China.[49]

46. *Sanguo zhi* 2.86.

47. *Baopuzi waipian* 50.644–721; *Baopuzi neipian*, 336; see also the translations by Sailey, *Master Who Embraces Simplicity*, 241–72, and Ware, *Alchemy, Medicine, Religion*, 6–27; as well as the analysis in Wells, *To Die and Not Decay*.

48. *Baopuzi waipian* 50.665–66.

49. See his biography in *Jin shu* 72.1911–14; Sailey, *Master Who Embraces Simplicity*, 521–32.

The Body in the Paratext   101

Although Ge Hong is primarily associated with the *Inner Chapters* of the *Master Who Embraces Simplicity*, this aspect of his scholarly and religious persona remains in the background of his "Self-account" in the *Outer Chapters*. Following the model set by Sima Qian, though never mentioning that model, Ge Hong begins with a description of his family history, but he is swifter than his predecessor to move on to his own life. Despite his elite background and southern pride, Ge characterizes his youth and education as socially and geographically disadvantaged. Living in relative poverty after his father's early death and growing up in the south, away from the culturally dominant north, Ge was aware of his incomplete access to northern cultural productions:

[The Han dynasty book catalogs] "Separate Records" and "Monograph on Arts and Letters" list 13,299 scrolls in all. But since the beginning of the Wei dynasty [220–266], various kinds of literature have been proliferating, and there are now several times as many books as in the past. So I knew myself that the books I had not yet seen were many. Because not all books were available south of the Yangtze River, in the past I wanted to visit the capital [Luoyang] to search for rare books. I happened to run into some great unrest, though, and had to return when I was not yet halfway there, which I have often regretted. Now that I am approaching the age of "not being confused anymore" and my old intentions are declining and crumbling, I only hope to "diminish and diminish again, pursuing no pursuits,"[50] and to live out my days plowing my fields in the countryside. At this time, a wide-ranging scholarship has already come to an end for me.

案別錄、藝文志，衆有萬三千二百九十九卷。而魏代以來，群文滋長，倍於往者。乃自知所未見之多也。江表書籍，通同不具。昔欲詣京師索奇異，而正值大亂，半道而還，每自嘆恨。今齒近不惑，素志衰穨，但念損之又損，為乎無為，偶耕藪澤，苟存性命耳。博涉之業，於是日沮矣。[51]

50. The sentence combines allusions to *Lunyu* 2.4: "At forty, I was no longer confused" (四十而不惑), and *Laozi* 48.192: "If you pursue learning you grow day by day, if you pursue the Way you diminish day by day. By getting diminished and diminished again, you get to the point of having no pursuits. Having no pursuits, there is nothing that is not pursued" (為學日益，為道日損，損之又損之，以至於無為，無為無不為).

51. *Baopuzi waipian* 50.660. Ge Hong set out twice to travel to Luoyang, but he never made it there. Nevertheless, he traveled extensively during his life, mostly in southern China.

102   *Chapter One*

This passage is not only rich in implications for Chinese book history but Ge Hong also provides another instance of thinking about one's intellectual life in terms of age. We might interpret it as Ge Hong bidding a voluntary farewell to classical learning at forty—the age when Confucius, in his epigrammatic "autobiography" in the *Analects*, described himself as no longer confused. This interpretation is especially apt since Ge rejects devotion to learning in favor of devotion to the Way, using words from the *Canon of the Way and Virtue*, ingeniously combining allusions to central texts of the Confucian and the Daoist traditions.

Considering the discourse on the decline of vital breath throughout one's life and its influence on intellectual powers that we discussed in part 1, Ge Hong's midlife change of path could also be seen in another light. Ge, now in his late thirties, might have doubted his ability to cope with the extensive reading necessary to excel in classical learning and thus decided to focus on the Daoist arts of longevity instead.

Ge Hong continues by describing himself as lacking in natural endowments, presenting a mix of physical and mental defects: "As a person, I am slow-witted and rustic; I am dull by nature and halting of speech, and my appearance is disagreeable" (洪之為人也而騃野, 性鈍口訥, 形貌醜陋).[52] However, with each imperfection, Ge Hong associates himself with historical figures who were also described as lacking quick-wittedness, verbal facility, and good looks but had shown themselves to be intellectually and morally superior. To single out his halting speech aligns him with Confucius, who commended this trait (as noted in part 1). By characterizing himself in this way, Ge Hong tacitly joins an illustrious group of men described as halting of speech or even stuttering, including eminent literati like Sima Xiangru, Yang Xiong, Guo Pu, and Zuo Si.[53]

Ge Hong further emphasizes his unconventional nature by admitting his disregard for fashionable or even clean clothes. These and other elements of his autobiography also occasionally appear in the chapters of the *Master Who Embraces Simplicity* itself. In addition, the main chapters contain passages that are decidedly autobiographical in character and

---

52. *Baopuzi waipian* 50.662.

53. While we have no information on the physical looks of Yang Xiong and Guo Pu, Zuo Si's biography mentions that "he was of ugly appearance and spoke haltingly" (貌寢, 口訥, *Jin shu* 92.2376).

The Body in the Paratext 103

supply information not mentioned in the preface itself, highlighting the interconnectedness of the authorial preface with the main text.[54]

Ge Hong, explaining that his aversion to small talk led to his sobriquet "Master Who Embraces Simplicity," which he himself then embraced and used to title his two collections, adds another detail about his physical condition, claiming that he "was infirm and frail by nature and also often sick" (洪稟性尪羸, 兼之多疾).[55] Following a passage on his contentment with poverty and his dislike of mindless social intercourse, Ge elaborates on how persistent ill health affects his mood and social practices, continuing to refer to himself by his personal name, Hong:

> When it comes to offering my condolences after the death of someone's parent or paying sickbed visits, I want to overcome my aversion [to social interaction] with all my heart, and I feel that it is quite out of the question that I do not go. But being sick and in poor health myself, I usually don't manage. Whenever my critics blame me for that, I admit my fault, but I do not take their criticism to heart. The only reason I am not feeling ashamed of myself is that I am all intent [on making these visits], but then my illness thwarts my desires.
>
> 至於弔大喪, 省困疾, 乃心欲自勉強, 令無不必至, 而居疾少健, 恒復不周, 每見譏責於論者, 洪引咎而不恤也。 意苟無餘, 而病使心違, 顧不媿己而已。[56]

Ge Hong describes a universal experience: being unwell makes him irritable, which in turn makes him disinclined to fulfill his social and ritual obligations, such as the duty to visit the sick and the bereaved—a topic discussed in more detail in part III. Remarkably, Ge does not blame his reluctance to socialize solely on illness, which would be the most broadly recognized "objective" reason to escape one's responsibilities. Instead, he complicates the picture by introducing intermediate psychological steps, thus creating a fuller image of himself as an individual and achieving

---

54. On Ge Hong's rejection of fashionable clothes, see the Outer Chapters (Baopuzi waipian 26.11). Chapter 19 of the Inner Chapters, "The Long View" ("Xia lan" 遐覽), is rich in autobiographical information (Baopuzi neipian 19.303–10).

55. Baopuzi waipian 50.664.

56. Baopuzi waipian 50.665–66.

104   *Chapter One*

greater authenticity. This passage is also one of many examples in early medieval literature in which the words *ji* 疾 and *bing* 病 are used interchangeably.

Continuing to reflect on his restraint in social interactions, Ge admits to being overly critical when forming friendships while also expressing gratitude for a network of "friends who help out when I am short of food or urgently need to prepare a medical concoction" (至於糧用窮匱, 急合湯藥, 則喚求朋類).[57] In this part of his autobiography, he also writes about his relationships with his students and his teaching philosophy. After this detailed characterization of his personal disposition, Ge returns to major events of his adult life, especially his involvement in military campaigns between 303 and 306, his resignation from office, his literary activities, and the contents of the two parts of his *Master Who Embraces Simplicity*.

Toward the end of his preface, Ge Hong mentions previous self-accounts, including those of Wang Chong and Cao Pi, which evidently circulated among educated readers. Surprisingly, Ge does not mention Sima Qian's preface or his letter despite expressing admiration for the historian in the *Inner Chapters*.[58] Commenting on Cao Pi's tendency to brag—an observation that Liu Zhiji would echo four hundred years later—Ge Hong offers a mocking response: a lengthy list of things he claims not to be good at, which, however, soon turns into a boast about his own martial prowess.[59]

Two other aspects of Ge Hong's preface are noteworthy in our context. First, illness and impairment are present in various other respects as well. For example, Ge recounts that military action caused an ancestor to sustain "injuries all over his body and a wound that cost him his right eye" (瘡痍周身, 傷失右眼). Another forefather "withdrew from the world claiming illness" (稱疾自絕於世), and his father "resigned from office on grounds of illness" (以疾去官).[60] On the lexical level, it is remarkable how frequently Ge uses illness metaphors, such as *ji* 疾, in the sense of "to

---

57. *Baopuzi waipian* 50.670.

58. See the chapter "Illuminating the Root" ("Ming ben" 明本), *Baopuzi neipian* 10.167–68.

59. *Baopuzi waipian* 50.702.

60. All three quotations from *Baopuzi waipian* 50.645–46.

trouble" or "to dislike." Although it is difficult to ascribe specific authorial intentions to this feature of Ge's prose, it infuses the text with notions of ill health for the reader.[61]

Ge Hong's ostentatious display of his physical deficiencies, unappealing looks, and rejection of social graces is rhetorically complex. On the one hand, he taps into a rich reservoir of Confucian biographical motifs, befitting an authorial preface to the *Outer Chapters* of the *Master Who Embraces Simplicity* that seemingly seeks to construct an image of sincerity and profundity, setting himself apart from what he describes as the superficial zeitgeist: "My abilities are not in accord with my time, my conduct runs counter to this age" (用不合時, 行舛於世). In fashioning this persona of an erudite nonconformist, Ge, who refers to himself as "the least of the Confucians" (儒者之末),[62] also draws on Daoist traditions, evoking the physically impaired but flourishing figures we know from the *Zhuangzi*, such as Zhili Shu 支離疏 and Shushan Wuzhi 叔山無趾, as well as from some of the hagiographies in his own *Traditions of Divine Transcendents* (*Shenxian zhuan* 神仙傳).[63]

In the preface to the *Inner Chapters* Ge reaffirms this stance, comparing his strength to that of a fly, his strategies to that of a limping turtle, his looks to the famously ill-favored wife of the Yellow Emperor, and his assets to sand and gravel:

> How could I dare, having the strength of a fly, to dream of undertakings such as surging up to the sky? Or, whipping a limping turtle to follow in the tracks of [the legendary steed] "Flying Rabbit"? Or, with the ugliness of a

---

61. Describing his adversaries' behavior toward him, Ge Hong writes, "They all dislike (*ji*) me because I am different from them, so I was exposed to their fault-finding (*ci*) and slander" (共疾洪之異於己而見疵毀). About his own inclinations, he states, "I particularly dislike people who have no propriety" (洪尤疾無義之人), and "Vulgar people hated me for disliking them" (俗人憎洪疾己). See *Baopuzi waipian* 50.668, 50.673, and 50.676, respectively.

62. These two quotations are from *Baopuzi waipian* 50.721 and 50.666.

63. *Zhuangzi* 4.180 and 5.202. These figures have been discussed from different perspectives; see, e.g., Milburn, "Marked Out for Greatness?," 18, and "Disability in Ancient China"; Chapman, "Unwholesome Bodies," 16–24; Galvany and Graziani, "Legal Mutilation and Moral Exclusion," 34–54. On *Traditions of Divine Transcendents*, see Campany, *To Live as Long*.

106   *Chapter One*

dressed-up Momu, to seek charming conversation in pursuit of a mate? Or, pushing worthless sand and gravel, demand a thousand pieces of gold at [the legendary jade expert Bian] He's shop?

豈敢力蒼蠅而慕冲天之舉，策跛鼈而追飛兔之軌，飾嫫母之陋醜求媒揚之美談，推沙礫之賤質，索千金於和肆哉。[64]

By flaunting this outwardly gauche and deficient persona, Ge may have pursued a dual objective appropriate to the two parts of his work: to justify his unsatisfactory official career—here we see parallels with Wang Chong—and to legitimize his expertise in alchemy, pharmacology, and other longevity techniques, which are central to the *Inner Chapters* and his works *Traditions of Divine Transcendents* and *Formulas to Keep Up One's Sleeve in Preparation of Emergencies* (*Zhouhou beijifang* 肘後備急方).[65] Ge certainly succeeded at writing himself into two lineages: the tradition of scholarly learning associated with Confucius and the tradition he himself helped to establish through his *Traditions of Divine Transcendents*.

Xiao Yi: Coming to Terms with Illness and Impairment

Another fragmentarily preserved authorial preface, written by a future emperor, makes room for the author's body: the final chapter in Xiao Yi's work *Master of the Golden Tower*.[66] Xiao Yi, who briefly ruled as Emperor Yuan of the Liang dynasty between 552 and 555, may today be best known as the passionate book collector who, in 554, set his enormous library on fire to prevent it from falling into the hands of Western Wei troops led by Yuwen Tai 宇文泰 (507–556). Whether Xiao was indeed personally responsible for the conflagration or not, the fire must have caused a

---

64. *Baopuzi neipian*, 336.

65. There are many indications that Ge Hong felt close to Wang Chong: he defended Wang against critics complaining about the length of his texts (*Baopuzi waipian* 43.423–26); he argued for breadth of learning (32.98–120); he resumed and developed Wang's argument that generations are equal (30.65–78); and so on.

66. *Jinlouzi* 14.1343–69. Beatrice Spade's translation of the self-account is helpful but only partly convincing; see her "Life and Scholarship of Emperor Yuan," 26–31. See also Tian, "Twilight of the Masters," 478–85.

The Body in the Paratext   107

momentous loss to the Chinese literary heritage.[67] Xiao spent his adult life working on his magnum opus, *Master of the Golden Tower*, which he finished a year before his death at the hands of the Western Wei. The book, only transmitted in fragments, is a voluminous collection of writings on diverse topics still awaiting full discovery.

Unlike Cao Pi, Xiao Yi does not boast about his physical fitness. Instead, he recalls the early onset of maladies that stayed with him for life. Living with illness from an early age may have influenced Xiao to open his preface with reflections on the transitoriness of life, unlike Wang Chong, who closed with such reflections. Life being as fleeting as it is, "How could I not write a self-account?" (豈可不自序也),[68] writes Xiao, revealing his belief that self-accounts serve as an antidote to mortality and significantly contribute to an author's posthumous reputation. Although Xiao Yi also appears elsewhere in *Master of the Golden Tower*, this prefatorial chapter, dedicated to his intellectual development, may be seen as a particularly effective imprint of himself.

Again unlike Cao Pi, Xiao Yi focuses on his literary activities. He notes that he began composing poetry at five years old and compares his teenage reading habits to those of Ge Hong, quoting Ge's self-account. He also quotes Cao Pi's self-account but less favorably, mentioning Cao's proficiency at pellet chess to denounce games and other extravagances, as Ge Hong had done before him.[69] Illness is first mentioned in connection with a literary activity of a particular kind: Xiao Yi's attempt to memorize a genealogical handbook at thirteen. The identity of the *Genealogies of a Hundred Families* (*Bai jia pu* 百家譜) is uncertain, but if it was indeed the book that Xiao's father, Emperor Wu of Liang (梁武帝, r. 502–549, Xiao Yan 蕭衍, 464–549), had commissioned Wang Sengru to revise, as many commentators assume, it was likely a voluminous work ranging from at least fifteen to possibly eighty scrolls.[70] Xiao Yi reports that he nearly memorized this text but that the effort made him sick with a disorder he calls "heart *qi*" (心氣). He notes that this illness was acute at the time but

---

67. On the events surrounding the loss of the Liang library and a historiographical analysis of the records, see Dudbridge, *Lost Books of Medieval China*, 38–44.

68. *Jinlouzi* 14.1343–44.

69. *Jinlouzi* 14.1348.

70. *Jinlouzi* 14.1351–52, 52n2.

108 Chapter One

improved as he grew up—which tells us that it must have stayed with him for several years—only to recur during personal crises later in his life:

> When I grew up, [this disorder] improved incrementally. But when I then had to bury five sons in quick succession,[71] I was so filled with grief that I was in a state of confusion, and I suffered cruelly in my mind.[72] At home, I felt dead inside; out and about, I didn't know where to turn. There were times when I felt as if my spirit was outside of my body and no longer belonged to me. When my eldest son [Fangdeng 方等, 528–549] did not return from the Southern Campaign, followed by the demise of my father, my thoughts became ashen destruction, and I was at my wits' end.
>
> 及長漸善, 頻喪五男, 銜悲怳忽, 心地荼苦。居則常若尸存, 行則不知所適。有時覺神在形外, 不復附身。及以大兒為南征不復, 繼奉國諱, 隨念灰滅, 萬慮盡矣。[73]

Xiao Yi follows this stunning admission with a philological and historical inquiry into his condition. In its attempt to create a cohort of fellow sufferers, Xiao's excursus evokes Sima Qian's list of suffering writers:

> Since I suffer from heart *qi*, I repeatedly asked experts where the name "heart *qi*" came from, but most of them did not have answers. I believe that Zhuangzi was describing heart *qi* when he wrote, "crying out without being sick, laughing as if being startled."[74] Manqian [Dongfang Shuo 東方朔, 154–93 BCE] once said. "When yin and yang [*qi*] fight with each other, then heart *qi* moves; when heart *qi* moves, then the spirit disperses."[75] Hua Tan

---

71. Xu Yimin 許逸民, compiler of *Master of the Golden Tower*, concludes that it is impossible to decide who the sons are that Xiao Yi refers to here.

72. As is his practice throughout much of *Master of the Golden Tower*, Xiao Yi uses a term with Buddhist connotations but not in a strictly terminological way. The "ground" in *xin di* stands for "the place where the seeds of Buddhahood are planted and cultivated," as A. Charles Muller suggests in his entry of the related term *xintian* 心田, "mind field," in the *Digital Dictionary of Buddhism*.

73. *Jinlouzi* 14.1351.

74. Since this quotation is not part of the transmitted *Zhuangzi* and we lack information about its context, my translation can only be tentative.

75. In a conversation recorded in his biography, Dongfang Shuo discusses the physiological effects of joy and grief in similar terms; see *Han shu* 65.2852.

[d. 322] said, "If liver *qi* is faint, one's face looks green; if heart *qi* moves, one's face looks red."[76] Zuo Qiuming mentioned that "King [Jing] of Zhou died of heart illness" and that "Zichong perished of heart illness."[77] Cao Zhi [d. ca. 288] also had heart illness.[78] Yin Shi, who was the father of Yin Zhongkan [d. 399/400], had this illness.[79] More recently, Zhang Siguang [Zhang Rong 張融, 444–497] also suffered from this illness after mourning his parents.[80] Zhao Fei, Grand Astrologer of the state of [Northern] Liang, who worked on creating the Qiandu calendar for thirty years, died of a heart disorder.[81] And wasn't Ruan Kan of the Jin dynasty, who was called Gentleman Mad, another one?[82]

既感心氣, 累問通人, 心氣之名, 當為何起, 多無以對。余以為莊子云：「無疾而呼, 其笑若驚」, 此心氣也。曼倩有言：「陰陽爭則心氣動, 心氣動則精神散。」華譚曰：「肝氣微則面青, 心氣動則面赤。」左氏云：「周王心疾終」, 「子重心疾卒。」曹志亦有心疾。殷師者, 仲堪之父也, 有此病。近張思光居喪之後, 感此病。涼國太史令趙畟造乾度曆三十年, 以心疾卒。晉阮侃謂士狂者, 豈其餘乎?[83]

76. This quotation is not part of Huan Tan's *New Discourses* in its transmitted form.

77. *Zuozhuan* Xiang 3: "Zichong was so distressed by this that he came to be afflicted with a sickness of the heart and died" (子重病之遂遇心病而卒) and Zhao 22: "The king developed an acute heart ailment" (王有心疾乙丑崩于榮錡氏); as translated in Durrant, Li, and Schaberg, *Zuo Tradition*, 901 and 1609.

78. *Jin shu* 50.1391: "When his mother died, he exaggerated the mourning rites and as a result became seriously ill. He lost his emotional balance and died in the ninth year [of the Taikang 太康 period]" (遭母憂, 居喪過禮, 因此篤病, 喜怒失常。九年卒).

79. According to *Traditional Tales and Recent Accounts*, "Yin Zhongkan's father suffered from palpitations of the heart caused by a deficiency of heart *qi*. Hearing ants move under his bed, he thought they were oxen fighting" (殷仲堪父病虛悸, 聞牀下蟻動, 謂是牛鬭, *Shishuo xinyu* 34.6). Liu Xiaobiao, in his commentary to this passage, cites Tan Daoluan's 檀道鸞 largely lost *Continued Annals of Jin* (*Xu Jin yangqiu* 續晉陽秋), which describes Yin Shi as suffering from "lost heart illness" (*shixin bing* 失心病). In *Jin shu* 84.2194, Yin Shi's illness is called auditory hypersensitivity (*er cong* 耳聰). On Yin Zhongkan, also see part 1.

80. Zhang Rong's intense filiality is described in *Nan Qi shu* 41.728.

81. The transmitted sources do not have information on Zhao Fei's medical condition.

82. On Ruan Kan, see Liu Xiaobiao's commentary to *Shishuo xinyu* 19.6; also see *Taiping yulan* 739.6b. In changing the name from Ruan Yu 阮裕 to Ruan Kan 阮侃, I follow the emendation suggested in *Jinlouzi* 14.1356n20.

83. *Jinlouzi* 14.1351; see also Tian, "Twilight of the Masters," 479.

110   *Chapter One*

Xiao Yi's exemplars, drawn from ancient and recent history alike in something of an act of retroactive diagnosis, are more of a motley crew than Sima Qian's lists, but they give us a better understanding of Xiao's condition than the term "heart *qi*" can, emphasizing emotional suffering and mental instability during periods of mourning and other challenging biographical events. We lack sufficient information to correlate Xiao's heart *qi* meaningfully with any specific biomedical diagnosis or a clear diagnosis within Chinese medicine. The biography of the Northern Zhou physician Yao Sengyuan 姚僧垣 (499–583) describes Xiao Yi as "frequently suffering from disorders in the chest and abdomen" (嘗有心腹疾) and that Yao successfully treated him using purging techniques following a pulse diagnosis. Despite this, our understanding of Xiao Yi's condition remains vague.[84]

Xiao Yi himself attributed his heart *qi* disorder to his excessive dedication to study as a boy. This self-diagnosis connects with our earlier discussion about Xiao Yi's list of writers who suffered illness or even death due to intense intellectual exertion, such as Yan Hui, Jia Yi, Yang Xiong, and Cao Zhi. While available sources do not specifically describe these men as afflicted with heart *qi*, other texts blame this ailment on mental overexertion, as seen in the story mentioned in part 1 of the Buddhist monk Zhu Fayi.

Although zealous religious dedication is more commonly documented in Buddhist contexts than in Daoist ones, the biography of the scholar-official Shen Yanzhi 沈演之 (397–449) could be a case in point. According to the *History of the Song Dynasty* (*Song shu* 宋書), Shen was known for his fondness for learning as a child and reportedly "read the *Laozi* a hundred times a day" (讀老子日百遍). This claim about Shen Yanzhi raises questions about his reading practices. If he read the *Laozi* anywhere close to a hundred times a day, he likely read silently rather than aloud. Alternatively, the phrase might be figurative, indicating that he spent all day reading the *Laozi*. We might wonder whether he read

---

84. *Zhou shu* 47.841. This case is also mentioned in Goldschmidt, *Medical Practice in Twelfth-Century China*, 71. The early sixth-century work *Treatises on the Origins and Symptoms of All Illnesses* (*Zhubing yuanhou lun* 諸病源候論, 610), attributed to Chao Yuanfang 巢元方 (fl. 605–616), mentions heart *qi* disorders, both deficiency and overabundance of heart *qi* (*xin qi xu/sheng* 心氣虛/盛), in various contexts, including those characterized by emotional instability. See, e.g., *Zhubing yuanhou lun* 15.466.

The whole text from beginning to end, silently or aloud, and whether he read from a manuscript. Given the text's brevity, it is unlikely Shen struggled to memorize it, as Xiao Yi did with the considerably longer *Genealogies of a Hundred Families*. Instead, Shen may have pondered the text obsessively. Unfortunately, the historian's intention was not to provide a realistic image of Shen's childhood but to characterize him as an ardent student, leaving many questions unanswered. Shen's biography also notes that he died in his early fifties, "having suffered from a heart *qi* disorder for many years" (素有心氣疾病歷年).[85]

In the next section of his reconstructed self-account, Xiao Yi reflects on his younger years, possibly when he was around twelve years old, providing a glimpse into his life that seems to confirm his image as a dedicated student:

> When I was young, during summer evenings, I would lower the red curtains and, within the mosquito nets where I kept a silver cup filled with sweet wine from Shanyin, I would read while lying in bed, sometimes until dawn. I reckon this had become my routine. I also suffered from a rash that left my elbows and knees festering all over. In the more than thirty years since, I have broadly cherished more than ten thousand books.
>
> 吾小時, 夏日夕中下絳紗蚊絢中有銀甌一枚, 貯山陰甜酒。臥讀有時至曉, 率以為常。又經病瘡, 肘膝爛盡。比以來三十餘載泛玩衆書萬餘矣。[86]

What in Xiao Yi's preface reads like an almost idyllic scene of indulging in drink and literature takes on a more somber color in light of recollections offered by Yan Zhitui in the *Family Instructions of the Yan Clan*. Yan introduces pain into the picture and turns the sweet wine from Shanyin into a medicinal—an explanation consistent with Xiao's aversion to alcohol mentioned elsewhere in his preface:

> Emperor Yuan of the Liang [i.e. Xiao Yi] once told me: "In the past, when I was in Kuaiji and only twelve years old, I was already fond of learning. At the time, I was also afflicted with a rash so bad I could not close my hands

---

85. *Song shu* 63.1685–86.
86. *Jinlouzi* 14.1357.

112 Chapter One

or bend my knees.[87] I would shut myself in my study, sitting all by myself behind drawn kudzu curtains to keep out the flies, often sipping from a silver cup filled with sweet wine from Shanyin to ease the pain. I had set my heart on reading history books by myself, twenty scrolls a day. I was reading without a teacher, and I sometimes did not know a character or understand a phrase. Then I would go over the text again by myself, and I never got tired of this."

梁元帝嘗為吾說: 「昔在會稽, 年始十二, 便已好學。時又患疥, 手不得拳, 膝不得屈。（閑）〔閉〕齋張葛幃避蠅獨坐, 銀甌貯山陰甜酒, 時復進之, 以自寬痛。率意自讀史書, 一日二十卷, 既未師受, 或不識一字, 或不解一語, 要自重之, 不知厭倦。」[88]

Assuming Yan Zhitui's memory is accurate, this recollection not only adds details about the severity and discomfort of Xiao Yi's skin condition but also suggests that Xiao freely discussed his illnesses. To go a step further, this openness indicates that it was not particularly unusual to bring up such topics in conversation. This interpretation is supported by the context of the anecdote in the *Family Instructions*: Yan Zhitui did not cite Xiao Yi's case to emphasize his painful complaint but rather to highlight the young prince's dedication to learning.

Unfortunately, neither Xiao Yi in *Golden Tower* nor Yan Zhitui in *Family Instructions* mentions whether they associate the former's skin disorder with his nightly reading. Was the rash a result of the imbalance caused by overexerting his mental faculties? Or did the pain prevent him from sleeping, thus causing him to read all night? According to one fragment in *Master of the Golden Tower*, Xiao Yi continued his nocturnal work habits later in life. Following his mother's exhortation to prioritize serving his people over personal literary pursuits, he began doing administrative work by candlelight and only retired at midnight.[89]

Xiao Yi continues his self-account by introducing yet another significant health issue linked to his fondness for learning:

---

87. I follow Jeffrey Riegel in understanding *jie* 疥 as "a scabby itch rather than the parasitic skin disease caused by the itch mite *Sarcoptes scabiei*" ("Curing the Incurable," 228n8). In his note, Riegel also refers to Harper, *Early Chinese Medical Literature*, 285n6.

88. *Yanshi jiaxun* 8.197; see also Tian, *Family Instructions*, 151.

89. *Jinlouzi* 13B.1334.

In the past thirty-something years, I have leafed through more than ten thousand books. When I was fourteen, a troubling eye disorder became chronic, and my eyesight turned dim, so I could not read books myself anymore. For the past twenty-six years, I have always ordered attendants to recite them for me.

比以來三十餘載, 泛玩眾書萬餘矣。 自余年十四, 苦眼疾沈痼, 比來轉暗, 不復能自讀書。 二十六年來, 恒令左右唱之。[90]

Continuing the pattern established above—reading all night at twelve while suffering from a severe rash, and at thirteen developing a heart *qi* disorder due to excessive memorization—Xiao Yi associates his eye disorder with his reading as well, emphasizing that his visual difficulties nevertheless did not deter him from his studies.

However, the specifics of his visual impairment remain unclear. It seems unlikely that he experienced sustained or complete vision loss, as we know that Xiao Yi was an accomplished painter and calligrapher. We also know that he expressed disdain for the collaborative work that led to compilations such as the *Annals of Lü Buwei* and the *Master Huainan* (*Huainanzi* 淮南子) and that he prided himself on working and writing his *Master of the Golden Tower* alone.[91] These activities would have required at least partial vision, suggesting that his eyesight had its good moments or that he could see to some degree, possibly both. Writing about his extensive reading, Xiao may have intentionally chosen the phrase *fanwan* 泛玩, which has strong tactile connotations meaning "to leaf through and cherish," rather than a term that emphasizes reading in visual terms.

Elsewhere in *Master of the Golden Tower*, Xiao Yi evokes the sheer quantity of books waiting to be read:

Masters literature arose during the Warring States, and literary collections flourished during the two Han dynasties. Now, we have arrived at a situation where every family has their writings and every individual their collected works. While the best succeed in relating true intentions and honoring customs, the worst only cram writing tablets and wear out later generations. While the books written in the past are already piling up, new books are

---

90. The emendations of 三 to 二 follows *Jinlouzi* 14.1358n5.
91. *Jinlouzi* 9A.8010–11; see also Tian, "Twilight of the Masters," 479.

114   *Chapter One*

written all the time. Even if you set all your heart to learning when you are young, by the time your hair has turned white, you still will not have read them all.[92]

諸子興於戰國, 文集盛於二漢, 至家家有製, 人人有集。其美者足以叙情志, 敦風俗; 其弊者祗以煩簡牘, 疲後生。往者既積, 來者未已。翹足志學, 白首不徧。[93]

Although this passage from the chapter "Establishing Words" does not explicitly connect the overwhelming amount of reading to Xiao Yi's physical condition, it complements the image he created in his preface of a man who is severely challenged yet uniquely persevering. From this angle, the evocations of physicality in the prefaces of both Cao Pi and Xiao Yi contribute to the fashioning of these (future) emperors' self-images as capable rulers and writers despite their apparent differences. While Cao Pi exhibits physical prowess as a martial counterpart to his literary persona, Xiao Yi highlights what it takes to conquer physical infirmity and mental challenges—namely, genius and supreme determination.[94] Moreover, he associates his illnesses and impairments with filial duty. How he frames the flaring up of his heart *qi* disorder after his father's death is reminiscent of Sima Qian's grander strategy to preserve his moral integrity in the face of physical injury. Xiao Yi's grief over the death of his sons also fits into this framework. However, reducing the illness narratives in the *Master of the Golden Tower* to mere self-fashioning for posterity does not do justice to their prevalence. The preface is not the only place where Xiao Yi writes about his physical condition, and he does so in greater detail than previously seen by other writers. It seems that with Xiao Yi, the writer's body has truly come into its own.

When considering an autobiographer's wish to control the image

92. *Zhi xue* 志學 connotes Confucius's "autobiographical" sketch in *Lunyu* 2.4, which describes the age of fifteen as dedicated to learning.

93. *Jinlouzi* 9A.852; see also the translation by Tian in "Literary Learning," 132.

94. In certain ways, Xiao Yi's unfavorable self-presentation resembles that of Alexander Pope (1688–1744): he too described his own physique in unflattering terms, was ridiculed by his contemporaries, and had his illnesses attributed to "his perpetual application," that is, the severity of his studies. See Nicolson and Rousseau, *"This Long Disease, My Life"*, 14; see also 7–82.

The Body in the Paratext   115

of themselves left to future generations, Xiao Yi's case offers a sobering perspective on the potential failure of such efforts. Despite his consistent attempts to link his infirmity with his intense dedication to study and to emphasize his perseverance in the face of physical challenges, the official record casts him in a different light. According to his biography in the *History of the Liang Dynasty* (*Liang shu* 梁書), for instance, Xiao Yi's eye complaint was a birth defect, with its prenatal roots substantiated by a prophetic dream of his father, Emperor Wu. The emperor reportedly tried to cure his seventh son himself but eventually failed and caused Xiao Yi to lose sight in one eye.[95] Another biography presents an utterly vindictive view of Xiao Yi's nightly reading as an adult, emphasizing how harshly he treated the attendants tasked with reading aloud for him, thus tainting the image of ardent study and selfless work.[96] Biographical sources such as these have played a dominant role in shaping Xiao Yi's historical image, all but obliterating the persona of the hard-studying, persevering prodigy that the Master of the Golden Tower tried to establish for himself.

95. *Liang shu* 5.135. If we are to believe the historical record, Xiao Yi was teased cruelly for his affliction, not only by his half-brother, Xiao Lun 蕭綸 (519–551), but also by his wife, Xu Zhaopei 徐昭佩 (d. 459); see Lu Qinli, *Xian Qin Han Wei Jin Nanbeichao shi*, 2030; *Nan shi* 12.341. See also Tian, "Twilight of the Masters," 479.

96. *Nan shi* 8.243.

CHAPTER TWO

Corresponding Bodies

Health and Illness in Epistolary Genres

> The patient is at once a sort of traveler and investigator,
> a human observatory which finds itself, involuntarily, in
> other realms—he does not travel idly (as it were, to the
> Riviera), but to a massive, existential encounter with the
> wholly Other, an encounter which after the initial shock
> comes to contain strong elements of exploration and
> investigation.
>
> —Oliver Sacks, "Clinical Tales"

Writing a letter is not automatically an autobiographical enterprise. A significant portion of the rich epistolary corpus from early medieval China covers diverse topics, from politics and diplomacy to literary and religious issues. However, because letters can accommodate all kinds of topics and literary forms, they also provide a convenient space for writers to turn to their own lives as subject matter. As we discussed in our analysis of Sima Qian's response to Ren An in the previous chapter, letters are particularly well suited for autobiographical purposes. The epistolary form, grounded in the reciprocal—if not always equal—relationship between writer and addressee, inherently encourages self-disclosure and self-reflection. These could be brief, formulaic references to oneself and the recipient, as required by many correspondence subgenres, or more substantial life-writing in the main body of a letter. In line with epistolary conventions and expectations, letter writers rarely offer extended or consecutive self-narratives but instead report specific life events, evoke shared memories, or respond to specific requests or inquiries made by the addressee, as seen in Sima Qian's letter to Ren An.

Alluding to Lejeune's "autobiographical pact," which assumes an agreement between author and reader to accept the truth claims of a first-person narrative by a narrator bearing the author's name, Janet Altman has suggested the term "epistolary pact" to characterize the specific communication in letters. Altman, who understands epistolarity as "the use of the letter's formal properties to create meaning," emphasizes the role of the addressee, "whose presence alone distinguishes the letter from other first person forms." In the reciprocality of the epistolary experience, "the original *you* becomes the *I* of a new utterance." For Altman, the epistolary pact consists in this "call for response from a specific reader within the correspondent's world."[1]

Although most correspondences from early medieval China have only been transmitted fragmentarily, so that we rarely have series or even pairs of letters, traces of the epistolary pact can also be detected in individual letters removed from their original context of back-and-forth communication. In the case of Sima Qian, for instance, we do not have the letter from Ren An to which Sima Qian apparently replied, nor do we know if Sima Qian's letter ever reached its addressee. Still, Sima Qian undoubtedly wrote within the framework of an epistolary pact: he conveys the idea that Ren An awaited an answer, which he eventually provided, regardless of whether Ren An ever read his reply or not. For us as later readers, not part of the original circle of correspondents, recognizing this aspect of the epistolary pact—letter writers calling for responses from specific addressees—is an important tool to situate the self-accounts we find in seemingly isolated letters within larger communications, even when these larger contexts have not been transmitted.

The broad range of personal experiences reflected in epistolary self-narratives from early and medieval China also includes health and illness. This is unsurprising, as our physical condition can have a profound impact on our being in the world and, consequently, our writing. Often, it also affects the relationship between correspondents. Reflecting once more on Sima Qian, we see that his letter to Ren An not only allowed him to evoke how

---

1. Altman, *Epistolarity*, 6, 87–89, 117.

118   Chapter Two

his physical impairment defined him as an individual body and a social being but also that the letter provided a platform to contest this social definition and to project an alternative, superior self. This new self was fully functional in both familial and social terms, as a dutiful son who, despite his physical impairment, fulfilled his moral responsibilities toward his ancestors, contemporary cultural community, and posterity.

If correspondence is such an effective medium for communicating about health and illness, why then do we see so little of it in the letters transmitted from early medieval China? And what are the reasons behind its presence in certain branches of epistolary literature? This second chapter of part II on autobiographical accounts of health and illness first introduces what we can expect from early and early medieval Chinese epistolary health reports in general. It then turns to the epistolary texts of five writers active between the fourth and sixth centuries. Each of these texts exemplifies an important facet and distinct mode of epistolary self-writing about health and illness: Huangfu Mi's memorial to the throne declining an appointment, Wang Xizhi's numerous casual notes to family members and friends, Tao Qian's single testamentary letter to his sons, another memorial to the throne by the calligrapher Yu He, and a personal letter by Shen Yue advocating his retirement from office, along with his deathbed memorial.[2] As we will see, the distinct subgenres of correspondence result in different types of epistolary pacts and health reports.

Omitted, Obscured, Edited Out:
Health and Illness in Letter-Writing

Health-related information is unevenly distributed in the letters that have come down to us from early medieval China. In the brief, casual letters preserved for their calligraphic value, health and illness are mentioned

---

2. Research on health and illness reports in Chinese letters is scarce. Bruce E. Carpenter has translated an astonishingly detailed report of an illness and recovery in a letter by a certain Zhou Wen 周閏, collected in Zhou Lianggong's seventeenth-century anthology *Chidu xinchao* 11.269; see Carpenter, "Seventeenth-Century Chinese Anthology," 179–80. For a brief overview of the features of autobiographical letters in the European tradition, with no particular focus on illness, see Enenkel, "Epistolary Autobiography."

frequently and often in harsh and drastic detail. These letters, labeled *tie* 帖 (notes), were preserved regardless of their content and typically survived in their entirety, with their epistolary frames intact. Based on these notes, it appears that health reports, health inquiries, and health wishes were a conventional component of casual, quotidian correspondence. They are regularly found in the inner frame that surrounds the main body of a letter, that is, the proem, which is concerned with the previous relationship between the correspondents, and the epilogue, where writers look toward the future. It appears that expressing interest in the correspondent's health and sharing information about one's own health were important for maintaining relationships, akin to other matters typically covered in the epistolary frame, such as letters received or missed and the lament of continued separation between the correspondents.[3]

In contrast, letters transmitted for their content, literary merit, or because they were written by notable individuals rarely mention health and illness. If they do, it is usually in a formulaic or stylized manner.[4] These pieces of correspondence, labeled *shu* 書 (letters), survived because they were incorporated into historical works, anthologies, and commonplace books. During this process, editors routinely removed more immediate epistolary features from these documents, including the outer and inner letter frames, which they deemed inconsequential to the main content. The systematic loss of the inner frames, where health reports, inquiries, and valedictions typically appear, deprives us of a great amount of valuable information, including information beyond the immediate sphere of health and illness. Editors usually only transmitted the main body or excerpts of the main body of a letter, often in a revised form. What remains about the writer's health or other quotidian topics serves the rhetorical purpose of emphasizing the close connection between correspondents but in a restrained manner that prioritizes literary form and convention over raw, truthful exchange.

The scarcity of the topic of health and illness in literary letters is not solely the result of editorial intervention. Knowing that letters had become an established literary genre in the Han dynasty, we can also assume that

---

3. On the epistolary frame in general, see Richter, *Letters and Epistolary Culture*, 76–93 and 101–9; on health-related topics, see esp. 90–93 and 104–5.

4. See also Yang Li, "Dunhuang shuyi 'wenji shu.'"

120   *Chapter Two*

many of the surviving pieces were written for an audience broader than just the designated addressee—Sima Qian's letter to Ren An may well be a case in point. As more or less public writings with a literary, political, or religious agenda, these letters either omitted or obscured any unsavory health conditions that might have been included in private correspondence. A letter written by Lu Yun (262–303) to his friend Yang Yanming exemplifies this very well:

> Yanxian [i.e., Gu Rong 顧榮 (270–312 or 322)] told me that his illness is becoming increasingly severe. It frightens me deeply that he might be declining. If someone gets a serious illness, we should still hope they live until a hundred years old. Even if we must never doubt this, those close to the patient will still feel woeful. I hope [Yanxian] will be diligent at taking his medicine and get better in due course. I myself have long been frail, and recently I have been unwell all the time. I am feeling worse by the day, and it costs me a lot of energy to put up with this. Because of my official duties, a meeting between us is hard to arrange. My feelings of longing for you, how weary they make me.[5] Take good care of yourself and let me hear from you often.
>
> 彥先相說。疾患漸欲增廢。深為怛然。行向衰。篤疾來應百年之望。雖未必此為疑。然親親所以相卹之一感耳。想懃服藥。行復向佳耳。吾既常羸。閒來體中亦恆少賴。日爾勿勿。則堪自力。未遽待罪。會期難剋。情之戀想。何勞之多。好自愛。屢相聞。[6]

Lu Yun's letter, as it has come down to us, lacks the outer frame of prescript and postscript. While remnants of the inner frame are still present in the form of an epilogue, the proem appears to have been completely edited out. Lu Yun's vagueness in describing both the illness of his young friend and brother-in-law Gu Rong and his own fatigue might easily be overlooked, not least since we come away from reading this letter with a distinct impression of the severity of Gu Rong's condition and of Lu Yun's anxiety about his own health. A closer examination reveals that we, as later and unintended readers, are left in the dark about

---

5. Variants of this phrase are used in other transmitted letters as well. It alludes to the line "How can I describe the weariness of longing that I feel?" (我勞如何) in the ode "Tiny Bird" ("Mianman" 綿蠻, *Mao shi* no. 230).

6. Lu Yun, "Yu Yang Yanming shu" 與楊彥明書 no. 4, in *Quan Jin wen* 103.2b.

the specific nature of either man's ailment. The biographies in the *History of the Jin Dynasty* (*Jin shu* 晉書) do not provide additional details. Gu Rong's biography mentions illness only once, together with his love of drinking. He is quoted as saying to a friend that wine could dispel worries, but it could also make one sick like nothing else.[7] It is unclear from this remark whether Gu was known as someone who knowingly jeopardized his health by drinking excessively or if he avoided alcohol because of its negative effects.

The surviving correspondence between Lu Yun and his elder brother Lu Ji suggests that Lu Yun was often unwell, possibly due to his intense focus on literary pursuits. Mental overexertion may have contributed to the fatigue he mentions in his letter to Yang Yanming.[8] Although Lu Yun frequently wrote to his brother about not feeling well enough to think clearly or compose to his satisfaction, he never specified a particular disorder. In the case of letters between brothers, this was probably not due to decorousness or a desire to obscure something distasteful but rather to the allusiveness and ellipsis of intimate communication, where certain things are left unsaid because they are familiar to both correspondents. In twentieth-century scholarship, Qian Zhongshu has written about the common difficulty of reading letters not addressed to us in terms of the "universe of discourse" (語言天地) shared by the correspondents: "Trivial family matters, scattered words between relatives and friends, casual jottings, rough and careless, but the recipients understood" (家庭瑣事, 戚友碎語, 隨手信筆, 約略潦草, 而受者了然).[9]

According to Gu Rong's biography, he and the Lu brothers, all hailing from Wu, became known as the Three Prodigies (*san jun* 三俊) after their arrival in Luoyang in 289. The celebrated "Note on Recovery" ("Pingfu tie" 平復帖), attributed to Lu Ji's hand and considered the oldest surviving calligraphic letter in Chinese history, may further illustrate the connection between these men. Written in cursive script, the exact content of the "Note on Recovery" is difficult to determine. Scholars debate how to transcribe and interpret large portions of the text, including the identity

---

7. *Jin shu* 68.1811.

8. On Lu Yun's tendency to torture himself during literary composition, see part 1.

9. Qian Zhongshu, *Guanzhui bian*, 1109. See also the translation in Egan, *Limited Views*, 236–38.

122   *Chapter Two*

of "Yanxian" mentioned in the letter. Given the beginning of the "Note on Recovery"—"Yanxian is frail and suffering, and I fear he may not recover" (彥先羸瘵, 恐難平復)—Gu Rong is a likely candidate.[10] We know that Gu Rong was a decade younger than the Lu brothers and barely over thirty at the time Lu Yun's letter to Yang Yanming was written. We also know that Gu Rong did indeed recover, eventually outliving his friends, who were both executed in 303, by many years.

Apart from complaints about his own health, Lu Yun's letters also provide examples of health-related inquiries and wishes. He asks Yang Yanming, as seen above, to take good care of himself (好自愛), inquires about his brother's well-being (兄體中佳者), and writes in a letter to Dai Jifu, "May illness give you a wide berth" (疾病處遠).[11]

To illustrate how health-related information was embedded into other epistolary themes, consider the opening of a letter by Liu Chengzhi 劉程之 (ca. 360–416), which survives with a more complete epistolary frame. Liu Chengzhi, better known as Liu Yimin 劉遺民 ("recluse Liu"), abandoned his official career to spend the last twelve years of his life as a lay disciple of the eminent monk Huiyuan 慧遠 (334–416) on Mount Lu.[12] From there, he wrote to Sengzhao 僧肇 (374–414), a principal member of the translation team around Kumārajīva 鳩摩羅什 (344–413) in Chang'an, to ask several doctrinal questions about Sengzhao's recent "Discourse on *prajñā* as Not Knowing" ("Banruo wu zhi lun" 般若無知論). Liu Chengzhi's letter begins as follows:

> Yimin obeisantly salutes you: Since I recently feasted on excellent news from you [probably referring to the "Discourse on *prajñā* as Not Knowing"], I cherish a longing for you from afar. How is your health during the severe cold at the end of the year? When the transmission of letters was cut off, I had to store up my increasing longing for you. Your disciple is seriously unwell here in the wilderness, frequently ravaged by illness. As the monk Huiming is

10. See Qi Gong, "Pingfu tie shuo bing shiwen."
11. "Yu xiong Pingyuan shu" no. 7 and "Yu Dai Jifu shu" 與戴季甫書 no. 1, in *Quan Jin wen* 102.2b, 103.1a.
12. See Zürcher, *Buddhist Conquest*, 217–24. Zürcher gives Liu's dates as 354–410. On Liu Yimin's biographical sources and dates, see also Streif, *Erleuchtung des Nordens*, 154–61.

about to travel north, I write to you to share my feelings. The ancients did not let their relationships become indifferent because they were physically separated; the experience of enlightenment made them feel close to one another. Therefore, even if we are separated by rivers and mountains and cannot meet at this time, when it comes to my longing for your demeanor, emulation of your mind, and following of your tracks, the diligence of my yearning and admiration is great indeed. For a very long time, there will be no opportunity to meet you. As I gaze at the roseate clouds, I take a long sigh. In accordance with the seasons, take good care of your honorable health.

遺民和南, 頃餐徽聞, 有懷遙佇, 歲末寒嚴, 體中如何? 音寄雍隔, 增用抱蘊。弟子沈病草澤, 常有弊療, 邇因慧明道人北游, 裁通其情, 古人不以形疏致淡, 悟涉則親, 是以雖復江山悠邈, 不面當年, 至於企懷風味, 鏡心象跡, 佇悅之勤, 良以深矣。糸丏然無因, 瞻霞永嘆, 順時愛敬。[13]

Although we cannot be sure about the degree of editorial intervention, the inner frame of Liu Chengzhi's letter appears to have been transmitted in its entirety. Liu Chengzhi inquires about Sengzhao's health, mentions his own ill health, and expresses wishes for the continued well-being of his addressee. These health-related remarks are interwoven with expressions of admiration for Sengzhao's superior insight and a longing for further communication. The remainder of the letter's proem describes life on Mount Lu, including accolades for Huiyuan. Liu Chengzhi then moves on to the main subject of his letter. He reveals that it was Daosheng 道生 (ca. 360–434) who had brought Sengzhao's "Discourse on *prajñā* as Not Knowing" to Mount Lu "at the end of last summer" (去年夏末),[14] that is, in 408. He praises the treatise for its style and insight and finally lists his questions, also on behalf of other members of the Mount Lu community, asking Sengzhao to provide further explanations.

We do not know how long it took the messenger monk Huiming to traverse the more than a thousand kilometers between Chang'an

13. "Zhi shu Shi Sengzhao qing wei 'Banruo wu zhi lun' shi" 致書釋僧肇請為般若無知論釋, in *Quan Jin wen* 142.5b–7a, *Zhao lun* 肇論 1.154–55. See also the translations by Liebenthal, *Book of Chao*, 86–95, and Felbur, *Essays of Sengzhao*, 87–90. The Buddhist salutation *henan* is a rendering of the Sanskrit term *vandanam* (prostration, bow, to worship).

14. *Quan Jin wen* 142.6a.

124   *Chapter Two*

and Mount Lu (in modern-day Jiangxi Province). We only know that Liu wrote in the twelfth month and that Sengzhao responded in the eighth month of the following year, 410, with a letter more than twice the length of Liu's.[15] Sengzhao's proem perfectly mirrors that of the letter he had received from Mount Lu. Sengzhao, too, expresses longing for Liu and admiration for his letter and other writings. He inquires about Liu's health (頃常如何), mentions that he himself has often been unwell (貧道勞疾多不佳耳), and expresses good wishes (厚自保愛) and a desire for further letters.[16] Sengzhao also matches Liu's sketch of his current circumstances by describing recent activities in Kumāra-jīva's circle, writing about several collaborators and scripture transla-tion projects. After duly praising earlier works by Liu and Huiyuan and requesting more to be sent, he mentions his commentary on the *Vimalakīrti Sutra*,[17] which he encloses with his letter (今因信持一本往南). Following detailed responses to Liu's questions, Sengzhao closes the letter with an epilogue contemplating the limits of language and imploring Liu to continue the correspondence. Unfortunately, there is no further evidence that the epistolary exchange between Liu Yimin and Sengzhao continued.

Comparing the health-related remarks in the proems of the two letters, we detect slight differences. While Sengzhao, the much younger man who may not have experienced serious illness himself, remains squarely within the realm of conventional set phrases, the older Liu Yimin brings up his ill health in a less formulaic and more emphatic way. Beyond the simple difference in age, which often comes with more experience of being unwell, Liu Yimin's different approach to writing about his condition could also reflect the self-perception of a man who seems to have suffered from ill health throughout much of his life. According to a miracle tale in the fifth-century *Records Proclaiming Divine Manifestation* (*Xuan yan ji* 宣驗記), Liu Yimin was "frequently sick" (多病), but intense meditation last-

---

15. "Da Liu Yimin shu" 答劉遺民書, in *Quan Jin wen* 164.1a–4b; Liebenthal, *Book of Chao*, 96–109; Felbur, *Essays of Sengzhao*, 90–99.

16. *Quan Jin wen* 164.1a.

17. This *Commentary on the "Vimalakīrti Sutra"* (*Zhu Weimojie jing* 注維摩詰經) collects comments by Sengzhao, Kumārajīva, Daosheng, and Daorong 道融.

ing many months eventually brought him healing (因遂病差).[18] A later source, Chen Shunyu's 陳舜俞 (d. 1074) *Records of Mount Lu* (*Lushan ji* 盧山記), describes Liu Yimin's intense meditation practice in similar terms but presents it as his way of preparing for his approaching death, stating that Liu undertook this meditation when he started feeling ill in the first month of his twelfth year at Mount Lu (自正月感疾。便依念佛三昧), which led to his passing half a year later.[19]

We find similar sentiments about health and illness expressed in the frames of letters throughout the corpus of early and early medieval epistolary literature, whether in formulaic or more poetic terms and in both familiar and high registers. The most basic inquiry after the correspondent's health, "May you be without complaint" (無恙), appears in ordinary family letters and polite exchanges alike. This phrase is used in the earliest extant Chinese personal letters, dated to around 224 BCE, which include the following series of health inquiries followed by health reports: "Heifu and Jing bow repeatedly and send their best greetings to Zhong: Is mother without complaint? Heifu and Jing are without complaint" (黑夫、驚敢再拜問中: 母毋恙也? 黑夫、驚毋恙也).[20] Similar phrases appear in the only surviving letter-writing guide from early medieval China, Suo Jing's 索靖 (239–303) *Monthly Etiquette* (*Yueyi* 月儀).[21] Several of the high-register model letters in this guide express health wishes, either straightforwardly, "May you be unharmed; this would be very fortunate" (無恙幸甚), or more elaborately, "May you, in a warm house or wearing a thick fur coat, harmonize your vital breath and nurture your spirit; may you rest well, this would be very fortunate" (溫室重裘, 和氣養神, 休宜幸甚).[22]

Although we must assume that most information about health and illness was either omitted, obscured, or edited out in early and early medie-

---

18. Cited after Falin's 法琳 (572–640) "Discourse on Determining What Is Correct" ("Bian zheng lun" 辯正論) 7.538.

19. *Lushan ji* 3.1039.

20. These letters were discovered in 1975–1976 in tomb no. 4 of Shuihudi in Hubei Province; see *Yunmeng Shuihudi Qin mu*, 25–26, figs. 167–68. On the phrase *wuyang*, see Harper, "Conception of Illness," 227.

21. *Quan Jin wen* 84.8b–10b.

22. On Suo Jing's *Monthly Etiquette*, see Richter, *Letters and Epistolary Culture*, 140–45.

126 *Chapter Two*

val Chinese epistolary literature, Qianshen Bai was certainly right when he noted that "in ancient times, one major function of the letter was to report on the writer's health."[23] The rare extant sources are still rich and worth exploring, even if they only constitute the tip of the iceberg, as is always the case with the literature of this period.

The Ailing Doctor: Huangfu Mi's Memorial Declining the Summons to Office

The literary scholar, medical expert, and lifelong recluse Huangfu Mi (215–282) has already made an entrance as a "book maniac" in part I. According to biographical records, he was not only an ardent reader but also a prolific writer, active in fields ranging from literature to history, biography, hemerology, and medicine.[24] The two autobiographical texts he wrote, titled "Self-Account" ("Zi xu" 自序) and the *Annals of the Master of Arcane Tranquility* (*Xuanyan chunqiu* 玄晏春秋—"Arcane Tranquility" being a sobriquet of Huangfu Mi's), only survive in fragments. However, several other texts that include autobiographical references and self-accounts of illness have been transmitted. This unusually rich record is due to three interconnected elements in Huangfu Mi's biography: personal experience with illness, medical expertise, and steadfast "substantive" reclusion—a term suggested by Alan Berkowitz to describe reclusion that is "more than an occasional act, more than mere rhetoric, more than insincere posturing, and more than a state of mind."[25] Based on Huangfu Mi's consistent record of declining appointments throughout his life, his literary work dedicated to the lives of recluses, including the *Biographies of Eminent Gentlemen* (*Gaoshi zhuan* 高士傳), and the praise of reclusion dispersed throughout his oeuvre, Berkowitz has even

23. Bai, "Illness, Disability, and Deformity," 161.

24. For a descriptive bibliography of Huangfu Mi's works, see Nagel-Angermann, "*Diwang shiji*," 41–54. On his life and literary oeuvre, see Declercq, *Writing Against the State*, 159–205. On his testamentary essay ("Duzhong lun" 篤終論), see Knapp, "Heaven and Death." On the reception of Huangfu Mi in medical history, see Brown, *Art of Medicine in Early China*, 130–50.

25. Berkowitz, *Patterns of Disengagement*, 147.

suggested that Huangfu Mi "should be seen as the greatest advocate of substantive reclusion in early-medieval China."[26]

Biographical sources suggest that Huangfu Mi developed a debilitating illness in his thirties, which led him to the study of medicine and later to the compilation of medical handbooks. In the preface to his *ABC of Acupuncture and Moxibustion* (*Zhenjiu jiayijing* 針灸甲乙經), Huangfu Mi makes this connection himself, mentioning that he started compiling the book during the Ganlu period (256–260) after recovering from a wind stroke and concomitant deafness, which took several months to cure (病風加苦聾百日).[27] The importance of personal experience of illness to Huangfu Mi's approach to medicine becomes clear when he adapts a proverb known from the *Zuo Tradition*: "When you have broken your arm three times, you know how to practice good medicine" (三折肱, 知為良醫).[28] Describing his own medical qualifications, Huangfu Mi writes, "It is not that I am just saying 'I can.' Isn't it true that 'he who broke his arm three times becomes a doctor'?" I was not born knowing, experience also played its part" (匪曰我能也, 蓋三折臂者為醫, 非生而知之, 試驗亦其次也).[29] In his emphasis on personal experience as the basis of one's scholarship, Huangfu Mi resembles Wang Chong, who wrote *Nurturing Inborn Nature* almost two centuries earlier, and Liu Xie, whose chapter "Nurturing the Vital Breath" took shape more than two centuries later.

While the connection between Huangfu Mi's poor health and his interest in medicine seems unambiguous, it is more difficult to discern why he never accepted an official appointment. Was he truly unable to serve, or did he have other motives for avoiding involvement in politics? The turbulent political situation during much of his adult life—characterized by the decline of the Wei dynasty after Cao Pi's death in 226 and the rise of the Sima family, leading to the foundation of the Jin dynasty in 266— would certainly have provided ample reason to shun official engagements

26. Berkowitz, *Patterns of Disengagement*, 160.

27. *Huangdi zhenjiu jiayijing*, 655. See also the translation in Yang and Chace, *Systematic Classic*, xx.

28. *Zuozhuan* Ding 13; Durrant, Li, and Schaberg, *Zuo Tradition*, 1813.

29. Quoted in *Zhubing yuanhou lun* 6.178. Brown translates this passage in *Art of Medicine in Early China*, 139. Huangfu Mi's "I can" (我能也) may reverberate with *Zhuangzi* 17.594.

128   *Chapter Two*

for reasons of self-preservation. Illness might have served as "an opportune excuse."[30] While we cannot verify the truthfulness of Huangfu Mi's various professions of being too sick to serve, his writings offer insight into how he presented himself as ailing.

In the context of epistolary reflections on health and illness, one of his compositions is especially pertinent: the "Memorial Declining the Summons" ("Rang zhengpin biao" 讓徵聘表), which Huangfu Mi submitted to Sima Yan 司馬炎 (236–290) in 267, just a year after Sima had established the Jin dynasty and declared himself Emperor Wu (Jin Wudi 晉武帝, r. 266–290). As one of several types of official communication to superiors, memorials to the throne are a well-established epistolary genre: written in the first person and addressed to a single recipient, they are not part of regular correspondence like personal letters but are nevertheless reciprocal, typically receiving a reply from the emperor or someone in the administration. Unlike literary letters (*shu*), which operate with the deceit of being addressed to a particular recipient of one's own social standing but are intended for a larger audience (as Sima Qian's letter might have been), memorials to superiors (*biao* 表, also *shangshu* 上書/疏) were openly public within the limits of the court and the upper echelons of the administration, serving as a crucial platform for literati to make their voices heard.

As we know from examples transmitted in historical works, anthologies, and commonplace books, memorials were written on a wide variety of subjects, including the writer himself.[31] Although an exclusive focus on the writer was rare, authors of memorials frequently used autobiographical material to support their main rhetorical objectives.[32] This characteristic turn to the writer's life and experience aligns with Liu Xie's description

---

30. Declercq, *Writing Against the State*, 178.

31. Well-known examples include Cao Zhi's "Memorial Seeking to Prove Myself" and Li Mi's 李密 (227–287) "Memorial Expressing My True State" ("Chen qingshi biao" 陳情事表). See *Wen xuan* 37.1675–84 and 37.1693–96.

32. Many of the memorials included in chapters 37–38 of the *Selections of Refined Literature* incorporate autobiographical material. Memorials have not been extensively studied as sources of autobiographical literature; one exception is Robert Joe Cutter's "Letters and Memorials in the Early Third Century: The Case of Cao Zhi." For an introduction to the types and features of letters to the throne and the process of memorializing, with a focus on the Eastern Han, see Giele, *Imperial Decision-Making*, 83–200.

of the genre in *Literary Mind*. Based on the core meanings of *biao* 表, Liu viewed memorials as "externalizations" of the writerly self, depicting them as texts that "state one's request outright" (表以陳請) and can be seen as "guideposts" (表者標也).[33]

The introduction to Huangfu Mi's "Memorial Declining the Summons" in the *History of the Jin Dynasty* notes that, following repeated imperial appointments, Huangfu Mi "submitted a memorial claiming to be a 'servant in the wilderness'" (諡上疏自稱草莽臣), using a phrase that describes countryfolk in the *Mengzi*.[34] The memorial, in its transmitted form, opens as follows:

> Your servant, riddled with ailments and maladies, has lost his taste for the Way. Owing to my illness, I have pulled out my hairpin to loosen my hair in the forests and hills. Without access to human society, I keep the company of birds and beasts. Your Majesty, who has been parting the undergrowth to gather orchids, has, together with them, also reaped weeds.
>
> 臣以尪瘵。迷于道趣。因病抽簪。散髮林阜。人綱否閉。鳥獸為群。陛下披榛采蘭。并收蒿艾。[35]

Huangfu Mi raises the main issue of his memorial to Emperor Wu at the beginning: the effects of his ill health on his ability to serve in an official position. His emphasis is not so much on his physical limitations—these will make an impressive entrance later in the text—but on the accompanying loss of urbanity and courtliness. He presents himself with unbound, possibly unkempt hair, having long abandoned the hairpin that characterized the appearance expected of any respectable adult in public at the time. He further emphasizes his detachment from polite society by placing himself among animals in the wilderness, associating his "ailments and maladies" with the loss of culture and even humanity.

33. *Wenxin diaolong* 22.406.

34. *Mengzi* 5b7.

35. *Quan Jin wen* 71.4a–b. The text was reconstructed by Yan Kejun, mainly following the differently abridged versions in Huangfu Mi's biography in *Jin shu* 51.1415 and in *Yiwen leiju* 37.665. See also the translations in Declercq, *Writing Against the State*, 185–88, and Nagel-Angermann, "Diwang shiji," 31–33 (as part of her full translation of Huangfu Mi's biography, 15–41).

130   *Chapter Two*

When he then depicts himself as a humble weed among exquisite orchids, however, Huangfu Mi's choice of imagery is ambiguous. While the fragrant orchid (*lan* 蘭) clearly represents values associated with the court, the weeds he mentions are not as lowly as they first appear. Artemisia (*hao* 蒿) and moxa (*ai* 艾) were well-established medicinal plants that we can only read as images of the writer's medical expertise. In a few lines, Huangfu Mu thus skillfully retreats to the margins of civilization and then moves back toward the cultural center, where the medical arts have long held a place.

After this shrewd self-introduction, where he presents himself as both unworthy of officialdom *and* a worthy medical man, Huangfu Mi continues with a passage of adulation. He compares his addressee, Emperor Wu, with legendary rulers of the past and assures him of his subject's absolute loyalty. Returning to the topic of his unsuitability for office, Huangfu Mi delves deep into his own past, providing a detailed account of his physical infirmity:

> Moreover, "this petty person is not good."[36] I attract disaster and invite misfortune. I have long been suffering from a serious illness that has left half of my body numb and my left foot smaller than my right foot. This has been going on for nineteen years. I also took Cold-Food medicine, but because I violated the medication rules, I suffered cruelly.[37] That was seven years ago. In midwinter, although I stripped naked and ate ice, I was in the same distress as during a case of Summerheat. In addition, I was coughing and suffering from counterflow,[38] sometimes feeling feverish and other times as if I had cold damage. Floating *qi* caused swellings that made my limbs feel sore and heavy.
>
> 而小人無良。致災速禍。久嬰篤疾。軀半不仁。右腳偏小。十有九載。又服寒食藥。違錯節度。辛苦荼毒。于今七年。隆冬裸袒

36. An allusion to a statement made by King Wu of the Zhou dynasty (周武王, trad. r. 1046–1043 BCE) in the *Book of Documents*; see *Shangshu* 11.70b.

37. The phrase 違錯節度, literally "run contrary and incorrectly to regularity and measurement," could also be understood to mean that the drug did not agree with Huangfu Mi's predisposition, as the biographical narrative about the side effects of his Cold-Food Powder use suggests; see *Jin shu* 51.1415.

38. Huangfu Mi probably referred to the reversed flow of the stomach *qi*, which may cause symptoms such as vomiting or hiccups; see Sivin, *Traditional Medicine*, 222.

食冰。當暑煩悶。加以咳逆。或若溫瘧。或類傷寒。浮氣流腫。
四肢酸重。[39]

Huangfu Mi's illness report focuses on two periods of his life that contribute to his current infirmity. Not at all vague about the onset of his complaints—usually interpreted as a form of hemiplegia—he carefully counts the years of his suffering, stating that it started in 248, just a year before the military coup of Sima Yi 司馬懿 (179–251), which ushered in the decline of the Wei dynasty. Huangfu Mi then jumps twelve years ahead, from his early thirties to his mid-forties, to describe how he suffered from the side effects of Cold-Food medicine, also known as Cold-Food Powder (*hanshi san* 寒食散). As striking as the symptoms he lists may appear, they are fairly conventional when it comes to reports about this notorious composite drug, as we know from other medieval texts, among them a treatise by Huangfu Mi himself.[40] Similar to the beginning of the memorial, this passage operates with a mix of self-deprecation and self-praise. While overtly admitting to a self-medication blunder, Huangfu Mi simultaneously alludes to his medical expertise by demonstrating his powers of (self-)diagnosis and his facility with medical terminology.

The next passage turns to the more immediate present of the now fifty-two-year-old writer:

> To this day, I suffer badly. [Sometimes when I] gasp for breath, the family elders come out to see me, and my wife and children bid me farewell forever. Pressed by the heavenly [imperial] power, I was unable to tarry and forced myself up to get on the road, which made my suffering even more severe. I could not bear to start on my way. Accepting my faith and awaiting punishment, I put my head on the pillow and heave a sigh.

于今困劣。救求呼嚙。父兄見出。妻息長訣。仰迫天威。不能淹留。扶輿就道。所苦加篤。不任進路。委身待罪。伏枕歎息。[41]

---

39. *Quan Jin wen* 71.4a.

40. Fragments of Huangfu Mi's *Discourse on Cold-Food Powder* (*Lun hanshisan fang* 論寒食散方, a work in two chapters, composed together with Cao Xi 曹翕) are transmitted in chapter 6 of the *Treatises on the Origins and Symptoms of All Illnesses* and in commonplace books. See also Richter and Chace, "Trouble with Wang Xizhi," 86–89.

41. *Quan Jin wen* 71.4a.

132   Chapter Two

After this dramatic description of his abandoned attempt to travel to the capital Luoyang, Huangfu Mi introduces another passage of praise for the emperor while at the same time deprecating himself, interweaving his narrative with allusions to classical literature. He then continues to deepen the narrative of his own unworthiness, again referring to his ill health:

> I have respectfully heard that the other gentlemen who shared my fate [of being summoned to court] have all managed to arrive. Only your servant is ill and ailing, confined to his bed, nursing his offense. Although I desire [to serve] in this enlightened age, I fear I would have lost my life by the roadside. But even if I were not ill, since we are already living as in the age of Yao and Shun, I could hold on to my resolve of Mount Ji [where the legendary recluse Xu You lived] and would still be pardoned.[42] Your servant has heard: If there is an enlightened and sagacious ruler above, the servants below will be altruistic and sincere; if there is a government "acting with leniency" above,[43] the people below will be abiding and true. I sincerely wish that Your Majesty may ... not allow dirt and filth [such as myself] to muddy the clear stream [of your rule] forever.
>
> 竊聞同命之士。咸以畢到。唯臣疾疚。抱釁床蓐。雖貪明時。懼斃命路隅。設臣不疾。已遭堯舜之世。執志箕山。猶當容之。臣聞上有明聖之主。下有輸實之臣。上有在寬之政。下有委情之人。仰唯陛下...無令泥滓。久濁清流。[44]

When he expresses the fear of losing his life "by the roadside" even in "the age of Yao and Shun," Huangfu Mi comes dangerously close to suggesting that he was avoiding official positions for reasons of self-preservation rather than due to illness. His next rhetorical move ingeniously blunts this suspicion by linking the sagacity of the ruler with the sincerity of the servant: if you, my sovereign, are as virtuous as you believe, the writer of

---

42. Xu You 許由, "the classic recluse," is said to have withdrawn to the foot of Mount Ji when the legendary Emperor Yao offered him the throne; see Declercq, *Writing Against the State*, 393–96. Huangfu Mi uses the same argument in his "Discourse on Dispelling Exhortation" ("Shiquan lun" 釋勸論), written in 266, also in response to summonses he had received; see *Jin shu* 51.1411; Nagel-Angermann, "*Diwang shiji*," 19; see also Declercq, *Writing Against the State*, 181–84.

43. Alluding to an instruction given by the legendary Emperor Shun; see *Shangshu* 3.18c.

44. *Quan Jin wen* 71.4b.

this memorial cannot be devious. Judging by the emperor's response to the memorial, Huangfu Mi navigated these treacherous rhetorical waters well. His biography in the *History of the Jin Dynasty* reports that not only did he manage to evade this and subsequent appointments without alienating Emperor Wu, but the emperor even fulfilled Huangfu Mi's wish to borrow books by sending him a cartload, which "Huangfu Mi, frail and sick as he was, perused untiringly" (謐雖羸疾, 而披閱不怠), in accordance with his image as a "book maniac."[45]

In his only surviving personal letter, part of an exchange with his contemporary Xin Kuang 辛曠 about reclusion, Huangfu Mi wrote that "illness and glory are in competition" (疾與榮競).[46] If he was implying that his own illness would keep him from glory, history would most certainly prove him wrong. In this way, he resembles Sima Qian. While both men failed to keep their bodies intact, the "beginning of filial duty," they clearly succeeded in establishing their names for future generations, thus fulfilling the "end of filial duty."

Not a Digression: Pretending to be Sick in Chinese Literature

Huangfu Mi's "Memorial Declining the Summons" aligns him with a well-established discursive practice. Since the beginning of the Han dynasty, citing illness to evade official duties or politically sensitive situations had become commonplace. By the Eastern Han period, this tactic was "a standard feature of the rhetoric of reclusion and a form of political protest."[47] The frequency of such withdrawals from official service on the pretext of illness is underscored by the case of Xie Fei 謝朏 (439–506), who, upon ostentatiously leaving the capital just before Emperor Gao of the Qi dynasty (Qi Gaodi 齊高帝, r. 479–482) ascended the throne, made it clear that his motives were political by explicitly declaring, "I am not sick" (我無疾).[48]

Memorials declining appointments, requesting temporary leave, or peti-

---

45. *Jin shu* 51.1415; Nagel-Angermann, "*Diwang shiji*," 34; see also Declercq, *Writing Against the State*, 188.

46. "Da Xin Kuang shu" 答辛曠書, in *Yiwen leiju* 37.667, *Quan Jin wen* 71.4b–5a. For the two surviving letters by Xin Kuang, see *Yiwen leiju* 37.666.

47. Farmer, "Calling in Sick," 82.

48. *Liang shu* 15.262.

134   Chapter Two

tioning for permanent retirement had a limited repertoire of justifications. The first excuse was pleading filial duty, that is, caring for frail parents or mourning their deaths. As the central ethical value since the Han dynasty, filial duty could override many other public obligations. The second excuse was pleading illness, suggesting physical or mental incapacity to fulfill official duties. Given these limited options and the ease with which one could feign certain physical ailments, it is unsurprising that illness was often used as a pretext and that declarations of being ill were typically viewed with distrust and suspected as self-serving. Falsely claiming that one's parents were sick or deceased, on the other hand, must have been unacceptable for most. An anecdote from *Traditional Tales and Recent Accounts* illustrates the danger of such fabrications: the Eastern Han official Chen Shi 陳寔 (104–187) once sentenced a clerk to death because he had "fraudulently claimed that his mother was ill in order to get a leave of absence" (詐稱母病求假).[49]

There are famous, likely legendary, rejections of appointments and withdrawals from office on the grounds of illness in earlier historical and philosophical literature. To cite just two examples: Confucius's instruction about how to excuse oneself from an archery ceremony as transmitted in *Records about Ritual* (*Liji* 禮記) and the rejection of the throne by Zichou Zhifu and Zichou Zhibo in the *Zhuangzi*. Confucius advised, "When a gentleman is asked to shoot an arrow but is not able to do so, he declines on account of illness" (孔子曰士使之射不能則辭以疾). In the *Zhuangzi*, Zichou Zhifu and Zichou Zhibo famously play with the double meaning of *zhi* 治, "to cure" and "to govern": "Zichou Zhifu said, 'Make me the Son of Heaven?— That would be all right, I suppose. But I happen to have a deep-seated and worrisome illness that I am just now trying to put in order. So I have no time to put the empire in order'" (我適有幽憂之病, 方且治之, 未暇治天下也).[50]

The rhetorical practice of pleading illness to avoid public service arose during the Han dynasty in connection with the development of the central state and its bureaucracy. Government service was the norm for the male elite, and careers typically began with an appointment followed by a series of promotions. Each step required navigating administrative networks

49. *Shishuo xinyu* 3.1; Mather, *Shih-shuo hsin-yü*, 85.
50. *Liji* 25.220c; *Zhuangzi* 28.965.

with their own rules. The same adeptness at navigating administrative procedures and personal preferences of policymakers was required if one did not seek government service but wanted to avoid it. Attempts to escape service were often interpreted as declarations of disloyalty to the ruler and regarded with suspicion, whether someone outside the administration rejected an appointment, as in the case of Huangfu Mi, or an officeholder sought to retire, as we will see in the case of Shen Yue.

In this context, pleading illness seemed to offer an innocuous way out. As Li Jianmin has shown, claiming to be unfit for service on grounds of illness in the Han dynasty could serve a variety of ulterior motives apart from avoiding office. Pleading illness could also express political dissent, further one's official career, or prompt an "inverse audience," that is, a sickbed visit by the emperor.[51] Li emphasized that the formal process of pleading illness involved preparing a written application, which would then receive an official response. Historical sources include many biographical or autobiographical narratives that relate events surrounding the literati's attempts to plead illness. Occasionally, the official communications themselves have survived as well. Especially if a famous scholar pleaded illness, their petitions might be included in their official biographies or collected in another source. In even fewer cases, we also have the text (or part of the text) of the official response in the form of an imperial edict.[52]

Anyone who set out to write a memorial to the throne pleading illness must have faced significant rhetorical pressure, regardless of whether they were genuinely suffering from a debilitating illness and seeking conditions that would allow them to recover or were in good health but looking to avoid a situation they perceived as precarious for other reasons. To be persuasive,

51. Based on studies of the *History of the Han Dynasty* and the *History of the Later Han Dynasty*, Li Jianmin identified more than two hundred cases of officials claiming to be ill. He also affirmed Yan Shigu's (581–645) understanding that the formal process of claiming to be ill involved the preparation of a written application (移病, 謂移書言病也); see Li Jianmin, *Shengming shixue*, 127–48; *Han shu* 58.2613. He Bian's study of sick leave petitions in the early eighteenth century presents a different spectrum of strategies to utilize illness for one's career, among them the attempt to make a complaint appear less serious than it was to avoid dismissal; see He Bian, "Too Sick to Serve," 54. On sickbed visits, see part III.

52. Guihua Xie's study "Han Bamboo and Wooden Medical Records" demonstrates that administrative rules about reporting and dealing with sickness were also in place for lower social orders, such as soldiers; see esp. 92–93.

136   Chapter Two

such petitions needed to balance graphic details of physical impairment with plausibility and literary decorum. In this respect, Huangfu Mi was an exception. As a medical scholar, he was not only excused from the restrictions that applied to other writers but might even have been expected to discuss illness, including his own, more extensively and in technical terms. Nevertheless, memorials pleading illness are among the most explicit self-narratives of illness found in Chinese letter-writing of the period.

Wang Xizhi's Notes: Self-portrait of the Artist as a Sick Man

That we know so much about the ill health of Wang Xizhi (303–361) is largely due to "calligraphic fortuity" (書法幸).[53] The appreciation of handwriting had been on the rise in China since the latter half of the Han dynasty, and by the fourth century, calligraphy was recognized as the supreme art form. It epitomized the key values and qualities of the superior scholar and was believed to channel transcendental powers.[54] Among the handwritten documents that became coveted collector's items, casual letters held a special place. Although seemingly written spontaneously and without artistic intention, their lively, vibrant cursive was seen to embody calligraphy at its most inspired. Appearing unstudied and artless, yet achievable only after years of exacting practice, the calligraphy of these notes was seen as reflecting their writers' character and mood perfectly. While Wang Xizhi was admired for his handwriting during his lifetime, his reputation continued to grow after his death and was sealed in the seventh century when Emperor Taizong (唐太宗, r. 626–649) of the Tang dynasty declared him the greatest of all calligraphers.[55]

Wang's letters were preserved not for their original ideas or literary beauty—as most surviving *shu* letters were—but for their handwriting; hence they were labeled *tie*, a term also used for other calligraphy models.

53. I owe this term to Qi Xiaochun's book *Mai shi zhi feng*.
54. On the early development of calligraphy, see Nylan, "Calligraphy, the Sacred Text," esp. 34–57.
55. See Ledderose, *Mi Fu and the Classical Tradition*, esp. 1–44; Qi Xiaochun, *Mai shi zhi feng*.

Corresponding Bodies 137

This process of selection and transmission has resulted in an epistolary corpus that is distinct in several ways. Comprising more than six hundred notes, mostly addressed to Wang's friends and relatives and focused on everyday matters, it is both much larger than that of any of his contemporaries and decidedly different in content. As has occasionally been remarked, it largely lacks substantial content, consisting instead of material that might be deemed too trivial and personal to be of historical relevance. However, considering how fragmentary and biased toward elite culture most literary sources from early medieval China are, Wang's "trivial" notes are highly valuable, granting us glimpses into the quotidian and ephemeral aspects of life during that period.[56]

The supposed ephemerality of Wang Xizhi's notes nevertheless raises questions about their status as autobiographical writings.[57] Can we read Wang's epistolary health reports as self-writing at all? Is everything we write about ourselves in a letter autobiographical? How we answer these questions depends on our understanding of the term "autobiography." Judging by the intentionality of writing and an author's ambition to define their historical image, Sima Qian's letter in reply to Ren An certainly ranks higher than Wang's everyday notes. However, given Wang's literary and art-historical standing in Chinese history, it would seem inappropriate to disregard his epistolary oeuvre as purely accidental. We can reasonably assume that Wang, fully aware of his calligraphic virtuosity, wrote at least some of his letters not only as "epistolary gifts" but also as "calligraphic gifts," expecting them to be preserved by their recipients and possibly transmitted to posterity.[58] Wang Xizhi was undoubtedly part of many different epistolary pacts, as evidenced by his surviving notes, which show that he expected answers from his correspondents and knew that they had similar expectations of him.

Among the insights we owe to "calligraphic fortuity," Wang Xizhi's ill health is particularly relevant to our inquiry. More than a hundred brief notes attributed to him mention fatigue, insomnia, belly aches, diarrhea,

---

56. Although we are focusing on Wang Xizhi here, other calligraphic letters from the period also merit scholarly attention, among them those by Wang's most famous son, Wang Xianzhi.

57. On this issue of "autobiography" versus "ego document," see Enenkel, "Epistolary Autobiography," 565–66.

58. Liz Stanley illustrates this idea in "Epistolary Gift."

138 *Chapter Two*

cold damage, pain, and other ailments. As I have pointed out elsewhere, Wang's notes represent "the earliest sizable corpus of personal health reports in Chinese literature."[59] They allow us to see the celebrated artist as a man who was often sick and who shared his suffering with a wide range of correspondents, sometimes with remarkable frankness and detail. The following examples hint at the spectrum and severity of the ailments that plagued Wang and demonstrate the most typical epistolary strategies he employed:

On the twelfth day of the first month, Xizhi writes again: Having received your letter of the twenty-sixth of last month, I felt comforted. Have you been fairly well lately? Your servant's diarrhea is persistent and won't stop. I have not the slightest appetite, and if I eat something, it is never digested. All my maladies are so bad. I do not know how to get any relief. I am absolutely perplexed. I cannot go into details. This is what Xizhi lets you know.

初月十二日。羲之累書。至得去月二十六日書。為慰。比可不。僕下連連不斷。無所一欲。噉輒不化消。諸弊甚。不知何以救之。罔極然。及不一一。羲之白。[60]

This morning was extremely cold. Having received your instruction, I know that your wife has a slight cough again and does not get much sleep but tosses and turns ever more. I hope she will soon be better. What medicine has she been given? Thinking of you, I am deeply worried. Are you fairly well? I vomited heavily again last night. When I ate a little something, it happened again. Only in the morning did I begin to feel fairly well again. I gratefully acknowledge your affection. Wang Xizhi knocks his head on the ground.

旦極寒。得示。承夫人復小欬。不善得眠。助反側。想小爾。復進何藥。念足下猶悚息。卿可否。吾昨暮復大吐。小噉物便爾。旦來可耳。知足下念。王羲之頓首。[61]

---

59. I have written about Wang Xizhi more extensively in two articles, "Beyond Calligraphy" and, with Charles Chace, "The Trouble with Wang Xizhi." Some of the translations and reflections I present here appeared in these two articles, including this quotation from "Trouble with Wang Xizhi," 35.

60. "Chu yue tie" 初月帖 (aka "Xizhi lei shu tie" 羲之累書帖), in *Quan Jin wen* 23.12b. See also the translations by Morino Shigeo and Satō Toshiyuki in *Ō Gishi zen shokan*, no. 344.

61. "(Dan) ji han tie" (旦) 極寒帖, in *Quan Jin wen* 23.6b; *Ō Gishi zen shokan*, no. 329.

I hope the reply I sent this morning has arrived. Has your ailment gotten better? I am concerned about you. Your servant's legs cannot bear this deeply overcast weather. The heavy pain is beyond words. I don't know how to cure it, which worries me deeply. Despite all my efforts, I cannot be comprehensive. Wang Xizhi knocks his head on the ground.

旦反想至。所苦差不。耿耿。僕腳中不堪沈陰。重痛不可言。不知何以治之。憂深。力不具。王羲之頓首。[62]

Because I lately had a letter from someone in your neighborhood, I was wondering about the swelling of the face you suffered from. Are you better now? Although my appetite has improved in the last [few] days, my shins have not. I suffer intensely from this and can hardly do anything involving physical exertion. Just a few words to let you know what's going on.

近因得里人書。想至知故面腫。今差不。吾比日食意如差。而骭中故不差。以此為至患。至不可勞力。數字令弟知聞耳。[63]

Xizhi lets you know: I am not cognizant of the recent state of your venerable body. I am waiting respectfully to receive further announcements. I, Xizhi, am miserable because of a Cold strike. I will soon write to you again. This is what Xizhi lets you know.

義之白。不審尊體比復何如。遲復奉告。義之中冷無賴。尋復白。義之白。[64]

These five notes illustrate the use of conventional set phrases alongside astonishingly detailed, concrete statements and questions, from the generic "Have you been fairly well lately?" (or the very general "May you be without complaint" mentioned in the first section of this chapter[65]) to the very specific "Your servant's diarrhea is persistent and won't stop" or "What medicine has she been given?" The notes also demonstrate that

---

62. "Dan fan tie" 旦反帖, in *Quan Jin wen* 25.11a; *Ō Gishi zen shokan*, no. 360.

63. "De liren shu tie" 得里人書帖, in *Quan Jin wen* 22.9b; *Ō Gishi zen shokan*, no. 635.

64. "Bu shen zun ti tie" 不審尊體帖 (aka "Heru tie" 何如帖), in *Quan Jin wen* 26.7a; *Ō Gishi zen shokan*, no. 286.

65. For example, "May everyone in your family be without complaint" (上下無恙), which appears in "Congmei jia ye tie" 從妹佳也帖, in *Quan Jin wen* 25.5a; *Ō Gishi zen shokan*, no. 205.

140   *Chapter Two*

discussions about illness were not restricted to casual letters between equals but extended to polite and even deferential communication with superiors. This is evident from Wang's use of different registers, personal pronouns, and designations for the letters he had received from the addressee ("letter" *shu* 書, "instruction" *shi* 示, "announcement" *gao* 告, etc.). Wang, like Lu Yun in his letter to Yang Yanming, not only writes about his own health and that of his correspondents but also about the ailments of mutual acquaintances. As we can see, letter-writing, in addition to conversation and gossip, played a significant role in the exchange of vital information within correspondents' social networks.

Wang's notes, straightforward and casual as most of them are, convey his suffering and distress with great intensity. This is partly because he is not reluctant to share raw details of his conditions, from gastrointestinal trouble to aches and exhaustion. But there is also another part to Wang's intensity: he frequently expresses a sense of speechlessness. Examples would be that he is "not writing in detail," "cannot be comprehensive," or that he describes pain as "beyond words."[66] Although references to the limits of language and writing are common epistolary topoi, as discussed earlier in relation to Sima Qian's letter, they ring especially true in the context of illness and suffering. For Wang, the ineffability of suffering, whether related to his own illnesses or those of relatives and friends, was a central concern.

Demonstrating knowledge of his addressees' health conditions and those of their family members and others in the community was an important element in Wang Xizhi's rhetorical repertoire. The notes quoted above suggest that epistolary etiquette required writers to put themselves last. They were expected first to acknowledge the addressees' situation and health, often connected with remarks on the arrival of letters and the season. Only after due attention had been paid to the addressee would writers raise their own issues, including their ailments. Despite this prevalent convention, also evident in the letters by Lu Yun and Liu Yimin quoted earlier, there are also notes by Wang Xizhi that focus entirely on his own health. It is difficult to tell if these are excerpts of originally longer texts or complete notes where Wang disregarded the claims of etiquette, perhaps overwhelmed by the intensity of his own suffering:

66. See Richter, "Beyond Calligraphy," 391–95.

Toward the winter solstice, I became aware of a stirring of Wind.[67] It worsened every day until the tenth of last month, when it was at its most critical. Everything was the same as last spring, only a bit lighter. Since then, it got a little better, but I certainly cannot overcome it. [This Wind has caused] a deep stagnation, which waxes and wanes. Consequently, I am much diminished in *qi* and flesh, which worries me very deeply. Today, I managed to sit up and so I am in fairly good spirits again. This is an incessant illness that I cannot get rid of, and that does not allow me any relief day or night. I do not know when I will get some temporary respite or even be able to convey [?]. Now, my vision is blurred, and my hand is also so bad that I cannot write this letter [well?]. This is what I wanted to let you know.

吾涉冬節。便覺風動。日日增甚。至去月十日。便至委篤。事事如去春。但為輕微耳。尋得小差。固爾不能轉勝。沈滯進退。體氣肌肉便大損。憂懷甚深。今尚得坐起。神意為復可耳。直疾不除。晝夜無復聊賴。不知當得暫有閒。還得□其寫不。如今忽忽目前耳。手亦惡。欲不得書示。令足下知問。[68]

The "stirring of Wind" at the beginning of the note could have caused blurred vision as well as tremors, both of which would have made writing difficult. This is one of only two letters in which Wang connects his illnesses with his handwriting. In the second letter, he mentions a bad shoulder in connection with writing difficulties:

Your latest letter has arrived. Having received your letter of the eighteenth, I feel comforted. How has everyone's health been recently in this rainy, steaming weather? Is the Adjutant better? I am concerned about you. My shoulder blade hurts intensely and has not responded to moxibustion. I suffer extremely and can hardly write. Despite all my efforts, I cannot write more than a few words.

近書至也。得十八日書。為慰。雨蒸比各可不。參軍轉差也。懸耿。吾胛痛劇。灸不得力。至患之。〔欲〕不得書。自力數字。[69]

---

67. On the two medical terms mentioned in the letter, pathogenic excess Wind (*feng* 風) and deep stagnation (*chen zhi* 沈滯), see Richter and Chace, "Trouble with Wang Xizhi," 60–64, esp. note 84 for further background information.

68. "Wu zhi dongjie tie" 吾涉冬節帖, in *Quan Jin wen* 24.1b–2a; *Ō Gishi zen shokan*, no. 345. The emendation of 日 to 目 follows *Ō Gishi zen shokan*.

69. "Jin shu zhi ye tie" 近書至也帖, in *Quan Jin wen* 23.11a; *Ō Gishi zen shokan*, no. 217.

142   *Chapter Two*

Considering Wang Xizhi's calligraphic eminence, these notes about his difficulties in writing while sick raise many questions. From a biographical perspective, we have no way of knowing at what time of his life he wrote these notes and for how long he suffered from the complaints he mentions. From an artistic perspective, we must wonder how his maladies influenced his art, especially since Chinese calligraphy is profoundly physical. Writing with an ink brush on extremely absorbent and thus quite unforgiving paper or silk, any impairment of the artist's health could easily register in their performance and product.[70] The potential of calligraphy to reveal the writer's body and mind was, after all, at the heart of the Chinese reverence of the art form, which regarded handwriting as an extension of the body, a manifestation of a writer's vital energies, *qi*, or as John Hay puts it, "a line of energy, materializing through the brush into the ink-trace."[71] This means that Wang's handwriting could have betrayed much more than just the obvious problems with his hands and shoulders but also other complaints, including intense grief or distress.[72]

Wang Xizhi's biography in the *History of the Jin Dynasty* mentions illness only once, in a thoroughly conventional manner, reporting that Wang left his position at the commandery claiming to be ill (*cheng bin* 稱病).[73] The loss of the memorial to the throne that he must have written on this occasion is regrettable. But while it is intriguing to imagine what Wang might have written to substantiate his claim, as he would have been expected to do, we would not expect a higher order of truthfulness from this type of official communication than from personal letters, as discussed in connection with Huangfu Mi above. Another detail mentioned in Wang's official biography that is interesting for us is his halting speech as a child (*ne yu yan* 訥於言), which is described in *Traditional Tales and Recent Accounts*

---

70. This becomes quite explicit in an unusual letter by the Ming author and artist Xu Wei 徐渭 (1521–1593) about his difficulties in producing calligraphy while sick; see Ryor, "Fleshly Desires," 124.

71. Hay, "Human Body as a Microcosmic Source," 88.

72. See Eugene Wang's "The Taming of the Shrew," an analysis of the calligraphy in Wang Xizhi's "Sang luan tie" 喪亂帖 (*Ō Gishi zen shokan*, no. 151.1) as reflecting Wang Xizhi's anguish at learning about the destruction of his family's ancestral tombs.

73. *Jin shu* 80.2101.

as severe.[74] This could, of course, be a historiographical motif (as discussed in part 1), introduced to mark him out for greatness and to create a contrast with Wang Xizhi's fluid and graceful handwriting later in life.

Another reported affliction of the young Wang Xizhi is similarly multivalent in its historiographical connotations. According to an anecdote in Pei Qi's 裴啟 fragmentarily transmitted *Forest of Conversations* (*Yulin* 語林, ca. 363), Wang suffered from *dian* 癲. While this medical term was used to refer to a broad range of physical and mental disorders, the anecdote in the *Forest of Conversations* describes Wang Xizhi not as melancholic or insane but as afflicted with seizures:[75]

When he was young, Wang Xizhi often suffered from seizures. This went on for one or two years. Once, when he was just about to respond to a poem by Xu Xun and a seizure struck again, he received this twenty-word poem: "Taking pleasure in benevolence, wisdom, and music, / I entrust myself to the shady sides of mountains and rivers. / Clear and rippling the mountain stream coming down the rapids; / Honest and upright the forest of pines and bamboo." Upon coming to his senses again, he recited it to those around him. When he had finished his declamation, he sighed: "What does a seizure have to do with the perfection of virtuous things?"

王右軍少嘗患癲, 一二年輒發動。後答許詢詩, 忽復惡中得二十字云: 取歡仁智樂, 寄暢山水陰。清泠澗下瀨, 歷落松竹林。既醒, 左右誦之, 讀竟, 乃歎曰: 癲何預盛德事耶?[76]

---

74. *Jin shu* 80.2093; *Shishuo xinyu* 26.5.

75. On this aspect of *dian* see *Lingshu* 22.218–19. Also see Chiu "Mind, Body, and Illness," esp. 43–44, 246, 290–92. It is also possible that this anecdote refers to Wang Xizhi's contemporary and distant relative Wang Huzhi 王胡之 (*zi* Xiuling 修齡), whose biography mentions that he suffered from frequent, possibly epileptiform seizures (called *fengxuan ji* 風眩疾, "Wind dizziness illness"), which reportedly did not affect his intelligence; see *Jin shu* 76.2005.

76. Cited from the commentary to *Shishuo xinyu* 26.5. Also see *Taiping yulan* 739.9b; Lu Qinli, *Xian Qin Han Wei Jin Nanbeichao shi*, 896. Lu Qinli added one couplet to the poem, based on a quotation in a commentary to *Selections of Refined Literature*; see *Wen xuan* 22.1056. The phrase *ji chang* 寄暢 appears only three times in early medieval and Tang sources: apart from Wang Xizhi's seizure poem, it is used twice in the Lanting poems: once by Wang himself and once by Yu Yue 虞說; see Lu Qinli, *Xian Qin Han Wei Jin Nanbeichao shi*, 895 and 916.

144 Chapter Two

Unsurprisingly, Wang mentions none of these childhood conditions in his notes. Why would he when, as an adult, he was plagued by so many recent and more serious ailments? The anecdote about his childhood seizures, unconfirmed by any other source, is also colored by the fact that Pei Qi, the historian who reported it, was occasionally accused of unreliability. Nonetheless, the link the story creates between exceptional creativity and illness forms an intriguing, albeit tentative, addition to the self-portrait of the artist as a sick man that emerges from Wang's letters.[77] Within Chinese history, the episode connects Wang Xizhi with a tradition of writers who received literary inspiration in dreams, such as the renowned early medieval poets Xie Lingyun (385–433) and Jiang Yan (444–505), mentioned in part 1. In light of the biomedical interpretation of certain forms of *dian* as "falling sickness" or epilepsy, the anecdote could even link Wang Xizhi to a lineage of supposed fellow sufferers through the ages, from Socrates to Dostoevsky.

Speculating about the role that physical suffering may have played in Wang Xizhi's calligraphy is tempting. Did he achieve mastery despite persistent ill health, or did his genius depend on it to some extent? Could some of the most admired features of Wang Xizhi's handwriting, such as the "sudden changes of speed and brush direction," noted by Robert E. Harrist,[78] be attributed to his suffering, perhaps even to specific health conditions? Was he able to balance the ineffability of suffering through his calligraphy? In Europe, questions about the influence of physical and mental impairment on artistic creation have been posed since the age of Romanticism.[79] Similar inquiries have been pursued in both Chinese and

---

77. See Temkin, *Falling Sickness*. In neurological discussions, the apparently involuntary composition of poetry triggered by a seizure is called hypergraphia.

78. Harrist, "Reading Chinese Calligraphy," 5.

79. See, e.g., Lawlor, *Consumption and Literature*; Byrne, *Tuberculosis and the Victorian Literary Imagination*. One of the most prominent representatives of this movement was the German psychiatrist and philosopher Karl Jaspers (1883–1969), perhaps best known in Chinese studies as the originator of the idea of the "Axial Age." Jaspers built on Friedrich Nietzsche (1844–1900), who in *The Gay Science* (*Die fröhliche Wissenschaft*, first published 1882) praises illness, pain, and suffering. Jaspers, himself sickly throughout most of his life, also posed the question whether illness was not only destructive but might also contribute positively to an artist's creativity; see his *General Psychopathology*, first published in 1913 and last revised in 1942 (*Allgemeine Psychopathologie*, 611). In addition to general observations

Western art history of the early modern period, where well-documented biographies allow for partial reconstruction of artists' medical histories. A prominent example is J. M. William Turner (1775–1851), whose illnesses, particularly his vision disorders, have been shown to have significantly impacted his art.[80] Even if we cannot speak with the same certainty about the much earlier and much more elusive Wang Xizhi, it is worthwhile to consider what role illness may have played in his art. This perspective might enhance our understanding of the complex and still obscure conditions of artistic creation.

Life-Changing Illness in Tao Qian's Letter to His Sons

Similar to Wang Xizhi, whose calligraphy was cherished during his lifetime but only became truly canonical long after his death, Tao Qian's 陶潛 (Tao Yuanming 陶淵明, 365–427) poetry also experienced a significant posthumous rise in appreciation. In the sixth century, Zhong Rong included him in his *Poetry Gradings*, assigning him a middle rank, and Xiao Tong expressed his admiration for Tao by including his poems in the *Selections of Refined Literature* and editing a collection of his works, complete with biography and preface. Tao Qian's poetic reputation continued to grow in the centuries that followed, akin to that of Wang Xizhi, although in Tao's case, it took until the Song dynasty (960–1279) before he was recognized widely.[81]

Tao Qian's epistolary record is slim. A "Letter to Yan and My Other Sons" ("Yu zi Yan deng shu" 與子儼等書) is the only piece of correspondence that has survived. Given its nature as a testamentary familial admonition, it may never have been a letter in the narrow sense of correspondence mailed to a spatially separated recipient. Instead, it should be read as a memento in letter form, left for his five sons to cherish and

---

about the relationship between illness and artistic creativity, Jaspers also published case studies on figures such as the painter Vincent van Gogh (1853–1890) and the playwright August Strindberg (1849–1912).

80. See, e.g., Cahill, "'Madness' in Bada Shanren's Paintings"; Scholtz and Auffarth, "William Turner."

81. On the historical reception of Tao Qian through the ages, see Tian, *Tao Yuanming*; Swartz, *Reading Tao Yuanming*.

146   *Chapter Two*

contemplate after his death.[82] In terms of the epistolary pact and the reciprocity of the relationship between writer and addressee, it is unlikely that Tao Qian wrote this letter expecting a written reply but rather in the hope that his sons would heed his advice.

Tao's letter follows generic conventions that set admonitory letters (*jie zi shu* 戒子書) apart from regular personal correspondence.[83] Written to younger family members, that is, to inferiors, familial admonitions identify the addressees by their personal names in the prescript and characterize the communicative act they are performing as a "notification" or "announcement." Admonitory letters also forgo the epistolary courtesy of a proem, common in letters to equals or superiors, and often start *in medias res*. Tao's letter begins with these words:

> [Tao Qian] notifies [his sons] Yan, Si, Fen, Yi, and Tong.
>
> Heaven and earth bestow life. Where there is birth, there must also be death. Of the ancient sages and worthies, was there a single one who could escape this fate?
>
> 告儼、俟、份、佚、佟。夫天地賦命。有生必有終。自古聖賢。誰能獨免。[84]

This beginning sets the testamentary tone of the letter. In the subsequent passages, Tao Qian, "more than fifty years old" (吾年過五十), first reflects on his own life before offering this urgent advice to his sons: never forget that you are brothers. The transition he employs between these two parts of his letter is particularly significant for our exploration of the role of illness in autobiographical writing:

---

82. The biography of Lei Cizong 雷次宗 (386–448), author of another testamentary admonition written around the same time, spells out this motive: "He wrote to his nephews so that his words would be kept [or observed]" (與子姪書以言所守, *Song shu* 93.2293).

83. I discuss the features of this genre in more detail in "Letters of Familial Admonition," esp. 245–47 and 256–57.

84. "Yu zi Yan deng shu" 與子儼等書, in *Quan Jin wen* 111.7b–8a, *Yiwen leiju* 23.424, *Song shu* 93.2289–90; see also the translations by Davis, *T'ao Yüan-ming*, 1:228–30, and by Hightower in "Letter to His Sons." Tao Qian's five sons also appear in his "Poem Blaming My Sons" ("Ze zi shi" 責子詩); see Lu Qinli, *Xian Qin Han Wei Jin Nanbeichao shi*, 1002–3. See also my "Letters of Familial Admonition," 263–65.

Days and months keep going by. Cleverness and artfulness are truly far from me now. When I muse on the past, how nebulous it all seems. Since I got ill, I have slowly been declining and diminishing. Relatives and friends have not forgotten me; they have all come with medicines to help me get better. But I myself fear that my allotted time is drawing to a close.

日月遂往。機巧好疏。緬求在昔。眇然如何。疾患以來。漸就衰損。親舊不遺。每以藥石見救。自恐大分將有限也。[85]

Tao Qian concludes the autobiographical section of the letter by reflecting on an illness that has left him increasingly diminished, altering both his daily life and his outlook on the future. Death had already played an important role in Tao Qian's work, especially after the loss of his mother and sister about ten years earlier (in 401 and 405, respectively), when he was in his early forties. His inability to recover from this later illness must have thrown the finiteness of his own life into much sharper relief, prompting him to reflect on his mortality in practical terms, including the fate of his children, which led him to compose this testament for his sons.

The life-changing, lingering illness that divides Tao Qian's biography into one part where dying is still a remote possibility and another part where death has drawn close plays a similarly pivotal role in the text. It acts as the hinge between the letter's first, autobiographical part, and its second, cautionary part. In epistolary terms, Tao's report on the reason why he chose to address his sons at this time is a perfectly appropriate move since letters generally include self-referential or metanarrative elements.

Although Tao Qian does not specify when he first became ill, how long ago that was, or what his ailment was, it is tempting to connect this passage in the letter to biographical information found in other sources. The earliest of these is Yan Yanzhi's 顏延之 (384–456) eulogy on Tao Qian, which claims that the poet "when he was in middle age suffered from intermittent fevers" (年在中身, 疾維痁疾).[86] Yan's eulogy also locates illness earlier in his subject's life, describing the young Tao Qian as "poor and sick" (少而貧病).[87]

---

85. *Quan Jin wen* III.7b.

86. "Eulogy on Summoned Gentleman Tao, with a Preface" ("Tao zhengshi lei bing xu" 陶徵士誄并序), in *Wen xuan* 57.2474; see also *Quan Song wen* 38.3a. On *shan* 痁 (intermittent fevers, often translated as malaria), see Li Hao, "Tao Yuanming," 58–59.

87. *Wen xuan* 57.2470.

148   *Chapter Two*

His first biography in a standard history, Shen Yue's account in the *History of the Song Dynasty*, completed in the late fifth century, provides further context, attributing Tao Qian's resignation from his initial position and his decision to sustain himself by "plowing the fields" as reasons for the "frailty and sickness" he later developed (躬耕自資, 遂抱羸疾). As Xiaofei Tian has pointed out, these explanations should be read within the contemporary discourse of reclusion rather than as a realistic representation of Tao Qian's life.[88] Another illness-related passage in Shen Yue's biography has a higher chance of being based on more than historiographical topicality. It shows Tao Qian being unable to walk due to a "foot illness" (*jiaoji* 脚疾) and being carried by two of his sons and a retainer in a wicker sedan chair (*lan yu* 籃輿) on his way to Mount Lu.[89] Later biographical sources include the episode as well, and the seventh-century *History of the Jin Dynasty* even adds another story in which Tao himself explains to an interlocutor, "I have long been suffering from foot illness, so I came here riding in a wicker sedan chair" (素有脚疾, 向乘籃輿).[90]

While illness or impairment was rarely depicted in Chinese visual art, the motif of Tao Qian in a carrying basket gained popularity due to the concurrent rise in prominence of Tao Qian and of Pure Land Buddhism in the late Tang and Song dynasties. Pure Land Buddhism had come to regard Huiyuan as their first patriarch and the White Lotus Society, which the eminent monk is said to have inaugurated at Mount Lu, as the fountainhead of their tradition.[91] Legends about Mount Lu and the gatherings of the Lotus Society proliferated, often figuring Tao Qian as a protagonist, whether in literature or in other art forms. Of the three

88. *Song shu* 93.2287; also see Tian, *Tao Yuanming*, 71–73.

89. *Song shu* 93.2288. On Bai Juyi's poetic response to this ailment of Tao Qian's, see his poem "Foot Illness" ("Zu ji" 足疾), in *Quan Tang shi* 458.5205–6; also see Swartz, *Reading Tao Yuanming*, 65.

90. *Jin shu* 94.2462; also see Tian, *Tao Yuanming*, 81–83. In Tao Qian's biography of his maternal grandfather, Meng Jia 孟嘉, feet are mentioned as well: Tao describes his grandfather as "returning home on foot" (步歸家) after resigning his post as a young man and later in life as "retiring because of foot illness" (辭以脚疾). See "Biography of His Excellency Meng, Former Chief of Staff to the Jin Generalissimo for Subduing the West" ("Jin gu zhengxi dajiangjun changshi Meng fujun zhuan" 晉故征西大將軍長史孟府君傳), in *Quan Jin wen* 112.6b and 112.7a.

91. See Zürcher, *Buddhist Conquest*, 219–21; Jones, *Chinese Pure Land Buddhism*.

main motifs in which the poet occurs in Chinese painting since the Song dynasty, two are connected with Mount Lu: apart from being carried to a gathering of the Lotus Society, Tao Qian was also depicted as one of the "Three Laughers at Tiger Brook" (虎溪三笑). This motif is based on an anecdote that shows Huiyuan seeing off Tao Qian and the Daoist master Lu Xiujing 陸修靜 (406–477) after a visit to Mount Lu. All three broke into laughter when the roar of a tiger made them realize that Huiyuan had accidentally crossed the bridge over Tiger Brook with his friends and thus broken his vow never to leave his Mount Lu sanctuary. Fictional as the gathering of these three men undoubtedly is, it "came to represent the harmonious coexistence of the three schools of thought," Buddhism, Daoism, and Confucianism.[92] Claiming Tao Qian as a Confucian is, of course, a questionable construct.

Depictions of Tao Qian in a carrying basket on his way to Mount Lu, or, as other versions have it, leaving Mount Lu with a disapproving frown on his face,[93] are similarly imbued with meaning well beyond Tao Qian's bad feet. The role that his imperfect health plays in the mix of significations and connotations of paintings such as Li Gonglin's 李公麟 (1049–1106) *Lotus Society* is exemplary. Marginal and ancillary to dominant social and religious values as it may be, ill health still claims its place in the cultural *imaginaire*, whether this was intended by authors and painters or not.[94]

Returning to Tao Qian's own works, it is notable that illness is absent from several of his writings that are typically regarded as autobiographical, such as the "Biography of the Master of Five Willows" ("Wu liu xiansheng zhuan" 五柳先生傳), the "Imitations of Coffin Puller's Songs" ("Ni wan'ge ci" 擬挽歌辭), and the "Sacrificial Offering to My Younger Sister, Madame Cheng" ("Ji Chengshi mei wen" 祭程氏妹文). In his "Sacrificial Offering to Myself" ("Ziji wen" 自祭文), Tao Qian's poetic self is depicted

92. Nelson, "Bridge at Tiger Brook," 258. On the depiction of Tao Qian in Chinese art, also see Nelson, "Catching Sight of South Mountain" (on the association of Tao Qian with Mount Lu) and "Revisiting the Eastern Fence" (on Tao Qian's love of chrysanthemums).

93. See Nelson, "Bridge at Tiger Brook," 263–80.

94. On Li Gonglin's *Lotus Society* paintings, see Pan, *Painting Faith*, 173–281. The image on the dust jacket showing Tao Qian being carried in a basket is a detail of the large handscroll The Lotus Society, traditionally attributed to Li Gonglin, but probably of sixteenth-century origin.

150 Chapter Two

as walking joyfully and without impediment, unencumbered by any "foot illness."[95]

However, several of Tao Qian's poems do mention illness. Stephen Owen, who described poems as "a presentation of self that potentially carried strong autobiographical dimensions," had good reason to call Tao Qian "the first great poetic autobiographer."[96] In one of his "Miscellaneous Poems," for instance, Tao uses imagery that echoes the sentiments expressed in his letter to his sons:

	弱質與運頹	My feeble constitution declines with time's passing;
	玄鬢早已白	The black hair on my temples is early white.
	素標插人頭	Now the white sign is set upon my head,
8	前塗漸就窄	The way in front gradually becomes narrow.[97]

While this poem is difficult to date, another composition, "To Secretary Zhou, Zu, and Xie," was likely written circa 417, around the time Tao wrote the letter to his sons:

	負痾頹簷下	Burdened with sickness under tumbling eaves,[98]
	終日無一欣	In a whole day I have not a single joy.
	藥石有時閑	From medicines sometimes there's a respite,
4	念我意中人	and I think of you who are in my mind.[99]

---

95. *Quan Jin wen* 120.9b. This suggests that the "Sacrificial Offering to Myself" might have been composed earlier in Tao's life, possibly soon after the "Sacrificial Offering to My Younger Sister, Madame Cheng" (written in 407), as Timothy Wai Keung Chan and others have suggested; see Chan, *Considering the End*, 106–12. A curious echo of Tao Qian's evocation of his own death is found in Bao Zhao's 鮑照 (ca. 414–466) "Ballad of the Pine and Cyprus, with a Preface" ("Song bo pian bing xu" 松柏篇并序); see Lu Qinli, *Xian Qin Han Wei Jin Nanbeichao shi*, 1264–65.

96. Owen, "The Self's Perfect Mirror," 74, 78.

97. "Za shi" 雜詩 no. 7, in Lu Qinli, *Xian Qin Han Wei Jin Nanbeichao shi*, 1007; as translated by Davis, *T'ao Yüan-ming*, 1:131–32.

98. The phrase "burdened with sickness" (負痾) also appears in "To Chief of Staff Yang" ("Zeng Yang changshi shi" 贈羊長史詩), possibly written at about the same time; Lu Qinli, *Xian Qin Han Wei Jin Nanbeichao shi*, 976; Davis, *T'ao Yüan-ming*, 1:72.

99. "Shi Zhou yuan [Zhou Xuzhi, 377–427] Zu [Qi] Xie [Jingyi]" 示周掾祖謝 (aka "Shi Zhou Zu Qi Xie Jingyi san lang shi san ren gong zai chengbei jiang li jiao shu shi" 示周

In this poem, we again see the intertwining of sickness with straightened circumstances and the resulting loss of joy. Tao Qian also expresses gratitude for medicine, raising the possibility that the friends to whom he addressed this poem were among the benefactors he mentions in the letter to his sons. In the preface to a slightly later poem, "Reply to Aide Pang," written in 423—just a few years after his letter to his sons—Tao echoes ideas expressed in the letter: "I have been nursing an illness for many years and no longer write. From the first I was not gifted, and now I am old and sick as well" (吾抱疾多年。不復為文。本既不豐。復老病繼之).[100] The preface and poem together, written on the occasion of Pang's departure from Tao's neighborhood, are unmistakably infused with epistolary features, from Tao's appreciation of the letter he had received from Pang to the celebration of their friendship, the sorrow of parting, and the expression of hope for the other's well-being and a future reunion.

Whatever the specific circumstances of Tao Qian's ill health may have been, it is clear that he lived with illness and impairment during certain periods of his life and chose to reflect aspects of these experiences in his literary works.[101] Comparing the ephemeral notes of Wang Xizhi about his day-to-day suffering with Tao Qian's testamentary letter, which was openly written with a view to posterity, reveals a significant contrast. Tao's letter was intended not only as a future family heirloom but also as a document supporting the image of the reclusive poet that emerges from his overall

---

續之祖企謝景夷三郎時三人共在城北講禮校書詩), in Lu Qinli, *Xian Qin Han Wei Jin Nanbeichao shi*, 975; Davis, *T'ao Yüan-ming*, 1:54.

100. "Da Pang congjun shi" 答龐參軍詩, in Lu Qinli, *Xian Qin Han Wei Jin Nanbeichao shi*, 976–77; the quotation here is based on the translation by Davis, *T'ao Yüan-ming*, 1:60–61.

101. The scholar Li Hao has suggested a more definitive depiction of Tao Qian's medical history than might be warranted, given the insufficient and partly contradictory information available. Li portrays Tao as a man who ruined his already weak constitution through excessive mourning and retired from office because he was too ill to serve, suffering from "foot *qi*" (*jiao qi* 腳氣). Several of Li's points are nevertheless worth considering; for example, Tao may have consumed (chrysanthemum) wine for its pain-relieving qualities (we saw a similar use of wine as an analgesic in Xiao Yi's case), he went barefoot because wearing shoes caused him pain, and the walking stick frequently mentioned in Tao's later poems may be related to his difficulties walking. See Li Hao, "Tao Yuanming." On the difficulties of identifying "foot *qi*," see Smith, *Forgotten Disease*, esp. 25–42.

152   Chapter Two

oeuvre. It can hardly be a coincidence that the sentiments and imagery in his only surviving letter align seamlessly with his poetry.

In this respect, Tao Qian's letter to his sons is much closer to Sima Qian's letter to Ren An. Both men experienced life-defining impairments that changed them physically and mentally (despite the dissimilarity of their experiences) and chose to write about them in a letter. While Sima Qian insists on having regained a fully functional social self after his mutilation, Tao Qian shows acceptance of his decline once he realizes he will not recover from his illness contracted in middle age. In contrast, Wang Xizhi's notes do not revolve around a single life-changing event but rather detail the daily grind of ill health in its various, ever-changing forms.

Illness and Recovery as a Time to Grow: Yu He's Memorial about Calligraphy

Yu He's 虞龢 "Memorial Discussing Calligraphy" ("Lun shu biao" 論 書表) presents another notable pattern of illness in literature. While biographical information on Yu He is limited, most scholars agree that the memorial was submitted to Emperor Ming (宋明帝, r. 466–472) of the Liu Song dynasty in 470 in response to an imperial command. Emperor Ming is said to have called on Yu and other scholars to help him assess the quality of his calligraphy collection. Yu responded with an account detailing the development of calligraphy and the history of collecting and appreciating calligraphic works.[102] The text of the memorial itself indicates that Yu He submitted it alongside several scholarly works, including revised editions of two earlier texts on calligraphy and catalogs of calligraphic works by Wang Xizhi and others, possibly in the imperial collection.[103]

In contrast to Huangfu Mi's memorial, which is imbued with references to physical and medical matters to justify his declining of an appointment, Yu He's "Memorial Discussing Calligraphy" assigns illness a different and

---

102. On the uncertainties surrounding the dates of Yu He and the creation of the text, see Zhang Weiwei, *Lun shu biao*, 1–7; see also Qi Xiaochun, *Mai shi zhi feng*, 50–51.

103. *Quan Song wen* 55.5a; Zhang Weiwei, *Lun shu biao*, 44–45.

subtler role. Following generic conventions in memorial writing, where autobiographical passages often have an ancillary function in the writer's argument, Yu He introduces his own life experience to affirm his authority in calligraphic matters.[104] Illness appears right at the beginning of this autobiographical interlude:

> Your servant retired from office on grounds of illness to the "Eastern Bank." I roamed and relished mountains and rivers, "staying plain," and finding pleasure in quietude.[105] I "searched for my purpose" in "wooded canyons."[106] Through "hurrying and stumbling" encounters, I found those who graced me with their dignified concern.[107] Together, we went on outings, scaling mountains and drifting on water. Side by side, we explored the subtleties of writing and declamation. Whenever I saw a fine piece of calligraphy, I perused it at my pleasure. My humble penchant for calligraphy deepened, and little by little, I developed a rudimentary understanding of it. Upon meeting [Your Majesty], your servant became thoroughly immersed in kindness and guidance.
>
> 臣謝病東皋。遊玩山水。守拙樂靜。求志林壑。造次之遇。遂紆雅顧。預陟泛之遊。參文咏之末。其諸佳法。恣意披覽。愚好既深。稍有微解。及臣遭遇。曲沾恩誘。[108]

104. Since autobiographical interludes supporting the author's authority are also a common component of topical essays, it is interesting to compare different legitimization strategies. In the field of calligraphy, for instance, Sun Qianli (ca. 648–702), who included two autobiographical passages in his *Manual of Calligraphy* (written in 687), chose to focus first on the childhood origins of his calligraphy practice and the many years he spent practicing, and second on his ways of dealing with criticism of his own calligraphy. See *Shupu* 2, 6–7.

105. Yu He may be alluding to Tao Qian's poetry here, in particular the poems "Back Home Again" ("Gui qu lai xi ci" 歸去來兮辭) and "Returning to Live in Gardens and Fields" ("Gui yuantian ju" 歸園田居 no. 1); see Lu Qinli, *Xian Qin Han Wei Jin Nanbeichao shi*, 988 and 991.

106. This sentence combines allusions to *Lunyu* 16.11 and Xie Lingyun's (385–433) poem "Written on the Lake on My Way Back from the Retreat at Stone Cliffs" ("Shibi jingshe huan huzhong zuo" 石壁精舍還湖中作); see Lu Qinli, *Xian Qin Han Wei Jin Nanbeichao shi*, 1165.

107. An allusion to *Lunyu* 4.5.

108. *Quan Song wen* 55.2a. For the emendation of 涉 to 陟, see Zhang Weiwei, *Lun shu biao*, 19–20, 20n2.

154   *Chapter Two*

Yu He's memorial exhibits many of the stylistic features characteristic of the genre. It is written in high-register literary language, partly in a densely allusive parallel style, and maintains the humble, submissive tone appropriate for official communication addressed to the ruler. The specific moment Yu He chose for his autobiographical interlude—a time when he had retired from office due to illness—is particularly intriguing for our inquiry. He does not specify the nature of his illness in the memorial, and the sparse biographical data available do not provide such details either. The elated description of his life on "sick leave" allows for three interpretations.

Two of these interpretations involve biographical speculation. One could speculate that Yu He was perfectly well and enjoyed time off from the office pretending to be sick. Alternatively, he might have indeed been recuperating from a serious illness that prevented him from fulfilling his official duties but chose to spare his imperial reader the unpleasant details of his condition. Both interpretations are plausible. As we have noted, illness, as one of the few accepted excuses to evade serving in office, was often used as a pretext.[109] Omitting unseemly details about an illness from polite communication was equally common. Yu He would certainly have been aware that the explicit illness narratives found, for example, in Wang Xizhi's notes had no place in a polite letter, much less in a memorial to the throne—unless, of course, the memorial was written to decline an appointment or request retirement.

Yu He ensures that the period he describes does not come across as a dreary recovery but rather as a time of elegant reclusion. The coherence and density of the allusions in the first few sentences underscore this. Identified with quotation marks in my translation, these allusions evoke passages in praise of reclusion in the *Analects* and in poems by Tao Qian and Xie Lingyun. Although pleading illness was often the first step for an official who wanted to withdraw from office, reclusion itself was by no means always associated with ill health. Conventionally, retiring due to a bodily complaint might even devalue a recluse's loftier motives. As Alan Berkowitz has suggested, reclusion should ideally stem from purely moral

---

109. To cite Thomas Mann's (1749–1832) literary character Goethe, as he muses in the 1939 novel *Lotte in Weimar*, "Krankheit hat ja auch ihr Vorteilhaftes, sie ist ein Dispens und eine Befreiung" ("after all, illness has its benefits too, it is a dispensation and a liberation"). See Mann, *Lotte in Weimar*, 289.

reasons and be "a way of life pursued by choice."[110] At least in literature, life in reclusion, far from the potentially sickening and often lethal places of political power, was chiefly associated with good health. This is evident in legendary figures such as the hale and hearty Rong Qiqi 榮啟期, roaming Mount Tai at ninety years of age.[111] Even some of Tao Qian's writings, like the "Sacrificial Offering to Myself" mentioned in the previous section, depict the recluse as a healthy, energetic man who easily copes with the physical labor of gardening, fetching water, and carrying firewood. It is thus no surprise that later historians struggled to reconcile reports of Tao Qian's ill health with the motives of his reclusion.

While it is difficult to determine which of the two biographical interpretations of Yu He's retirement on the grounds of illness is accurate, a third interpretation, rooted in literary developments of the time, offers a more compelling explanation for why Yu He might have chosen to situate his growth in calligraphic appreciation during this period of his life. In the fifth century, the personal experience of illness began to find a place in Chinese poetry. Although detailed descriptions of physical suffering were still uncommon, poets started to write about themselves as "lying sick" (*wo ji/bing* 臥疾/病). As we will discuss in part III, one common pattern was to describe illness and recovery not in harsh medical terms but as periods of leisure and opportunities for intellectual and spiritual growth, often in the company of friends.

While memorials may have originated as a relatively plain, utilitarian genre (*bi* 筆), they increasingly became associated with refined literature (*wen* 文), especially from the Jin dynasty onward, as Liu Xie asserted in his *Literary Mind* (although there is no indication that he included Huangfu Mi). Sketching the development of memorials as a genre, Liu explicitly demands that "their style must be fanned by proper understanding and their beauty driven by pure literariness" (必雅義以扇其風, 清文以馳其麗).[112] Although Liu wrote half a century after the "Memorial Discussing Calligraphy" was submitted, we can assume that Yu He, a literatus closely associated with the Liu Song dynasty court and its literary milieu, was deeply familiar with these developments.

110. Berkowitz, *Patterns of Disengagement*, 7.
111. See, e.g., *Liezi* 1.22–23.
112. *Wenxin diaolong* 22.408.

156   *Chapter Two*

Yu He likely embraced both the rising literary status of the memorial and the incorporation of illness in refined literature. He may have consciously employed the novel feature of writing while sick in his memorial, possibly drawing inspiration from the models provided by Tao Qian and Xie Lingyun. It is this reflection of recent literary trends in depicting health and illness that distinguishes Yu He's "Memorial Discussing Calligraphy" rather than the autobiographically insubstantial remarks on his recuperation in the countryside.

Far From Reticence: Shen Yue's Epistolary Modes of Self-Revelation

Until we are sick, we understand not.
—John Keats, "Letter to J. H. Reynolds, 3 May 1818"[113]

Shen Yue's (441–513) letter to Xu Mian 徐勉 (466–535) ostensibly presents itself as a personal message to a friend, but its underlying purpose as a memorial to Emperor Wu of the Liang dynasty (r. 502–549) is hardly concealed. This letter is noteworthy for its rare urgency in describing the author's failing health and a narrative flow that is unmatched in contemporary literature. The letter certainly runs counter to Shen Yue's reputation for reticence, a quality implied by the posthumous name "Yin" (隱) bestowed upon him by Emperor Wu.[114] Shen Yue wrote it in 510, toward the end of a long and successful career serving three southern dynasties, at the height of his recognition as one of the preeminent literary authorities of his time.

Today, Shen Yue is best remembered for his advancements in prosody, particularly those documented in the postface he added to Xie Lingyun's biography in his *History of the Song Dynasty* (submitted in 488). These contributions had a lasting influence on the development of Chinese poetry from the Tang dynasty onward.[115] In addition to his acclaimed

---

113. Scott, *Selected Letters of John Keats*, 123. While not directly concerned with Keats's illness, Donald C. Goellnicht's book *The Poet-Physician: Keats and Medical Science* is an excellent analysis of how Keats's poetry was inspired by his medical studies and practice.

114. *Liang shu* 13.243.

115. For a comprehensive study of Shen Yue's life and work, see Richard Mather's

historical writings, poems, and rhapsodies, Shen Yue also left behind prose writings in various genres, among them an autobiographical letter in which the sixty-nine-year-old Shen Yue implicitly asks his young friend and benefactor Xu Mian, who was close to Emperor Wu, to intercede with the emperor on his behalf, aiding him in his desire to retire from an onerous official position:

> In my youth, I was left fatherless and destitute, without a close relative to rely on.[116] I was on the point of falling to the ground, toiling and staggering,[117] miserable from morn to night, hobbling along with meager appointments. My aim was not selfish, but I looked forward to receiving some small emolument and, depending on this, to returning east [to my native Wuxing]. More than ten years went by before I undeservedly got an appointment in Xiangyang Prefecture [in modern-day Hubei Province]. Public and private planning is not my forte, but to keep my body supplied with material needs, I could not avoid taking responsibility for human affairs.
>
> At the end of the Yongming era [483–493], when I left the capital to become Grand Warden of Dongyang, my intention consisted in "stopping when I had had enough."[118] But when the Jianwu era [494–498] began its cycle, the human world once more crowded in on me. To leave the court then once and for all, never to return, was not yet easily accomplished. At the beginning of the reign of the Dark Suspicious One,[119] there were many factions within the royal government, and for this reason planning to retire seemed almost attainable. [At the time,] I commissioned you to convey my feelings to Director Xu.[120] I suppose you remember this and have not forgotten it.

---

magisterial *The Poet Shen Yüeh (441–513): The Reticent Marquis.* On matters of prosody, see esp. 37–84, where Mather also translates Shen Yue's postface to the biography of Xie Lingyun.

116. When Shen Yue was twelve years old, his father Shen Pu 沈璞 (416–453) was executed during the turmoil following the assassination of Liu Yilong 劉義隆 (407–453), Emperor Wen of the Liu Song dynasty (宋文帝, r. 424–453).

117. The last phrase combines allusions to the *Book of Odes* and the *Changes of Zhou;* see "The Beating of Drums" ("Ji gu" 擊鼓, *Mao shi* no. 31) and *Zhou yi* 3.7c.

118. *Laozi* 44A.180.

119. Xiao Baojuan 蕭寶卷 (483–501), penultimate emperor (Donghun hou 東昏侯, r. 498–501) of the Qi dynasty.

120. Xu Xiaosi 徐孝嗣 (453–499), who was Director of the Department of State Affairs from 497 to 499.

158 Chapter Two

When the way of the Sages was restored [in 502, when the Liang dynasty was established], quite by mistake I met with good fortune and my past resolve and former intention once more became sidetracked. At the beginning of this year, when we had reached the New Year ceremonies, my request for retirement was denied because of the emperor's kindness. I am truly unable to promote or proclaim morality or good government or to gloriously unfold the politics of the court. But I still would like to search out and explore texts and documents to find the similarities and differences in contemporary discussions.

However, since the beginning of the year, my illness has worsened, and my anxieties [have grown more] piercing. This is doubtless due to the fact that my vitality is limited and my work has been excessive. Surely, this decline and exhaustion is due to my advanced years. Dragging my staff, now walking, now halting, I exert my strength to work as conscientiously as I can. Looking in from outside, watching from the sidelines, I still appear to be a whole man. But whenever I want to apply myself to anything, I find that my body and bones are not coordinated. I constantly find it necessary to strenuously gather myself before I can put forth any energy. When I take off my clothes to go to bed, I feel as if my limbs no longer have any relation to the rest of my body. My upper body is hot, my lower body is cold; every month it gets worse, every day more intense. If I take something warm, I feel overheated, and if I ingest something cool, I invariably suffer from diarrhea. The later recovery never comes up to the earlier recovery, while the later severity is always greater than the earlier. Every hundred days or every few weeks, I have to shift to a new hole in my leather belt. When I grasp my arm with my hand, I figure that every month it is smaller by half a degree.[121]

Estimating my prognosis from this, how can I last much longer? If it goes on like this day after day without stopping, I will leave behind for my Sage Lord [i.e., Emperor Wu] an irrevocable regret. I rashly desire to petition, pleading for an official rank for my retirement and old age [and ask you to investigate the prospect of such a petition]. If Heaven lends me the years that I may return to my normal health, when I was able to employ my talents and strength, this is all I would ever want.

吾弱年孤苦, 傍無朞屬, 往者將墜於地, 契闊屯邅, 困於朝夕, 崎嶇薄宦, 事非為已, 望得小祿, 傍此東歸。 歲逾十稔, 方忝襄陽縣, 公私情

---

121. If used as a unit of length, *fen* 分 (part) refers to a tenth of an inch (*cun* 寸). Since a change of "half a *fen*" would hardly be detectable when grasping one's arm, it is likely that Shen Yue is speaking metaphorically.

計，非所了具，以身資物，不得不任人事。永明末，出守東陽，意在止足；而建武肇運，人世膠加，一去不反，行之未易。及昏猜之始，王政多門，因此謀退，庶幾可果，託卿布懷於徐令，想記未忘。聖道聿興，謬逢嘉運，往志宿心，復成乖爽。今歲開元，禮年云至，懸車之請，事由恩奪，誠不能弘宣風政，光闡朝猷，尚欲討尋文簿，時議同異。而開年以來，病增慮切，當由生靈有限，勞役過差，總此凋竭，歸之暮年，牽策行止，努力祗事。外觀傍覽，尚似全人，而形骸力用，不相綜攝。常須過自束持，方可僶俛。解衣一臥，支體不復相關。上熱下冷，月增日篤，取煖則煩，加寒必利，後差不及前差，後劇必甚前劇。百日數旬，革帶常應移孔；以手握臂，率計月小半分。以此推算，豈能支久？若此不休，日復一日，將貽聖主不迫之恨。冒欲表聞，乞歸老之秩。若天假其年，還得平健，才力所堪，惟思是策。[122]

Shen Yue's letter is unusual for a literary letter (*shu*). Although the editors of the *History of the Liang* evidently stripped it of the epistolary features it must have once had—all that is left is a single intimate "you" (*qing* 卿) addressing Xu Mian—they decided not to tone down Shen Yue's harrowing account of his physical decline. This part of the letter, preserved in all its graphic detail, likely remained because of its literary mastery and central conceit of being an appeal not so much to the letter's primary addressee Xu Mian but rather to Emperor Wu.

Epistolary self-writing typically focuses on specific life events rather than presenting an entire life. Shen Yue's letter, however, combines these autobiographical modes. Prompted by his current physical distress and his desire to withdraw from his position, he offers readers the long view of his long life, leading up to the time since the beginning of the new year. After a succinct and elegant self-account of his official merits, depicted against a backdrop of reluctance to assume official positions, he turns to his present condition, describing it in a highly original, idiosyncratic voice—a stark contrast to Wang Chong's prosaic and restrained self-account of aging in the preface to *Discourses Weighed in the Balance*, which, as we saw in the previous chapter, simply states, "My hair turned white, my teeth fell out, and I became older every day."

Shen Yue lists an array of ailments: declining strength, failing thermo-

---

122. "Yu Xu Mian shu" 與徐勉書, in *Quan Liang wen* 28.7b–8a, *Liang shu* 13.235–36. My translation largely follows Mather, *Shen Yüeh*, 132–34.

160   *Chapter Two*

regulation, and a body struggling to coordinate movements and palpably withering away. These symptoms would be daunting for anyone, but they may have been especially frightening for Shen Yue, who had led an exceptionally active life and apparently always enjoyed good health. His biography in the *History of the Liang* suggests that his mother had a hand in this. Concerned about his excessive fondness for learning and worried that he might sicken himself by staying up all night, she is said to have rationed the oil for his lamp. Although this only prevented him from nighttime reading and not from reciting in the dark, his mother's caution may have helped Shen Yue build a foundation for good health by preventing early exhaustion.[123]

Another image of robust health appears in Shen Yue's "Statement of Confession and Repentance" ("Chanhui wen" 懺悔文), a singular piece of early medieval self-writing, composed around 487 when Shen was in his mid-forties.[124] Although this type of confession is a specifically Buddhist genre, Shen Yue, born into a family following the Celestial Masters, must have been familiar with Daoist traditions of confession as well.[125] Religious confessions share certain features with letters: they are written in the first person, addressed to specific recipients (the Buddha or the celestial authorities), and implicitly also address other members of the writer's religious community. However, they differ in one decisive element of epistolarity, that is, their view of reciprocity, since the reply expected of a confession is not a letter back but rather a response from a numinous power. Apart from these similarities with the epistolary pact, confessions of course also follow distinct genre requirements in other respects.

In his confession, Shen Yue vividly describes intense physicality—ranging

---

123. *Liang shu* 13.233.

124. *Quan Liang wen* 32.1b–2b. The text was originally collected in Daoxuan's 道宣 (596–667) *Guang Hongming ji* 28.331. For context and a translation, see Mather, *Shen Yüeh*, 166–73.

125. Pei-Yi Wu introduced the development of Daoist confessions of sin in his 1979 article "Self-Examination and Confession of Sins in Traditional China" and in his 1990 book *Confucian's Progress*, 209–34; see also Bauer, *Antlitz Chinas*, 209–25. On Shen Yue's background in Celestial Masters Daoism and his later turn to the Shangqing school, see Mather, *Shen Yüeh*, 85–126. For a comprehensive discussion of *chanhui*, see also Greene, *Chan Before Chan*, 159–204.

from gluttony to killing animals, stealing food and books, and promiscuous sex with both men and women. This may appear to fit the genre's requirement to detail all sorts of improprieties. Curiously, though, other writers often remained bland and noncommittal in their confessions (as far as we can tell from surviving examples), whereas Shen Yue delivers cascades of carnal misdeeds in dazzling literary beauty, again eschewing the reticence that later became the emblem of this writer. Despite the passionate remorse and self-reproach expressed, Shen Yue's "Statement of Confession and Repentance" can also be read as a fervent self-celebration of a man reveling in the abundant energy and health that allowed him to commit the many transgressions he so masterfully lists. In this respect, his confession is reminiscent of Cao Pi's self-portrait as a young and healthy athlete discussed earlier.

Returning to Shen Yue's letter to Xu Mian, written twenty-five years later, the memories of his lost vigor must have compounded Shen's dismay. Rather than presenting a dry list of symptoms, he provides detailed observations that lend depth and credibility to his descriptions: his halting walk, the effort required to gather himself before moving, and his unsuccessful attempts to regulate how hot or cold he feels. Shen even takes readers to his bedside to show them his naked, diminished body, and he does so by sharing his own perceptions: the anxious gaze at his waist and the apprehensive probing of his arms—an intimate perspective unmatched in early medieval literature. In doing so, Shen not only removed what Richard Mather calls the "self-protective mask" he wore throughout most of his life but also literally bared himself to his addressees.[126]

Shen Yue's blatant violation of the contemporary conventions of refined literature can only be interpreted as a drastic gesture of sincerity aimed at counteracting the skepticism that surrounded any attempt to retire from office. Why, then, was Shen Yue's supplication not ultimately granted? From the *History of the Liang*, we know that Xu Mian did indeed petition for Shen Yue to be relieved of his duties and granted a sinecure, but Emperor Wu declined this request. The exact reasons for the emperor's decision remain unknown, but it is conceivable that the letter, despite its

---

126. Mather, *Shen Yüeh*, 12. In this way, Shen Yue comes close to the medieval Christian motif of *ostentatio vulnerum*, the display of Jesus's wounds received on the cross, which also became a motif in European autobiographical writing.

162   *Chapter Two*

persuasive power, may have offended its secondary recipient, assuming that Xu Mian shared the letter with the emperor (which seems likely).

One potential issue was Shen Yue's strategy of circumventing the rules of decorum by changing genres. He could not have been as blunt and direct in a formal memorial to the throne as he was in a letter to a friend. While we might admire this move as ingenious, the emperor might have been offended by this very gesture of being addressed vicariously. Additionally, there is an incongruity between Shen Yue's professions of illness and the "literary health" of his brilliant letter, whose eloquence could have been interpreted as betraying his claims of physical decline.[127]

Another problematic aspect is Shen Yue's implicit comparison of his current situation with the reign of the last emperor of the Qi dynasty, another time in his life when he sought to withdraw from office. Finally, Shen Yue's letter contains a subtle hint of coercion when he suggests that if the emperor does not permit his retirement, the emperor could soon be left with "irrevocable regret," essentially holding the sovereign accountable for his subject's eventual death.

Despite his literary might and originality, She Yue was undoubtedly aware of his literary predecessors. When composing the letter to Xu Mian, he may have been inspired by writings he himself included during the compilation of the *History of the Song Dynasty*. One of them is a letter with a similarly indirect rhetorical strategy, quoted in the biography of Xie Zhuang 謝莊 (421–466). In this letter, written in 454, Xie Zhuang expresses his desire to temporarily withdraw from office on the grounds of illness, addressing Liu Yigong 劉義恭 (413–465) in the hope that Liu would convey his intentions to Emperor Xiaowu (宋孝武帝, r. 453–464, Liu Jun 劉駿, 430–464).[128] If Shen Yue did indeed emulate Xie Zhuang's mode of indirect address, he also adapted and modified his predecessor's rhetorical strategy. The thirty-five-year-old Xie used the conventional narrative that only the best should serve—familiar from our discussion of

---

127. Alan Elbaum made a similar observation about this paradox when he asked, "Can a person write limpid prose when roiled by pain?" See Elbaum, "Fire in My Heart," 148.

128. Xie Zhuang, "Memorandum to Yigong, Prince of Jiangxia" ("Yu Jiangxia wang Yigong jian" 與江夏王義恭牋), in *Song shu* 85.2171–72; *Quan Song wen* 35.5b–6b. The memorandum has been discussed and partly translated by Cynthia L. Chennault; see her "Lofty Gates or Solitary Imprisonment?," 295–99.

Huangfu Mi—and presented himself as not only sickly from childhood but also doomed to die early due to his short-lived lineage. In contrast, Shen Yue, twice as old as Xie Zhuang, focuses on the achievements of his long, healthy life in service to three different courts and depicts his ailments as a recent development.[129]

The comparison between Xie Zhuang's memorandum and Shen Yue's letter raises an intriguing question about the relationship between narratives of illness and narratives of old age. Qian Zhongshu has pointed out that "writing about being old and declining is not the same as writing about being old and sick" (寫老而衰, 非寫老而病), citing a letter by the aged Bai Juyi (772–846), in which Bai mentions that he has not been ill lately.[130] Qian's main argument—that one can recover from illness but not from the normal process of aging—is obviously correct. However, it does not fully account for cases like that of Wang Chong, who mistook an illness for aging, subsequently recovered, and later experienced a reversal of the decline he had initially attributed to aging.

Unfortunately, our understanding of how aging was experienced in early and early medieval China is limited. Most autobiographical compositions from the period come from much younger writers, as mentioned earlier in connection with Wang Chong's self-account. Shen Yue and Wang Chong are exceptional in reporting from old age, as they lived longer than the authors of the other illness narratives discussed here: Wang Chong wrote after retirement at around seventy, while Shen Yue was still in office at seventy-two. Assuming Shen Yue represented his symptoms truthfully, the cluster of symptoms he describes in his letter might indicate a specific disorder rather than mere aging.

In other texts composed during the last years of his life, Shen Yue also

---

129. Shen Yue may also have been inspired by another plea for retirement on grounds of poor health quoted in the *History of the Song Dynasty*, Yan Yanzhi's "Memorial Expressing Myself" ("Zi chen biao" 自陳表), written in 452, when Yan was sixty-eight years old, and submitted to Emperor Wen (宋文帝, r. 424–453). Yan writes that an attack of Summer-heat he had suffered during the summer had become chronic and left him with numerous complaints: dizziness, toothaches, coldness and numbness in his limbs, a bad left shoulder, and loss of appetite (自去夏侵暑, 入此秋變, 頭齒眩疼, 根痼漸劇, 手足冷痺, 左胛尤甚。素不能食, 頃向減半, *Song shu* 33.1903).

130. Qian Zhongshu, *Guanzhui bian*, 1404.

164   *Chapter Two*

mentions his ill health, sometimes lamenting them as the effects of aging. In a late-life letter to a friend forty years his junior, the poet Wang Yun 王筠 (481–549), Shen Yue twice contrasts Wang Yun's youthful poetry with his own past youth, highlighting his current state as an old man for whom "a general decay has arrived" (爛然總至) and who has "suddenly found himself worn out and old" (倏焉疲暮).[131] He expresses a similar sentiment in a very different type of text, a vow made for a Buddhist assembly, also known as a maigre feast, which he hosted in 513. Beginning with reflections on the ephemerality of human life, he eventually mentions that he was stricken with an illness the summer before (約以往夏, 遘罹病疾).[132]

For an account of Shen Yue's final illness, we must turn to his biography in the *History of the Liang*. According to this account, Shen Yue suffered a shock after an unpleasant conversation with Emperor Wu, followed by a fall later that night and a "dream that Emperor He of the Qi cut off his tongue with a sword" (夢齊和帝以劍斷其舌).[133] As Richard Mather has suggested, the memory of the execution of the young Emperor He (齊和帝, r. 501–502, Xiao Baorong 蕭寶融, 488–502), which Shen Yue had advised, likely "haunted him to his dying day."[134] Upon waking from this nightmare, Shen Yue first "called in a shaman to interpret the dream" (召巫視之), and then "called for a Daoist priest to submit a red petition on his behalf to the celestial authorities" (乃呼道士奏赤章於天). In the petition, he claimed that the deposition of the Qi dynasty had not been his own idea. Reportedly, the emperor "sent his personal physician, Xu Zhuang, to examine Shen Yue" (高祖遣上省醫徐奘視約疾). The biography also notes that the emperor was infuriated when he learned about the Daoist petition, as it implied that Shen was trying to absolve himself from blame for the last emperor of the Qi dynasty's death, thereby implicitly accusing Emperor Wu.[135]

We do not know if Shen Yue composed his "Testamentary Deathbed Memorial" ("Linzhong yibiao" 臨終遺表) during his final illness, as

---

131. "Letter in Reply to Wang Yun" ("Bao Wang Yun shu" 報王筠書), in *Quan Liang wen* 28.6b–7a; Mather, *Shen Yüeh*, 217.

132. "Prayer Text for a Thousand-Monk Assembly" ("Qian seng hui yuanwen" 千僧會願文), in *Quan Liang wen* 32.2a–3b; Mather, *Shen Yüeh*, 161.

133. *Liang shu* 13.243.

134. Mather, *Shen Yüeh*, 131.

135. *Liang shu* 13.243. See also Mather, *Shen Yüeh*, 221–22.

described in his official biography. Letters, poems, edicts, epitaphs, and other texts composed when one's "end was approaching" (臨終) were part of a long literary tradition. It was not uncommon for writers to plan their "last words" ahead of time, to be prepared for all eventualities.[136] There are indications that Shen Yue might have composed his memorial earlier; he may not have been able to write or even dictate while in the state of acute physical and mental distress suggested by the narrative in the *History of the Liang Dynasty*. On the other hand, the memorial reads like an impromptu composition written during a time of imminent fear that his end was near. It certainly lacks the polish and "literary health" of his letter to Xu Mian, though this could of course be an intentional effect. Whenever it was composed, the memorial again revolves around illness as a humbling and disconcerting experience:

Your servant Yue says: Your servant nurses an illness that is "pervasive and lingering" [and has brought me to my deathbed].[137] So far I have not yet transformed [i.e., died], but my body and spirit have been on the verge of separation more than a dozen times this month alone. I have been in extreme pain and utmost distress, and I have no words to describe this. Back in my normal days, when I was in good health, I didn't think it would be like that. Comparing how I feel right now with falling on swords or sitting on daggers would make it sound too easy. Your Majesty has entered deeply into the Dharma Gate [of Buddhist teachings] and strictly follows austere practices. On the inside, you are compassionate, and on the outside, you are forgiving—this is truly your original heavenly nature. I humbly wish that Your Majesty's sagely heart could dwell on this and expand [your compassion] even further. Your petty servant can then face the road that lies ahead without harboring regrets. Although [my words] embarrassingly cannot achieve the "goodness" [of a dying person's speech], I hope they at least equal "the sorrowful cries [of a dying bird]."[138] Respectfully put forward.

---

136. As mentioned, for example, by Wei Xiong 韋夐 (502–578), who tells his sons on his deathbed, "I have always been afraid that my end would come swiftly, that's why I prepared these words beforehand to admonish you" (吾常恐臨終恍惚, 故以此言預戒汝輩, *Zhou shu* 31.546).

137. Alluding to the deathbed speech by King Cheng of the Zhou dynasty (周成王, r. 1042/1034–1006 BCE). See "Gu ming" 顧命, in *Shangshu* 18.125c.

138. This is an allusion to *Lunyu* 8.4: "The cries of a bird that is about to die are sorrowful; the words of a man who is about to die are good." (鳥之將死, 其鳴也哀; 人之將死, 其言也善).

166 Chapter Two

臣約言。臣抱疾彌留。迄今未化。形神欲離。月已十數。窮楚極
毒。無言以喻。平日健時。不言若此。據刀坐劍。比此為輕。仰
為深入法門。屬茲苦節。內矜外恕。實本天懷。伏願復留聖心。
重加推廣。微臣臨塗。無復遺恨。雖慚也善。庶等鳴哀。謹啟。[139]

Shen Yue's testamentary memorial deviates from the typical deathbed requests for specific funeral arrangements or favors for descendants. His primary intention seems apologetic; appealing to Emperor Wu's "sagely heart," he is asking for clemency (*shu* 恕). Shen Yue's explicit acknowledgments of the emperor's Buddhist faith are interwoven with implicit references to the Confucian canon through allusions. He evokes both the oldest transmitted deathbed text in China, the chapter "Testamentary Charge" ("Gu ming" 顧命) in the *Book of Documents*, and a saying by the dying Zengzi 曾子 in the *Analects*, which underscores the value of words spoken by those facing death.[140]

Shen Yue's apology appeals to the emperor's empathy for a man suffering from a cruel illness that has robbed him of his former, healthy self, including his facility with language and literary expression. These abilities must have been central to his social identity and self-conception. Shen Yue, who had been eloquent all his life, now writes that he has "no words to describe" his pain and reflects that "back in my normal days, when I was in good health, I didn't think it would be like that." He depicts his illness not only as a disruption of life as he knew it but also as a threat to his identity as a brilliant man of letters.

In this respect, Shen Yue's illness contrasts with that of Tao Qian. Tao expressed resigned acceptance, perhaps because he had time to adjust to the loss of physical vitality he suffered in middle age. In contrast, the much older Shen Yue grapples with the recent, unexpected loss of mental autonomy, and his declarations of trust in Buddhist teachings sound feeble and uncertain. As G. Thomas Couser has remarked, "bodily dysfunction is perhaps the most common threat to the appealing belief that one controls one's destiny."[141]

---

139. *Quan Liang wen* 27.6b–7a.

140. See also part III on the representation of sickbed visits.

141. Couser, *Recovering Bodies*, 9.

Selfhood, Public Persona, and Health in Early Medieval Self-Narratives

Early medieval authors wrote about their health in a broad range of texts, contexts, and representational modes. While their voices varied depending on communicative purpose and genre conventions, they shared similar concerns across different forms of self-writing.

The first-person illness narratives introduced in the first chapter of part II share basic literary features and exhibit a certain rhetorical homogeneity. This is because the prefaces in which they are embedded all serve the same function: to present the authors of the collections to which they were attached in the most favorable light, which in turn should ensure the favorable reception of the book. Despite the rhetorical similarities between these self-narratives of strength and grandeur, the prefaces differ in why and how they present their authors' physical conditions. The court official Sima Qian asserts his filial duty and individual value after surviving punitive mutilation. The provincial scholar Wang Chong emphasizes his exceptional physical and intellectual vigor, which allowed him to defy old age. The future emperor Cao Pi celebrates his athletic and martial prowess to demonstrate his readiness for the throne. The southern savant Ge Hong flaunts physical imperfections to set himself apart from the crowd and lay claim to medical and alchemical expertise. Prince Xiao Yi insists that illness and impairment were integral to his achievements as a writer, scholar, and future emperor.

The epistolary texts discussed in the second chapter are more diverse in character and style than the prefaces because they represent different types of communication by letter, ranging from formal and quasi-public memorials to the throne to familial testamentary letters, semi-personal letters, and intimate notes. Each of these subgenres operates within different hierarchical relationships, requiring different types of epistolary etiquette, including different conventions of discussing health matters and different reasons for bringing them up in the first place. The persona created in correspondence is generally not as openly public as that in the prefaces, although most surviving letters, while ostensibly based on the reciprocity of epistolary communication between writer and specific addressee, were likely written with an eye toward wider audiences, including posterity.

168   *Chapter Two*

We have seen that writers did not need to delve into raw physical details to emphasize the importance of illness or impairment in their lives. Sima Qian's letter, for instance, was vague about his life after mutilation, instead relying on the reader's imagination to grasp the significance of surviving such severe corporal punishment. Similarly, a few words in Tao Qian's letter to his sons make it clear that the illness he suffered in middle age was a life-changing experience, one he wanted his sons to understand. Yu He, who only hinted at the illness and recovery that granted him the leisure to pursue calligraphy, may have included this information only to signal his awareness of recent literary developments—developments that increasingly granted illness experiences a space in refined literature.

As we observed in the high-register memorials to the throne by Huangfu Mi and Shen Yue, as well as in Wang Xizhi's informal notes to friends and family, explicit descriptions of physical distress appear in different epistolary genres, serving distinct functions. Memorials pleading illness often instrumentalize and perform ill health to advance the professional goals of their authors. In contrast, informal notes include health matters not so much for persuasive purposes but for relational ones. Writing about illness in these notes aims to affirm close personal relationships and alleviate the burden of illness for either the correspondents or others in their circle. Shen Yue's deathbed memorial acknowledges the power of illness to shake one's identity, underscoring the overwhelming importance of health for the literati officeholder.

Early medieval authors clearly saw their bodies as a constitutive part of their identities. The anxiety that illness and impairment might prevent them from fulfilling their familial and social roles is evident across prefaces and letters. These obligations ranged from filial or paternal duties to the responsibilities of office, scholarly self-expectations, and a ruler's conception of his duties. This observation connects early medieval self-writing about health and illness with Liu Xie's exhortation that writers "nurture their vital breath," as discussed in part 1. Although the main thrust of Liu's essay in *Literary Mind* was concerned with preserving and cultivating one's literary creativity, Liu also aimed his advice at literati officeholders who were tasked with churning out official documents in vast numbers and various genres and whose health was often of no concern to their superiors.

What difference does it make if we consider how early medieval writers represented their physical condition in their self-writings? When we read these well-known texts not merely as disembodied voices speaking across the centuries but as accounts of full-blooded physical beings subject to the onslaught of time and mortality, our understanding of these works deepens significantly. First, paying attention to literary representations of health and illness broadens our perception of the spectrum of human experience preserved in these texts. It is easy to overlook the ubiquity of individual illness and suffering in medieval literature. By focusing on these aspects, we gain a more comprehensive view of the lived realities of the authors and their contemporaries.

Additionally, these self-accounts highlight important aspects of literary practice and the development of literature in early medieval China, including evolving notions of authorship and what constituted refined literature. Sima Qian's self-accounts are particularly notable for being among the first to depict authorship as deeply rooted in the writer's physical condition. The other prefaces and letters we discussed all display variations of this rootedness and suggest that health and illness became increasingly accepted as integral parts of an author's identity and public persona. The thematic scope of subjects considered appropriate for refined literature expanded during early medieval China. Illness, once marginal, gradually became an established topic, even in the highest-register form of refined literature, poetry, an evolution that shall be explored further in part III.

Ultimately, the greatest gain for our understanding of early medieval literature may be the realization that health and illness *were* integrated into self-writing, whether knowingly or incidentally. Despite the scarcity and restraint of these accounts, they deserve to be incorporated into our understanding of early medieval discourses about selfhood and identity.

PART THREE

Teaching from the Sickbed

Notions of Health and Illness in the *Vimalakīrti Sutra* and Chinese Poetry

At that time, Mañjuśrī asked Vimalakīrti: "How should bodhisattvas comfort bodhisattvas who are ill?" Vimalakīrti said, "Explain that the body is impermanent, but do not teach that one should despise or abandon one's body."

—*Vimalakīrti Sutra*, chap. 5[1]

The two chapters in this part of the book explore the notions of health and illness expressed in the *Vimalakīrti Sutra* and examine how Chinese poets from the fourth century onward responded to these themes. I propose that the sutra enriched Chinese literature through not only its various translations from the Sanskrit and its powerful poetic descriptions of health and illness but also its principal narrative conceit of the sickbed setting. This setting resonated deeply with the long Chinese literary tradition of describing sickbed visits—whose narrative patterns and motifs are explored in a brief digression below—and helped make illness a more acceptable poetic topic in China.

Early medieval poets familiar with the sutra realized the poetic and intellectual potential of the sickbed setting and began experimenting with

---

1. *Weimojie suo shuo jing* 5.544c; McRae, *Vimalakīrti Sutra*, 110. The original text reads: 爾時文殊師利問維摩詰言：「菩薩應云何慰喻有疾菩薩？」維摩詰言：「說身無常, 不說厭離於身」.

172 *Part Three*

this form, most famously and influentially Xie Lingyun. Deeply engaged with the *Vimalakīrti Sutra*, Xie may have been the first Chinese poet to write a poem while "lying sick" (*wo ji/bing* 臥疾/病). Once early medieval poets established writing from the sickbed as an accepted poetic space, Tang dynasty poets further developed the potential for writing about personal illness with increasing boldness. This ensured that poetry written while lying sick remained a thriving subgenre throughout the remainder of the imperial period.

Thus, facilitating the articulation of ideas and anxieties concerning illness as an essential part of the human condition and each individual life emerges as one of the *Vimalakīrti Sutra*'s most profound influences on Chinese literature.

CHAPTER THREE

Health and Illness in the Vimalakīrti Sutra

The *Vimalakīrti-nirdeśa-sūtra*, the "scripture of the teaching of Vimal-akīrti," was one of the most popular and influential Buddhist sutras in medieval China, inspiring generations of literati and artists after its arrival in the second century CE. Scholars have identified various reasons for the Chinese fascination with this text and its main protagonist, the Buddhist layman Vimalakīrti. Vimalakīrti famously manifested illness to create an opportunity to engage those who flocked to his sickbed in discussions of Mahāyāna Buddhist teachings and ultimately guide them toward enlightenment.

In the late 1950s, Erik Zürcher emphasized the sutra's "highly philosophical contents," particularly its discussions on emptiness (*kong* 空; Skt. *śūnyatā*) and nonduality (*bu er* 不二; Skt. *advaya*). He also praised the text's "remarkable literary qualities," especially "a certain dramatic tension," which attracted early medieval Chinese literati who were steeped in Pure Conversation (*qingtan* 清談) and Dark Learning (*xuanxue* 玄學).[1] A few years later, Paul Demiéville became the first Western scholar to provide a detailed overview of the sutra's wide reception in Chinese thought, literature, and visual art.[2] Building on the insights of Zürcher and Demiéville, Richard Mather, in the late 1960s, elaborated on the sutra's appeal to the Chinese gentry, who might have found it easier to identify with a wealthy, respected lay believer like Vimalakīrti than with a more conventional bodhisattva figure.[3]

---

1. Zürcher, *Buddhist Conquest*, 50, 131, 132.

2. Demiéville, "Vimalakīrti in China."

3. However, Mather also emphasized that "both the intention and actual influence of the sutra were ... strongly supportive of the Saṅgha" and that "no statement in the sutra, however radical, was ever felt to pose a threat to the institution of monasticism." Mather, "Vimalakīrti and Gentry Buddhism," 73 and 69.

174   Chapter Three

Jonathan Silk, more recently, has suggested that the existence of a plot may have been a crucial aspect of the text's allure.[4] He also challenges the prevalent idea that the *Vimalakīrti Sutra* primarily targeted laypersons. Instead, he posits that, in its original cultural context, the sutra was intended for an Indian monastic audience, who would have understood the depiction of a wondrous layman outsmarting bodhisattvas as another paradox in a text full of paradoxes, thus recognizing Vimalakīrti as "a dramatic embodiment of the teaching of paradoxical non-duality."[5]

While the origins of the *Vimalakīrti Sutra* are not well documented—it may have emerged in India in the first or early second century CE[6]—the history of its Chinese translations and commentaries is better known. The first recorded translation, Zhi Qian's 支謙 *Weimojie jing* 維摩詰經 (ca. 222–229), was followed by several others, and by the fourth century, multiple translations circulated, including a synoptic version, which served as a sort of critical edition.[7] These earlier renditions were all superseded at the beginning of the fifth century by the translation completed by Kumārajīva (ca. 344–413) and his team of eminent collaborators.[8] Their rendering

4. Silk, "Taking the *Vimalakīrtinirdeśa* Seriously," 161–63, 171–72. On the literary features of the sutra, see also Hamlin, "Magical *upāya*"; Cui Zhongtai, "*Weimojie jing* de xiju ticai"; Gómez, "On Buddhist Wonders"; Orsborn, "Vimalakīrti's Aporia."

5. Silk, "Taking the *Vimalakīrtinirdeśa* Seriously," 177. William R. LaFleur has pointed out that Kamo no Chōmei's 鴨長明 (1155–1216) attraction to the *Vimalakīrti Sutra*, as expressed in his *Account of My Ten-Foot-Square Hut* (*Hōjōki* 方丈記), was also not based on the appeal of the layman and householder as opposed to the monk but rather on that of the recluse who "moves deliberately and emphatically out of society and into isolation and solitude." LaFleur, *Karma of Words*, 111.

6. See Lamotte, *Teaching of Vimalakīrti*, lxxxix–xcviii. Apart from a few fragments, the Sanskrit original of the *Vimalakīrti Sutra* had long been assumed lost when a complete manuscript, dated to the eleventh to thirteenth century, was discovered at Potala Palace in Lhasa in 2001. See Huang Baosheng, *Fan Han duikan*. For the English translation of this text, see Harrison and Gómez, *Vimalakīrtinirdeśa*.

7. For a basic introduction to the sutra's translations and commentaries, see Lamotte, *Teaching of Vimalakīrti*, xxvi–xxxvii; Zhou Shujia, *Zhou Shujia Foxue lunzhu ji*, 2:975–80. On Zhi Mindu's 支愍度 *He Weimojie jing* 合維摩詰經 (ca. 290–307), see Lamotte, *Teaching of Vimalakīrti*, xxx–xxxi; Zürcher, *Buddhist Conquest*, 99–100, 352n80.

8. Unless stated otherwise, references to Chinese-language passages from the *Vimalakīrti Sutra* in this chapter are to Kumārajīva's translation, *Weimojie suo shuo jing* 維摩詰所說經, completed in 406. The two other surviving translations are Zhi Qian's *Weimojie jing*

Health and Illness in the Vimalakīrti Sutra 175

remains the most popular and influential version of the sutra in Chinese; Demiéville has called it one of the most brilliant texts in the Chinese Buddhist canon.[9]

In modern times, Kumārajīva's translation of the *Vimalakīrti Sutra* into Chinese, along with the only surviving complete translation in Tibetan, has been rendered into English, French, and other Western languages.[10] Research on the *Vimalakīrti Sutra* has flourished, focusing extensively on the sutra's translations and commentaries, Mahāyāna doctrine as discussed in these texts, and the sutra's influence on Chinese Buddhism, literature, and visual art. Dunhuang studies, in particular, has shown a keen interest in the *Vimalakīrti Sutra* due to the historical period covered by Dunhuang manuscripts and paintings, which coincides with the time when the sutra was most prominent in China.[11]

The crucial role of illness in the *Vimalakīrti Sutra* is most distinctly addressed in a unique Japanese institution known as the Assembly on the *Vimalakīrti Sutra* (Yuima-e 維摩會). In this assembly, the sutra, when recited, "is ingested aurally as medicinal and curative, a substance able to transform and heal the human body."[12] This event was first held as a healing ritual for Fujiwara no Kamatari 藤原鎌足 (b. 614) in 656 or 657 and was repeated annually until Kamatari's death in 669. In 706, following an illness of Kamatari's son Fuhito 不比等 (659–720), the annual assembly, revolving around a weeklong reading of the sutra, was resumed. It was held on the anniversary of Kamatari's death and, since 712, has been hosted in the Fujiwara clan temple Kōfukuji in Nara.[13]

---

and Xuanzang's 玄奘 *Shuo Wugoucheng jing* 說無垢稱經 (ca. 649–650). Variants of the sutra's title are discussed in Lamotte, *Teaching of Vimalakīrti*, lxv–lx.

9. Demiéville, "Vimalakīrti in China," 186.

10. For an excellent comparative study of translations of the *Vimalakīrti Sutra* into English, see Nattier, "*Teaching of Vimalakīrti*." My own English translations in this chapter are largely based on John R. McRae's translation of the Kumārajīva version, with occasional modifications. McRae, *Vimalakīrti Sutra*.

11. See the annotated bibliography covering publications in English and Chinese from 1900 to 2011 by Cheng and Tse, "Thematic Research," as well as Felbur, "*Vimalakīrtinirdeśa*."

12. Eubanks, *Miracles of Book and Body*, 82.

13. See Groner, *Ryōgen and Mount Hiei*, 129–39. On the sutra's reception in Japan, see also LaFleur, *Karma of Words*, 107–15; Bauer, "Yuima-e as Theater of the State." To mention just one work from the sutra's long history in Japan: the great advocate of Buddhism

176 Chapter Three

Content and Narrative Features of the *Vimalakīrti Sutra*

The opening frame of the *Vimalakīrti Sutra* is set on the outskirts of the ancient Indian city of Vaiśālī, where the Buddha preaches to a great assembly of disciples, bodhisattvas, and devas in a garden donated by the female devotee Āmrapālī. Setting the tone for the entire sutra, the Buddha performs magical feats to elucidate his teachings, such as creating an immense canopy from many small ones and manifesting the intrinsic beauty and purity of the buddha land. The skillful means (*fangbian* 方便; Skt. *upāya*) employed by the Buddha in this opening scene also dominate the second chapter, which takes us to the residence of the householder Vimalakīrti within Vaiśālī. Vimalakīrti decides to manifest illness to teach those who visit his sickbed about the fragility of the human body, which is inherently prone to sickness and suffering, in contrast with the perfection and indestructibility of the Tathāgata's body.

The following two chapters return to Āmrapālī's garden, where the Buddha, aware of Vimalakīrti's somewhat guileful wish that the luminary staying in the suburbs would acknowledge his illness, seeks someone from his entourage to visit the ailing householder on his behalf. However, both disciples and bodhisattvas decline, each recounting a previous encounter with Vimalakīrti in which he outwitted them in doctrinal understanding and debate. At the beginning of chapter 5, the bodhisattva Mañjuśrī agrees to visit Vimalakīrti, accompanied by thousands curious about the debate between the youthful bodhisattva of wisdom and the sagacious householder. Upon their arrival, they miraculously all fit into a room that Vimalakīrti, anticipating this host of visitors, had emptied of servants and furniture, save for his bed. Mañjuśrī and Vimalakīrti then discuss doctrinal questions, principal among them the concepts of emptiness—prompted by the empty room—and nonduality, as well as illness.

In chapter 6, another magical feat takes center stage: Vimalakīrti summons thousands of magnificent lion-thrones from the distant universe of Merudhvaja to seat his audience, who then receive his teachings on

---

Shōtoku Taishi 聖德太子 (574–622) composed a commentary on Kumārajīva's translation of the *Vimalakīrti Sutra*, titled *Yuimagyō gisho* 維摩經義疏; see Hubbard, *Expository Commentary*. See also Kawaguchi Ekai's translation *Kan Zō taishō kokuyaku Yuimagyō* 漢藏對照國譯維摩經, which takes various Chinese and Tibetan translations into account.

"inconceivable liberation" (*bu ke siyi jietuo* 不可思議解脫; Skt. *acintya-mukta*). The next chapter features a famous contest of discursive and magical powers between a goddess residing in Vimalakīrti's house and the monk Śāriputra, a member of Mañjuśrī's entourage. Although Śāriputra is renowned as one of the Buddha's most eminent disciples, in the *Vimalakīrti Sutra* he represents dualistic and outdated ideas and is repeatedly ridiculed and proven wrong—this time by being temporarily transformed into a woman.

Chapters 8 and 9 focus on discussions about the paths to achieving buddhahood and nonduality. The debate culminates when Mañjuśrī asks Vimalakīrti to explain his understanding of nonduality, to which Vimal-akīrti responds with his famous "thundering silence." The following chapter once more connects the assembly to another universe: to feed his numerous guests, Vimalakīrti creates a bodhisattva who travels to the distant world of Sarvagandhasugandhā, governed by a buddha named "Accumulation of Fragrances." The bodhisattva returns with fragrant rice and millions of curious bodhisattvas who join the congregation in Vimalakīrti's sickroom.

In chapter 11, Vimalakīrti magically transports the entire assembly back to the Buddha in Āmrapālī's garden, thus closing the narrative frame where it started. A discussion about buddha lands and indestructible liberation ensues. In chapter 12, the Buddha reveals that Vimalakīrti spent his previous life in the buddha land of Abhirati ("Wondrous Joy"). When he asks Vimalakīrti to manifest this land to the audience, the householder conjures up Abhirati in his right hand and takes his audience there. The last two chapters are dedicated to extolling the sutra itself, elaborating on the superiority of the Dharma offering (*fa gongyang* 法供養; Skt. *dharma-pūjā*) in chapter 13 and presenting the formal bestowal of the sutra text in the concluding chapter 14.

This summary illustrates the rudimentary plot running through the *Vimalakīrti Sutra*: one main character (Vimalakīrti) creates an occasion for a showdown, albeit benign; the second main character (the Buddha) responds by sending a deputy (Mañjuśrī); the ensuing, imaginatively designed encounter allows both the agent provocateur and the deputy to shine, sometimes at the expense of supporting characters (the closest we get to antagonists); the grand finale brings everyone together, absolving the apparent troublemaker and confirming his apotheosis. The huge and

178 *Chapter Three*

colorful cast of dramatis personae includes humans, buddhas, gods, and extraterrestrial beings, who at times respond as a group to the action and dialogue, as a Greek chorus might.

The narrative is enriched by sparkling, often humorous conversations (occasionally presented as flashbacks), dramatic changes of setting (from a small empty room to another universe and back again), spectacular magical feats, and grandiose imagery. Repetition and formulaic elements in themes, phrases, and embedded subplots provide rhetorical coherence and lend a pleasing rhythmic quality to the text.

All narrative elements, redundant and tangential as they may seem, serve the text's primary purpose: the exposition and propagation of Mahāyāna Buddhist ideas. The staggering hyperboles, frequent narrative digressions, and other ostensibly gratuitous rhetorical practices all make sense if understood within the context of the Buddhist concept of skillful means, that is, as expedient devices designed to engage a broad audience, facilitate their understanding of complex doctrinal ideas, and ultimately guide them toward enlightenment.[14]

However, we should not dismiss the sutra's storytelling elements as mere tools to captivate the uneducated. The artful composition of the *Vimalakīrti Sutra* must, on another level, also have appealed to a learned audience capable of grasping a purely discursive text about the doctrinal matters discussed in the sutra. On this other level, the *Vimalakīrti Sutra* truly does as it tells—not an easy thing to do, as the writers among the sutra's readers must have recognized—by integrating religious doctrine with storytelling. By perfectly merging these two aspects, the text dissolves any hypothetical dualism, demonstrating how to enter the gate of nonduality through narrative.

Before delving into the topic of health and illness in the *Vimalakīrti Sutra*, a brief digression into the representation of sickbed visits in earlier Chinese literature is necessary to provide the literary background for our discussion.

---

14. For a discussion on the concept of skillful means, most closely associated with the *Lotus Sutra*, see Pye, *Skilful Means*; on the *Vimalakīrti Sutra*, see esp. 83–100. While Pye does not discuss textual features as skillful means, Luis Gómez does, for example, when he talks about the "wonder of persuasion"; see Gómez, "On Buddhist Wonders," 545–47.

Digression: Sickbed Visits in Early Chinese Literature—Everyday Practice and Exceptional Opportunity

> All at once, Ziyu fell ill. Zisi went to ask how he was. . . . Dragging himself haltingly to the well and taking in his reflection, Ziyu said: "My, my! So the Creator is making me all crooked like this!"—"Do you resent it?" asked Zisi. "Why no, what would I resent!"
>
> 俄而子輿有病, 子祀往問之。 . . . 跰𨇤而鑑於井,
> 曰: 「嗟乎! 夫造物者又將以予為此拘拘也! 」
> 子祀曰: 「女惡之乎? 」曰: 「亡,予何惡! 」
>
> —Zhuangzi, "The Great and Venerable Teacher"[15]

Scholars studying the *Vimalakīrti Sutra* have discussed the sutra's central setting as a reflection of Buddhist practice. Étienne Lamotte, the French translator of the Tibetan version, simply states that "visiting the sick is a Buddhist tradition."[16] Buddhist scriptures trace the duty to care for sick monks back to the Buddha's teaching and his exemplary attendance to ailing monks. As Koichi Shinohara has shown in his analysis of the Vinaya commentary "Attending to the Sick and Sending Off the Dead" ("Zhanbing songzhong" 瞻病送終) by the early Tang monk Daoxuan (596–667), the duty of care was very practical, aiming to make the sick as comfortable as possible. It also involved elements of teaching to ensure critically ill monks were well prepared for a favorable death and future rebirth. Stories of the Buddha visiting a sick monk or sending someone else to visit in his stead are common throughout sutra literature and may have been familiar motifs for early medieval readers of the *Vimalakīrti Sutra*.[17]

While there is no doubt that visiting the sick was an established Buddhist tradition, sickbed visits had long been an important part of the indigenous Chinese tradition as well, both in practice and in rhetoric. Early Chinese historical and Masters literature is full of scenes set at someone's sickbed.

---

15. *Zhuangzi* 6.258–59; translation adapted from Watson, *Complete Works of Zhuangzi*, 47.

16. Lamotte, *Teaching of Vimalakīrti*, 33n20.

17. See Shinohara, "Moment of Death," esp. 111. See also the chapter on attending to the sick ("Zhan bing" 瞻病) in *Fayuan zhulin* 95.3.985–86.

180   *Chapter Three*

While much can happen in this particular narrative setting, the illness itself that brought one protagonist to their sickbed and prompted another protagonist to visit is rarely mentioned, let alone described in detail. Despite this vagueness in medical terms, exploring these scenes sheds unique light on perceptions of health and illness. Literary sickbed visits illuminate ill health as a phenomenon that called for the performance of the participants' social duties, whether they be the patient, the visitor, or the attendants.

As I will show below, early Chinese historical and didactic texts, including ritual instructions, *prescribed* sickbed visits as a matter of decorum. These prescriptions detailed whom to visit, when, how often, what to bring as a gift, and so on. These long-established ritual conventions form the backdrop for *descriptions* of sickbed visits in historical texts and anecdotal literature. For example, sick calls often serve to characterize the moral fiber of the visitor, measured by their adherence to ritual propriety. While sickness, as an inauspicious omen, may signal disorder on either the individual level or, in the case of a ruler, the level of the realm, sickbed visits can function as auspicious correctives that help to restore order.

From the perspective of historical and semi-historical storytelling, sickbed visits provide an especially productive setting to perform certain values because they facilitate meetings that would not have been possible had all protagonists been in good health. Another productive feature of sickbed visits is their dual nature. One part is highly public, as access to the sick person must be mediated by family members or officials and can thus be intentionally performed by the visitor to create a certain public impression. The other part takes place in the relative seclusion of the sickroom with a very limited audience, possibly just the patient and the visitor. Sickbed visits feature in stories involving the assassination of either the sick person or the visitor, sometimes with yet another motif, the pretense of illness, thrown in for good measure. They also provide occasions for famous last words of rulers or ministers or for final conversations between friends.

The phrase "sickbed visit" translates the similarly imprecise Chinese terms *wen ji* 問疾 or *wen bing* 問病. Both the English and Chinese phrases can cover a spectrum of activities from a polite, formal call—sometimes even by a representative on behalf of a more exalted person—to intimate, everyday acts of attending to the sick person's needs. These two ends of the spectrum were occasionally differentiated. For instance, the *Guanzi* lists the "Nine Kindnesses" (九惠) expected of a ruler, which include "caring for the sick" (養疾) and "visiting the sick" (問病) as numbers four and six.[18] Prescriptions about visiting the sick in early Chinese texts, often found in handbooks of ritual propriety, emphasize the duty to make sickbed visits or pay condolence calls (*wen ji diaosang* 問疾弔/吊喪) for two main reasons: ensuring the integration of the sick into society and providing concrete support in a situation that usually presents a crisis for a sick person's family in many ways, not least financially.

Attention to the sick can be read as an attempt to counterbalance the danger and inauspiciousness associated with impending mortality and the general reluctance to face illness and death—perhaps even a broad sense of fear of contagion. Consider the famous anecdote of Confucius visiting his sick disciple Ran Boniu 冉伯牛:

> When Boniu had an illness, the master visited him and held his hands through the window. He said, "We will lose him. It must be destiny. Such a man, and that he has such an illness! Such a man, and that he has such an illness!"
> 伯牛有疾, 子問之, 自牖執其手。曰: 亡之, 命矣夫! 斯人也而有斯疾也! 斯人也而有斯疾也![19]

While Confucius not entering Boniu's house could be interpreted as a desire to maintain a safe distance from a very sick person, the anecdote alleviates any suspicions about the master's detachment by showing him holding his disciple's hands through a window, creating a vivid image of liminality that mixes intimacy and distance.[20]

---

18. *Guanzi* 54.870. Alternative and partly synonymous phrases include *kan ji* 看疾, *tan bing* 探病, *xing bing* 省病, *xing ku* 省苦, and *xunwen bingqing* 詢問病情. Phrases that indicate the actual nursing of a sick person, apart from *yang ji*, include *hou bing* 候病, *zhan bing* 瞻病, and *shi ji* 侍疾.

19. *Lunyu* 6.10. In his commentary on this passage, Zhu Xi refrains from pronouncing a retrospective diagnosis himself, but he mentions that "earlier Confucians assumed that [Boniu] suffered from leprosy" (先儒以為癩也; see *Sishu zhangju jizhu*, 87). On early Chinese notions of contagion, see Kuriyama, "Epidemics, Weather, and Contagion."

20. Li Ling also mentions the possibility that Confucius, while not concerned with contagion, was dismayed that his disciple, by all accounts a man of morality and integrity,

182   *Chapter Three*

The regulations concerning sickbed visits and condolence calls may also reflect the communicative and psychological challenges experienced by the sick and their visitors. Between pity and dread on both sides, self-expression can become difficult, and the assistance of social etiquette is appreciated. This is not only true for actual visits but also in writing, as evidenced by the high formulaity of "calling cards" announcing sickbed visits and letters inquiring about the correspondent's health.[21]

Early Chinese texts also mention more concrete elements of decorum. An expanded form of this prescription in the *Records about Ritual* states that the household of the sick was expected to "clean in and around the house," and, as the commentary adds, "for the esteemed visitors that would come for a sickbed visit" (疾病, 外內皆掃, 為賓客將來問疾也).[22] From prescriptions such as these, it appears that announcing one's illness practically amounted to a call for visitors. The familiarity with this practice may well have contributed to the plausibility of Vimalakīrti's "pretense" or manifestation of illness and to the popularity of the *Vimalakīrti Sutra* in China.

Gifts also seem to have been an important part of the sickbed visit.[23] The standard histories are full of lists of gifts given by emperors to sick ministers, often including medicine, substantial sums of money, and other valuables.[24] The rank of the sick person would, of course, be taken into account. A passage from the *Xunzi* demonstrates this by prescribing the frequency of visits and alluding to a similar statement in the *Records about Ritual*: "The feudal lords do not visit their ministers' houses unless it is to make a sickbed visit or to pay a condolence call" (諸侯非問疾弔喪

---

contracted an "impure" illness. Li Ling, *Sang jia gou*, 133. On the moral connotations of certain illnesses, see my "Stories of Coping with Sickness," 178–79.

21. On calling cards (*ye* 謁 or *ci* 刺), see Korolkov, "'Greeting Tablets' in Early China," esp. 309. On formulaity in illness letters, see part II of this book.

22. *Taiping yulan* 738.2a.

23. See, e.g., the injunction in the *Records about Ritual*: "If you are making a sickbed visit but cannot leave gifts behind, don't ask the sick what they desire" (問疾弗能遺, 不問其所欲, *Liji* 3.4).

24. Two excellent studies of Han dynasty sickbed visits are Li Jianmin, *Shengming shixue*, 127–48 (chapter 5, "Han dai 'yi bing' yanjiu"), and Qu Bingrui and Li Yang, "Qin Han tanbing de zhengzhi wenhua." Both focus on the political implications of sickbed visits as represented in historical sources, especially standard histories.

臣之家).[25] This instruction highlights the exceptional nature of illness overall: due to its potentially life-altering and life-threatening character, illness overrides many usual practices based on social roles and differences in social status.

Sickbed visits facilitate exceptional meetings for both parties. On the one hand, they bring visitors to a house they would otherwise not frequent, creating opportunities for what we might call inverse audiences. On the other hand, sickbed visits grant access to a sick person's inner sphere that would otherwise be out of reach for the visitor. Two anecdotes from the *Traditional Tales and Recent Accounts* illustrate this.

In the first anecdote, Xie An is on his way to visit the sick Huan Wen 桓溫 (312–373). "Catching sight of him from afar, Huan sighed, 'It has been a long time since I saw such a man in my gate'" (桓公遙望, 歎曰吾門中久不見如此人).[26] Here, being sick grants Huan Wen a potentially politically beneficial meeting. The second anecdote tells the well-known story of an aborted sickbed visit, illustrating that visitors have special access to someone's inner quarters during illness. Six years after the death of her husband, Cao Cao, in 220, Dowager Empress Bian 卞 (159–230) emerged from seclusion to visit her son Cao Pi on his sickbed. It was only on this occasion that she realized her son had taken over all his father's palace women to serve as his own attendants. Appalled, Dowager Empress Bian broke off her visit and, supposedly, did not even attend her son's funeral soon after.[27]

While it is impossible to do full justice to the many different narrative uses of the sickbed,[28] two associations deserve particular mention: the sickbed as a stage to perform filial duty and as an opportunity to teach.

---

25. *Xunzi* 27.622; see also *Liji* 21.15.

26. *Shishuo xinyu* 8.105; Mather, *Shih-shuo hsin-yü*, 254. On the relationship between these two men, also see Spiro, *Contemplating the Ancients*, 110–14; Chen, *Anecdote, Network*, 180–85.

27. *Shishuo xinyu* 19.4; Mather, *Shih-shuo hsin-yü*, 365.

28. Referring to a small group of these narratives, Jeffrey Riegel has even spoken of "a small subgenre of tales that involve a sick ruler consulting with a sage-like individual about the source of his sickness and what should be done to treat it." See Riegel, "Curing the Incurable," 226. For an anecdote about Wang Yan 王衍 (256–311) visiting Pei Kai 裴楷 (237–291) on his sickbed, see Richter, "Stories of Coping with Sickness," 179–80.

184   *Chapter Three*

The association with filial duty is due to the dominant interpretation of an anecdote about Zengzi, the disciple of Confucius most closely associated with the core value of filiality. The anecdote appears in various forms in a number of early Chinese texts, but its most influential instantiation is found in the *Analects*: "When Zengzi was sick, he called his disciples and said, 'Uncover my feet, uncover my hands'" (曾子有疾, 召門弟子曰：啟予足, 啟予手).[29] Zengzi's request is open to interpretation, especially given the semantic range of the word *qi* 啟 (to open, unfasten), but in the most traditional reading, Zengzi wishes to demonstrate to his disciples that he had kept his limbs intact throughout his life.[30] This, in turn, was connected with Confucius's exhortation to preserve one's corporeal integrity, pronounced in conversation with Zengzi in the *Canon of Filial Duty*, which we mentioned in part II in connection with Sima Qian.[31]

The *Canon of Filial Duty* describes how filial sons should be "extremely anxious if their parents are sick" (孝子之事親也 . . . 病則致其憂).[32] As a result, sickbed scenarios connected with filial duty frequently appear in historical accounts and anecdotes, depicting children, from rulers to commoners, taking care of their sick parents, sometimes even at the risk of their own health.[33] Emperor Wen of the Han dynasty (漢文帝, r. 180–157 BCE) is among the best-known filial sons since his service to his sick mother ensured him a place among the *Twenty-Four Filial Exemplars* (*Ershisi xiao* 二十四孝), a group of filial children whose deeds were presented in popular collections starting from the Tang dynasty.[34] According to one of his

29. *Lunyu* 8.3.

30. In his discussion of this passage, Li Ling has shown how tenuous the traditional interpretation is and suggested reading it as the very sick Zengzi's wish to reassure himself of his four limbs; see Li Ling, *Sang jia gou*, 164–65. See also the different take on this situation in *Xunzi*: "When Zengzi was ill, Zeng Yuan held (*chi* 持) his feet" (曾子病, 曾元持足, *Xunzi* 30.658). Depicting Zengzi's son holding his dying father's feet creates an atmosphere of familial intimacy rather than public-facing self-justification.

31. Wang Chong offers this interpretation explicitly, citing Zengzi's request in the form of "uncover my feet" (開予足). See *Lunheng* 23.971.

32. *Xiaojing* 6.17c.

33. To mention just one historical example: Gao Yan 高演, Emperor Xiaozhao of the Northern Qi (齊孝昭帝, r. 560–561), possibly hastened his own death through excessive worry at his mother's sickbed. See *Yanshi jiaxun* 8.187; Tian, *Family Instructions*, 151.

34. On narratives of filial duty in early medieval China, see Knapp, *Selfless Offspring*; on

ministers, Yuan Ang 袁盎 (d. 148 BCE), Emperor Wen surpassed even Zengzi in attending to his mother during her prolonged illness: "His Majesty would not close his eyes, not take off his clothes, and not allow his mother to take any medicine he had not tasted himself before" (太后嘗病, 三年, 陛下不交睫, 不解衣, 湯藥非陛下口所嘗弗進).[35] Another account presents Emperor Wen in a different light, as the sick person in need of care. Suffering from carbuncles, he found relief in Deng Tong 鄧通, one of his favorites, who sucked the pus from the sores—a service that the emperor's own son reportedly provided only unwillingly.[36]

As mentioned in part II in connection with Shen Yue's "Testamentary Deathbed Memorial," the perception of the sickbed as an opportunity to teach can also be traced to Zengzi. The *Analects* passage that follows the one just discussed about Zengzi uncovering his limbs to his disciples has the sick Master Zeng saying, "The words of men who are about to die are excellent" (人之將死, 其言也善).[37] While many last words spoken at a sickbed, by either the visitor or the sick person, have a clear political dimension,[38] other sickbed visits described in Chinese Masters literature strike a different tone.

An outstanding example is found in the *Zhuangzi*, in the chapter "The Great and Venerable Teacher" ("Da zong shi" 大宗師), which describes two sickbed visits among the friends Zisi 子祀, Ziyu 子輿, Zili 子犁, and Zilai 子來. In these visits, both the sick and their visiting friends— who are as yet spared their friends' fate when they come to visit—share important teachings that transcend any immediate political agenda or concern with ritual propriety. Instead, they celebrate friendship by placing what might easily be dry pronouncements about the human condition in the mouths of intimate friends. The friends take turns in telling us (and each other) that it would be futile to resent what illness can do to us and that we better face the changes we inevitably undergo during our lives with equanimity and even appreciation. The easy back and forth in

---

the development of "a new genre of popular works called *The Twenty-Four Filial Exemplars*," see esp. 4–5.

35. *Shi ji* 101.2739.

36. *Taiping yulan* 88.4b; Knapp, *Selfless Offspring*, 12.

37. *Lunyu* 8.4.

38. See, e.g., the cases discussed by Charles Sanft in "Moment of Dying."

186   *Chapter Three*

their striking exchanges about the acceptance of illness, disfigurement, and death is hard to forget.[39] In these scenes, social etiquette either remains in the background or is subverted to highlight the interaction between close friends. A related text, the *Liezi*, similarly celebrates friendship in the face of illness and death, as illustrated in an anecdote where Yang Zhu 楊朱 visits a sick friend.[40] Both the *Zhuangzi* and the *Liezi* agree on accepting illness and impairment as integral parts of life, possibly even considering them a higher form of health.[41]

Many more examples could be cited to demonstrate that in Chinese literature, the sickbed was seen as a stage for instruction and gaining insights well before the *Vimalakīrti Sutra* was first translated into Chinese. As Eve Kosofsky Sedgwick notes, the sickbed is "a privileged scene of teaching" and a setting where "the assignment of pedagogical roles is unstable."[42] In this respect, the *Vimalakīrti Sutra* certainly found fertile ground when it began to circulate among Chinese writers in the fourth and fifth centuries.

Vimalakīrti Teaching about Illness

The *Vimalakīrti Sutra* deals with illness in an exemplary way, both by taking a sickbed visit as its main setting and by offering explicit observations about the human body's propensity for illness and decay throughout the text. Despite this, the theme of health and illness has remained marginal in the otherwise rich field of scholarship on the *Vimalakīrti Sutra*. One reason for this could be that talk of health and illness discourse is so abundant in Buddhist texts that it is easy to dismiss it as mere background noise. As early as the 1930s, Paul Demiéville pointed out that both Buddhist and medical thought are rooted in the deliverance from suffering: "Diagnosis, etiology, recovery, therapeutics—these four principles that summarize all of medicine can be substituted for the Buddhist Four Truths in a natural and straightforward transposition."[43] This closeness and the perva-

39. *Zhuangzi* 6.258–62.
40. *Liezi* 6.204–5.
41. Bauer, "Krankheit und Heilung bei Lieh-tzu," 4–10.
42. Sedgwick, "Pedagogy," 183.
43. Demiéville, *Buddhism and Healing*, 1. See also Demiéville's foundational entry on

sive "physician's point of view" make medical imagery more dominant in Buddhism compared with other religious, philosophical, or literary texts.[44]

Medical tropes in the *Vimalakīrti Sutra* appear as they do in countless other Buddhist writings. Metaphors of illness describe the lack of enlightenment (眾生病), the process of achieving enlightenment is compared to healing (療眾病), bodhisattvas appear as medicinal plants (現作諸藥草), and they are encouraged to be "medicine kings" who heal all illnesses (醫王療治眾病).[45] What makes the *Vimalakīrti Sutra* special, however, is not its use of medical imagery but the crucial and constitutive role that illness plays in its narrative and doctrinal message. This is all the more remarkable since Vimalakīrti's illness does not follow the conventional arc of illness and healing or decline, where a sick person emerges either healed or deceased at the end of the narrative. Nor does any of the narrative action within the sutra connote the suffering, somberness, and urgency usually associated with illness. On the contrary, Vimalakīrti appears powerful, dynamic, and spirited throughout the sutra, which contrasts sharply with his conventional depiction as a frail old man in much of Chinese painting.[46]

The key question concerns the nature of Vimalakīrti's illness. Is he really ill or just pretending? And how could he be ill, given his advanced stage on the path to buddhahood? Three approaches to this question are possible. The first and doctrinally most sophisticated approach would be to point out that the *Vimalakīrti Sutra* aims to shatter a dualistic view of its protagonist's health or nonhealth, along with other dualities, such as: Is

---

illness (Jap. *byō* 病) in the Buddhist encyclopedia *Hōbōgirin* 法寶義林, esp. 26–30. On Buddhist medical metaphors, see also Salguero, *Translating Buddhist Medicine*, 67–83; Moretti, "'Eight Sufferings,' and the Medical Metaphor," 89.

44. Compare the Lord as the healer in the Jewish tradition (e.g., Exodus 15:26, Psalm 30:2), which inspired the idea of Jesus as the healer ("Christus Medicus") in Christianity (e.g., Matthew 8:5–17). See Arbesmann, "Christus Medicus." In Islam, God as well as the Qur'an itself are regarded as a source of healing (at-Tawbah 9:14; al-Fussilat 41:44). For more on religious healing in Islam, see Dols, *Majnūn*, 211–60.

45. For these phrases, see *Weimojie suo shuo jing* 1.537a, 5.544c, and 8.550a. Also, see the pithy descriptions of the suffering caused by old age and sickness in the possibly apocryphal *Sutra of the Five Kings* (*Wu wang jing* 五王經); Moretti, "'Eight Sufferings' and the Medical Metaphor," 81–82.

46. On the implications of depicting Vimalakīrti as old and fragile, see also Richter, "Literature and the Arts."

188   Chapter Three

he a layman or not? Is he alone at home or not? Is his house big enough for his many visitors or not? These and similar questions all fade in the light of nonduality.

Two further approaches to understanding Vimalakīrti's illness are suggested in the second chapter of the sutra itself. The text states briefly but explicitly that Vimalakīrti, "using skillful means, manifested as being ill" (其以方便, 現身有疾).[47] The verb *xian* 現 chosen by Kumārajīva (as well as by Zhi Qian before and Xuanzang after him) means "to show, reveal, appear, manifest." This can be interpreted in two ways, depending on the underlying notion of the householder's body.

If we assume that Vimalakīrti has the body of a mortal human, *xian* suggests that his illness need not be created, pretended, or feigned. Rather, it was already present when Vimalakīrti decided to show it, to make it visible. Illness would thus be revealed as an essential part of the human condition, even if it is not always obvious. This idea is a key message in many Buddhist writings, not just in the *Vimalakīrti Sutra*. A prominent example is the "Four Sights" (*sixiang* 四相) episode in the biography of the historical Śākyamuni Buddha. According to several of Śākyamuni's life stories, the first three excursions taking him outside of the city gates confronted the young prince Siddhārtha Gautama with a sick man, an old man, and a corpse, thus introducing him for the first time in his sheltered life to the reality of impermanence and human suffering. The fourth encounter, with a *śramaṇa*, pointed him toward his future path. In the Śākyamuni Buddha's life story, the insight gained outside the city gates prompts the young man's Great Departure (*chujia* 出家) from his sheltered home and anticipates the enlightenment he was to experience years later.[48]

If we assume, as it increasingly appears toward the end of the *Vimalakīrti Sutra*, that Vimalakīrti is enlightened—that is, fully a buddha—we could, in a third approach, interpret the body that is present and presented on the sickbed as his corporeal, transient, docetic transformation body (*huashen* 化身; Skt. *nirmāṇakāya*). The appearance of the transformation body could be freely chosen depending on the specific salvific needs of those around him. In the Mahāyāna doctrine of the Buddha's "Three Bodies" (*san*

47. *Weimojie suo shuo jing* 2.539b; McRae, *Vimalakīrti Sutra*, 83.

48. On old age and illness in Buddhist hagiography and early medieval poetry, see Richter, "Four Gates, Eight Poets, Sixteen Poems."

shen 三身; Skt. *trikāya*), the other two bodies are the eternal, transcendent Dharma body, which lacks form (*fashen* 法身; Skt. *dharmakāya*), and the after-enlightenment body of reward or recompense, also called the body of bliss (*baoshen* 報身; Skt. *saṃbhogakāya*).[49] This approach would allow us to regard the householder's manifested illness as a skillful means in response to those in need of liberation.

In Erik Zürcher's reading, which describes "the loving and saving power of the Bodhisattva" as "the one basic theme of the whole sutra," Vimalakīrti "voluntarily undergoes the 'disease of existence' for the sake of all beings."[50] As with all important ideas in the sutra, this concept recurs later in the text, especially in chapter 5, discussed in detail below, where it is central to the discourse unfolding during the sickbed visit. In chapter 8, when the house-holder describes the path to buddhahood and thus also his own path, he emphasizes the manifestation of decrepitude and illness as skillful means by mentioning it twice, first in prose—"he numinously reveals entering old age and sickness, yet forever eradicates the roots of illness" (示入老病, 而永斷病根)—and later in verse—"he may numinously reveal old age, illness, and death / to accomplish [the liberation of] the hosts of sentient beings" (或示老病死, 成就諸群生).[51] This time, he uses the verb *shi* 示, which is close in meaning to *xian*, including connotations of teaching.

The condensed characterization of Vimalakīrti's illness in chapter 2 is followed by the passage that seems to have fascinated medieval Chinese writers the most: the cascade of similes of the body in Vimalakīrti's first speech to those who came to visit him on his sickbed:

Sirs, this body is impermanent, without strength, without power, without solidity. Given the way it rapidly disintegrates, it cannot be trusted. Alternately suffering and vexatious, it accumulates a host of illnesses. Sirs, the wise do not rely on such a body. This body is like a bit of foam that cannot be grasped. This body is like bubbles that do not last very long. This body is like

---

49. For a concise delineation of the development of this important Mahāyāna concept, see Nagao, "On the Theory of Buddha Body." Also see the extensive work on the topic by Michael Radich, among them his "Problems and Opportunities in the Study of the Bodies of the Buddha."

50. Zürcher, *Buddhist Conquest*, 131.

51. *Weimojie suo shuo jing* 8.549a and 550a; McRae, *Vimalakīrti Sutra*, 134 and 138.

190   *Chapter Three*

a mirage, generated from thirst. This body is like a banana tree, with nothing solid within. This body is like a phantasm arising from confused [views]. This body is like a dream, an illusory view. This body is like a shadow, manifested through karmic conditions. This body is like an echo, dependent on causes and conditions. This body is like a cloud, which changes and disappears in an instant. This body is like lightning, unstable from one moment to another.

諸仁者！是身無常、無強、無力、無堅、速朽之法, 不可信也！為
苦、為惱, 眾病所集。諸仁者！如此身, 明智者所不怙; 是身如聚
沫, 不可撮摩; 是身如泡, 不得久立; 是身如炎, 從渴愛生; 是身如
芭蕉, 中無有堅; 是身如幻, 從顛倒起; 是身如夢, 為虛妄見; 是身
如影, 從業緣現; 是身如響, 屬諸因緣; 是身如浮雲, 須臾變滅; 是
身如電, 念念不住。

Following the first and most famous "Ten Similes," the text enumerates several more in a different, less regular pattern. Retaining the striking anaphora "this body" (*shi shen* 是身) fourteen times, this repetition builds to a veritable crescendo:

This body is without master, like the earth. This body is without self, like fire. This body is without lifespan, like the wind. This body is without person, like water. This body is insubstantial, being housed in the four elements. This body is empty, leaving self and the qualities of self behind. This body is ignorant, like plants and rubble. This body is inactive, being turned by the power of the wind. This body is impure, replete with defilements. This body is deceptive, since even though one washes, clothes, and feeds it, it will necessarily disintegrate. This body is a disaster, vexed by a hundred and one illnesses. This body is like a well on a hill, pressed by age. This body is unreliable, dying in spite of being needed. This body is like a poisonous snake, a vengeful bandit, an empty aggregation. It is the composite of the *skandhas*, sensory realms, and sensory capacities.[52] Sirs, this [ordinary body] being so calamitous and repugnant, you should wish for the body of the Buddha. Why? The body of the Buddha is the body of the Dharma.

是身無主, 為如地; 是身無我, 為如火; 是身無壽, 為如風; 是身無
人, 為如水; 是身不實, 四大為家; 是身為空, 離我我所; 是身無知,

---

52. The phrase *yin jie (zhu)ru* 陰界(諸)入 refers to the five aggregates (Skt. *skandha*, i.e., form, feeling, perception, impulse, and consciousness), the eighteen sensory realms (Skt. *dhātu*) or elements of cognition, and the twelve sense fields or bases (Skt. *āyatana*).

如草木瓦礫；是身無作，風力所轉；是身不淨，穢惡充滿；是身為虛偽，雖假以澡浴衣食，必歸磨滅；是身為災，百一病惱；是身如丘井，為老所逼；是身無定，為要當死；是身如毒蛇、如怨賊、如空聚，陰界諸入所共合成。諸仁者！此可患厭，當樂佛身。所以者何？佛身者即法身也。[53]

Étienne Lamotte, who studied the origin of these similes (*piyu* 譬喻; Skt. *upamāna*) in Buddhist literature, counted thirty-five of them throughout the *Vimalakīrti Sutra*.[54] They compare the body to a diverse range of phenomena, from objects or circumstances in the natural world—such as the elements (most prominently water), the weather, fauna, and flora—to mental phenomena like illusions and dreams, to illness and even emptiness. The most common *tertium comparationis* is impermanence, which emphasizes the dependent origination of the body (as well as every other phenomenon), closely followed by insubstantiality and intangibility. Notably, impurity plays only a marginal role.[55]

The teaching about the body is resumed and complemented in chapter 3, where the Buddha's disciples, one after another, relate why they would rather not visit the sick Vimalakīrti. Embedded in Ānanda's tale about his encounter with the householder, the teaching about the body now focuses on the superiority of the Tathāgata's body. When Vimalakīrti learns that Ānanda is begging for milk to cure an illness of the Buddha,[56] he instructs

53. *Weimojie suo shuo jing* 2.539b–c; McRae, *Vimalakīrti Sutra*, 83. Vimalakīrti repeats a similar list at the beginning of chapter 7 in response to Mañjuśrī's question about how a bodhisattva should view sentient beings.

54. Lamotte, *Teaching of Vimalakīrti*, 34n23. See also Salguero, *Translating Buddhist Medicine*, 70–73, and Akira Sato's study of a similar set of similes in "Kamalaśīla's Interpretation of Eight Similes."

55. As Sue Hamilton has shown, this markedly contrasts with attitudes toward the human body in Theravāda Buddhism. See Hamilton, "From the Buddha to Buddhaghosa," 58–61.

56. On various doctrinal interpretations of the illnesses of the Buddha, see Lamotte, *Teaching of Vimalakīrti*, 294–98; Demiéville, *Buddhism and Healing*, 22–30 (including the illnesses of the bodhisattvas); Strong, "Explicating the Buddha's Final Illness." Among scriptural sources, see especially the discussion of the Buddha's illnesses in terms of skillful means in chapter 18 ("Xian bing pin" 現病品) of the *Nirvana Sutra* (*Mahāparinirvāṇa-sūtra*; *Da banniepan jing* 大般涅槃經) 18.669–73.

Chapter Three

the young disciple about the nature of his master's body in no uncertain terms:

> Stop, stop, Ānanda! Do not speak thus. The Tathāgata's body is the embodiment of [adamantine] *vajra*. In it the evils are already eradicated and the host of good qualities are universally assembled. What illness could it have, what vexation could there be? Go silently, Ānanda—do not revile the Tathāgata, and do not let anyone else hear such coarse talk. . . . If brahmans in the heterodox paths hear this, they will think, "Who is this teacher, who is unable to save himself from illness but would save others of their ills?" Sir, go quietly and quickly, and do not let anyone hear this.
>
> 止, 止! 阿難! 莫作是語! 如來身者, 金剛之體, 諸惡已斷, 眾善普會, 當有何疾? 當有何惱? 默往, 阿難! 勿謗如來, 莫使異人聞此麤言。 ...外道梵志, 若聞此語, 當作是念: 「何名為師? 自疾不能救, 而能救諸疾?」 仁可密速去, 勿使人聞。

Ānanda reports that he "then heard a voice from space" (即聞空中聲) that confirmed Vimalakīrti's words but softened their rebuke by presenting the Buddha's illness as a skillful means befitting this corrupted age:

> Ānanda, it is as the householder has said. It is just that the Buddha has appeared in this evil age of the five corruptions and manifests his Dharma to emancipate sentient beings. Go, Ānanda. Take the milk without shame.
>
> 阿難! 如居士言。 但為佛出五濁惡世, 現行斯法, 度脫眾生。 行矣, 阿難! 取乳勿慚。[57]

The longest and most explicit discussion of the doctrinal implications of illness takes place in chapter 5, titled "Visiting the Sick" ("Wenji pin" 問疾品), during Mañjuśrī's visit to Vimalakīrti's house. After Mañjuśrī politely inquires about his health and conveys the Buddha's regards, Vimalakīrti elaborates on the origination and characteristics of his illness and addresses "how bodhisattvas should comfort ill bodhisattvas" (菩薩應云何慰喻有疾菩薩) and "how ill bodhisattvas should control their minds" (有疾菩薩

---

57. *Weimojie suo shuo jing* 3.542a; McRae, *Vimalakīrti Sutra*, 95–96. On this part of the sutra, see also Mather, "Vimalakīrti and Gentry Buddhism," 63–64; Pye, *Skilful Means*, 89–90.

云何調伏其心).[58] Vimalakīrti's teachings are embedded in references to fundamental Buddhist or Mahāyāna Buddhist doctrines such as compassion (*bei* 悲; Skt. *karuṇā*), impermanence (*wuchang* 無常; Skt. *anitya*), nonself (*wu/fei wo* 無/非我; Skt. *anātman*), suffering (*ku* 苦; Skt. *duḥkha*), and emptiness. When Mañjuśrī asks about the cause of his illness, for instance, Vimalakīrti responds that it arose from "great compassion" (大悲) and explains: "Since all sentient beings are ill, therefore I am ill" (以一切眾生病, 是故我病) and "Because there is samsara, there is illness" (有生死則有病).[59]

When asked how bodhisattvas should comfort ill bodhisattvas, Vimalakīrti advises that one should "teach that the body is impermanent, but not that one should despise or abandon one's body" (說身無常, 不說厭離於身).[60] This equitable attitude toward the body aligns with the lack of emphasis on the body's impurity seen in the similes discussed earlier, distinguishing it from the emphasis on the loathsomeness or impurity of corporeal embodiment prevalent in many other Buddhist writings.[61] This relative affirmation of the body in the *Vimalakīrti Sutra* recalls another episode from the life story of the historical Śākyamuni Buddha: his decision to abandon the severe asceticism he had practiced for many years, a decision that turned out to be crucial for his enlightenment.

---

58. *Weimojie suo shuo jing* 5.544b–545b; McRae, *Vimalakīrti Sutra*, 108–13.

59. *Weimojie suo shuo jing* 5.544b; McRae, *Vimalakīrti Sutra*, 108.

60. *Weimojie suo shuo jing* 5.544c; McRae, *Vimalakīrti Sutra*, 110.

61. Sue Hamilton has proposed that "the Buddha's attitude to the body . . . is neither positive nor negative" and one was expected "to have a purely analytical attitude towards one's body"; see her "From the Buddha to Buddhaghosa," 52, 54–55. However, the contemplation of the inherent impurity of the body, whether one's own body or those of others, was an established meditation practice (*bujing guan/xiang* 不淨觀/想; Skt. *aśubha-bhāvanā*). See Mrozik, *Virtuous Bodies*, 87–92; Greene, *Secrets of Buddhist Meditation*, 26–29, 114–70 (a translation of the *Chan mi yao fa jing* 禪祕要法經).

CHAPTER FOUR

Emulating Vimalakīrti in Early Medieval Chinese Poetry

The fascination with the *Vimalakīrti Sutra* has left traces throughout medieval Chinese literature and visual art. Richard Mather has noted "hundreds of traceable allusions . . . in the writings of fourth- and fifth-century gentlemen and gentlemen-monks of the lower Yangtze area" alone, and it is unlikely that even the recent thousand-page tome dedicated to "Studies in the Belief in Vimalakīrti in Medieval China" by the modern scholar He Jianping covers them all.[1] In this chapter, I focus on one particular element of the reception of the *Vimalakīrti Sutra*: early medieval poetry with a sickbed setting. After presenting a catalog of extant pre-Tang sickbed poems (*wo ji/bing shi* 臥疾/病詩), the chapter concludes with a section looking ahead at the development of sickbed poetry in the Tang dynasty.

Poems Written While Lying Sick: An Overview

Only a small number of poems surviving from the pre-Tang period are set at a sickbed. The following list includes all twelve poems that mention this particular setting in the title. Going by extant poems, Wang Xiuzhi was the first poet to explicitly use the phrase "lying sick" in a title. The list also includes sixteen poems that thematize illness in the poem proper, but does not include poems that merely mention illness in passing or use it metaphorically.[2] The

---

1. Mather, "Vimalakīrti and Gentry Buddhism," 72; He Jianping, *Zhongguo zhonggu Weimojie xinyang.*

2. An example of the first case is Dao Qia's 到洽 (477–527) "Presented to Ren Fang" ("Zeng Ren Fang shi" 贈任昉詩); examples of the latter are two poems by Bao Zhao (ca.

Emulating Vimalakīrti 195

selection criteria focus on poems that refer to the author's or persona's own illness, not that of others (with the exception of certain exchange poems). In addition to poems about being sick, I also include poems about recovering from illness.

Liu Zhen 劉楨 (d. 217)
"Four Poems Presented to the Central Commander of the Five Guards" no. 2 ("Zeng wuguan zhonglangjiang shi si shou" 贈五官中郎將詩四首)

Zhi Yu 摯虞 (d. 311)
"Rhapsody on Recovering from Illness" ("Ji yu fu" 疾愈賦)

Tao Qian 陶潛 (365–427)
"To Secretary Zhou, Zu, and Xie" ("Shi Zhou Zu Xie" 示周掾祖謝, ca. 417)[3]

Xie Lingyun 謝靈運 (385–433)
"Stopping by My Villa in Shining" ("Guo Shining shu shi" 過始寧墅詩, 422)
"Reading in My Study" ("Zhai zhong du shu shi" 齋中讀書詩, 422)
"Commanding Scholars to Discuss Books [with Me]" ("Ming xueshi jiang shu shi" 命學士講書詩, 423)
"Climbing the Tower by the Pond" ("Deng chishang lou shi" 登池上樓詩, 423)
"Visiting South Pavilion" ("You nan ting shi" 遊南亭詩, 423)
"On Returning to My Old Gardens, for Perusal by the Imperial Secretaries Yan Yanzhi and Fan Tai" ("Huan jiu yuan, zuo jian Yan Fan er zhongshu shi" 還舊園作見顏范二中書詩, 426 or 428)
"When I First Arrived in the Capital" ("Chu zhi du shi" 初至都詩, 426, fragment)
"In Response to My Younger Cousin Huilian" ("Chou congdi Huilian shi" 酬從弟惠連詩, 430)

414–466), "Ballad of the Pine and Cyprus, with a Preface" and "Farewell Poem for Attendant Gentleman Wu" ("Yu Wu shilang bie shi" 與伍侍郎別詩). See Lu Qinli, *Xian Qin Han Wei Jin Nanbeichao shi*, 1786, 1264–65, 1288.

3. See the discussion in part II.

196   *Chapter Four*

Wang Xiuzhi 王秀之 (422–494)
"Expressing My Intent While Lying Sick" ("Wo ji xu yi shi" 臥疾敍
意詩, before 493)

Jiang Yan 江淹 (444–505)
"I Lament Parting from Head Scribe Liu While Lying Sick" ("Wo ji
yuan bie Liu changshi shi" 臥疾怨別劉長史詩)

Xie Tiao 謝朓 (464–499)
"Companion Piece to a Poem Written While Lying Sick by Senior
Administrator Wang [Xiuzhi]" ("He Wang changshi wo bing
shi" 和王長史臥病詩)
"Poem Presented to Minister Shen [Yue] While Lying Sick in My
Commandery" ("Zai jun wo bing cheng Shen shangshu shi" 在
郡臥病呈沈尚書詩, 496)
"Claiming Illness, I Return to My Garden, Notifying My Relatives
and Associates" ("Yi bing huan yuan shi qinshu shi" 移病還園示
親屬詩, 498)

Shen Yue 沈約 (441–513)
"Companion Piece to a Poem by Left Assistant Yu Gaozhi [441–
491] Requesting Sick Leave" ("He zuocheng Yu Gaozhi yi bing
shi" 和左丞庾杲之移病詩, before 491)
"In Response to Xie Tiao's [Poem Written While Lying Sick]"
("Chou Xie Xuancheng Tiao shi" 酬謝宣城朓詩, 496)

Liu Xiaochuo 劉孝綽 (481–539)
"[Observing] the Autumn Rain While Lying Sick" ("Qiu yu wo ji
shi" 秋雨臥疾詩, fragment)

Pei Ziye 裴子野 (469–530)
"Rhapsody Written While Lying Sick" ("Wo ji fu" 臥疾賦, fragment)

Xiao Gang 蕭綱 (503–551)
"Poem Written While Lying Sick" ("Wo ji shi" 臥疾詩, fragment)
"Poem on the Joy of Convalescence" ("Xi ji liao shi" 喜疾瘳詩)

Liu Xiaowei 劉孝威 (496–549)
"Companion Piece to Emperor Jianwen's Poem Written While
Lying Sick" ("He Jianwen di wo ji shi" 和簡文帝臥疾詩)

Zhu Chaodao 朱超道 (fl. 520–539)
"Poem Written at the End of the Year While Seriously Ill" ("Sui wan chen ke shi" 歲晚沈痾詩)

Yu Xin 庾信 (513–581)
"Poem Written While Lying Sick and in Deep Distress" ("Wo ji qiong chou shi" 臥疾窮愁詩)

Wang Zhou 王冑 (558–613)
"Describing the Meaning of the *Vimalakīrti Sutra* While Lying Sick in Min-Yue, with a Preface" ("Wo ji Min Yue shu *Jingming* yi bing xu" 臥疾閩越述淨名意并序, 603/604?)

Shi Huijing 釋慧淨 (578–ca. 645)
"Poem Sent to My Old Companions from a Winter's Day in Puguang Temple Where It Was Snowing While I Was Lying Sick" ("Yu dong ri Puguang si wo ji zhi xue jian zhu jiuyou shi" 於冬日普光寺臥疾值雪簡諸舊遊詩)

Xie Lingyun: "Lying Sick with Much Happy Leisure"

Xie Lingyun (385–433) was one of the most prominent Chinese readers and admirers of the *Vimalakīrti Sutra*. A member of an eminent aristocratic family, Xie was a brilliant poet, master of prose, painter, and calligrapher. He was also, as Richard Mather remarks, "one of the most vocal lay protagonists of Buddhism in his generation."[4] Mather and others have speculated that Xie may have been among the very few in early medieval China with some knowledge of Sanskrit. Although much of Xie's writing has been lost, it is clear that he engaged with Buddhism throughout his adult life. He composed Buddhist inscriptions, such as the one on the image of the Buddha at Mount Lu in 413,[5] epitaphs for Buddhist monks

---

4. Mather, "Landscape Buddhism," 67. For a brief summary of Xie Lingyun's Buddhist associations, see also Zürcher, *Buddhist Conquest*, 412n125.

5. "Inscription on the Buddha-Shadow" ("Fo ying ming" 佛影銘, written in 413), in *Quan Song wen* 33.5a–6a; Mather, "Vimalakīrti and Gentry Buddhism," 77–78; Frodsham, *Murmuring Stream*, 1:179–81.

198   *Chapter Four*

like the great Huiyuan (334–416),[6] and the "Discourse on Distinguishing What Is Essential" ("Bianzong lun" 辨/辯宗論) in 422, a treatise in a question-and-answer format on the doctrinal debate about sudden versus gradual enlightenment.[7] Xie also wrote a commentary on the *Diamond Sutra* (*Vajracchedikā-prajñāpāramitā*; *Jingang banre jing* 金剛般若經注) and collaborated with Buddhist monks to revise the stylistically poor translation of the *Nirvana Sutra* (*Mahāparinirvāṇa-sūtra*; *Da banniepan jing* 大般涅槃經) by Dharmakṣema (Tanwuchen 曇無讖 / Tanmochen 曇摩讖, 385–433), probably between 430 and 432.[8]

The closest association of Xie Lingyun with the *Vimalakīrti Sutra* in popular memory rests on an anecdote about the end of his life. In 433, Xie was accused of plotting rebellion and sentenced to be publicly beheaded in the marketplace of Guangzhou. On his way to the execution ground, Xie is said to have cut off his reportedly beautiful beard and donated it to the Jetavana Monastery in Nanhai, where it was affixed to an image of Vimalakīrti.[9] Apart from this colorful but possibly spurious anecdote, we also have a wealth of literary references that speak to Xie Lingyun's relationship with the *Vimalakīrti Sutra*, including the monumental, self-annotated "Rhapsody on Living in the Mountains" ("Shan ju fu" 山居賦).[10] His best-known poetic reference to the sutra is a group of eight encomia or eulogies (*zan* 贊) about the first ten similes of the body from chapter 2 of the *Vimalakīrti Sutra*. Xie wrote them in 424, during his first period of retirement from office on his family estate in Shining.[11] Beyond their potential to

6. "Epitaph on Dharma Teacher Huiyuan of Mount Lu" ("Lushan Huiyuan fashi lei" 廬山慧遠法師誄, written in 417), in *Quan Song wen* 33.7b–8a.

7. *Quan Song wen* 32.5a–11a; Bodde in Fung, *History of Chinese Philosophy*, 2:274–84.

8. See Frodsham, *Murmuring Stream*, 1:71–73. The *Nirvana Sutra* proposes the presence of Buddha-nature (*fo xing* 佛性; Skt. *buddhatā*) in everyone. The notion that everyone has the capacity for enlightenment, including those described as *icchāntika* (*chanti* 闡提), who were earlier assumed incapable of attaining enlightenment, was an idea that Xie Lingyun had advocated in his "Inscription on the Buddha-Shadow."

9. *Song shu* 67.1777; *Taiping guangji* 405.3268.

10. *Quan Song wen* 31.1a–11a.

11. "Encomia on the Ten Similes of the *Vimalakīrti Sutra*" ("Weimojing shi pi zan" 維摩經十譬贊), in *Quan Song wen* 33.4a–5a. Two of the encomia—the first on foam and bubbles and the sixth on shadow and echo—treat two similes simultaneously. On Kamo no Chōmei's interpretation of these similes in his *Hōjōki*, see LaFleur, *Karma of Words*, 112.

Emulating Vimalakīrti 199

illuminate certain Buddhist doctrines, these similes seem to have attracted Xie for their poetic potential, perhaps due to the close connection between transience and beauty in the Chinese poetic tradition.[12]

The seventh encomium, dedicated to "floating clouds" (浮雲), is an excellent illustration of Xie's poetic approach to the sutra's terse similes:

	泛濫明月陰	Floating and drifting, they conceal the bright moon,
	蒼蔚南山雨	"Billowing and swelling," they drench "South Hill."[13]
	能為變動用	While we can enjoy their alterations,[14]
4	在我竟無取	The self ultimately cannot grasp them.
	俄已就飛散[15]	Soon they are already flown away and dispersed,
	豈復得攢聚	How could one gather them together again?
	諸法既無我	When all dharmas are without "self,"[16]
8	何由有我所	From where could "the qualities of self" arise?[17]

Xie Lingyun augments the sutra's brief text—"This body is like a floating cloud, changing and disappearing in an instant" (是身如浮雲，須臾變滅 [18])—both poetically and doctrinally. He adds allusive images and notions that emphasize the clouds' impermanence and transmutability, and he explicitly interprets the simile in light of the doctrine of nonself.

Surprisingly, none of Xie Lingyun's eight encomia mentions illness, the

---

12. On the motif of the ephemerality of human life in early Chinese poetry, see Kroll, "Literary Criticism and Personal Character," 529–32.

13. This line alludes to a couplet in the ode "The Men at Waiting" that describes the rising mist at South Hill ("Hou ren" 候人, *Mao shi* no. 151). Quotation marks in my translations of poetry indicate either allusions or Buddhist terms.

14. My tentative translation of this line leaves open whether the alterations refer to the changing shape of clouds or to the rain these clouds may eventually produce, which in turn would determine how we "use" (*yong* 用) them: enjoying the visual spectacle that clouds present or the benefits of precipitation.

15. The emendation from 己 to 已 follows most editions of Xie Lingyun's works. See, e.g., *Xie Lingyun ji*, 445.

16. According to Muller's *Digital Dictionary of Buddhism*, *zhu fa* 諸法 are "all the factors that comprise an individual," while the phrase *zhu fa wu wo* 諸法無我 means that "nothing has a self, or is independent of the law of causation."

17. *Quan Song wen* 33.4b.

18. *Weimojie suo shuo jing* 2.539b; McRae, *Vimalakīrti Sutra*, 83.

200　Chapter Four

fallibility of the human body, or indeed the body as such. Similarly, other poems about the similes transmitted in the "Buddhist" chapters of *Collection of Literature Arranged by Categories* do not mention these themes. These include Kumārajīva's "Poem about the Ten Similes" ("Shi yu shi" 十喻詩), which likely predates Xie Lingyun's poems, and the much later poems by two Liang emperors. *Collection of Literature* quotes a "Poem on the Ten Similes of Illusion" ("Shi yu huan shi" 十喻幻詩) and a "Poem on Being Like a Mirage" ("Ru yan shi" 如炎詩) by Xiao Yan, who ruled as Emperor Wu of the Liang dynasty between 502 and 549, as well as six poems on individual similes, such as the echo or the shadow, by Xiao Gang, who succeeded him as Emperor Jianwen of the same dynasty (梁簡文帝, r. 549–551).[19] While the original phrase "this body is like" may still resonate when reciting these poems, their authors have shifted away from the stark realities of physical frailty and impermanence toward loftier, more dignified spheres in choosing their poetic imagery.

Xie Lingyun, deeply engaged with the *Vimalakīrti Sutra*, may have also been the first Chinese poet to write a poem while lying sick. Xie's "Reading in My Study," written during his first banishment from the capital to Yongjia in the winter of 422, is the earliest transmitted Chinese poem to use the phrase "lying sick" (*wo ji* 臥疾). However, the speaker does not dwell on his illness but rather adopts a jubilant tone, as the following excerpt from the sixteen-line poem demonstrates:

	臥疾豐暇豫	Lying sick with much happy leisure,
8	翰墨時間作	I often take up brush and ink.
	懷抱觀古今	Intent on reading [books] old and new,
	寢食展戲謔	In bed and during meals I spread them out, where they make me "quip and joke."[20]

In this poem, illness is depicted as a gift of leisure, providing time to pursue personal interests and express aspects of one's personality that would

---

19. See *Yiwen leiju* 76.1294–95; Lu Qinli, *Xian Qin Han Wei Jin Nanbeichao shi*, 1084, 1532, 1937–38.

20. Lu Qinli, *Xian Qin Han Wei Jin Nanbeichao shi*, 1168. See also the translation in Frodsham, *Murmuring Stream*, 1:170. The allusion to the *Book of Odes* lends the "quipping and joking" a respectable air; see "Recesses of the Qi" ("Qi ao" 淇奧, *Mao shi* no. 55).

otherwise (i.e., when in good health) be set aside for the sake of official duties. Similarly, in another of Xie's Yongjia poems, "Commanding Scholars to Discuss Books [with Me]," written about a year later in the fall of 423, the specifics of the speaker's indisposition remain obscure. The poet declares himself to be "lying sick like the Governor of Huaiyang" (臥病同 淮陽), alluding to the Han official Ji An 汲黯 (d. 112 BCE) who famously declined (albeit to no avail) an appointment by Emperor Wu of the Han on grounds of illness.[21] In "Commanding Scholars to Discuss Books [with Me]," illness emerges again as little more than a period of socially accepted idleness and an opportunity to pursue intellectual endeavors, often in the company of friends.[22] In the introduction to his "Discourse on Distinguishing What Is Essential," Xie Lingyun draws a similar connection, attributing the composition of this text to the benefits of being sick, likely in the winter of 422/423, describing himself as "lying sick on my pillow with few concerns and many days of leisure" (余枕疾務寡, 頗多暇日).[23] As we saw in part II, half a century later Yu He would tap into this same spirit in his "Memorial Discussing Calligraphy."

The formal similarities between Vimalakīrti's use of illness and Xie Lingyun's poems are evident. Both the sutra and Xie's poems leverage the exceptional nature of illness: Vimalakīrti adheres to the rules of etiquette that demand visiting the sick, while the speakers in Xie's poems take advantage of the dispensation from their duties during illness. Another significant commonality is that neither Vimalakīrti nor the speakers in Xie's poems reap the "benefits" of their illnesses solely for themselves; instead, they share these moments with an audience. Illness, therefore, appears less as a personal affliction and more as an opportunity to connect with others, if for different purposes. Like Vimalakīrti, Xie Lingyun does not seem to be suffering from his illness but rather appears well enough to enjoy reading and socializing fully.

Xie expresses a similar sentiment in his "Rhapsody on Living in the Mountains." In the preface, he writes, "Nursing an illness, I have entered a retirement where I can be in harmony with my predisposition and inner

---

21. *Shi ji* 120.3110.

22. Lu Qinli, *Xian Qin Han Wei Jin Nanbeichao shi*, 1169; Frodsham, *Murmuring Stream*, 1:132.

23. *Quan Song wen* 32.5a.

202   Chapter Four

state. Daring to indulge my pleasure, I have composed a rhapsody" (抱疾就閑, 順從性情, 敢率所樂, 而以作賦). He continues in this vein, embarking on the rhapsody proper with the words, "Master Xie was lying sick on a mountain peak, perusing a book passed down by men of old. Feeling in accord with their sentiments, I smiled and said . . ." (謝子臥疾山頂, 覽古人遺書, 與其意合, 悠然而笑曰 . . .).[24] Xie mentions his illness several more times throughout the rhapsody, yet he consistently comes across as physically, intellectually, and poetically vigorous.

Unlike Vimalakīrti's docetic illness, which remains more of an abstract concept in the sutra, Xie's poems are often read as autobiographically authentic, used to reconstruct the poet's medical history. For instance, "Reading in My Study" is interpreted as evidence of Xie's prolonged illness during the winter of 422, while "Climbing the Tower by the Pond," his most famous poem, written in the early spring of 423, is read as evidence of his recovery.[25] While there is no reason to doubt the autobiographical dimension of these poems, it is important to remember the long Chinese tradition of writing in certain personas, in both poetry and prose. Assuming the persona of a sick man would not have been difficult for most writers, not only because everyone is familiar with illness in one way or another but also because of the long tradition of pleading illness to leave office or reject a position, as we discussed in part II. Illness, being one of the few legitimate excuses allowing one to escape official duties, almost on par with taking care of or mourning one's parents, should thus make us cautious when interpreting poems written "while lying sick" as strictly autobiographical.

The prominence of sickness in Xie Lingyun's poetry may stem not only from his familiarity with the *Vimalakīrti Sutra* and his own experiences with illness and recovery but also from his profound engagement with

24. *Quan Song wen* 31.1a. The translation, with emendations, is based on Westbrook, "Landscape Description," 186, 190. For other references to the *Vimalakīrti Sutra*, see 31.6b, 9a.

25. See, e.g., *Xie Lingyun ji*, 91–99, 580. Other poems mentioning the speaker's sickness and recovery that are usually interpreted as autobiographical include "Stopping by My Villa in Shining" (422), "Visiting South Pavilion" (423), "On Returning to My Old Gardens, for Perusal by the Imperial Secretaries Yan Yanzhi and Fan Tai" (426 or 428), and "When I First Arrived in the Capital" (426).

Jian'an poetry.[26] He must have known Liu Zhen's (d. 217) "Four Poems Presented to the Central Commander of the Five Guards." The second of these poems can be read as written after a sickbed visit and addressed to the departing visitor, in this case, Cao Pi. The first half of the poem reads as follows:

	余嬰沉痼疾	Since I have been suffering from a serious and persistent illness
	竄身清漳濱	I have been lying low at the banks of the Clear Zhang,
	自夏涉玄冬	From summer all the way into dark winter
4	彌曠十餘旬	It has been more than a dozen weeks.
	常恐游岱宗	I often feared that my soul would travel to Mount Tai [the netherworld]
	不復見故人	And I would never see my old friend again.
	所親一何篤	You, my dear one, are so devoted
8	步趾慰我身	That you took the trouble to come and comfort me.
	清談同日夕	In clear conversation lasting all day and all night,
	情盻叙憂勤	Through heartfelt glances, you expressed worry and concern.[27]

We do not know when Liu Zhen wrote the poem, but it is unlikely that the protracted illness he describes here was the one that led to his death during the often-evoked 217 epidemic.[28] Liu Zhen's reference to the banks of the river Zhang (Zhang *bin* 漳濱) was to become one of the most productive allusions to illness starting in the Liang dynasty, appearing in eight pre-Tang poems and rhapsodies and nine pieces of patterned prose, and thriving in the Tang dynasty, where it occurs in 154 *shi*-poems and nineteen pieces of patterned prose.[29] Reflecting on the narratives and motifs of sick-

26. See Xiaofei Tian's inspiring interpretation of Xie's poems on the Jian'an masters in *Halberd at Red Cliff*, 30–58.

27. *Wen xuan* 23.1111–12; Lu Qinli, *Xian Qin Han Wei Jin Nanbeichao shi*, 369–70; see also Fusheng Wu, "I Rambled and Roamed," esp. 628–29, for a translation of this poem.

28. See Jiao Peimin, Liu Chunyu, and He Yuxin, *Zhongguo zaihai tongshi: Qin Han juan*, esp. 95–109, 429. Also see Zhang Meili, Liu Jixian, and Jiao Peimin, *Zhongguo zaihai tongshi: Wei Jin Nanbeichao juan*.

29. To mention only two Liang dynasty examples: Xie Tiao uses the phrase "banks of

204   Chapter Four

bed visits in early Chinese literature discussed earlier, the poem joins the tradition of celebrating friendships from the sickbed seen in the *Zhuangzi* and *Liezi*.

In Xie Lingyun's appropriation of Liu Zhen's poem, Xie assumes the role of Liu, but the visitor who comforted him at his sickbed is not an imperial family member or superior; rather, it is his favorite young relative, Xie Huilian 謝惠連 (407–433). Here are the first two stanzas of the five-stanza poem, responding to an earlier poem sent by Huilian:[30]

	寢瘵謝人徒	Bedridden with sickness I withdrew from human company,
	滅迹入雲峯	Obliterating my traces I entered the cloud-hung peaks.
	巖壑寓耳目	Crags and gorges sheltered my eyes and ears,
4	歡愛隔音容	The ones I loved separated from me in voice and appearance.
	永絕賞心望	Cut off forever from the prospect of being with an understanding heart,
	長懷莫與同	Always regretting that no one is with me.
	末路值令弟	At the end of the road I came upon you, my esteemed young cousin,
8	開顏披心胸	Who brought a smile on my face and opened up the heart in my breast.
	心胸既云披	When the heart in my breast had opened up,
	意得咸在斯	My mind's content entirely rested in this.
	凌澗尋我室	You crossed mountain streams to seek my house,

---

the Zhang" in his "Rhapsody Requiting a Kindness" ("Chou de fu" 酬德賦) addressed to Shen Yue; see *Quan Qi wen* 23.4a. However, it is difficult to tell if this is simply an allusion or a concrete autobiographical reference. Mather assumes the latter in his "Poetic Essay Requiting a Kindness," 613. The banks of the Zhang also appear in Li Jingyuan's 李鏡遠 poem "The Eastern Gate: Illness" ("Dong chengmen bing" 東城門病), part of a group composition at an Eight Precepts Fasting Ceremony led by Xiao Gang ("Baguanzhai ye fu si chengmen geng zuo" 八關齋夜賦四城門更作); see Lu Qinli, *Xian Qin Han Wei Jin Nanbeichao shi*, 2008.

30. Xie Huilian, "Poem Offered to Kangle upon Encountering a Storm at Lake Xiling" ("Xiling yu feng xian Kangle shi" 西陵遇風獻康樂詩); see Lu Qinli, *Xian Qin Han Wei Jin Nanbeichao shi*, 1193. The poem features a figurative reference to illness in the penultimate line: "The grief I have accumulated makes me ill" (積憤成疚痗).

12	散帙問所知	You opened my books and questioned me on them.
	夕慮曉月流	At night I feared the moon was gliding on to dawn,
	朝忌曛日馳	By day I resented the sun's flight into the dusk.
	悟對無厭歇	We were never tired of being together,
16	聚散成分離	But the gathering and scattering would complete our parting.[31]

The social dimension that emerges in Liu Zhen's and Xie Lingyun's poems is a recurring theme in many later poems written "while lying sick." These poems often address friends or colleagues, as seen in Xie Tiao's "Poem Presented to Minister Shen [Yue] While Lying Sick in My Commandery," written in 496.[32] Like his clansman Xie Lingyun in "Commanding Scholars to Discuss Books," Xie Tiao begins with a reference to the Han dynasty official Ji An, known for his poor health and his continued excellent governance while laid up with illness.[33] The speaker presents himself as cheerfully negligent of his illness, reducing it to a delightful treat of time and leisure. He describes the fine bream, green-ant wine, summer plums, and autumn lotus root he enjoyed and ends on a note of longing for his old friend Shen Yue.

As if to confirm Xie Tiao's indifference to the illness that prompted the poem, Shen's poetic response does not mention illness either, not even in the form of a veiled get-well wish; instead, Shen focuses on his young friend's official career.[34] The two Xies' nonchalance about health may also be related to their relative youth when they wrote these poems, both being

31. "In Response to My Younger Cousin Huilian" (430), in *Wen xuan* 25.1199; see Lu Qinli, *Xian Qin Han Wei Jin Nanbeichao shi*, 1175. English translation, with adaptations, by Frodsham, *Murmuring Stream*, 1:149. Also see the discussion and translation in Williams, "A Conversation in Poems," 495–99. Line 16 alludes to the passage "gathering together and scattering bring it all to completion" (聚散以成) in *Zhuangzi* 25.914; Watson, *Complete Works of Zhuangzi*, 224.

32. Lu Qinli, *Xian Qin Han Wei Jin Nanbeichao shi*, 1427. Also see translations by Frodsham, *Anthology of Chinese Verse*, 162–63; Mather, *Age of Eternal Brilliance*, 2:252–53. The poem was written in 495 or 496 when Xie served as Governor of Xuancheng in present-day Anhui. Mather suspects the illness might have been "a recurrence of the malaria he picked up in Chiang-ling"; see "Poetic Essay Requiting a Kindness," 604.

33. See Mather, *Age of Eternal Brilliance*, 2:253n2; *Xie Lingyun ji*, 137–39nn2, 5.

34. "In Response to Xie Tiao's [Poem Written While Lying Sick]"; see Lu Qinli, *Xian Qin Han Wei Jin Nanbeichao shi*, 1634; Mather, *Age of Eternal Brilliance*, 1:222–24.

206   *Chapter Four*

in their thirties and likely not overly concerned about a momentary lapse in their health.

There are also early medieval sickbed poems that do not so much celebrate the extra leisure time granted by a minor ailment but rather express distress and apprehension, possibly in response to more serious ailments or the experience of a general physical decline later in life. Wang Xiuzhi (442–494) may well have been around fifty when he wrote "Expressing My Intent While Lying Sick" (sometime before 493), the first known poem to use the phrase "lying sick" in its title (seventy or so years after Xie Lingyun first used it in a poetic line). While Wang does not specify his ailments, he speaks of his worry about advancing age and deteriorating health.[35] Interestingly, Xie Tiao's companion piece to this poem does not replicate Wang Xiuzhi's melancholic mood but strikes a lighter tone, probably out of politeness.[36] He quotes a line from the *Changes of Zhou* that implies that his friend's illness is undeserved and would clear up without medicine. Richard Lynn translates this line as: "If an illness strikes the one who practices No Errancy here, let him not resort to medication, for then there will be joy" (勿藥有喜). Following the commentary, Lynn explains that an illness "that one does not bring on oneself should not be treated for it is accidental or brought about by the processes of nature. One should, in effect, wait it out, and health will return of its own accord."[37] As we have seen, a similar idea is also expressed in the *Zhuangzi* and *Liezi*.

Similar to Wang Xiuzhi's "Expressing My Intent While Lying Sick," the somber, autumnal mood of Jiang Yan's (444–504) "I Lament Parting from Head Scribe Liu While Lying Sick," apparently written after a friend's sickbed visit, also reflects the poet's awareness of his mortality, even if he does not detail his condition.[38]

---

35. Lu Qinli, *Xian Qin Han Wei Jin Nanbeichao shi*, 1477; Mather, *Age of Eternal Brilliance*, 2:81n1.

36. "Companion Piece to a Poem Written While Lying Sick by Senior Administrator Wang [Xiuzhi]"; see Lu Qinli, *Xian Qin Han Wei Jin Nanbeichao shi*, 1444; Mather, *Age of Eternal Brilliance*, 2:80–83. Also see Xie Tiao's "Claiming Illness, I Return to My Garden, Notifying My Relatives and Associates" (498), a poem that, apart from the title, does not mention illness at all; see Lu Qinli, *Xian Qin Han Wei Jin Nanbeichao shi*, 1435; Mather, *Age of Eternal Brilliance*, 2:276–77.

37. *Zhou yi* 3.28a; Lynn, *Classic of Changes*, 296, 298.

38. Lu Qinli, *Xian Qin Han Wei Jin Nanbeichao shi*, 1563.

The notion that illness, aside from pain and suffering, can provide opportunities such as leisure time inspired poems like Liu Xiaochuo's (481–539) fragmentarily received "[Observing] the Autumn Rain While Lying Sick."[39] In this poem, not only does the ailing speaker have all the time in the world to watch a torrential downpour, but his acute observations of his surroundings suggest that the enforced idleness of lying sick may have heightened his perceptiveness. Sickness has often been depicted as reducing one's interaction with the outside world, which in turn has been credited for an increase in one's sensitivity. Xie Lingyun's poem "Climbing the Tower by the Pond" supports this view: after recovering from a long illness, the speaker famously perceives the world anew.[40]

Huijing: "Suffering Brought Me to a Halt"

The motif of portraying illness as an opportunity is also evident in the work of the monk Huijing (578–ca. 645). In his "Poem Sent to My Old Companions from a Winter's Day in Puguang Temple Where It Was Snowing While I was Lying Sick," Huijing extols the wonders of the falling snow. The poem paints a fascinating tableau, supported by allusions, reflecting the Buddhist monk's ecumenical taste in music and reading:

	臥病苦留滯	Lying sick,[41] my suffering brought me to a halt.
	闢戶望遙天	Opening the door, I look up into the vast sky.
	寒雲舒復卷	Cold clouds are stretching out and then furling again,
4	落雪斷還連	Falling flakes are sheering off and then connecting once more.[42]

39. Lu Qinli, *Xian Qin Han Wei Jin Nanbeichao shi*, 1842.

40. A small number of other poems about recovery have survived. See Zhi Yu's (d. 311) fragmentarily transmitted "Rhapsody on Recovering from Illness," in *Yiwen leiju* 75.1290; Xiao Gang's (503–551) "Poem on the Joy of Convalescence," in Lu Qinli, *Xian Qin Han Wei Jin Nanbeichao shi*, 1944.

41. *Wo ke* 臥病, synonymous to *wo ji*, is also used in Xie Lingyun's "Climbing the Tower by the Pond."

42. The pattern and wording of the second couplet seem inspired by Shen Yue's poem "Accompanying Emperor Wu of the Qi for a Military Review at Langye Fortress, Written upon Imperial Command" ("Cong Qi Wudi Langyecheng jiangwu yingzhao shi" 從齊武

208　　*Chapter Four*

凝華照書閣	Frozen flowers light up my book chamber,[43]
飛素婉琴弦	Flying fluff caresses the strings of my zither.
廻飄洛神賦	Fluttering about the "Rhapsody on the Luo River Goddess,"
8　皎映齊紈篇	And shimmering on the poem about Qi silk,
縈階如鶴舞	Whirling over the steps [into the courtyard] as cranes in dance,
拂樹似花鮮	And clinging to the trees like flowers in fresh bloom.[44]
徒賞豐年瑞	I praise this omen of a bounteous year,
12　沈憂終自憐	Deeply saddened I finally "nurse my sorrow."[45]

In this poem, written at a prominent Buddhist temple in Chang'an, likely toward the end of Huijing's life,[46] references to illness provide an apparently slim frame for a meditation on the beauty of the falling snow. This meditation is extended through allusions to two poems in the fourth couplet: Cao Zhi's "Rhapsody on the Luo River Goddess" ("Luo shen fu" 洛神賦) and the "Song of Resentment" ("Yuange xing" 怨歌行) attributed to Ban Jieyu 班婕妤 (d. ca. 6 BCE), both of which mention snow.

While we can be sure that Huijing knew it, the *Vimalakīrti Sutra* is never mentioned. Nonetheless, the revelation of perfect beauty during

---

帝瑯瑯城講武應詔詩). In Mather's translation, the sixth couplet reads: "The windblown pennants are unfurled and furl again / The clouds and roseate mists have cleared and seem to swirl" (風斾舒復卷, 雲霞清似轉). See Lu Qinli, *Xian Qin Han Wei Jin Nanbeichao shi*, 1631; Mather, *Age of Eternal Brilliance*, 1:89.

43. The "frozen flowers" may also be a reference to Shen Yue's poem "Climbing the Terrace to Gaze at the Autumn Moon" ("Deng tai wang qiu yue" 登臺望秋月). See Lu Qinli, *Xian Qin Han Wei Jin Nanbeichao shi*, 1663; Mather, *Age of Eternal Brilliance*, 1:173–75.

44. This seems to be an allusion to an almost verbatim line in the "Poem on a Firefly" ("Yong ying shi" 詠螢詩) by Xiao Gang; see Lu Qinli, *Xian Qin Han Wei Jin Nanbeichao shi*, 1961.

45. Lu Qinli, *Xian Qin Han Wei Jin Nanbeichao shi*, 2772. The final line alludes to the "Nine Changes" ("Jiu bian" 九辯) in the *Songs of Chu*; see *Chu ci buzhu* 8.183.

46. Lu Qinli includes Huijing in his collection of Sui dynasty poetry, citing that he "was famous in the Kaihuang [581–600] and Daye [605–618] periods" (著名於開皇、大業之際). Lu Qinli, *Xian Qin Han Wei Jin Nanbeichao shi*, 2772. According to Huijing's biography in *Continued Biographies of Eminent Monks* (*Xu Gaoseng zhuan* 續高僧傳) by Daoxuan 道宣 (596–667), the composition may have taken place in the early Tang; see *Xu Gaoseng zhuan* 3.441.

what appears to be mortal illness evokes a miraculous feat described in the sutra's first chapter. To disprove the doubts the Buddha himself had planted in Śāriputra's mind about the purity of this land, "The Buddha touched the earth with his toe, and instantly the great chiliocosm was as if gloriously ornamented with a hundred thousand jewels" (於是佛以足指按地, 即時三千大千世界, 若干百千珍寶嚴飾).[47] The revelation of the innate beauty and perfection of *this* buddha land—that is, the world we inhabit, as blemished and defiled as it may appear most of the time—is the sutra's first strong statement about nonduality. Read in this light, Huijing's evocation of the seemingly insignificant beauty of a snowy day serves as a powerful affirmation of life in the face of suffering.

Wang Zhou: "In the City of Vaiśālī Lived an Elder"

The first transmitted sickbed poem explicitly mentioning the *Vimalakīrti Sutra* was composed by Wang Zhou (558–613, courtesy name Chengji 承基), a member of the Langye Wang clan. Wang may have written the poem in 603 or 604 while on a military expedition against Linyi 林邑 in what is now Vietnam.[48] Titled "Describing the Meaning of the *Vimalakīrti Sutra* While Lying Sick in Min-Yue, with a Preface," the poem is divided into two parts, though the rhyme continues. The first part details the miseries of lying ill in more depth than seen so far in any of our examples of pre-Tang poetry, while the second part extols the teachings of the *Vimalakīrti Sutra*:

> When I was lying sick at the coast of Min with a "pervasive and lingering illness" for a fortnight,[49] my good friend, Dharma Teacher Yong, urged me to control my body and mind with the *Vimalakīrti Sutra*, this marvelous [Mahāyāna] canon. I made an effort, in my illness, to roughly lay out its meaning, and respectfully send Dharma Teacher [Yong] the following words.
>
> 余臥疾閩海。彌留旬朔。善友顒法師。勸余以淨名妙典調伏身心。力疾粗陳其意。敬簡法師云爾。

---

47. *Weimojie suo shuo jing* 1.538c–539a; McRae, *Vimalakīrti Sutra*, 78–79.

48. See Knechtges and Chang, *Ancient and Early Medieval Chinese Literature*, 1283.

49. Note the allusion, mentioned earlier in part II, to the deathbed speech by King Cheng of the Zhou dynasty; *Shangshu* 18.125c.

210   Chapter Four

客行萬餘里	This stranger has traveled ten thousand miles and more,
眇然滄海上	Afar on the blue-green sea.
五嶺常炎鬱	The Southern Five Ranges are forever sweltering,
4　百越多山瘴	The Hundred Yue states abound in mountain miasma.
兼以勞形神	All this has worn out my body and spirit,
遂此嬰疲恙	And caused me to become sick from exhaustion.
桐雷邈已遠	[The doctors] Tong and Lei are men of the far distant past,[50]
8　砭石良難訪	[The fabled] acupuncture stones [of old] are difficult to find indeed.
抱影私自憐	"Hugging my shadow," and "nursing a private sorrow,"
霑襟獨惆悵	"My tear-stained lapels" bespeak lonely "despair."[51]
毗城有長者	"In the city of Vaiśālī lived an elder,"[52]
12　生平夙所尚	Whom I have revered all my life.
復藉大因緣	Devoting myself anew to the great [law of] "causes and conditions,"[53]
勉以深迴向	I strive for the profound "transference of merit."[54]
心路資調伏	My "mind-road" [of discursive thought] directed at "self-control,"[55]

50. Lord Jun 桐君 and Duke Lei 雷公 are said to have been contemporaries of the Yellow Emperor. See Tao Hongjing's 陶弘景 (452–536) "Preface to *Materia Medica*" ("*Bencao xu*" 本草序), in *Quan Liang wen* 47.2b.

51. Each line of this couplet employs two allusions to the *Songs of Chu*: "hugging my shadow" alludes to "Alas That My Lot Was Not Cast" ("Ai shi ming" 哀時命), with strong connotations of homesickness; "nursing a private sorrow" and "despair" to "Nine Changes"; and "tear-stained lapels" to "Nine Laments" ("Jiu tan" 九歎). See *Chu ci buzhu* 17.319, 8.183, and 16.306, respectively. "Nurse a private sorrow" is David Hawkes's translation; see *Songs of the South*, 209.

52. A reference to the *Vimalakīrti Sutra*'s introduction of its main protagonist; see *Weimojie suo shuo jing* 1.539a.

53. The law of dependent origination (*yuanqi* 緣起), mentioned frequently in the *Vimalakīrti Sutra*. See, e.g., *Weimojie suo shuo jing* 1.537a, 1.537c, 2.539b, 7.548a.

54. The idea of transferring one's merit to benefit the salvation of others is also discussed in the sutra. See, e.g., *Weimojie suo shuo jing* 1.538b and 9551b.

55. While the term "mind-road" does not occur in the *Vimalakīrti Sutra*, the idea of "self-control" or "discipline" plays an important role. See, e.g., *Weimojie suo shuo jing* 1.538a, 1.538b, 4.543c, 5.544c, 5.545a, 5.545b.

16	於焉念實相	I contemplate the "true characteristics."[56]
	水沫本難摩	Foam on water is by nature difficult to seize,[57]
	乾城空有狀	The heavenly musicians' mirage city is "empty of existence."[58]
	是生非至理	This life is not the ultimate truth,
20	是我皆虛妄	This self is all "hollow deception."
	求之不可得	Seeking [the ultimate truth] in these, it cannot be obtained,
	誰其受業障	Everyone suffering from the "hindrance of karma."
	信矣大醫王	Indeed, great is the "Medicine King,"[59]
24	茲力誠難量	His merciful power is truly hard to fathom.[60]

The first five couplets of Wang Zhou's poem are devoted to the speaker's illness. We learn that the sickness arose from arduous travel and the harsh climatic conditions in the insalubrious south, a self-diagnosis consistent with contemporary medical beliefs. The speaker expresses a profound sense of distress and an inability to find effective treatment. This evocation of despair and loneliness far from home is articulated using phrases familiar from the *Songs of Chu*. This has a curiously ambiguous effect: on one hand, the references to the expressive *Songs of Chu* amplify the urgency of the suffering described; on the other hand, they also temper and domesticate the suffering by presenting the speaker's despair within the framework of conventional, culturally approved ways of expression.

56. The notion of "true characteristics" or "reality"—as contrasted with "hollow deception" (i.e., "delusion") in line 20—is also frequently discussed in the *Vimalakīrti Sutra*. See, e.g., *Weimojie suo shuo jing* 3.541a, 4.544a, 9.551b.

57. Kumārajīva's translation of the *Vimalakīrti Sutra* has "a clump of foam" (*jumo* 聚沫); *Weimojie suo shuo jing* 2.539b, 7.547b.

58. The term *qian cheng* 乾城 (an abbreviated form of *qiantapo cheng* 乾闥婆城, "gandharva city") does not occur in the *Vimalakīrti Sutra*. However, the mirage itself (*huan* 幻) figures in the list of similes (*Weimojie suo shuo jing* 2.539b) and elsewhere.

59. As mentioned above, the term Medicine King is used several times in the sutra. See, e.g., *Weimojie suo shuo jing* 1.537a, 5.544c, and 8.550a.

60. Lu Qinli, *Xian Qin Han Wei Jin Nanbeichao shi*, 2701. See the alternative title in the "Preface to a Poem sent to Dharma Teacher Yong While I am Lying Sick at the Coast of Min" ("Wo ji Min hai jian Yong fashi shi xu" 臥疾閩海簡顒法師詩序), in *Quan Sui wen* 14.7b.

212 Chapter Four

After this surprisingly detailed account of hardship, the poem abruptly shifts focus. The remaining seven couplets concentrate on the speaker's long-standing reverence for the *Vimalakīrti Sutra*. Only the opening line of this second part, "In the city of Vaiśālī lived an elder," however, is specific to the sutra. While the doctrines mentioned in the rest of the poem—such as the law of dependent origination and the transference of merit—are indeed found in the *Vimalakīrti Sutra* (as my annotations show), they are also essential teachings of Mahāyāna Buddhism present in numerous other scriptures. This aligns with Erik Zürcher's astute characterization of the *Vimalakīrti Sutra* as "a real compendium of Mahāyāna doctrine."[61]

It is unclear from the text of the poem which translation of the sutra Wang Zhou knew. The terminology he uses points to Kumārajīva rather than Zhi Qian. However, the use of the name Vimalakīrti translated as Jingming 淨名 ("clean name" or "impeccable reputation") instead of the transliteration Weimojie 維摩詰 suggests that he might have known the sutra through a different translation, possibly one of the four that have not survived. While Xuanzang's mid-seventh-century translation of the name as Wugoucheng 無垢稱 ("unsoiled name") never gained significant popularity, "Jingming" is widely found in Tang literature. This name can be traced back to sources from the early fifth century but only attained traction during the Liang dynasty.[62] Wang Zhou might also have been familiar with the *Treatise on the Profundity of the "Vimalakīrti Sutra"* (*Jingming xuan lun* 淨名玄論) by his contemporary Jizang 吉藏 (549–623).

Looking Ahead: The Flourishing of Sickbed Poetry in the Tang

While little more than two dozen early medieval sickbed poems have survived, a much larger number exist from the Tang dynasty and later

---

61. Zürcher, *Buddhist Conquest*, 181. Zürcher (at 364n258) also cites Kumārajīva's words to that effect, as transmitted in a commentary on the sutra edited by Sengzhao and containing annotations by himself, Kumārajīva, Daosheng, and Daorong. See *Zhu Weimojie jing* 10.413c.

62. The first transmitted record of the name "Jingming" seems to be in the *Commentary on the "Vimalakīrti Sutra,"* where Kumārajīva remarks on the meaning of the householder's name. See *Zhu Weimojie jing*, preface, 327b.

periods. A cursory search of *The Complete Tang Poems* (*Quan Tang shi* 全唐詩) reveals more than three hundred poems with titles containing phrases like "lying sick" (臥疾/病) or "in sickness" (病中). This does not even include the numerous poems dealing with illness without such explicit titles or the considerable number of poems about sick nonhuman beings.[63] The greatest poets of the Tang era wrote about being sick, from early figures like Lu Zhaolin 盧照鄰 (ca. 635–684)[64] and Chen Zi'ang 陳子昂 (661–702) to Meng Haoran 孟浩然 (689–740) and Wang Wei 王維 (699–761)—who famously chose the style name Mojie 摩詰 in honor of Vimalakīrti—to Du Fu 杜甫 (712–770), Meng Jiao 孟郊 (751–814), and Li He 李賀 (790–816). Many of their poems are moving in their openness about physical suffering and decline, contrasting sharply with the restraint seen in early medieval China.[65]

Since even a brief account of Tang sickbed poetry in the context of the *Vimalakīrti Sutra* would exceed the scope of this chapter, a few remarks on a small number of poems by Bai Juyi (772–846) will have to suffice to illustrate the flourishing of this genre during the Tang period. That Bai Juyi is exceptional in many ways, not least in the number of poems written while ill that he left us, does not skew the picture but rather emphasizes how much had changed in the poetic depiction of illness since the sixth century. One such example is his "Sitting Quietly in My Sickness" ("Bing zhong yanzuo" 病中宴坐), here presented in Arthur Waley's poetical rendering:[66]

---

63. These poems are mostly allegorical; see, e.g., Jia Dao's 賈島 (749–843) "Sick Cicada" ("Bing chan" 病蟬) or Du Fu's "Sick Cypress" ("Bing bai" 病柏), in *Quan Tang shi* 219.2306 and 573.6658.

64. On Lu Zhaolin, see Kroll, "Memories of Lu Chao-lin," esp. 590, and "Aid and Comfort."

65. See, e.g., Florence Hu-Sterk's exploration of illness in Tang poetry ("Maladie et poésie sous les Tang"). Hu-Sterk focuses on Du Fu, Bai Juyi, and Li He, arguing that the topic became more prominent in connection with a turn to private life after the An Lushan Rebellion. For an overview of the *Vimalakīrti Sutra*'s literary reception during the Tang dynasty, see Sun Changwu, *Zhongguo wenxue zhong de Weimo*, 157–193 and 261–316. See also the study of women's poetry on illness in the Ming and Qing dynasties, Fong, "Writing and Illness."

66. Waley's translation in *Life and Times of Po Chü-i* (p. 200) omits the fifth couplet, which I have thus translated here. Since this couplet clarifies that the speaker is sitting

214 *Chapter Four*

有酒病不飲	I have got wine, but am not well enough to drink.
有詩慵不吟	I have got poems, but am too weak to chant them.
頭眩罷垂鉤	My head is giddy, I have had to give up fishing;
4　手痺休援琴	My hand is stiff, I have stopped playing my lute.
竟日悄無事	All day the silence is never broken;
所居閒且深	No worries reach me in my place of quiet retreat.
外安支離體	My body is reconciled to its crippled state;
8　中養希夷心	My heart finds refuge in its own mysteries.[67]
窗戶納秋景	My windows let in the autumn scenery,
竹木澄夕陰	Bamboo and trees limpid in the setting sun.
宴坐小池畔	Sitting quietly on the edge of the small pond,
12　清風時動襟	A gentle wind is stirring the lapels of my dress.[68]

None of the early medieval poems resembles this piece in its apparent autobiographical candor or physical explicitness: from head and hand and body and heart to the swaying lapels, it introduces a level of personal detail that was previously uncommon. The poem also surprises by the absence of any outside agenda: illness is no longer merely an opportunity or excuse to write about something else. As Stephen Owen suggested in an early article on poetry as autobiography, Bai's poem can confidently be read as "a privileged document of inner life, a presentation of self that potentially carried strong autobiographical dimensions."[69]

Bai Juyi not only wrote dozens of poems about the illnesses he suffered throughout his life and his physical decline in old age,[70] but he also frequently

---

inside a building rather than outside, as suggested by Waley's rendering of the last couplet, the translation of the last couplet is also my own. *Yanzuo* in the title could also refer to meditation, as it also appears in the *Vimalakīrti Sutra* (see, e.g., *Weimojie suo shuo jing* 2.539c). Waley's choice of "sitting quietly" is as open to interpretation as the original Chinese term.

67. Two allusions enliven this couplet: the first is to Zhili Shu 支離疏, one of the famous "sage cripples" in the *Zhuangzi* (4.180, mentioned earlier in part II), and the second is to a characterization of the mysterious in chapter 14 of the *Laozi*: "Looking at it and not seeing it, this is called invisible; listening for it but not hearing it, this is called inaudible" (視之不見, 名曰夷; 聽之不聞, 名曰希, *Laozi* 14.52).

68. *Quan Tang shi* 459.5218.

69. Owen, "The Self's Perfect Mirror," 72.

70. See Fan Ka-Wai's analysis of representations of Bai Juyi as a sick man from a medical perspective in *Zhonggu shiqi de yizhe yu bingzhe*, 200–222.

invoked the *Vimalakīrti Sutra* in various contexts, from illness to the study of Buddhist texts and even drinking. In the poem "The Lyric of Fallen Teeth" ("Chiluo ci" 齒落辭), for instance, Bai reflects on the loss of two of his teeth. He gives a voice to these teeth, letting them cite, among other things, the simile of the cloud, which is quoted verbatim from Kumārajīva's translation, to comfort their former master: "Haven't you heard the Buddha's teachings? / That this body is like floating clouds, / and changes and vanishes in an instant" (又不聞諸佛說, 是身如浮雲, 須臾變滅).[71]

A common conceit in several of Bai's poems is his identification with the famous householder. This identification can be expressed directly, such as when Bai refers to himself as "Minister Bai, the elder from Vaiśālī" (毗耶長者白尚書), or when he describes the dwelling where he is recuperating as a "ten-foot-square small pavilion" (小亭方丈).[72] This epithet of Vimalakīrti also appears in one of the "Fifteen Poems Written in Sickness" ("Bing zhong shi shiwu shou" 病中詩十五首), composed in 839, after Bai appears to have suffered a mild stroke that paralyzed his left leg. In this poem, addressed to a friend who had come to visit him, Bai identifies his sickbed visit with that in the *Vimalakīrti Sutra*, identifying himself as the householder and his visitor, a monk, as Mañjuśrī.[73]

However, illness is not the only point of comparison for Bai Juyi. He also likens himself to Vimalakīrti during times of joyful drinking, for example, in one of his "Songs on Myself" ("Zi yong" 自詠).[74] According to the sutra's second chapter, Vimalakīrti was unaffected by his engagement with all the spheres of secular life and benefited everyone he met, even in wine shops and brothels.

---

71. *Quan Tang shi* 461.5250; Tian, "Old Things in Mid-Tang China," 341.

72. See "On My Retirement as Minister of Justice" ("Xingbu shangshu zhiren" 刑部尚書致仕, 842), in *Quan Tang shi* 460.5235, and "On Sick Leave, Leisurely Gazing from the Southern Pavilion" ("Bingjia zhong nanting xianwang" 病假中南亭閒望), in *Quan Tang shi* 428.4714. The association of Vimalakīrti with his "ten-foot [dwelling]" (*fang zhang zhi shi* 方丈之室) seems to have become common in the sixth century. See, e.g., Xiao Gang's "Confession on the Six Faculties" ("Liugen chanwen" 六根懺文), in *Quan Liang wen* 14.7a.

73. "Responding to Monk Xian Who Came to Inquire Why I Suffer from a Wind Disorder" ("Da Xian shangren lai wen yinhe fengji" 答閑上人來問因何風疾), in *Quan Tang shi* 458.5198.

74. In the poem, Bai describes himself as "half walking around singing and drunk, half sitting in meditation" (半醉行歌半坐禪). See *Quan Tang shi* 454.5139–40.

216   *Chapter Four*

In "Giving Up Moxibustion" ("Ba jiu" 罷灸), another one of the "Fifteen Poems Written in Sickness," Bai Juyi adopts a different approach by envisioning Vimalakīrti almost as a close friend. He imagines this friend's words of warning—Vimalakīrti's speech about the similes of the body—and anticipates the sharp-witted householder's censure, as described in chapters 3 and 4 of the sutra, should Bai become too attached to a particular medical treatment. In Waley's free yet brilliant translation, the poem reads:

病身佛說將何喻	In Buddhist teachings what parable should guide me now that I am ill?
變滅須臾豈不聞	Have I not heard that the body in a trice changes and disappears?
莫遣淨名知我笑	Lest Vimalakīrti should look and laugh, I have given up my treatment;
4 休將火艾灸浮雲	What use to take fiery mugwort and cauterize a cloud?[75]

The second line of the poem already anticipates the simile—"This body is like a floating cloud, changing and disappearing in an instant" (是身如浮雲，須臾變滅)—that will be spelled out at the end of line 4. Here, Bai identifies not with the enlightened Vimalakīrti but with a floating cloud. Although this choice cannot really be called humble either, it acknowledges the vulnerability and impermanence of the poet's body and demonstrates the enlightened flexibility of Bai Juyi's self-image. By simultaneously presenting such diverse ideas about his own body and illnesses, he appears to be doing or even embodying what the *Vimalakīrti Sutra* does, shattering any dualistic views his readers might hold about him.

Four hundred years before Bai Juyi, Xie Lingyun, an admirer of the *Vimalakīrti Sutra*, first used the words "lying sick" in a poem, potentially paving the way for the emergence of a poetic space for illness. Though this space was initially explored rather hesitantly over the following century and a half, much of this hesitance dissipated during the Tang dynasty. In this period, illness increasingly became a poetic topic, openly acknowledged as an inevitable part of life.

75. *Quan Tang shi* 458.5198; Waley, *Life and Times of Po Chü-i*, 195.

Reflecting on the flourishing of sickbed poetry in the Tang dynasty and beyond, we might ask why it would matter that a new type of poem came into existence. While it may, at first sight, seem like a minor development in the history of Chinese literature, the creation of a recognized literary form to express thoughts, feelings, and anxieties about health and illness represents a major step in the ongoing quest for human self-expression and dialog.

The early medieval writers who originated this form used it in a somewhat limited way, mainly focusing on the gift of leisure time that minor illness can provide, allowing them to engage in activities that their official duties might preclude. This exuberance about a few days off should be understood in the context of literati concerns about overwork, as discussed in the first part of this book. However, from the early seventh century onward, the Tang successors of the early medieval writers fully realized the potential of the sickbed setting to foreground the body and its weaknesses and ailments, creating poems that allow readers to connect with their writers' physicality in an unprecedented way.

The early medieval encounter with Buddhist practices, ideas, and texts left a profusion of enduring traces on Chinese culture. Some of these traces are prominent and well-studied, such as the establishment of monastic culture (also beyond Buddhism) and the rise of new concepts about rebirth and the afterlife, along with their ethical implications for this life. These momentous developments affected various social, cultural, and intellectual spheres, from devotional practices and welfare politics to architecture and painting.

Significant as these broad strokes are, however, they do not constitute the whole historical picture, which for depth and intricacy also relies on an abundance of finer yet equally enduring lines. One such detail is the literary phenomenon discussed here: the Chinese establishment of a poetic subgenre, not invented but certainly influenced by a particular Buddhist sutra. As explored in the discussion of sickbed visits in early Chinese literature, the ground was well prepared for this development. The encounter with the *Vimalakīrti Sutra* helped to bring the personal experience of illness into Chinese poetry, sparking a literary tradition—sickbed poetry—that is not primarily dedicated to religious matters or discourses.

Remarkably, this process was not so much driven by the most import-

218   *Chapter Four*

ant doctrinal matters expounded in the *Vimalakīrti Sutra*, such as emptiness and nonduality, but rather by a literary feature of the text, the sickbed setting of its inner chapters, and by a recurring theme, our propensity to illness, which in the sutra itself plays an ancillary role in the exposition of fundamental doctrinal ideas. The case of the *Vimalakīrti Sutra's* influence on Chinese sickbed poetry thus illustrates how subtly and unobtrusively cultural influences can operate, extending well beyond the introduction of tropes and ideas. It also highlights how deeply embedded Buddhism had become in Chinese culture.

AFTERWORD

At year's end is there anything one can depend on?
Helter-skelter, grief and sickness come by turns.
Were it not for bath-leave, who could ever find relief?
How to preserve oneself has surely never been passed on.

—Shen Yue, "Companion Piece to a Poem by Left
Assistant Yu Gaozhi Requesting Sick Leave"[1]

In this book, I have taken my readers through a diverse array of literary texts from early medieval China. My aim was to explore how these texts address health and illness and how they weave these themes into their broader understanding of human existence, culture, and literature. As we have seen in the preceding pages, the interplay between individual, familial, and social experiences of health and illness shaped both lofty thought and down-to-earth politics in early medieval China. Not only are traces of this interdependence evident in a wider range of literary texts than we might have expected, but we have also seen that treating illness as a literary subject appears to have gained prominence throughout this period, even in high-register works of refined literature.

The couplets opening Shen Yue's companion piece to Yu Gaozhi's poem requesting sick leave encapsulate many of the themes explored in this book: the anxieties about maintaining creativity as writers and officials, as discussed in part 1; the varied forms of writing about personal health

---

1. Lu Qinli, *Xian Qin Han Wei Jin Nanbeichao shi*; Mather, *Age of Eternal Brilliance*, 1:9–10. The original text reads: 歲暮豈云聊 / 參差憂與疾 / 匪澣孰能賜 / 持身固無述.

220 Afterword

in correspondence and other autobiographical genres, examined in part II; and the struggle to accept illness as an intrinsic part of the human condition, and how to confront this challenge in life and poetry, as presented in part III. At the risk of reducing the many different voices cited in these pages, we shall finish with a summary of the book's main findings.

In part I, the close analysis and contextualization of the essay "Nurturing the Vital Breath" in Liu Xie's early sixth-century work *The Literary Mind and the Carving of Dragons* revealed the deep concern of early medieval writers with preserving and cultivating their literary creativity. For most of them, this creativity was inextricably linked to their social roles as officials in the government bureaucracy. Situating himself in the tradition of Wang Chong and Cao Pi, who wrote in the first and second centuries CE, Liu Xie located the root of literary creativity in the writer's body and its particular reservoir of vital energies. Rather than discussing health and illness in general terms, Liu took an occupational approach, addressing the specific challenges that early medieval writer-officials faced, especially overwork and excessive mental exertion, which he primarily blamed on misguided literary developments. Drawing on a Zhuangzian phrase, Liu Xie's advice to his fellow writers on how to "keep their blade like new" incorporated earlier Chinese notions of health and literary creativity found in canonical writings and works of Masters literature. Although primarily concerned with the workings of the mind, these works demonstrate beyond doubt that Chinese writers clearly understood themselves as living, thriving, aging, and often enough also suffering bodies.

Moving from the proclamation of apparently universal claims about health and illness expressed in Liu Xie's essay, part II turned to individual voices that had narrated their personal experiences of health and illness. We saw that writers of authorial prefaces, informal notes, formal letters, and official communications approached the depiction of their physical condition in ways that suited the rhetorical purposes of their texts. Whether legitimizing authorship (Sima Qian, Wang Chong, Cao Pi, Ge Hong, Yu He, Xiao Yi), maintaining close relationships with intimate friends or family members (Wang Xizhi, Tao Qian), or pleading illness to avoid office (Huangfu Mi, Shen Yue), these writers adapted their portrayals of health and illness to fit their needs. Health and illness can be obscured, as in Sima Qian's restrained accounts of his life after suffering corporal punishment in the second century BCE, or they can be flaunted, as in Cao Pi's early third-century account of himself as bursting with health and Shen Yue's early fifth-century memorial pleading illness and requesting retirement.

The analysis of Shen's memorial also revealed intriguing contradictions between a writer's physical health, as claimed in their writing, and the literary health of the texts themselves. The connection between illness and creativity also emerged in our discussions of Wang Xizhi's fourth-century letters and his calligraphic genius. The frequent claims of illness, whether based on actual ill health or as a pretext, in official or personal correspondence, can reflect the need of writers to carve out private space and leisure time—a concern that resonates with the anxieties about overwork later expressed by Liu Xie. Connecting Liu Xie's intent with Xiao Yi's surprising candor in divulging his physical challenges and mental distress in the middle of the sixth century highlights subtle changes in literary culture, suggesting that health and illness had become more accepted as part of an author's identity and public persona and that authors increasingly embraced these themes as subjects of refined literature.

In part III, this development was explored in greater detail by focusing on the emergence of sickbed poetry in early medieval China and beyond. While narratives about sickbed visits were already prevalent in early Chinese historical and Masters literature, the topic was only gradually adopted in poetry, the highest-register literary genre. Based on the surviving record, the early fifth-century poet Xie Lingyun may have played a vital role in establishing "lying sick" as a legitimate poetic theme, inspired by his immersion in Jian'an poetry and the *Vimalakīrti Sutra*, a Mahāyāna scripture set at a sickbed that discusses health and illness throughout the text.

In the works of Xie Lingyun and other early medieval poets, lying sick is often depicted as a gift of leisure, a time to read or to gather with friends—again connecting with Liu Xie's concerns and the practice of pleading illness. However, Tang dynasty poets took writing about lying sick in a different direction. Once the sickbed had been established as a poetic space in early medieval China, poems written "while lying sick" flourished during the Tang dynasty. In this period, poems dedicated to illness emerged in great numbers and different forms. Individual poets engaged more explicitly with their own illnesses and physical decline, often moving these matters from the margins of a poem—where they were usually relegated

222   Afterword

in early medieval poems—to its very center, thus fully realizing the poetic potential of this subgenre.

Despite the great variety and diversity of voices heard throughout this book, there is still much more to discover in the rich literary heritage of this period, whether in historical prose, poetry, or religious scriptures. Regarding early medieval—or more broadly, premodern—Chinese literature, the "unexploited mine" of writing about illness that Virginia Woolf identified a century ago has only begun to be explored. Health and illness are pervasive yet often overlooked topics that deserve to be made fully visible in Chinese studies, as well as for a wider audience in the health humanities and beyond.

It is my hope that scholars of Chinese literature, history, and religion will take up this line of inquiry, making new and varied discoveries beyond those I have introduced. Such work can bring us closer to a more comprehensive understanding of what it meant to be alive and well—or alive and unwell—in premodern China and what this understanding may imply for us as readers today. As we grapple with interpreting ancient literature and navigating the modern world, we need all the guidance we can get in the art of living.

ABBREVIATIONS

CSJC   *Congshu jicheng* 叢書集成

DZ   *Zhengtong Daozang* 正統道藏

SBBY   *Sibu beiyao* 四部備要

SSJ   *Shisanjing zhushu* 十三經注疏

T.   *Taishō shinshū Daizōkyō* 大正新修大藏經

BIBLIOGRAPHY

Allamand, Carole. "The Autobiographical Pact, Forty-Five Years Later." *European Journal of Life Writing* 7 (2018): 51–56.

Altman, Janet Gurkin (1945–2008). *Epistolarity: Approaches to a Form*. Columbus: Ohio State University Press, 1982.

Arbesmann, Rudolph. "The Concept of 'Christus Medicus' in St. Augustine." *Traditio* 10 (1954): 1–28.

Aronson, Jeffrey K. "Autopathography: The Patient's Tale." *British Medical Journal* 321 (2000): 1599–1602.

Avrahami, Einat. *The Invading Body: Reading Illness Autobiographies*. Charlottesville: University Press of Virginia, 2007.

Bai, Qianshen. "Illness, Disability, and Deformity in Seventeenth-Century Chinese Art." In *Body and Face in Chinese Visual Culture*, edited by Wu Hung and Katherine R. Tsiang, 147–70. Cambridge, MA: Harvard University Asia Center, 2005.

Baihutong shuzheng 白虎通疏證. Compiled by Chen Li 陳 (1809–1869). Beijing: Zhonghua shuju, 1994.

Baopuzi neipian jiaoshi 抱朴子外篇校釋. Compiled by Wang Ming 王明. Beijing: Zhonghua shuju, 1985.

Baopuzi waipian jiaojian 抱朴子外篇校箋. Compiled by Yang Mingzhao 楊明照. Beijing: Zhonghua shuju, 1996.

Bauer, Mikaël. "The Yuima-e as Theater of the State." *Japanese Journal of Religious Studies* 38 (2011): 161–79.

Bauer, Wolfgang (1930–1997). *Das Antlitz Chinas: Autobiographische Selbstdarstellungen in der chinesischen Literatur von ihren Anfängen bis heute*. Munich: Hanser, 1990.

———. "Krankheit und Heilung bei Lieh-tzu." In *Heilen und Schenken: Festschrift für Günther Klinge zum 70. Geburtstag*, edited by Herbert Franke and Walther Heissig, 1–11. Wiesbaden: Harrassowitz, 1980.

Bauman, Zygmunt. *Consuming Life*. Cambridge: Polity Press, 2007.

Beiji qianjin yaofang 備急千金要方 (652). Compiled by Sun Simiao 孫思邈 (581–682). Beijing: Renmin weisheng chubanshe, 1998.

Beitang shuchao 北堂書鈔. Compiled by Yu Shinan 虞世南 (558–638). Commentary by Kong Guangtao 孔廣陶. Taipei: Wenhai chubanshe, 1966.

226 *Bibliography*

Berg, Daria. *Perceptions of Lay Healers in Late Imperial China.* Durham, UK: Department of East Asian Studies, University of Durham, 2000.

Berkowitz, Alan J. (1950–2015). *Patterns of Disengagement: The Practice and Portrayal of Reclusion in Early Medieval China.* Stanford, CA: Stanford University Press, 2000.

Berry, Sarah L., Craig M. Klugman, Charise Alexander Adams, Anna-Leila Williams, Gina M. Camodeca, Tracy N. Leavelle, and Erin G. Lamb. "Health Humanities: A Baseline Survey of Baccalaureate and Graduate Programs in North America." *Journal of Medical Humanities* 44 (2023): 463–80.

Bian, He. "Too Sick to Serve: The Politics of Illness in the Qing Civil Bureaucracy." *Late Imperial China* 33, no. 2 (2012): 40–75.

"Bian zheng lun" 辯正論. Compiled by Falin 法琳 (572–640). In *T.* 2110.

Biggs, Robert D. "Medicine, Surgery, and Public Health in Ancient Mesopotamia." *Journal of Assyrian Academic Studies* 19, no. 1 (2005): 1–19.

Blair, Ann M. *Too Much to Know: Managing Scholarly Information before the Modern Age.* New Haven, CT: Yale University Press, 2010.

Blitstein, Pablo A. *Les fleurs du royaume : savoirs lettrés et pouvoir impérial en Chine, Ve– VIe siècles.* Paris: Les Belles lettres, 2015.

Bodman, Richard Wainwright (1947–2023). "Poetics and Prosody in Early Mediaeval China: A Study and Translation of Kūkai's *Bunkyō Hifuron.*" PhD diss., Cornell University, 1978.

Boyd, Kenneth M. "Disease, Illness, Sickness, Health, Healing and Wholeness: Exploring Some Elusive Concepts." *Medical Humanities* 26, no. 1 (2000): 9–17.

Brown, Miranda. *The Art of Medicine in Early China: The Ancient and Medieval Origins of a Modern Archive.* Cambridge: Cambridge University Press, 2015.

Byrne, Katherine. *Tuberculosis and the Victorian Literary Imagination.* Cambridge: Cambridge University Press, 2011.

Cahill, James. "The 'Madness' in Bada Shanren's Paintings." *Asian Cultural Studies* 17 (1989): 119–43.

Campany, Robert F. *Making Transcendents: Ascetics and Social Memory in Early Medieval China.* Honolulu: University of Hawai'i Press, 2009.

———. *Signs from the Unseen Realm: Buddhist Miracle Tales from Early Medieval China.* Honolulu: University of Hawai'i Press, 2012.

———. *To Live as Long as Heaven and Earth: A Translation and Study of Ge Hong's "Traditions of Divine Transcendents."* Berkeley: University of California Press, 2002.

Canguilhem, Georges (1904–1995). "Health: Crude Concept and Philosophical Question." Translated by Todd Meyers and Stefanos Geroulanos. *Public Culture* 20, no. 3 (2008): 467–77.

———. *The Normal and the Pathological.* Translated by Carolyn R. Fawcett, with an introduction by Michel Foucault. New York: Zone Books, 1991.

Carel, Havi, and Rachel Cooper, eds. *Health, Illness, and Disease: Philosophical Essays*. London: Routledge, 2014.

Carpenter, Bruce E. "A Seventeenth-Century Chinese Anthology of Letters." *Tezukayama University Review* 69 (1990): 176–90.

Celsus, Aulus Cornelius (25 BCE–50 CE). *Of Medicine*. Translated by James Greive. London: Wilson and Durham, 1756.

Chan mi yao fa jing 禪祕要法經. In *T*. 613.

Chan, Timothy Wai Keung. *Considering the End: Mortality in Early Medieval Chinese Poetic Representation*. Leiden: Brill, 2012.

Chang, Ch'ung-ho (張充和, 1914–2015), and Hans H. Frankel (1916–2003), trans. *Two Chinese Treatises on Calligraphy*. New Haven, CT: Yale University Press, 1995.

Chapman, Jesse. "Unwholesome Bodies: Reading the Sign of the Amputated Foot in Early China." *Asia Major* 30, no. 2 (2017): 1–26.

Charon, Rita. *Narrative Medicine: Honoring the Stories of Illness*. London: Oxford University Press, 2006.

Ch'en, Ch'i-yün (陳啟雲, 1933–2020), trans. *Hsün Yüeh and the Mind of Late Han China: A Translation of the "Shen-chien" with Introductions and Annotations*. Princeton, NJ: Princeton University Press, 1980.

Chen, Hsiu-fen. "Nourishing Life, Cultivation and Material Culture in the Late Ming: Some Thoughts on *Zunsheng bajian* 遵生八牋 (Eight Discourses on Respecting Life, 1591)." *Asian Medicine* 4 (2008): 29–45.

Chen, Jack. *Anecdote, Network, Gossip, Performance: Essays on the "Shishuo xinyu"*. Cambridge, MA: Harvard University Asia Center, 2021.

Chen Xiaolin 陳曉林. "Qiantan *Yanshi jiaxun* de yixue sixiang" 淺談顏氏家訓的醫學思想. *Zhongyiyao wenhua* 2 (2009): 23–25.

Cheng, Fung Kei, and Samson Tse. "Thematic Research on the *Vimalakīrti Nirdeśa Sūtra*: An Integrative Review." *Buddhist Studies Review* 31 (2014): 3–51.

Cheng Guiting 程桂婷. *Jibing dui Zhongguo xiandai zuojia chuangzuo de yingxiang yanjiu: Yi Lu Xun, Sun Li, Shi Tiesheng weili* 疾病對中國現代作家創作的影響研究: 以魯迅, 孫犁, 史鐵生為例. Beijing: Zhongguo shehui kexue chubanshe, 2015.

Chennault, Cynthia L. "Lofty Gates or Solitary Imprisonment? Xie Family Members of the Southern Dynasties." *T'oung Pao* 85 (1999): 249–327.

Chiang, Howard. *After Eunuchs: Science, Medicine, and the Transformation of Sex in Modern China*. New York: Columbia University Press, 2018.

Chidu xinchao 尺牘新鈔 (1662). Compiled by Zhou Lianggong 周亮工 (1612–1672). In *CSJC*.

Chiu, Martha Li. "Mind, Body, and Illness in a Chinese Medical Tradition." PhD diss., Harvard University, 1986.

Choy, Howard Y. F., ed. *Discourses of Disease: Writing Illness, the Mind and the Body in Modern China*. Leiden: Brill, 2016.

228 Bibliography

Chu ci buzhu 楚辭補注. Commentary by Wang Yi 王逸 (second century CE) and Hong Xingzu 洪興祖 (1090–1155). Beijing: Zhonghua shuju, 1983.

Chunqiu Gongyang zhuan zhushu 春秋公羊傳注疏. Commentary by He Xiu 何休 (d. 175) and Xu Yan 徐彥 (fl. late eighth and early ninth century). In *SSJ*.

Chunqiu Zuo zhuan zhengyi 春秋左傳正義. Commentary by Du Yu 杜預 (222–284) and Kong Yingda 孔穎達 (574–648). In *SSJ*.

Congshu jicheng 叢書集成. Shanghai: Commercial Press, 1935–1937.

Cook, Constance A. 2023. *Medicine and Healing in Ancient East Asia*. Cambridge: Cambridge University Press.

Cook, Kay. "Illness and Life Writing." In *Encyclopedia of Life Writing: Autobiographical and Biographical Forms*, edited by Margaretta Jolly, 456–58. Chicago: Fitzroy Dearborn, 2001.

Couser, G. Thomas. "Introduction: The Embodied Self." *a/b: Auto/Biography Studies* 6, no. 1 (1991): 1–7.

———. *Recovering Bodies: Illness, Disability, and Life Writing*. Madison: University of Wisconsin Press, 1997.

Csikszentmihalyi, Mark. "Allotment and Death in Early China." In *Mortality in Traditional Chinese Thought*, edited by Amy Olberding and Philip J. Ivanhoe, 177–90. Albany: State University of New York Press, 2011.

Csikszentmihalyi, Mark, and Michael Nylan. "Constructing Lineages and Inventing Traditions through Exemplary Figures in Early China." *T'oung Pao* 89 (2003): 59–99.

Cui Zhongtai 崔鍾太. "*Weimojie jing* de xiju ticai 維摩詰經的戲劇體裁." *Wenhua yishu yanjiu* 3 (2008): 78–79, 220.

Cullen, Christopher. "Patients and Healers in Late Imperial China: Evidence from the *Jinpingmei*." *History of Science* 31 (1993): 99–150.

Cunningham, Andrew. "Identifying Disease in the Past: Cutting the Gordian Knot." *Asclepio* 54, no. 1 (2002): 13–34.

Cutter, Robert Joe. "Letters and Memorials in the Early Third Century: The Case of Cao Zhi." In *A History of Chinese Letters and Epistolary Culture*, edited by Antje Richter, 307–30. Leiden: Brill, 2015.

———. "To the Manner Born? Nature and Nurture in Early Medieval Chinese Literary Thought." In *Culture and Power in the Reconstitution of the Chinese Realm, 200–600*, edited by Scott Pearce et al., 53–71. Cambridge, MA: Harvard University Asia Center, 2001.

Da banniepan jing 大般涅槃經. In *T.* 375.

Da Dai liji jinzhu jinyi 大戴禮記今註今譯. Commentary by Gao Ming 高明 (1909–1992). 3rd rev. ed. Taipei: Commercial Press, 1993.

Daode zhenjing yanyi shouchao 道德真經衍義手鈔. In *DZ* 717.

Dauncey, Sarah. *Disability in Contemporary China: Citizenship, Identity and Culture.* Cambridge: University of Cambridge Press, 2020.

Davis, A. R. (1924–1982). *T'ao Yüan-ming (AD 385–427): His Works and Their Meaning.* 2 vols. Cambridge: Cambridge University Press, 1983.

Declercq, Dominik. *Writing Against the State: Political Rhetorics in Third and Fourth Century China.* Leiden: Brill, 1998.

Demiéville, Paul (1894–1979). *Buddhism and Healing: Demiéville's Article "Byō" from "Hōbōgirin"* (1937). Translated by Mark Tatz. Lanham, MD: University Press of America, 1985.

———. "Vimalakīrti in China" (1962). Translated by Sara Boin-Webb. *Buddhist Studies Review* 21, no. 2 (2004): 179–96.

Deng Hanmei 鄧寒梅, ed. *Zhongguo xiandangdai wenxue zhong de jibing xushi yanjiu* 中國現當代文學中的疾病敘事研究. Nanchang: Jiangxi renmin chubanshe, 2012.

Despeux, Catherine, trans. *Prescriptions d'acuponcture valant mille onces d'or : traité d'acuponcture de Sun Simiao du VIIe siècle.* Paris: Guy Trédaniel, 1987.

Digital Dictionary of Buddhism. Edited by Charles A. Muller. 1995–. http://buddhism-dict.net/ddb/.

Dols, Michael W. *Majnūn: The Madman in Medieval Islamic Society,* edited by Diana E. Immisch. Oxford: Clarendon, 1992.

Dongguan Hanji jiaozhu 東觀漢記校注. Compiled by Wu Shuping 吳樹平. Zhengzhou: Zhongzhou guji chubanshe, 1987.

Donne, John (1572–1631). *Devotions upon Emergent Occasions,* London: Cambridge University Press, 1923.

Du, Heng. "The Author's Two Bodies: The Death of Qu Yuan and the Birth of *Chuci zhangju* 楚辭章句." In *Qu Yuan and the "Chuci": New Approaches,* edited by Martin Kern and Stephen Owen, 98–155. Leiden: Brill, 2024.

Dudbridge, Glen (1938–2017). *Lost Books of Medieval China.* London: British Library, 2000.

Duffy, Kay J. "The Third Day of the Third Month in Early Medieval China: Literary Composition as Ritualized Practice." PhD diss., Princeton University, 2019.

Durrant, Stephen W. *The Cloudy Mirror: Tension and Conflict in the Writings of Sima Qian.* Albany: State University of New York Press, 1995.

———. "Self as the Intersection of Traditions: The Autobiographical Writings of Ssu-ma Ch'ien." *Journal of the American Oriental Society* 106 (1986): 33–40.

Durrant, Stephen, Wai-Yee Li, Michael Nylan, and Hans van Ess. *The Letter to Ren An and Sima Qian's Legacy.* Seattle: University of Washington Press, 2016.

Durrant, Stephen, Wai-Yee Li, and David Schaberg, trans. *Zuo Tradition/Zuozhuan: Commentary on the "Spring and Autumn Annals."* Seattle: University of Washington Press, 2016.

Bibliography

Egan, Ronald C., trans. *Limited Views: Essays on Ideas and Letters by Qian Zhongshu*. Cambridge, MA: Harvard University Asia Center, 1998.

———. "Poet, Mind, and World: A Reconsideration of the 'Shensi' Chapter of *Wenxin diaolong*." In *A Chinese Literary Mind: Culture, Creativity, and Rhetoric in "Wenxin diaolong,"* edited by Zong-qi Cai, 101–26. Stanford, CA: Stanford University Press, 2001.

Elbaum, Alan. "'The Fire in My Heart and the Pain in My Eyes': Interdependence and Outburst in the Illness Letters of the Cairo Geniza." *Speculum* 98 (2022): 122–63.

Emeney, Johanna. *The Rise of Autobiographical Medical Poetry and the Medical Humanities*. Stuttgart: Ibidem, 2018.

Enenkel, Karl. "Epistolary Autobiography." In *Handbook of Autobiography/Autofiction*, edited by Martina Wagner-Egelhaaf, 565–78. Berlin: De Gruyter, 2019.

Eubanks, Charlotte. *Miracles of Book and Body: Buddhist Textual Culture and Medieval Japan*. Berkeley: University of California Press, 2011.

Fan Ka-Wai 范家偉. *Zhonggu shiqi de yizhe yu bingzhe* 中古時期的醫者與病者. Shanghai: Fudan daxue chubanshe, 2010.

Farmer, J. Michael. "Calling in Sick During the Reign of Gongsun Shu." *Journal of the American Oriental Society* 140 (2020): 81–94.

Fayuan zhulin 法苑珠林. In *T.* 2122.

Felbur, Rafal, trans. *Essays of Sengzhao (Taishō Volume 45, Number 1858)*. In *Three Short Treatises by Vasubandhu, Sengzhao, and Zongmi*, translated by John P. Keenan, Rafael Felbur, and Jan Yün-hua, 49–138. Moraga, CA: Bukkyō Dendō Kyōkai, 2017.

———. "*Vimalakīrtinirdeśa*." In *Brill's Encyclopedia of Buddhism*, vol. 1, edited by Jonathan A. Silk, 274–82. Leiden: Brill, 2015.

Ficino, Marsilio (1433–1499). *Three Books on Life: A Critical Edition and Translation with Introduction and Notes*. Translated by Carol V. Kaske and John R. Clark. Binghamton, NY: Center for Medieval and Early Renaissance Studies, State University of New York, 1989.

Fong, Grace S. "'Record of Past Karma' by Ji Xian (1614–1683)." In *Under Confucian Eyes: Writings on Gender in Chinese History*, edited by Susan Mann and Yu-yin Cheng, 135–46. Berkeley: University of California Press, 2001.

———. "Writing and Illness: A Feminine Condition in Women's Poetry of the Ming and Qing." In *The Inner Quarters and Beyond: Women Writers from Ming through Qing*, edited by Grace S. Fong and Ellen Widmer, 19–47. Leiden: Brill, 2010.

Forke, Alfred (1867–1944), trans. *Lun-hêng*. 2 vols. Leipzig: Harrassowitz, 1907 and 1911. Reprint, New York: Paragon, 1962.

Foucault, Michel (1926–1984). *The Birth of the Clinic: An Archaeology of Medical Perception*. Translated by A. M. Sheridan Smith. New York: Vintage, 1994.

Fung, Yu-Lan (1895–1990). *A History of Chinese Philosophy*. 2 vols. Translated by Derk Bodde. Princeton, NJ: Princeton University Press, 1952–53.

Frank, Arthur W. *The Wounded Storyteller: Body, Illness, and Ethics*. 2nd ed. Chicago: University of Chicago Press, 2013.

Frodsham, John David (1930–2016). *An Anthology of Chinese Verse: Han Wei Chin and the Northern and Southern Dynasties*. Oxford: Clarendon, 1967.

———. *The Murmuring Stream: The Life and Works of the Chinese Nature Poet Hsieh Ling-yün (385–433), Duke of K'ang-lo*. 2 vols. Kuala Lumpur: University of Malaya Press, 1967.

Fuehrer, Bernhard. "The Court Scribe's *Eikon Psyches*: A Note on Sima Qian and His Letter to Ren An." *Asian and African Studies* 6, no. 2 (1997): 170–83.

Gadamer, Hans Georg (1900–2002). "On the Enigmatic Character of Health." Translated by Jason Gaiger and Nicholas Walker. In *The Enigma of Health: The Art of Healing in a Scientific Age*, 103–16. Stanford, CA: Stanford University Press, 1996.

Galvany, Albert, and Romain Graziani. "Legal Mutilation and Moral Exclusion: Disputations on Integrity and Deformity in Early China." *T'oung Pao* 106 (2020): 8–55.

Gao Hao 高昊. "*Shanhaijing* 'Zhongshanjing' jibing jizai yanjiu" 山海經·中山經 疾病記載研究. MA thesis, Zhengzhou daxue, 2015.

Gardner, Daniel K., trans. *Learning to Be a Sage: Selections from the Conversations of Master Chu, Arranged Topically*. Berkeley: University of California Press, 1990.

Genette, Gérard (1930–2018). *Paratexts: Thresholds of Interpretation*. Translated by Jane E. Lewin. Cambridge: Cambridge University Press, 1997.

Giele, Enno. *Imperial Decision-Making and Communication in Early China: A Study of Cai Yong's "Duduan."* Wiesbaden: Harrassowitz, 2006.

Glauch, Sonja, and Katharina Philipowski. "Vorarbeiten zur Literaturgeschichte und Systematik vormodernen Ich-Erzählens." In *Von sich selbst erzählen: Historische Dimensionen des Ich-Erzählens*, 1–61. Heidelberg: Universitätsverlag Winter, 2017.

Goellnicht, Donald C. *The Poet-Physician: Keats and Medical Science*. Pittsburgh: University of Pittsburgh Press, 1984.

Goldschmidt, Asaf. *Medical Practice in Twelfth-Century China: A Translation of Xu Shuwei's Ninety Discussions [Cases] on Cold Damage Disorders*. Berlin: Springer, 2019.

Gómez, Luis O. (1943–2017). "On Buddhist Wonders and Wonder-Working." *Journal of the International Association of Buddhist Studies* 33 (2010/2011): 513–54.

Gómez, Luis, and Paul Harrison, trans. *Vimalakīrtinirdeśa—The Teaching of Vimalakīrti: An English Translation of the Sanskrit Text Found in the Potala Palace, Lhasa*. Berkeley, CA: Mangalam Press, 2022.

Bibliography

Gong Ailing 宫愛玲. *Shenmei de jiushu: Xiandai Zhongguo wenxue jibing xushi shixue yanjiu* 審美的救贖：現代中國文學疾病敘事詩學研究. Jinan: Shandong jiaoyu chubanshe, 2014.

Graham, Angus C. (1919–1991), trans. *The Book of Lieh-tzu*. London: Murray, 1960.

———, trans. *Chuang-tzu: The Seven Inner Chapters and Other Writings from the Book Chuang-tzu*. London: Allen and Unwin, 1981. Reprint, Indianapolis: Hackett, 2001.

Greene, Eric M. *Chan Before Chan: Meditation, Repentance, and Visionary Experience in Chinese Buddhism*. Honolulu: University of Hawai'i Press, 2021.

———. *The Secrets of Buddhist Meditation: Visionary Meditation Texts from Early Medieval China*. Honolulu: University of Hawai'i Press, 2021.

Groner, Paul. *Ryōgen and Mount Hiei: Japanese Tendai in the Tenth Century*. Honolulu: University of Hawai'i Press, 2002.

Guang Hongming ji 廣弘明集. Compiled by Daoxuan 道宣 (596–667). In *T*. 2103.

Guanzi jinzhu jinyi 管子今註今譯. Commentary by Li Mian 李勉 (1919–2015). Taipei: Commercial Press, 1990.

Guo, Liping. "An Overview of Narrative Medicine in China." *Chinese Medicine and Culture* 6, no. 2 (2023): 205–12.

Hamilton, Sue. "From the Buddha to Buddhaghosa: Changing Attitudes toward the Human Body in Theravāda Buddhism." In *Religious Reflections on the Human Body*, edited by Jane M. Law, 46–63. Bloomington: Indiana University Press, 1995.

Hamlin, Edward. "Magical *upāya* in the *Vimalakīrtinirdeśa-sūtra*." *Journal of the International Association of Buddhist Studies* 11 (1988): 89–121.

Han shu 漢書. Compiled by Ban Gu 班固 (32–92). Beijing: Zhonghua shuju, 1962.

Hanfeizi jishi 韓非子集釋. Commentary by Chen Qiyou 陳奇猷 (1917–2006). Shanghai: Shanghai renmin chubanshe, 1958.

Hanson, Marta. "Narrative Medicine in China and Chinese Sources for Narrative Medicine." *Chinese Medicine and Culture* 6, no. 2 (2023): 125–26.

Hanyu da cidian 漢語大詞典. Shanghai: Cishu chubanshe, 1991.

Harper, Donald. "The Conception of Illness in Early Chinese Medicine, as Documented in Newly Discovered 3rd and 2nd Century B.C. Manuscripts (Part 1)." *Sudhoffs Archiv* 74, no. 2 (1990): 210–35.

———. *Early Chinese Medical Literature: The Mawangdui Medical Manuscripts*. London: Kegan Paul, 1997.

Harrist, Robert E., Jr. "Reading Chinese Calligraphy." In *The Embodied Image: Chinese Calligraphy from the John B. Elliott Collection*, edited by Robert E. Harrist and Wen C. Fong, 2–29. Princeton, NJ: Art Museum, Princeton University, 1999.

Bibliography   233

Hausman, Daniel M. "Health and Well-Being." In *The Routledge Companion to Philosophy of Medicine*, edited by Miriam Solomon, Jeremy R. Simon, and Harold Kincaid, 27–35. New York: Routledge, 2017.

Hawkes, David (1923–2009), trans. *The Songs of the South: An Ancient Chinese Anthology of Poems*. Harmondsworth, Middlesex: Penguin, 1985.

Hawkins, Ann Hunsaker, and Marilyn Chandler McEntyre, eds. *Teaching Literature and Medicine*. New York: Modern Language Association of America, 2000.

Hay, John. "The Human Body as a Microcosmic Source of Macrocosmic Values in Calligraphy." In *Theories of the Arts in China*, edited by Susan Bush and Christian Murck, 74–102. Princeton, NJ: Princeton University Press, 1983.

He Jianping 何劍平. *Zhongguo zhonggu Weimojie xinyang yanjiu* 中國中古維摩詰信仰研究. Chengdu: Ba Shu shushe, 2009.

Heinrich, Ari Larissa. *The Afterlife of Images: Translating the Pathological Body Between China and the West*. Durham, NC: Duke University Press, 2008.

Henricks, Robert G. *Philosophy and Argumentation in Third-Century China: The Essays of Hsi K'ang*. Princeton, NJ: Princeton University Press, 1983.

Hightower, James R. (1915–2006), trans. "Letter to His Sons," by Tao Qian. *Renditions* 41–42 (1994): 15–17.

Hoeckelmann, Michael. "To Rot and Not to Die: Punitive Emasculation in Early and Medieval China." *T'oung Pao* 105 (2019): 1–42.

Hofmann, Bjørn. "Disease, Illness, and Sickness." In *The Routledge Companion to Philosophy of Medicine*, edited by Miriam Solomon, Jeremy R. Simon, and Harold Kincaid, 16–26. New York: Routledge, 2017.

Hou Han shu 後漢書. Compiled by Fan Ye 范曄 (398–446). Beijing: Zhonghua shuju, 1965.

Hu-Sterk, Florence. "Maladie et poésie sous les Tang." *Études chinoises* 24 (1995): 55–94.

Huang Baosheng 黃寶生. *Fan Han duikan "Weimojie suo shuo jing"* 梵漢對勘維摩詰所說經. Beijing: Zhongguo shehui kexue chubanshe, 2011.

Huangdi neijing Lingshu yijie 黃帝內經靈樞譯解. Compiled by Yang Weijie 楊維傑. Taipei: Tailian guofeng chubanshe, 1984.

Huangdi neijing Suwen yijie 黃帝內經素問譯解. Compiled by Yang Weijie 楊維傑. Taipei: Lequn chuban gongsi, 1977.

Huangdi zhenjiu jiayi jing 黃帝針灸甲乙經. In *Zhongyi shida jingdian quanlu* 中醫十大經典全祿, edited by Chen Zhenxiang 陳振相 and Song Guimei 宋貴美. Beijing: Xueyuan chubanshe, 1995.

Hubbard, J., trans. *Expository Commentary on the Vimalakīrti Sutra* (*Taishō Volume 56, Number 2186*). Berkeley: Bukkyō Dendō Kyōkai America, 2012.

Hucker, Charles O. (1919–1994). *A Dictionary of Official Titles in Imperial China*. Stanford, CA: Stanford University Press, 1985.

234 Bibliography

Idema, Wilt L. "Diseases and Doctors, Drugs and Cures: A Very Preliminary List of Passages of Medical Interest in a Number of Traditional Chinese Novels and Related Plays." *Chinese Science* 2 (1977): 37–63.

Illich, Ivan (1926–2002). *Medical Nemesis: The Expropriation of Health*. New York: Pantheon Books, 1976.

Ivanhoe, Philip J. "Death and Dying in the *Analects*." In *Mortality in Traditional Chinese Thought*, edited by Amy Olberding and Philip J. Ivanhoe, 137–51. Albany: State University of New York Press, 2011.

Jaspers, Karl (1883–1969). *Allgemeine Psychopathologie*. 8th ed. Berlin: Springer, 1965.

Jiao Peimin 焦培民, Liu Chunyu 劉春雨, and He Yuxin 賀予新. *Zhongguo zaihai tongshi: Qin Han juan* 中國災害通史：秦漢卷. Zhengzhou: Zhengzhou daxue chubanshe, 2009.

Jin shu 晉書. Beijing: Zhonghua shuju, 1974.

Jingming xuan lun 淨名玄論. Compiled by Jizang 吉藏 (549–623). In *T*. 1780.

Jingui yaolüe 金匱要略. Compiled by Li Keguang 李克光. Taipei: Zhiyin chubanshe, 1990.

Jinlouzi jiaojian 金樓子校箋. Compiled by Xu Yimin 許逸民. Beijing: Zhonghua shuju, 2011.

Jinlouzi shuzheng jiaozhu 金樓子疏證校注. Compiled by Chen Zhiping 陳志平 and Xiong Qingyuan 熊清元. Shanghai: Shanghai guji, 2014.

Jones, Charles B. *Chinese Pure Land Buddhism: Understanding a Tradition of Practice*. Honolulu: University of Hawai'i Press, 2019.

Jurecic, Ann. *Illness as Narrative*. Pittsburgh: University of Pittsburgh Press, 2012.

Kawaguchi, Ekai 河口慧海 (1866–1945), trans. *Kan Zō taishō kokuyaku Yuimagyō* 漢藏對照國譯維摩經. Tokyo: Sekai bunko kankōkai, 1928.

Keightley, David N. (1932–2017). "The 'Science' of the Ancestors: Divination, Curing, and Bronze-Casting in Late Shang China." *Asia Major* 14, no. 2 (2001): 143–87.

Kleinman, Arthur. *The Illness Narratives: Suffering, Healing, and the Human Condition*. New York: Basic Books, 1988.

Knapp, Keith N. "Heaven and Death According to Huangfu Mi, a Third Century Confucian." *Early Medieval China* 6 (2000): 1–31.

———. *Selfless Offspring: Filial Children and Social Order in Medieval China*. Honolulu: University of Hawai'i Press, 2005.

Knechtges, David R. *The Han Shu Biography of Yang Xiong (53 B.C.–A.D. 18)*. Tempe: Center for Asian Studies, Arizona State University, 1982.

———. "'Key Words,' Authorial Intent, and Interpretation: Sima Qian's Letter to Ren An." *Chinese Literature: Essays, Articles, Reviews (CLEAR)* 30 (2008): 75–84.

Knechtges, David R., and Taiping Chang, eds. *Ancient and Early Medieval Chinese Literature: A Reference Guide.* Vol. 2. Leiden: Brill, 2014.

Knechtges, David R., and Jerry Swanson. "Seven Stimuli for the Prince: The *Ch'i-fa* of Mei Ch'eng." *Monumenta Serica* 29 (1970/1971): 99–116.

Knight, D. Sabina. "Cancer's Revelations: Malignancies and Therapies in a Recent Chinese Novel." *Literature and Medicine* 28 (2009): 351–70.

Knoblock, John (1937–2018), trans. *Xunzi: A Translation and Study of the Complete Works.* 3 vols. Stanford: Stanford University Press, 1988, 1990, 1994.

Knoblock, John, and Jeffrey Riegel, trans. *The Annals of Lü Buwei.* Stanford, CA: Stanford University Press, 2000.

Kohn, Livia. *A Source Book in Chinese Longevity.* St. Petersburg, FL: Three Pines Press, 2012.

Korolkov, Maxim. "'Greeting Tablets' in Early China: Some Traits of the Communicative Etiquette or Officialdom in Light of Newly Excavated Inscriptions." *T'oung Pao* 98 (2012): 295–348.

Kroll, Paul W. "Aid and Comfort: Lu Zhaolin's Letters." In *A History of Chinese Letters and Epistolary Culture,* edited by Antje Richter, 829–52. Leiden: Brill, 2015.

———. "Literary Criticism and Personal Character in Poetry ca. 100–300 CE." In *China's Early Empires,* edited by Michael Nylan and Michael Loewe, 517–33. Cambridge: Cambridge University Press, 2010.

———. "The Memories of Lu Chao-lin." *Journal of the American Oriental Society* 109 (1989): 581–92.

———. "On Political and Personal Fate: Three Selections from Jiang Yan's Prose and Verse." In *Memory in Medieval China: Text, Ritual, and Community,* edited by Wendy Swartz and Robert Ford Campany, 388–404. Leiden: Brill, 2018.

Kümmel, Werner Friedrich. "Der Homo litteratus und die Kunst, gesund zu leben: Zur Entfaltung eines Zweiges der Diätätik im Humanismus." In *Humanismus und Medizin,* edited by Rudolf Schmitz and Gundolf Keil, 67–85. Weinheim: Acta humaniora, 1984.

Kuriyama, Shigehisa. "Epidemics, Weather, and Contagion in Traditional Chinese Medicine." In *Contagion: Perspectives from Pre-modern Societies,* edited by Lawrence I. Conrad and Dominik Wujastyk, 3–22. Aldershot: Ashgate, 2000.

LaFleur, William R. (1926–2010). *The Karma of Words: Buddhism and the Literary Arts in Medieval Japan.* University of California Press: Berkeley, 1983.

Lai, Chi-tim. "The Ideas of Illness, Healing, and Morality in Early Heavenly Masters Daoism." In *Philosophy and Religion in Early Medieval China,* edited by Alan K. L. Chan and Yuet-keung Lo, 173–201. Albany: State University of New York Press, 2010.

236 *Bibliography*

Lamotte, Etienne (1903–1983). *The Teaching of Vimalakīrti (Vimalakīrtinirdeśa): From the French Translation with Introduction and Notes (L'Enseignement de Vimalakīrti)* (1962). Translated by Sara Boin. London: Pali Text Society, 1976.

Laozi jiaoshi 老子校釋. Compiled by Zhu Qianzhi 朱謙之 (1899–1972). Beijing: Zhonghua shuju, 1984.

Lau, D. C. (1921–2010), trans. *Confucius: The Analects*. Hong Kong: Chinese University Press, 1992.

Lawlor, Clark. *Consumption and Literature: The Making of the Romantic Disease*. New York: Palgrave Macmillan, 2007.

Ledderose, Lothar. *Mi Fu and the Classical Tradition in Chinese Calligraphy*. Princeton, NJ: Princeton University Press, 1979.

Legge, James (1815–1897), trans. *The Chinese Classics*. 7 vols. London: Trübner, 1861–1872.

Lejeune, Philippe. *On Autobiography*. Edited by Paul John Eakin. Translated by Katherine Leary. Minneapolis: University of Minnesota Press, 1989.

———. "From Autobiography to Life-Writing, from Academia to Association: A Scholar's Story." Translated by Marie-Danielle Leruez. Plenary Lecture at the 58th Annual Kentucky Foreign Language Conference, April 22, 2005. https://www.autopacte.org/From%20Academy%20to%20Association.html.

Levy, Dore J. *Ideal and Actual in "The Story of the Stone."* New York: Columbia University Press, 1999.

———. "'Why Bao-yu Can't Concentrate': Attention Deficit Disorder in *The Story of the Stone*." *Literature and Medicine* 13 (1994): 255–73.

Li Hao 李浩. "Tao Yuanming shengping yu chuangzuo xinzheng: Jiyu 'shehui yiliao shi' shijiao de kaocha" 陶淵明生平与創作新證：基於"社會醫療史"視角的考察. *Shehui kexue luntan* 10 (2016): 52–65.

Li Jianmin 李建民. *Shengming shixue: Cong yiliao kan Zhongguo lishi* 生命史學：從醫療看中國歷史. Taipei: Sanmin shuju, 2005.

———. "They Shall Expel Demons: Etiology, the Medical Canon, and the Transformation of Medical Techniques before the Tang." In *Early Chinese Religion Part One: Shang Through Han (1250 BC–220 AD)*, edited by John Lagerwey and Marc Kalinowski, vol. 2, 1103–50. Leiden: Brill, 2010.

——— 李建民. "Zhongguo yixue shi yanjiu de xin shiye" 中國醫學史研究的新視野. *Xin shixue* 15, no. 3 (2004): 203–25.

Li Ling 李零. *Sang jia gou: Wo du "Lunyu"* 喪家狗：我讀論語. Taiyuan: Shanxi renmin chubanshe, 2007.

Li, Wai-yee. "Between 'Literary Mind' and 'Carving Dragons': Order and Excess in *Wenxin diaolong*." In *A Chinese Literary Mind: Culture, Creativity, and Rhetoric in "Wenxin diaolong,"* edited by Zong-qi Cai, 193–223. Stanford, CA: Stanford University Press, 2001.

———. "*Chi* 癡, *pi* 癖, *shi* 嗜, *hao* 好: Genealogies of Obsession in Chinese Literature." In *China and the World, the World and China: A Transcultural*

Perspective, vol. 1, edited by Barbara Mittler, Joachim Gentz, Natascha Gentz, and Catherine Vance Yeh, 213–31. Gossenberg: Ostasien Verlag, 2019.

Li Zong-kun 李宗焜. "Cong jiaguwen kan Shangdai de jibing yu yiliao" 從甲骨文看商代的疾病與醫療. *Zhongyang yanjiuyuan lishi yuyan yanjiusuo jikan* 72, no. 2 (2001): 339–91.

Liang shu 梁書. Beijing: Zhonghua shuju, 1973.

Liebenthal, Walter (1886–1982), trans. *The Book of Chao*. Peiping: Catholic University Press, 1948.

Liezi jishi 列子集釋. Compiled by Yang Bojun 楊伯峻 (1909–1992). Beijing: Zhonghua shuju, 1991.

Liji zhengyi 禮記正義. Commentary by Zheng Xuan 鄭玄 (127–200) and Kong Yingda 孔穎達 (574–648). In *SSJ*.

Lin Xiurong 林秀蓉, ed. *Zhong shen xian ying: Taiwan xiaoshuo jibing xushi yihan zhi tanjiu (1929–2000)* 眾身顯影：臺灣小說疾病敘事意涵之探究 (1929–2000). Gaoxiong: Chunhui chubanshe, 2013.

Liu Yuan-ju 劉苑如, Lo Pei-Hsuan 羅珮瑄, and Chiu Wan-Chun 邱琬淳. "Lidai sengzhuan jibing xushu de shuwei yanjiu: Cong sengren shoukao tanqi" 歷代僧傳疾病敘述的數位研究：從僧人壽考談起. *Zhongguo wenzhe yanjiu jikan* 30, no. 2 (2020): 5–29.

Lloyd, Geoffrey, and Nathan Sivin. *The Way and the Word: Science and Medicine in Early China and Greece*. New Haven, CT: Yale University Press, 2002.

Lo, Vivienne. "Self-Cultivation and the Popular Medical Traditions." In *Medieval Chinese Medicine: The Dunhuang Medical Manuscripts*, edited by Christopher Cullen and Vivienne Lo, 207–26. London: RoutledgeCurzon, 2005.

Lu Qinli 逯欽立, ed. *Xian Qin Han Wei Jin Nanbeichao shi* 先秦漢魏晉南北朝詩. Beijing: Zhonghua shuju, 1983.

Luhn, Clara. *Von Briefen und Kompilatoren: Zur Einbindung von Texten des Genres shu in Geschichts- und Sammelwerken*. Lun wen, vol. 26. Wiesbaden: Harrassowitz, 2022.

Lunheng jiaoshi 論衡校釋. Compiled by Wang Chong 王充 (27–ca. 100). Commentary by Huang Hui 黃暉. Beijing: Zhonghua shuju, 1990.

Lunyu zhushu 論語注疏. Commentary by He Yan 何晏 (190–249) and Xing Bing 邢昺 (931–1010). In *SSJ*.

Lushan ji 廬山記. Compiled by Chen Shunyu 陳舜俞 (d. 1074). In *T*. 2095.

Lüshi chunqiu 呂氏春秋. Commentary by Chen Qiyou 陳奇猷. Shanghai: Shanghai guji chubanshe, 2002.

Lynn, Richard John, trans. *The Classic of Changes: A New Translation of the I Ching as Interpreted by Wang Bi*. New York: Columbia University Press, 1994.

Ma Boying 馬伯英. *Zhongguo yixue wenhua shi* 中國醫學文化史. Shanghai: Renmin chubanshe, 1994.

Mann, Thomas (1875–1955). *Lotte in Weimar*. Berlin: Aufbau-Verlag, 1982.

Mao shi zhengyi 毛詩正義. Commentary by Mao Gong 毛公 (second century BCE), Zheng Xuan 鄭玄 (127–200), and Kong Yingda 孔穎達 (574–648). In *SSJ*.

Mather, Richard B. (1913–2014), trans. *The Age of Eternal Brilliance: Three Poets of the Yung-ming-Era*. 2 vols. Leiden: Brill, 2003.

———. "Hsieh T'iao's 'Poetic Essay Requiting a Kindness' (*Ch'ou-te fu*)." *Journal of the American Oriental Society* 110 (1990): 603–15.

———. "The Landscape Buddhism of the Fifth-Century Poet Hsieh Ling-yün." *Journal of Asian Studies* 18 (1958): 67–79.

———. *The Poet Shen Yüeh (441–513): The Reticent Marquis*. Princeton, NJ: Princeton University Press, 1988.

———, trans. *Shih-shuo hsin-yü: A New Account of Tales of the World*. 2nd ed. Ann Arbor: Center for Chinese Studies, University of Michigan, 2002.

———. "Vimalakīrti and Gentry Buddhism." *History of Religions* 8 (1968): 60–73.

McRae, John R. (1947–2011). *The Vimalakīrti Sutra*. In *The Sutra of Queen Śrīmālā of the Lion's Roar: The Vimalakīrti Sutra*, translated by Diana Y. Paul and John R. McRae, 55–181. Berkeley, CA: Numata Center for Buddhist Translation and Research, 2004.

Mengzi zhushu 孟子注疏. Commentary by Zhao Qi 趙岐 (d. 201) and Sun Shi 孫奭 (962–1033). In *SSJ*.

Metz, Bernhard. "Bibliomania and the Folly of Reading." *Comparative Critical Studies* 5, nos. 2–3 (2008): 249–69.

Miaofa lianhua jing 妙法蓮華經. In *T.* 262.

Milburn, Olivia. "Disability in Ancient China." In *Disability in Antiquity*, edited by Christian Laes, 106–18. New York: Routledge, 2016.

———. "Marked Out for Greatness? Perceptions of Deformity and Physical Impairment in Ancient China." *Monumenta Serica* 55 (2007): 1–22.

Moretti, Costantino. "The 'Eight Sufferings' and the Medical Metaphor in the *Sūtra of the Five Kings*." *Études chinoises* 34 (2015): 73–104.

Morino, Shigeo 森野繁夫, and Satō Toshiyuki 佐藤利行, trans. *Ō Gishi zen shokan* 王義之全書翰. 2nd ed. Tokyo: Hakuteisha, 1996.

Mrozik, Suzanne. *Virtuous Bodies: The Physical Dimension of Morality in Buddhist Ethics*. Oxford: Oxford University Press, 2007.

Nagao, Gadjin Masato 長尾雅人 (1907–2005). "On the Theory of Buddha Body (*Buddha-kāya*)." Translated by Hirano Umeyo. *The Eastern Buddhist* 6, no. 1 (1973): 25–53.

Nagel-Angermann, Monique. "Das *Diwang shiji* des Huangfu Mi (215–282)." PhD diss., University of Münster, 1999.

Nan Qi shu 南齊書. Beijing: Zhonghua shuju, 1972.

Nan shi 南史. Beijing: Zhonghua shuju, 1975.

Nattier, Jan. "*The Teaching of Vimalakīrti (Vimalakīrtinirdésa)*: A Review of Four English Translations." *Buddhist Literature* 2 (2000): 234–58.

Needham, Joseph (1900–1995). *Clerks and Craftsmen in China and the West.* Cambridge: Cambridge University Press, 1970.

Nelson, Susan E. "The Bridge at Tiger Brook: Tao Qian and the Three Teachings in Chinese Art." *Monumenta Serica* 50 (2002): 257–94.

———. "Catching Sight of South Mountain: Tao Yuanming, Mount Lu, and the Iconographies of Escape." *Archives of Asian Art* 51 (2000): 11–43.

———. "Revisiting the Eastern Fence: Tao Qian's Chrysanthemums." *The Art Bulletin* 83, no. 3 (2001): 437–60.

Nicolson, Marjorie (1894–1981), and G. S. Rousseau. *"This Long Disease, My Life": Alexander Pope and the Sciences.* Princeton, NJ: Princeton University Press, 1968.

Nugent, Christopher M. B. "Literary Media: Writing and Orality." In *The Oxford Handbook of Classical Chinese Literature (1000 BCE–900 CE)*, edited by Wiebke Denecke, Wai-Yee Li, and Xiaofei Tian, 46–60. Oxford: Oxford University Press, 2017.

Nunn, John Francis. 1996. *Ancient Egyptian Medicine.* Norman: University of Oklahoma Press, 1996.

Nylan, Michael. "Calligraphy, the Sacred Text and Test of Culture." In *Character and Context in Chinese Calligraphy*, edited by Cary Y. Liu, Dora C. Y. Ching, and Judith G. Smith, 16–77. Princeton, NJ: Art Museum, Princeton University, 1999.

———. *Yang Xiong and the Pleasures of Reading and Classical Learning in China.* New Haven, CT: American Oriental Society, 2011.

O'Malley, C. D. (1907–1970). "Jacobus Sylvius' Advice for Poor Medical Students." *Journal of the History of Medicine and Allied Sciences* 17, no. 1 (1962): 141–51.

Orsborn, Matthew (Shi Huifeng 釋慧峰). "Vimalakīrti's Aporia: Chiasmus & Apophasis in the *Vimalakīrtinirdeśa*." *Foguang xuebao* 2, no. 1 (2016): 199–264.

Ortiz de Montellano, Bernard R. "Disease, Illness, and Curing." In *Archaeology of Ancient Mexico and Central America: An Encyclopedia*, edited by Susan Toby Evans and David L. Webster, 215–20. New York: Garland, 2001.

Owen, Stephen, trans. *An Anthology of Chinese Literature: Beginnings to 1911.* New York: Norton, 1996.

———. *The End of the Chinese "Middle Ages": Essays in Mid-Tang Literary Culture.* Stanford, CA: Stanford University Press, 1996.

———. *The Making of Early Chinese Classical Poetry.* Cambridge, MA: Harvard University Press, 2006.

———. *Readings in Chinese Literary Thought.* Cambridge, MA: Council on East Asian Studies, Harvard University, 1992.

240   *Bibliography*

———. "The Self's Perfect Mirror: Poetry as Autobiography." In *The Vitality of the Lyric Voice: Shih Poetry from the Late Han to the T'ang*, edited by Lin Shuen-fu and Stephen Owen, 71–85. Princeton, NJ: Princeton University Press, 1986.

———. "Spending Time on Poetry: The Poetics of Taking Pains." In *Recarving the Dragon: Understanding Chinese Poetics*, edited by Olga Lomová, 157–78. Prague: Charles University and Karolinum Press, 2003.

Pan, An-Yi. *Painting Faith: Li Gonglin and Northern Song Buddhist Culture*. Leiden: Brill, 2007.

Peterson, Willard J. "Ssu-ma Ch'ien as Cultural Historian." In *The Power of Culture: Studies in Chinese Cultural History*, edited by Willard J. Peterson, Andrew W. Plaks, and Ying-shih Yü, 70–79. Hong Kong: Chinese University Press, 1994.

Petrarch's Remedies for Fortune Fair and Foul: A Modern English Translation of "De Remediis Utriusque Fortune". Vol. 1. Translated by Conrad H. Rawski. Bloomington: Indiana University Press, 1991.

Pitner, Mark G. "Stuttered Speech and Moral Intent: Disability and Elite Identity Construction in Early Imperial China." *Journal of the American Oriental Society* 137 (2017): 699–717.

Pokora, Timoteus (1928–1985). *Hsin-lun (New Treatise) and Other Writings by Huan T'an (43 B.C.–28 A.D.)*. Ann Arbor: Center for Chinese Studies, University of Michigan, 1975.

Pollard, David (1937–2024). "Ch'i in Chinese Literary Theory." In *Chinese Approaches to Literature from Confucius to Liang Ch'i-ch'ao*, edited by Adele Rickett, 43–66. Princeton, NJ: Princeton University Press, 1978.

Porter, Roy (1946–2002). "History of the Body Reconsidered." In *New Perspectives on Historical Writing*, 2nd ed., edited by Peter Burke, 233–60. University Park: Pennsylvania State University Press, 2001.

———. "The Patient's View: Doing Medical History from Below." *Theory and Society* 14, no. 2 (1985): 175–98.

Pregadio, Fabrizio, ed. *The Encyclopedia of Taoism*. London: Routledge, 2008.

Pritzker, Sonya. "Thinking Hearts, Feeling Brains: Metaphor, Culture, and the Self in Chinese Narratives of Depression." *Metaphor and Symbol* 22, no. 3 (2007): 251–74.

Pye, Michael. *Skilful Means: A Concept in Mahayana Buddhism*. London: Duckworth, 1978.

Qi Gong 啓功. "Pingfu tie shuo bing shiwen" 平復帖說並釋文. In *Zhongguo shufa quanji* 中國書法全集, vol. 20, edited by Liu Zhengcheng 劉正成, 18–20, 328. Beijing: Rongbaozhai, 1997.

Qi Liangde 戚良德. *Wenxin diaolong xue fenlei suoyin: 1907–2005* 文心雕龍學分類索引. Shanghai: Shanghai guji chubanshe, 2005.

Qi Xiaochun 祁小春. *Mai shi zhi feng: You guan Wang Xizhi ziliao yu renwu de zonghe yanjiu* 邁世之風：有關王羲之資料與人物的綜合研究. Taipei: Shitou chuban, 2007.

Qian Hanji 前漢紀. Compiled by Xun Yue 荀悅 (148–209). Taipei: Taiwan shangwu yinshuguan, 1971.

Qian Zhongshu 錢鍾書 (1910–1999). *Guanzhui bian* 管錐編. Beijing: Zhonghua shuju, 1986.

Qu Bingrui 曲柄睿 and Li Yang 李陽. "Qin Han tanbing de zhengzhi wenhua neihan" 秦漢探病的政治文化内涵. *Shixue yuekan* 7 (2012): 18–28.

Quan shanggu Sandai Qin Han Sanguo Liuchao wen 全上古三代秦漢三國六朝文, compiled by Yan Kejun 嚴可均 (1762–1843). Beijing: Zhonghua shuju, 1958.

Quan Tang shi 全唐詩. Beijing: Zhonghua shuju, 1979.

Quan Tang wen 全唐文. Beijing: Zhonghua shuju, 1983.

Radich, Michael. "Problems and Opportunities in the Study of the Bodies of the Buddha." *New Zealand Journal of Asian Studies* 9, no. 1 (2007): 46–69.

Richter, Antje. "Beyond Calligraphy: Reading Wang Xizhi's Letters." *T'oung Pao* 96 (2011): 370–407.

———. *Das Bild des Schlafes in der altchinesischen Literatur*. Hamburg: Hamburger Sinologische Gesellschaft, 2001. Reprint, Gossenberg: Ostasien Verlag, 2015.

———. "Empty Dreams and Other Omissions: Liu Xie's *Wenxin diaolong* Preface." *Asia Major* 25, no. 1 (2012): 83–110.

———. "Four Gates, Eight Poets, Sixteen Poems: Dependent Co-Authoring in Early Medieval Chinese Poetry." In *Authors, Authorship, and Authoring in Late Classical and Medieval China*, edited by Robert F. Campany and Wendy Swartz. Leiden: Brill, forthcoming.

———. *Letters and Epistolary Culture in Early Medieval China*. Seattle: University of Washington Press, 2013.

———. "Letters of Familial Admonition in Han and Six Dynasties China." In *A History of Chinese Letters and Epistolary Culture*, edited by Antje Richter, 239–75. Leiden: Brill, 2015.

———. "Literary Criticism in the Epistolary Mode: The Cao Brothers, Hofmannsthal, Keats, and Kolmar." *Journal of Epistolary Studies* 1 (2019): 5–37.

———. "Literature and the Arts." In *A Cultural History of Chinese Literatures*, Vol. 2: *The Medieval Period (200 CE–900 CE)*, edited by Jack Chen and Carlos Rojas. London: Bloomsbury, forthcoming.

———. "Stories of Coping with Sickness in Early Medieval China: Illness Narratives in Anecdotal Literature." *Chinese Medicine and Culture* 6, no. 2 (2023): 175–82.

Richter, Antje, and Charles Chace (1958–2018). "The Trouble with Wang Xizhi: Illness and Healing in a Fourth-Century Chinese Correspondence." *T'oung Pao* 103 (2017): 1–61.

Richter, Matthias L. "Must We All Have a Vast, Flowing *qi*? Revisiting *Mengzi* 2A2." *Nanyang Journal of Chinese Literature and Culture* 1 (2021): 25–43.

Riegel, Jeffrey. "Curing the Incurable." *Early China* 35–36 (2012–2013): 225–46.

Rojas, Carlos. "Introduction: 'The Germ of Life.'" *Modern Chinese Literature and Culture* 23, no. 1 (2011): 1–16.

Rothschild, Norman Harry (1969–2021). "The 'Tumor-Rash Axiom' and Beyond: Discursive Excrescences in Early in Medieval China." *Sino-Platonic Papers* 293 (2019): 1–28.

Ryor, Kathleen M. "Fleshly Desires and Bodily Deprivations: The Somatic Dimensions of Xu Wei's Flower Paintings." In *Body and Face in Chinese Visual Culture*, edited by Wu Hung and Katherine R. Tsiang, 121–45. Cambridge, MA: Harvard University Press, 2005.

Sacks, Oliver (1933–2015). "Clinical Tales." *Literature and Medicine* 5 (1986): 16–23.

———. *A Leg to Stand On*. New York: Vintage, 2020.

Sailey, Jay. *The Master Who Embraces Simplicity: A Study of the Philosopher Ko Hung, A.D. 283–343*. San Francisco, CA: Chinese Materials Center, 1978.

Salguero, C. Pierce. "A Flock of Ghosts Bursting Forth and Scattering: Healing Narratives in a Sixth Century Chinese Buddhist Hagiography." *East Asian Science, Technology, and Medicine* 32 (2010): 89–120.

———. *Translating Buddhist Medicine in Medieval China*. Philadelphia: University of Pennsylvania Press, 2014.

Sanft, Charles. "The Moment of Dying: Representations in Liu Xiang's Anthologies *Xin yu* and *Shuo yuan*." *Asia Major* 24, no. 1 (2011): 127–58.

———. "Rule: A Study of Jia Yi's *Xin shu*." PhD diss., University of Münster, 2005.

Sanguo zhi 三國志. Compiled by Chen Shou 陳壽 (233–597). Commentary by Pei Songzhi 裴松之 (372–451). Beijing: Zhonghua shuju, 1959.

Sato, Akira. "Kamalaśīla's Interpretation of Eight Similes in *Avikalpa-praveśadhāraṇīṭīkā*." *Journal of Indian and Buddhist Studies* 67, no. 3 (2019): 1148–53.

Scarry, Elaine. "Donne: But Yet the Body Is His Booke." In *Literature and the Body: Essays on Populations and Persons*, edited by Elaine Scarry, 70–105. Baltimore, MD: Johns Hopkins University Press, 1988.

Scholtz, Sibylle, and Gerd U. Auffarth. "William Turner." In *The Eye in History*, edited by Frank Joseph Goes, 269–71. London: Jaypee Brothers Medical Publishers, 2013.

Schonebaum, Andrew. *Novel Medicine: Healing, Literature, and Popular Knowledge in Early Modern China*. Seattle: University of Washington Press, 2016.

Schopenhauer, Arthur (1788–1860). *The World as Will and Representation*. Vol. 2. Translated by E. F. J. Payne. New York: Dover, 1958.

Scott, Grant F., ed. *Selected Letters of John Keats: Revised Edition*. Cambridge, MA: Harvard University Press, 2002.

Sedgewick, Peter R. "Nietzsche, Illness and the Body's Quest for Narrative." *Health Care Analysis* 21, no. 4 (2013): 306–22.

Sedgwick, Eve Kosofsky (1950–2009). "Pedagogy." In *Critical Terms for the Study of Buddhism*, edited by Donald S. Lopez, 162–87. Chicago: University of Chicago Press, 2005.

Seneca (d. 65). *Epistles*. Vol. 1. Translated by Richard M. Gummere. Loeb Classical Library, vol. 75. Cambridge, MA: Harvard University Press, 1917.

Shangshu zhengyi 尚書正義. Commentary by Kong Yingda 孔穎達 (574–648). In *SSJ*.

Shenjian 申鑒. Compiled by Xun Yue 荀悅. Commentary by Huang Xingceng 黃省曾 (1496–1546). Taipei: Shijie shuju, 1991.

Shi ji 史記. Compiled by Sima Qian 司馬遷 (ca. 145–ca. 87 BCE). Beijing: Zhonghua shuju, 1959.

Shi pin yishu 詩品譯注. Compiled by Zhong Rong 鐘嶸 (?–518). Commentary by Zhou Zhenfu 周振甫. Beijing: Zhonghua shuju, 1998.

Shih, Vincent Yu-chung (1902–2001), trans. *The Literary Mind and the Carving of Dragons: A Study of Thought and Pattern in Chinese Literature*. Hong Kong: Chinese University Press, 1983.

Shinohara, Koichi. "The Moment of Death in Daoxuan's Vinaya Commentary." In *The Buddhist Dead: Practices, Discourses, Representations*, edited by Bryan J. Cuevas and Jacqueline E. Stone, 277–309. Honolulu: University of Hawai'i Press, 2007.

Shisanjing zhushu 十三經注疏 (1816). Compiled by Ruan Yuan 阮元 (1764–1849). Beijing: Zhonghua shuju, 1980.

Shishuo xinyu jianshu 世說新語箋疏. Compiled by Liu Yiqing 劉義慶 (403–444). Commentary by Yu Jiaxi 余嘉錫 (1884–1955). Shanghai: Shanghai guji chubanshe, 1993.

Shitong tongshi 史通通釋. Compiled by Liu Zhiji 劉知幾 (661–721). Commentary by Pu Qilong 浦起龍 (1679–ca. 1762). In *SBBY*.

Shuijing zhu jiaoshi 水經注校釋. Compiled by Chen Qiaoyi 陳橋驛 (1923–2015). Hangzhou: Hangzhou daxue chubanshe, 1999.

Shuo Wugoucheng jing 說無垢稱經 (ca. 649–650). Translated by Xuanzang 玄奘 (602–664). In *T*. 476.

Bibliography

Shupu 書譜 (687). Compiled by Sun Qianli 孫虔禮 (ca. 648–702, zi Guoting 過庭). In *CSJC*.

Sibu beiyao 四部備要. Shanghai: Zhonghua shuju, 1927–1937.

Silk, Jonathan A. "Taking the *Vimalakīrtinirdeśa* Seriously." *Annual Report of the International Research Institute for Advanced Buddhology (ARIRIAB) at Soka University for the Academic Year 2013* 17 (2014): 157–88.

Sishu zhangju jizhu 四書章句集注. Commentary by Zhu Xi 朱熹 (1791–1855). Beijing: Zhonghua shuju, 1983.

Sivin, Nathan (1931–2022). "Emotional Counter-Therapy." In *Medicine, Philosophy and Religion in Ancient China: Researches and Reflections*, vol. 2, 1–19. Aldershot: Ashgate, 1995.

———. *Health Care in Eleventh-Century China*. Berlin: Springer, 2015.

———. *Traditional Medicine in Contemporary China: A Partial Translation of "Revised Outline of Chinese Medicine" (1972) with an Introductory Study on Change in Present-Day and Early Medicine*. Ann Arbor: Centre for Chinese Studies, University of Michigan, 1987.

Smith, Hilary A. *Forgotten Disease: Illness Transformed in Chinese Medicine*. Stanford, CA: Stanford University Press, 2017.

Smith, Kidder. "Sima Tan and the Invention of Daoism, 'Legalism,' et cetera." *Journal of Asian Studies* 62 (2003): 129–56.

Solomon, Andrew. "How a Mystery Illness Cost One Writer a Decade of Health." *New York Times*, March 6, 2022. https://www.nytimes.com/2022/03/01/books/review/invisible-kingdom-chronic-illness-meghan-orourke.html.

Song shu 宋書. Compiled by Shen Yue 沈約 (441–513). Beijing: Zhonghua shuju, 1974.

Song Zhenhao 宋鎮豪. "Shangdai de jihuan yiliao yu weisheng baojian" 商代的疾患醫療與衛生保健. *Lishi yanjiu* 2004.2: 3–26.

Sontag, Susan (1933–2004). *Illness as Metaphor*. New York: Farrar, Straus, Giroux, 1978.

Spade, Beatrice (1940–2012). "The Life and Scholarship of Emperor Yuan (508–555) of the Liang as Seen in the *Chin-lou-tzu*." PhD diss., Harvard University, 1981.

Spiro, Audrey (1927–2001). *Contemplating the Ancients: Aesthetic and Social Issues in Early Chinese Portraiture*. Berkeley: University of California Press, 1990.

Stanley, Liz. "The Epistolary Gift, the Editorial Third-Party, Counter-Epistolaria: Rethinking the Epistolarium." *Life Writing* 8, no. 2 (2011): 135–52.

Stein, Stephan. *Zwischen Heil und Heilung: Zur Frühen Tradition des Yangsheng in China*. Uelzen: Medizinisch-Literarische Verlagsgesellschaft, 1999.

Streif, Christian. *Die Erleuchtung des Nordens: Zum Disput zwischen Sengzhao and Liu Yimin über die Bodhisattva-Idee des Mahāyāna*. Wiesbaden: Harrassowitz, 2013.

Strong, John S. "Explicating the Buddha's Final Illness in the Context of his Other Ailments: The Making and Unmaking of Some *Jātaka* Tales." *Buddhist Studies Review* 29, no. 1 (2012): 17–33.

Sui shu 隋書. Beijing: Zhonghua shuju, 1973.

Sun Changwu 孫昌武. *Zhongguo wenxue zhong de Weimo yu Guanyin* 中國文學中的維摩與觀音. Beijing: Gaodeng jiaoyu chubanshe, 1996.

Susser, Mervin. "Editorial: Disease, Illness, Sickness; Impairment, Disability and Handicap." *Psychological Medicine* 20 (1990): 471–73.

Swartz, Wendy. *Reading Tao Yuanming: Shifting Paradigms of Historical Reception (427–1900).* Cambridge, MA: Harvard University Press, 2008.

Taiping guangji 太平廣記 (978). Compiled by Li Fang 李昉 (925–996) et al. Beijing: Zhonghua shuju, 1960.

Taiping yulan 太平御覽. Compiled by Li Fang et al. Beijing: Zhonghua shuju, 1960.

Taishō shinshū Daizōkyō 大正新修大藏經. Edited by Takakusu Junjirō 高楠順次郎 and Watanabe Kaigyoku 渡邊海旭. Tokyo: Taishō issaikyō kankōkai, 1924–29. Cited after http://tripitaka.cbeta.org.

Tan, Guanghui 譚光輝. *Zhengzhuang de zhengzhuang: Jibing yinyu yu Zhongguo xiandai xiaoshuo* 症狀的症狀: 疾病隱喻與中國現代小說. Beijing: Zhongguo shehui kexue chubanshe, 2007.

Targoff, Ramie. *John Donne, Body and Soul.* Chicago: University of Chicago Press, 2008.

Temkin, Owsei (1902–2002). *The Falling Sickness: A History of Epilepsy from the Greeks to the Beginnings of Modern Neurology.* Baltimore, MD: Johns Hopkins University Press, 1971.

———. "Health and Disease." In *Dictionary of the History of Ideas*, edited by Philip P. Wiener, 395–407. New York: Charles Scribner's Sons, 1974.

Ter Haar, Barend J. *Religious Culture and Violence in Traditional China.* Cambridge: Cambridge University Press, 2019.

Thesaurus Linguae Sericae: An Historical and Comparative Encyclopaedia of Chinese Conceptual Schemes. Edited by Christoph Harbsmeier et al. https://hxwd.org/index.html.

Thompson, Laurence G. "Medicine and Religion in Late Ming China." *Journal of Chinese Religions* 18 (1990): 45–59.

Tian, Xiaofei. *Beacon Fire and Shooting Star: The Literati Culture of the Liang (502–557).* Cambridge, MA: Harvard University Asia Center, 2007.

———. "The Cultural Politics of Old Things in Mid-Tang China." *Journal of the American Oriental Society* 140 (2020): 317–43.

———, trans. *Family Instructions for the Yan Clan and Other Works by Yan Zhitui (531–590s).* Berlin: De Gruyter, 2021.

246　*Bibliography*

———. *The Halberd at Red Cliff: Jian'an and the Three Kingdoms.* Cambridge, MA: Harvard University Asia Center, 2018.

———. "Literary Learning: Encyclopedias and Epitomes." In *The Oxford Handbook of Classical Chinese Literature (1000 BCE–900 CE),* edited by Wiebke Denecke, Wai-Yee Li, and Xiaofei Tian, 132–46. Oxford: Oxford University Press, 2017.

———. 田曉菲. "Tao Yuanming de shujia he Xiao Gang de yixue yanguang: Zhonggu de yuedu yu yuedu zhonggu" 陶淵明的書架和蕭綱的醫學眼光：中古的閱讀與閱讀中古. *Guoxue yanjiu* 37 (2016): 119–44.

———. *Tao Yuanming and Manuscript Culture: The Record of a Dusty Table.* Seattle: University of Washington Press, 2005.

———. "The Twilight of the Masters: Masters Literature (*zishu*) in Early Medieval China." *Journal of the American Oriental Society* 126 (2006): 465–86.

Tissot, Samuel (1728–1797). *An Essay on Diseases Incident to Literary and Sedentary Persons, With Proper Rules for Preventing Their Fatal Consequences, and Instructions for Their Cure.* Translated by James Kirkpatrick. London: Norse and Dilly, 1769.

Valentin, Karl (1882–1948). *Gar ned krank is a ned g'sund: Ein Erste-Hilfe-Lesebuch.* Edited by Gunter Fette. Munich: Piper, 2011.

Virchow, Rudolf (1821–1902). "Über die heutige Stellung der Pathologie (1869)." In *Rudolf Virchow und die Deutschen Naturforscherversammlungen,* edited by Karl Sudhoff, 77–97. Leipzig: Akademische Verlagsgesellschaft, 1922.

Wagner, Corinna. "Visual Translations: Medicine, Art, China and the West." *Fudan Journal of the Humanities and Social Sciences* 8, no. 2 (2015): 193–234.

Wagner, Rudolf G. (1948–2019). "A Building Block of Chinese Argumentation: Initial Fu 夫 as a Phrase Status Marker." In *Literary Forms of Argument in Early China,* edited by Joachim Gentz and Dirk Meyer, 37–66. Leiden: Brill, 2015.

Waley, Arthur (1889–1966). *The Life and Times of Po Chü-i.* London: Allen and Unwin, 1949.

Wang, Eugene Y. "The Taming of the Shrew: Wang Hsi-chih (303–361) and Calligraphic Gentrification in the Seventh Century." In *Character and Context in Chinese Calligraphy,* edited by Cary Y. Liu, Dora C. Y. Ching, and Judith G. Smith, 132–73. Princeton, NJ: Princeton University Art Museum, 1999.

Wang Gengsheng 王更生 (1928–2010). "Liu Xie *Wenxin diaolong* 'Yangqi'" lun yu daojiao" 劉勰文心雕龍養氣論與道教. *Wen yu zhe* 文與哲 12 (2006): 151–67.

Wang Yuanhua 王元化 (1920–2008). "Shi 'Yang qi pian' shuai zhi wei he shuo: Guanyu chuangzuo de zhijiexing" 釋〈養氣篇〉率志委和說：關於創

作的直接性. In *Wenxin diaolong jiangshu* 文心雕龍講疏, 255–74. Guilin: Guangxi shifan daxue chubanshe, 2004.

Ware, James R. (1932–2015), trans. *Alchemy, Medicine, Religion in the China of A.D. 320: The Nei P'ien of Ko Hung (Pao-p'u tzu)*. Cambridge, MA: MIT Press, 1966.

Watson, Burton (1925–2017), trans. *The Complete Works of Zhuangzi*. New York: Columbia University Press, 2013.

———, trans. *Ssu-ma Ch'ien, Grand Historian of China*. New York: Columbia University Press, 1958.

Weimojie jing 維摩詰經 (ca. 222–229). Translated by Zhi Qian 支謙 (fl. 220–252). In *T.* 474.

Weimojie suo shuo jing 維摩詰所說經 (406). Translated by Kumārajīva 鳩摩羅 什 (344–413). In *T.* 475.

Weingarten, Oliver. "'Self-Cultivation' (*xiu shen* 修身) in the Early Edited Literature: Uses and Contexts." *Oriens Extremus* 54 (2015): 163–208.

Wells, Matthew V. *To Die and Not Decay: Autobiography and the Pursuit of Immortality in Early China*. Ann Arbor, MI: Association for Asian Studies, 2009.

Wen xuan 文選. Compiled by Xiao Tong 蕭統 (501–531). Shanghai: Shanghai guji chubanshe, 1986.

Wenjing mifulun jiaozhu 文鏡祕府論校註. Compiled by Wang Liqi 王利器 (1912–1998). Taipei: Guanya wenhua, 1991.

Wenxin diaolong jiaozhu shiyi buzheng 文心雕龍校注拾遺補正. Compiled by Yang Mingzhao 楊明照 (1909–2003). Nanjing: Jiangsu guji chubanshe, 2001.

Wenxin diaolong yizheng 文心雕龍義證. Compiled by Zhan Ying 詹鍈 (1916–1998). Shanghai: Shanghai guji chubanshe, 1989.

Wenxin diaolong zhaji 文心雕龍札記. Compiled by Huang Kan 黃侃 (1886–1935) in 1926. Beijing: Zhonghua shuju, 1962.

Wenxin diaolong zhu 文心雕龍註. Compiled by Fan Wenlan 范文瀾 (1891–1969). Beijing: Renmin wenxue chubanshe, 1958.

Westbrook, Francis A. (1942–1991). "Landscape Description in the Lyric Poetry and '*Fuh* on Dwelling in the Mountains' of Shieh Ling-yunn." PhD diss., Yale University, 1973.

Williams, Nicholas Morrow. "A Conversation in Poems: Xie Lingyun, Xie Huilian, and Jiang Yan." *Journal of the American Oriental Society* 127 (2007): 491–506.

Wittgenstein, Ludwig (1889–1951). *Philosophical Investigations*. 2nd ed. Translated by G. E. M. Anscombe. Oxford: Blackwell, 1999.

Woolf, Virginia (1882–1941). "On Being Ill." In *The Essays of Virginia Woolf*, Vol. 4: *1925–1928*, edited by Andrew McNeillie, 317–29. Orlando, FL: Harcourt, 1994.

248   *Bibliography*

Wu, Fusheng. "'I Rambled and Roamed Together with You': Liu Zhen's (d. 2017) Four Poems to Cao Pi." *Journal of the American Oriental Society* 129 (2009): 619–33.

Wu, Pei-Yi (1927–2009). *The Confucian's Progress: Autobiographical Writings in Traditional China*. Princeton, NJ: Princeton University Press, 1990.

———. "Self-Examination and Confession of Sins in Traditional China." *Harvard Journal of Asiatic Studies* 39 (1979): 5–38.

Wu, Sujane. "Clarity, Brevity and Naturalness: Lu Yun and His Works." PhD diss., University of Wisconsin, Madison, 2001.

Wu Yue chunqiu jijiao huikao 吳越春秋輯校彙考. Commentary by Zhou Shengchun 周生春. Shanghai: Shanghai guji chubanshe, 1997.

Xiaojing zhushu 孝經注疏. Commentary by Li Longji 李隆基 (685–762), and Xing Bing 邢昺 (931–1010). In *SSJ*.

Xie, Guihua. "Han Bamboo and Wooden Medical Records Discovered in Military Sites from the North-Western Frontier Region." In *Medieval Chinese Medicine: The Dunhuang Medical Manuscripts*, edited by Christopher Cullen and Vivienne Lo, 78–106. London: RoutledgeCurzon, 2005.

Xie Lingyun ji jiaozhu 謝靈運集校注. Commentary by Gu Shaobo 顧紹柏. Taipei: Liren shuju, 2004.

Xin Tang shu 新唐書. Beijing: Zhonghua shuju, 1975.

Xinji Soushen ji xinji Soushen houji 新輯搜神記新輯搜神後記. Commentary by Li Jianguo 李劍國. Beijing: Zhonghua shuju, 2007.

Xinyi San zi jing 新譯三字經. Commentary by Huang Peirong 黃沛榮. Taibei: Sanmin shuju, 1995.

Xiong, Victor Cunrui, trans. *A Thorough Exploration in Historiography: "Shitong" by Liu Zhiji*. Seattle: University of Washington Press, 2023.

Xu Gaoseng zhuan 續高僧傳. Compiled by Daoxuan 道宣 (596–667). In *T.* 2060.

Xunzi jijie 荀子集解. Compiled by Wang Xianqian 王先謙 (1842–1918). Beijing: Zhonghua shuju, 1988.

Yang Li 楊莉. "Dunhuang shuyi 'wenji shu' de yuyan biaoxian" 敦煌書儀問疾書的語言表現. *Qinghai minzu xueyuan xuebao* 1 (2009): 125–30.

Yang, Shou-zhong and Charles Chace, trans. *The Systematic Classic of Acupuncture & Moxibustion by Huangfu Mi*. Boulder, CO: Blue Poppy Press, 1994.

Yanshi jiaxun jijie 顏氏家訓集解. Compiled by Yan Zhitui 顏之推 (531–ca. 591). Commentary by Wang Liqi 王利器 (1912–1998). Beijing: Zhonghua shuju, 1993.

Ye Shuxian 葉舒憲. *Wenxue yu zhiliao* 文學與治療. Beijing: Shehui kexue wenxian chubanshe, 1999.

Yim Chi-hung 嚴志雄. *Qian Qianyi "Bingta xiaohan zayong" lunshi* 錢謙益病榻消寒雜咏論釋. Taipei: Zhongyang yanjiuyuan, 2012.

Yim, Chi-hung 嚴志雄. "The 'Deficiency of Yin in the Liver': Dai-yu's Malady and *Fubi* in *Dream of the Red Chamber*." *Chinese Literature: Essays, Articles, Reviews (CLEAR)* 22 (2000): 85–111.

Yiwen leiju 藝文類聚 (624). Compiled by Ouyang Xun 歐陽詢 (557–641) et al. Commentary by Wang Shaoying 汪紹楹. Shanghai: Shanghai guji chubanshe, 1965.

Yu, Jimmy. *Sanctity and Self-Inflicted Violence in Chinese Religions, 1500–1700*. Oxford: Oxford University Press, 2012.

Yunmeng Shuihudi Qin mu 雲夢睡虎地秦墓. Edited by Yunmeng Shuihudi Qin mu bianxiezu 雲夢睡虎地秦墓編寫組. Beijing: Wenwu chubanshe, 1981.

Zhang Meili 張美莉, Liu Jixian 劉繼憲, and Jiao Peimin 焦培民. *Zhongguo zaihai tongshi: Wei Jin Nanbeichao juan* 中國災害通史：魏晉南北朝卷. Zhengzhou: Zhengzhou daxue chubanshe, 2009.

Zhang Weiwei 張薇薇. "*Lun shu biao" jiaozhu yu yanjiu* 〈論書表〉校注與研究. Hangzhou: Zhongguo meishu xueyuan chubanshe, 2010.

Zhanguo ce. Compiled by Liu Xiang 劉向 (79–8 BCE). Shanghai: Shanghai guji chubanshe, 1978.

Zhao lun 肇論. Compiled by Sengzhao 僧肇 (374–414). In *T.* 1858.

Zhengtong Daozang 正統道藏. Taipei: Xinwenfeng chubanshe, 1985.

Zhonghua bencao 中華本草. 10 vols. Edited by Guojia Zhongyiyao guanliju 國家中醫藥管理局. Shanghai: Shanghai kexue jishu chubanshe, 1998.

Zhou shu 周書. Beijing: Zhonghua shuju, 1971.

Zhou Shujia 周叔迦. *Zhou Shujia Foxue lunzhu ji* 周叔迦佛學論著集. 2 vols. Beijing: Zhonghua shuju, 1991.

Zhou yi zhengyi 周易正義. Commentary by Wang Bi 王弼 (226–249), Han Kangbo 韓康伯 (d. ca. 385), and Kong Yingda 孔穎達 (574–648). In *SSJ*.

Zhu Weimojie jing 注維摩詰經. In *T.* 1775.

Zhuangzi jishi 莊子集釋. Compiled by Guo Qingfan 郭慶藩 (1844–1896) and Wang Xiaoyu 王孝魚 (1900–1981). Beijing: Zhonghua shuju, 1995.

Zhubing yuanhou lun jiaozhu 諸病源候論校注. Compiled by Ding Guangdi 丁光迪. Beijing: Renmin weisheng chubanshe, 1992.

Zunsheng bajian 遵生八牋 (1591). Compiled by Gao Lian 高濂. Chengdu: Ba Shu shushe, 1992.

Zürcher, Erik (1928–2008). *The Buddhist Conquest of China: The Spread and Adaptation of Buddhism in Early Medieval China*. Leiden: Brill, 1959.

INDEX

acupuncture, 71–73, 210

ages: childhood and youth, 56, 92, 97–98, 101, 107–12, 142–44, 163; old age, 65–66, 92–97, 146–52, 156–67, 187–89, 214; old age *vs.* youth, 38–40, 124–25, 131, 164, 176, 205–6; premature aging, 17, 23, 54

Altman, Janet, 117

Āmrapālī, 176–77

Analects. See Lunyu

Ānanda, 191–92

appetite, lack of, 138–39, 163

Aronson, Jeffrey K., 80

"Attending to the Sick and Sending Off the Dead" ("Zhanbing songzhong" 瞻病送終) (Daoxuan), 179

autobiographical pact, 81–82, 85, 117, 146

autobiography. *See* self-writing

Bai jia pu 百家譜 (*Genealogies of a Hundred Families*), 107, 111

Bai Juyi 白居易 (772–846), 5n11, 148n89, 163, 213–16

Bai Juyi, works of: "Ba jiu" 罷灸 ("Giving Up Moxibustion"), 216; "Bing zhong shi shiwu shou" 病中詩十五首 ("Fifteen Poems Written in Sickness"), 215; "Bing zhong yanzuo" 病中宴坐 ("Sitting Quietly in My Sickness"), 213–14; "Bingjia zhong nanting xianwang" 病假中南亭閒望 ("On Sick Leave, Leisurely Gazing from the Southern Pavilion"), 215; "Chiluo ci" 齒落辭 ("The Lyric of Fallen Teeth"), 215; "Da Xian shangren lai wen yinhe fengji" 答閒上人來問因何風疾 " (Responding to Monk Xian Who Came to Inquire Why I Suffer from a Wind Disorder"), 215; "Xingbu

shangshu zhiren" 刑部尚書致仕 ("On My Retirement as Minister of Justice"), 215; "Zi yong" 自詠 ("Songs on Myself"), 215; "Zu ji" 足疾 (Foot Illness"), 148n89

Bai, Qianshen, 5, 126

Ban Gu 班固 (32–92), 91. See also *Han shu*

Ban Jieyu 班婕妤 (d. ca. 6 BCE), 208

Bao Xian 包咸 (6–65 BCE), 13

Bao Zhao 鮑照 (ca. 414–466), 150n95, 194n2

Baopuzi 抱朴子. *See* Ge Hong

Bauer, Wolfgang (1930–1997), 4, 80n

Bauman, Zygmunt (1925–2017), 81

Beiji qianjin yaofang 備急千金要方 (*Essential Prescriptions for Every Emergency Worth a Thousand in Gold*) (Sun Simiao), 67

Berkowitz, Alan (1950–2015), 126–27, 154–55

Bian 卞, Dowager Empress (159–230), 183

Bian Que 扁鵲 (fourth/fifth century BCE), 7n, 49

Bian zheng lun 宣驗記 (*Discourse on Determining What Is Correct*) (Falin), 125n18

book mania, 61–67

Book of Documents. See Shangshu

Book of Odes. See Shijing

Boyd, Kenneth M., 11

Bunkyō hifuron 文鏡祕府論 (*Secret Repository of Discourses on the Mirror of Literature*) (Kūkai), 70, 79

calligraphy, 3, 30, 39–42, 118–19, 136–38, 142–45, 152–55

Canguilhem, Georges (1904–1995), 9

252 Index

Canon of Filial Duty. See Xiaojing
Canon of Mountains and Seas. See Shanhai jing
Canon of the Way and Virtue. See Laozi
Cao Bao 曹褒 (d. ca. 102), 42–43
Cao Cao 曹操 (155–220), 39, 98–99, 183
Cao Pi 曹丕 (187–226, Emperor Wen of the Wei dynasty 魏文帝, r. 220–26): death, 95, 99–100, 127, 183; literary thought, 25, 30–31, 77, 220; self-writing, 39, 96–100, 104, 107, 114, 161, 167, 220–21; visiting the sick, 203; as a slow writer, 46
Cao Pi, works of: Dianlun 典論 (Classical Discourses), 39, 96–100; "Lun wen" 論文 ("Discourse on Literature"), 25, 30–31, 96–98; "Zi xu" 自敘 ("Self-account"), 39, 96–100
Cao Xi 曹羲, 131n40
Cao Zhen 曹真 (d. 231), 99
Cao Zhi 曹植 (192–232), 42–46, 53, 56, 98–99, 110, 128n31, 208
Cao Zhi 曹志 (d. ca. 288), 109
Canetti, Elias, 64
Celestial Masters Daoism, 5, 160, 164
Celsus, Aulus Cornelius (25 BCE–50 CE), 65–66
Chace, Charles, 5n
Changes of Zhou. See Zhou yi
Charon, Rita, 7
Chen Shi 陳寔 (104–187), 134
Chen Shunyu 陳舜俞 (d. 1074), 125
Chen Zi'ang 陳子昂 (661–702), 213
Cheng, emperor of the Han dynasty. See Liu Ao
Choy, Howard, 6
Chu ci 楚辭 (Songs of Chu), 37n44, 208n45, 210–11
Chunyu Yi 淳于意 (216–ca. 150 BCE), 7n
clouds: as image of impermanence, 190, 199, 204, 207–8, 215–16; roseate (xia 霞), 123, 207n42; in Wenxin diaolong, 25, 52
cold damage (shang han 傷寒), 130, 138
Cold-Food medicine (hanshi san/yao 寒食散/藥), 130–31
Collection of Essentials about Nurturing Life. See Yangsheng yaoji

Collection of Literature Arranged by Categories. See Yiwen leiju
compassion (bei 悲; Skt. karuṇā), 193
condolence, 103, 181–82
Confucius (Kongzi 孔子, trad. 551–479 BCE): and corporeal integrity, 59, 87–88, 184; on literature and learning, 30, 47, 52, 60, 100, 102; on pleading illness, 134; visiting the sick, 181; and Yan Hui, 51, 54–56, 96; and Zhou yi, 64. See also Lunyu
corporal punishment, 86–90, 168, 220
Couser, G. Thomas, 80, 166
Cui Weizu 崔慰祖 (d. 499), 62
Cullen, Christopher, 5
Cunningham, Andrew, 12

dao 道 (the Way), 61, 88, 101–2, 129
Daodejing 道德經. See Laozi
Daorong 道融, 124n17
Daosheng 道生 (ca. 360–434), 123–24, 212n61
Daoxuan 道宣 (596–667), 160n124, 179, 208n46
Daoyin tu 導引圖 (Tableau of Guiding and Pulling), 67
Dark Learning (xuanxue 玄學), 173
Demiéville, Paul, 173, 175, 186
Deng Tong 鄧通, 185
Dharma offering (fa gongyang 法供養; Skt. dharma-pūjā), 177
Dharmakṣema (Tanwuchen 曇無讖 / Tanmochen 曇摩讖, 385–433), 198
Diamond Sutra (Vajracchedikā-prajñāpāramitā; Jingang banre jing 金剛般若經注), 198
Dianlun 典論. See Cao Pi
diarrhea, 14, 137–39, 158
disability/impairment: Ge Hong, 104–5; Liezi, 186; and moral deficiency, 16, 81; Sima Qian, 87, 90, 100, 118, 168; Tao Qian, 148–52; terminology, 12, 17; Wang Xizhi, 142–44; Xiao Yi, 113–14, 167; Zhuangzi, 105, 186
Discourses Weighed in the Balance. See Wang Chong

Dong Zhongshu 董仲舒 (ca. 179–ca. 104 BCE)

Dongfang Shuo 東方朔 (154–93 BCE), 108

Donne, John (1572–1631), 79

dreams, 46–53, 77, 115, 144, 164, 190–91

Du Fu 杜甫 (712–770), 213

Du Qin 杜欽 (zi Zixia, fl. 33–22 BCE), 62–63

Du Yu 杜預 (222–285), 61, 64

Dubois, Jacques (ca. 1478–1555), 66

emptiness (kong 空; Skt. śūnyatā), 173, 176–78, 190–91, 193, 211, 218

epistolary pact, 81–82, 85, 117–18, 137, 160

Ershisi xiao 二十四孝 (Twenty-Four Filial Exemplars), 184

exacting study (ku xue 苦學), 59–60

exhaustion, mental: Bunkyō hifuron, 78; Cao Zhi 45; Confucius, 60; Gan Biao, 34; Ge Hong, 34–35; Lu Ji, 45; Lu Yun, 44–45; Sima Tan, 34; Wang Chong, 46, 55–56; Wang Zhou, 210; Yang Xiong, 48, 51, 67; in Wenxin diaolong, 24, 32, 35–38

Extended Reflections. See Shenjian

eye disorders, 62–63, 66, 77n174, 87, 113–14, 141, 145

Falin 法琳 (572–640), 125

Family Instructions of the Yan Clan. See Yanshi jiaxun

Fan Ka-wai 范家偉, 5n11, 214

Fan Ning 范甯 (ca. 339–401), 62–63

fatigue, 55, 120–21, 137, 140, 158–59

feng 風 (pathogenic wind), 13, 127, 141, 143n75, 215n73

fever, 130, 147

Ficino, Marsilio (1433–1499), 66

filial duty (xiao 孝): and sickbed visits, 16, 183–85; and retirement, 134; and self-harm, 23, 59, 77, 109; and self-writing, 84, 86–92, 114, 133, 167

Flaubert, Gustave, 64

fondness of learning, 39, 49, 53, 59–62, 110–12, 160

Fong, Grace, 5

foot illness (jiaoji 腳疾), 148–51

Fotudeng 佛圖澄 (d. 349), 49

friendship: and illness, 2, 120–22, 155, 180, 184–86, 220–21; Bai Juyi, 215–16; Ge Hong, 104; Shen Yue, 164; Tao Qian, 151; Xie Lingyun, 201–6

Fuchai, king of Wu (吳王夫差, r. 495–477 BCE), 57–58

Fujiwara no Fuhito 藤原不比等 (659–720), 175

Fujiwara no Kamatari 藤原鎌足 (b. 614), 175

Gadamer, Hans Georg (1900–2002), 9

Gao, emperor of the Qi dynasty. See Xiao Daocheng

Gao Biao 高彪 (d. ca. 184), 34

Gao Lian 高濂 (d. 1603), 67

Gaotang Long 高堂隆 (d. 237), 62–63

gastrointestinal disorders, 13–14, 44, 53, 110, 130, 137–40, 158

Ge Hong 葛洪 (ca. 283–343): illness metaphors, 13–14; on memory, 39–40; on physicians, 10–11; on old age, 95; self-writing, 100–107, 167, 200; yangsheng, 28, 34–35, 43n61

Ge Hong, works of: Baopuzi 抱朴子 (The Master Who Embraces Simplicity), 13, 28, 34–35, 39–40, 95, 98, 100–107, 220; Shenxian zhuan 神仙傳 (Traditions of Divine Transcendents), 105–6; Yuhan fang 玉函方 (Prescriptions from the Jade Case), 10–11; "Xu" 序 (Preface), 100, 105–6; Zhouhou beijifang 肘後備急方 (Formulas to Keep Up One's Sleeve in Preparation of Emergencies), 106; "Zi xu" 自敘 ("Self-account"), 100–106

Genette, Gérard (1930–2018), 83, 87

genre: autobiography, 80–82, 89–92, 167–69, 219–22; confession (chanhui wen 懺悔文), 160–61; and illness narratives, 2–3, 12, 15, 17–21, 91; letter (shu 書), 89–92, 116–26; memorial (biao 表, shangshu 上書/疏), 98, 126–136, 152–56, 164–68, 221; note (tie 帖), 118–22,

254   Index

138–42; authorial preface (*xu* 序), 83–84; self-account (*zi xu* 自序, *zi ji* 自記), 81–115, 117, 126, 159, 169; and speed of writing, 46. *See also* sickbed poetry

Goujian, king of Yue (越王句踐, r. 496–465 BCE), 57–58

Gu Rong 顧榮 (270–312 or 322), 120–22

Guanzi 管子, 29, 180–81

Guo Liping 郭莉萍, 7

Guo Pu 郭璞 (276–324), 52, 102

hair: beard, 198; and filial duty, 88–89; loosening, 129; and self-mortification, 59, 62; washing, 68–69; white, 54–55, 93–95, 114, 150, 159

halting speech, 46–47, 102, 142–43

Han shu 漢書 (*History of the Han Dynasty*) (Ban Gu), 29n13, 46–48, 64, 88–92, 135n51

Han Ying 韓嬰 (ca. 200–120 BCE), 29

Hanfeizi 韓非子, 87

Hanshi waizhuan 韓詩外傳 (*Outer Tradition of the Odes According to Han*) (Han Ying), 29

Harrist, Robert E., 144

Hay, John, 142

He, emperor of the Qi dynasty. See *Xiao Baorong*

He Jianping 何劍平, 194

"He Jianwen di wo ji shi" 和簡文帝臥疾詩 ("Companion Piece to Emperor Jianwen's Poem Written While Lying Sick") (Liu Xiaowei), 196

He Jiong 何炯, 15n

He Yan 何晏 (190–249), 13

heart disorders, 14, 49, 107–14

History of the Han Dynasty. See *Han shu*

History of the Jin Dynasty. See *Jin shu*

History of the Later Han Dynasty. See *Hou Han shu*

History of the Liang Dynasty. See *Liang shu*

History of the Song Dynasty. See *Song shu*

History of the Sui Dynasty. See *Sui shu*

Honglou meng 紅樓夢, 5

Hou Han shu 後漢書 (*History of the Later Han Dynasty*) (Fan Ye), 43, 46, 93n32, 135n51

Hua Tan 華譚 (d. 322), 108–9

Hua Tuo 華佗 (d. ca. 208), 49

Huai, prince of Liang. *See* Liu Yi

Huainanzi 淮南子, 113

Huan Tan 桓譚 (ca. 23 BCE–56 CE), 45–51, 76–78

Huan Wen 桓溫 (312–373), 183

Huangfu Mi 皇甫謐 (215–282): as a book maniac, 61, 64, 133; self-writing, 126–33, 135–36, 152, 163, 168, 220

Huangfu Mi, works of: "Da Xin Kuang shu" 答辛曠書 ("Letter in Reply to Xin Kuang"), 133; *Gaoshi zhuan* 高士傳 (*Biographies of Eminent Gentlemen*), 126; *Lun hanshisan fang* 論寒食散方 (*Discourse on Cold-Food Powder*), 131n40; "Shiquan lun" 釋勸論 ("Discourse on Dispelling Exhortation"), 132n42; "Rang zhengpin biao" 讓徵聘表 ("Memorial Declining the Summons"), 126–33, 155; *Xuanyan chunqiu* 玄晏春秋 (*Annals of the Master of Arcane Tranquility*), 126; *Zhenjiu jiayijing* 針灸甲乙經 (*ABC of Acupuncture and Moxibustion*), 127; "Zi xu" 自序 ("Self-account"), 126

Huijing 慧淨 (578–ca. 645), 197, 207–9

Huiyuan 慧遠 (334–416), 122–24, 148–49, 198

Idema, Wilt L., 4

illness: acceptance of, 152, 166, 185–86, 209, 220; in childhood, 56, 107–12, 142–44, 163; claiming/pleading, 16, 104, 133–42, 154–55, 168, 202, 220; feigning/pretending, 18–19, 133–36, 154, 180, 182, 187–88, 221; and friendship, 2, 120–22, 155, 180, 184–86, 220–21; as period of leisure, 155, 168, 197–207, 217, 221; metaphors, 3, 12–15, 73–74, 104–5, 187, 194; and old age, 151, 157–59, 163–64, 187–89, 214; terminology, 11–15

Index 255

impermanence (*wuchang* 無常; Skt. *anitya*), 171, 188–91, 193, 199–200, 216

inconceivable liberation (*bu ke siyi jietuo* 不可思議解脫; Skt. *acintya-mukta*), 177

injuries, 24, 87–90, 104, 114. *See also* self-harm

insomnia, 1, 137. *See also* sleep

Ji An 汲黯 (d. 112 BCE), 201, 205

"Ji yu fu" 疾愈賦 ("Rhapsody on Recovering from Illness") (Zhi Yu), 195, 207n40

Jia Yi 賈誼 (201–169 BCE), 53–56, 110, 206

Jiang Yan 江淹 (444–505), 52, 144, 196, 206

Jianwen, emperor of the Liang dynasty. *See* Xiao Gang

Jin Ping Mei 金瓶梅, 5

Jin shu 晉書 (*History of the Jin Dynasty*), 52–53, 61–63, 121, 129, 132–33, 142–43, 148

jing 精 (vital essence or energies), 31n20, 33, 51, 55, 68, 93

Jing, king of the Zhou dynasty (周景王, 544–520 BCE), 109

Jingming xuan lun 淨名玄論 (*Discourse on the Profundity of the* Vimalakīrti *Sutra*) (Jizang), 212

Jinlouzi. *See* Xiao Yi

Jishan 箕山 (Mount Ji), 132

Jizang 吉藏 (549–623), 212

Keats, John (1795–1821), 156

Koichi, Shinohara, 179

Kroll, Paul W., 96n40

Kūkai 空海 (774–835), 70, 79

Kumārajīva 鳩摩羅什 (344–413), 122, 174–76, 188, 200, 212

Lai, Chi-tim, 5

Laozi 老子, 1, 110

Lei yuan 類苑 (*Garden of Categories*), 62

Lejeune, Philippe, 85, 117

letter. *See* genre

Levy, Dore, 5

Li Gonglin 李公麟 (1049–1106), 149

Li He 李賀 (ca. 790–ca. 816), 53, 213

Li Jianmin 李建民, 135, 182n24

Li Ling 李陵 (d. 74 BCE), 86, 88

Li Ling 李零, 181n20, 184n30

Li Mi 李密 (227–287), 128n31

Li Shimin 李世民 (598–649, Emperor Taizong of the Tang dynasty 唐太宗, r. 626–649), 136

Li, Wai-yee, 36, 61n123

Liang shu 梁書 (*History of the Liang Dynasty*), 61–62, 115, 133, 157–61, 164–66

Liezi 列子, 4, 31, 60, 186, 204, 206

Liji 禮記 (*Records about Ritual*), 134, 182

Literary Mind and the Carving of Dragons, The. *See* Wenxin diaolong

Liu An 劉安 (179–122 BCE), 45n67

Liu Ao 劉驁 (51–7 BCE, Emperor Cheng of the Han dynasty 漢成帝, r. 33–7 BCE), 48

Liu Che 劉徹 (141–87 BCE, Emperor Wu of the Han dynasty 漢武帝, r. 141–87 BCE), 86, 90, 201

Liu Chengzhi 劉程之 (aka Liu Yimin 劉遺民, ca. 360–416), 122–25, 140

Liu Jun 劉峻 (*zi* Xiaobiao 孝標, 462–521), 61–62, 64

Liu Jun 劉駿 (430–464, Emperor Xiaowu of the Song dynasty 宋孝武帝, r. 453–464), 162

Liu Xiaochuo 劉孝綽 (481–539), 196, 207

Liu Xiaowei 劉孝威 (496–549), 196

Liu Xie 劉勰 (ca. 475–ca. 520). *See* Wenxin diaolong

Liu Yi 劉揖 (d. 169 BCE, Prince Huai of Liang 梁懷王, r. 178–169 BCE), 56

Liu Yigong 劉義恭 (413–465), 162

Liu Yilong 劉義隆 (407–453, Emperor Wen of the Song dynasty 宋文帝, r. 424–453)

Liu Yimin 劉遺民. *See* Liu Chengzhi

Liu Yiqing 劉義慶 (403–444), 49n83

Liu Yu 劉彧 (439–472, Emperor Ming of the Song dynasty 宋明帝, r. 466–472), 152

Liu Zhen 劉楨 (d. 217), 195, 203–6

256   Index

Liu Zhiji 劉知幾 (661–721). See *Shitong*
Liu Zhongying 柳仲郢 (d. 864), 57
longevity: Ge Hong, 29, 95, 105–6; *Shangshu* 14; Wang Chong, 56, 93–94; *Wenxin diaolong*, 19, 23, 75; Zhang Zhan, 62–63
Lotus Sutra (*Saddharma puṇḍarīka sūtra*; *Miaofa lianhua jing* 妙法蓮華經), 14, 49
Lu Ji 陸機 (261–303), 25, 36n40, 44–45, 69–70, 120–22
Lu Ji, works of: "Pingfu tie" 平復帖 ("Note on Recovery"), 121–22; "Wen fu" 文賦 ("Rhapsody on Literature"), 25, 36n40, 45n66, 69–70
Lu Xiujing 陸修靜 (406–477), 149
Lu Yun 陸雲 (262–303), 42–45, 69, 120–22, 140
Lu Yun, works of: "Yu Dai Jifu shu" 與戴季甫書 ("Letter to Dai Jifu"), no. 1, 122; "Yu xiong Pingyuan shu" 與兄平原書 ("Letters to his Elder Brother Lu Ji"), 44–45, 69, 122; "Yu Yang Yanming shu" 與楊彥明書 ("Letter to Yang Yanming"), no. 4, 120–22, 140
Lu Zhaolin 盧照鄰 (ca. 635–684), 213
Lü Buwei 呂不韋 (trad. 291–235 BCE), 87
Lüshi chunqiu 呂氏春秋 (*Annals of Lü Buwei*), 32n26, 38n46, 113
"Lun wen." See Cao Pi
Lunheng. See Wang Chong
"Lun shu biao" 論書表 ("Memorial discussing calligraphy") (Yu He), 152–56
Lunyu 論語 (*Analects*), 13, 47, 51–61, 102, 166, 181, 184–85
"Luo shen fu" 洛神賦 ("Rhapsody on the Luo River Goddess") (Cao Zhi), 208
Lushan 廬山 (Mount Lu), 122–25, 148–49, 197–98
Lushan ji 廬山記 (*Records of Mount Lu*) (Chen Shunyu), 125
Lynn, Richard, 206

Ma Boying 馬伯英 (1943–2023), 12
Ma Rong 馬融 (79–166), 63
Mahāyāna, 20, 173–78, 188, 193, 209, 212, 221
Mañjuśrī, 171, 176–77, 191–93, 215

Manual of Calligraphy. See *Shupu*
Mao shi. See *Shijing*
Donghun, marquess of the Qi dynasty. See Xiao Baojuan
Master of the Golden Tower. See Xiao Yi
Masters literature (*zishu* 子書), 2, 24, 83, 113, 179–86, 220–21
Mather, Richard, 161, 164, 173, 183, 194, 197
memorial. See genre
Meng Haoran 孟浩然 (689–740), 213
Meng Jiao 孟郊 (751–814), 213
Mengzi 孟子, 30n16, 36–37, 129
Mi Heng 禰衡 (ca. 173–198), 45
Ming, emperor of the Song dynasty. See Liu Yu
Miscellaneous Records from the Western Capital. See *Xijing zaji*
moxibustion, 141, 216

New Discourses. See *Xin lun*
Nirvana Sutra (*Mahāparinirvāṇa-sūtra*; *Da banniepan jing* 大般涅槃經), 191n56, 198
nonduality (*bu er* 不二; Skt. *advaya*), 20, 173–80, 187–88, 209, 216, 218
nonself (*wu/fei wo* 無/非我; Skt. *anātman*), 190, 193, 199
note. See genre
numbness, 130, 163n129
nurturing life. See *yangsheng*

O'Rourke, Meghan, 81
Outer Tradition of the Odes According to Han. See *Hanshi waizhuan*
overwork, 19, 42–56, 68, 110–12, 121, 217, 220
Owen, Stephen, 33, 46, 84–85, 150, 214

pain, 87, 90, 111–12, 137–40, 151n101, 165–66, 207
Pei Qi 裴啟, 143–43
Pei Songzhi 裴松之 (372–451), 97n41
persona: public, 19, 81, 92, 97, 114–15, 167–69; poetic, 149–50, 195, 202, 216, 221; religious, 101, 105–6
Petrarca, Franceso (1304–1374), 65–66

Ping, lord of Jin 晉平公 (r. 557–532 BCE), 72

Poetry Gradings. See Shi pin

Porter, Roy, 16–17

preface. *See* genre

Pure Conversation (*qingtan* 清談), 173

qi 氣 (vital breath or energies): calligraphy, 142; Cao Pi on, 96–98; as exhaustible, 29–32; Ge Hong, 102; health, 10, 23, 125; and literary creativity, 23–78, 220; Wang Chong, 93–96

Qian Zhongshu 錢鍾書 (1910–1999), 121, 163

"Qiu yu wo ji shi" 秋雨臥疾詩 ("[Observing] the Autumn Rain While Lying Sick") (Liu Xiaochuo), 196, 207–8

Qu Yuan 屈原 (trad. 340–278 BCE), 87, 91–92

Ran Boniu 冉伯牛, 181

skin disorders, 14, 111–13

reclusion, 126–27, 132–33, 148, 151, 154–55

Records about Ritual. See Liji

Records of the Invisible and Visible World. See Youming lu

Ren An 任安 (d. ca. 91 BCE), 88–92, 116–17, 120, 137, 152

ritual masters (*fangshi* 方士), 11

Rojas, Carlos, 6

Rong Qiqi 榮啟期, 155

"Ru yan shi" 如炎詩 ("Poem on Being Like a Mirage") (Xiao Yan), 200

Ruan Kan 阮侃, 109

Ruan Yu 阮瑀 (d. 212), 45n67

Sacks, Oliver (1933–2015), 116

Salguero, Pierce C., 5, 49

San zi jing 三字經 (*Three Character Canon*), 58–59

Śākyamuni Buddha, 160, 176–79, 188–93, 197, 209, 215

Śāriputra, 177, 209

scholar-physicians (*yi* 醫), 11, 16, 110, 127, 164

seizures (*dian* 癲), 143–44

self-account. *See* genre

self-harm, 19, 23–78

self-writing: Cao Pi, 96–100; Ge Hong, 100–106; Huangfu Mi, 126–33; and illness, 2–5, 16–20, 79–85, 116–20, 167–69, 202, 220; Liu Chengzhi, 122–25; Lu Yun, 120–22; Shen Yue, 156–66; Sima Qian, 85–92; Tao Qian, 145–52; Wang Chong, 27, 29, 43, 52, 92–96; Wang Xizhi, 136–43; Xiao Yi, 106–15; Yu He, 152–56

selfhood, 15, 19, 21, 83, 87, 116–18, 167–69. *See also* self-writing

Seneca (ca. 4 BCE–65 CE), 65

Sengyou 僧祐 (445–518), 28

Sengzhao 僧肇 (374–414), 122–25

Sengzhao, works of: "Banruo wu zhi lun" 般若無知論 ("Discourse on *prajñā* as Not Knowing"), 122–23; "Da Liu Yimin shu" 荅劉遺民書 ("Letter in Reply to Liu Yimin"), 124

shamans (*wu* 巫), 11, 164

shangshu 上書/疏. *See* genre

Shangshu 尚書 (*Book of Documents*), 14, 130n36, 132n43, 165–66, 209n49

Shanhai jing 山海經, 7n19

Shen Pu 沈璞 (416–453), 157n116

Shen Yanzhi 沈演之 (397–449), 110–11

Shen Yue 沈約 (441–513): final illness, 11, 164–66; friendship with Xie Tiao, 205; pleading illness, 135, 156–63, 168; poetry, 196, 207n42, 208n42, 219–21; compiler of *Song shu*, 148, 162–63

Shen Yue, works of: "Bao Wang Yun shu" 報王筠書 ("Letter in Reply to Wang Yun"), 164; "Chanhui wen" 懺悔文 ("Statement of Confession and Repentance"), 160–61; "Chou Xie Xuancheng Tiao shi" 酬謝宣城朓詩 ("In Response to Xie Tiao's [Poem Written While Lying Sick]"), 196, 205; "He zuocheng Yu Gaozhi yi bing shi" 和左丞庾杲之移病詩 ("Companion Piece to a Poem by Left Assistant Yu Gaozhi Requesting

258 Index

Sick Leave"), 196, 219–21; "Linzhong yibiao" 臨終遺表 ("Testamentary Deathbed Memorial"), 164–65, 185; "Qian seng hui yuanwen" 千僧會願文 ("Prayer Text for a Thousand-Monk Assembly"), 164; *Song shu*, 110, 148, 162–63; "Yu Xu Mian shu" 與徐勉書 ("Letter to Xu Mian"), 156–62, 165

shen 神 (spirit): and illness, 108–9, 141, 165–66, 210; and literary creativity, 25, 32–34, 38–42, 51, 69, 75–76; spirits of nature, 72; nurturing of, 54, 56, 63, 75–76, 125

Shenjian 申鑒 (*Extended Reflections*) (Xun Yue), 29, 73

Shi ji 史記 (*Records of the Historian*) (Sima Qian), 34, 58, 63, 85–92, 95, 184–85, 201

Shi pin 詩品 (*Poetry Gradings*) (Zhong Rong), 52, 145

"Shi yu huan shi" 十喻幻詩 ("Poem on the Ten Similes of Illusion") (Xiao Yan), 200

"Shi yu shi" 十喻詩 ("Poem about the Ten Similes") (Kumārajīva), 200

Shijing 詩經 (*Book of Odes*), 15n, 36–37, 43n59, 87, 120n5, 157n117, 199–200

Shishuo xinyu 世說新語 (*Traditional Tales and Recent Accounts*) (Liu Yiqing), 62, 109n79, 134, 142–43, 183

Shitong 史通 (*History Understood Thoroughly*) (Liu Zhiji), 84, 91–92, 98–99, 104

Shitou ji 石頭記, 5

shoulder, 141–42, 163n129

Shupu 書譜 (*Manual of Calligraphy*) (Sun Qianli), 39, 41–42, 153n104

Shuo Wugoucheng jing 說無垢稱經 (Xuanzang), 174n8, 188, 212

sickbed poetry (*wo ji/bing shi* 臥疾/病詩): pre-Tang dynasty, 19–20, 171–72, 194–97; Bai Juyi, 5n11, 148n89, 213–16; Chen Zi'ang, 213; Du Fu, 213; Huijing, 197, 207–9; Jiang Yan, 196, 206; Li He, 213; Liu Xiaochuo, 196, 207; Liu Xiaowei, 196; Liu Zhen, 203–6; Lu Zhaolin,

213; Meng Haoran, 213; Meng Jiao, 213; Pei Ziye, 196; Shen Yue, 196, 205–6; Tang dynasty, 212–18; Tao Qian, 150–51, 195; Wang Wei, 213; Wang Xiuzhi, 194, 196, 206; Wang Zhou, 197, 209–12; Xiao Gang, 196, 203n29, 207n40; Xie Lingyun, 195, 200–207; Xie Tiao, 196, 205; Yu Xin, 197; Zhu Chaodao, 197

sickbed visits (*wen ji/bing* 問疾/病): *Book of Documents*, 166; Confucius, 181; early China, 135, 179–86; and filial duty, 183–85; and friendship, 179, 185–86; Ge Hong, 103; *Guanzi*, 178–81; *Liji*, 182–83; *Vimalakīrti Sutra*, 19–20, 171–73, 176, 186–93; *Xiaojing*, 184–84; *Xunzi*, 182–84; Zengzi, 166, 184–85; *Zhuangzi*, 179, 185–86

Silk, Jonathan, 174

Sima Qian 司馬遷 (ca. 145–ca. 87 BCE): Confucius, 64; and fellow sufferers, 63–64, 108, 110; and filial duty, 86–92, 114, 133, 167–69; self-writing, 85–95, 100, 104, 116–20, 128, 137, 152, 220–21

Sima Qian, works of: "Bao Ren Shaoqing shu" 報任少卿書 ("Letter in Reply to Ren An"), 88–92, 116–20, 137, 152, 168–69; *Shi ji* 史記 (*Records of the Historian*), 34, 58, 63–64, 85–92, 95, 184–85, 201; "Taishigong zi xu" 太史公自序 ("Self-account of the Director of Archives"), 63–64, 85–92

Sima Tan 司馬談 (d. 110 BCE), 34, 86

Sima Xiangru 司馬相如 (179–117 BCE), 45–47, 91, 102

Sima Yan 司馬炎 (236–290, Emperor Wu of the Jin dynasty 晉武帝, r. 265–90), 61, 127–33

Sima Yi 司馬懿 (179–251), 131

Sivin, Nathan (1931–2022), 11n32, 14n44

skillful means (*fangbian* 方便; Skt. *upāya*), 176–78, 188–89, 192

sleep, 42–43, 57–59, 61–63, 112, 137–38, 160

Solomon, Andrew, 81

Song shu 宋書 (*History of the Song Dynasty*) (Shen Yue), 110, 148, 162–63

Songs of Chu. See Chu ci
spirit. See shen
Story of the Stone, The. See Shitou ji
Su Qin 蘇秦 (d. ca. 320 BCE), 58–59
suffering (ku 苦; Skt. duḥkha), 176, 186–90, 193, 207–9
Sui shu 隋書 (History of the Sui Dynasty), 29
"Sui wan chen ke shi" 歲晚沈痾詩 ("Poem Written at the End of the Year While Seriously Ill") (Zhu Chaodao), 197
Summerheat (shu 暑), 130–31, 163n129
Sun Jing 孫敬, 58–59
Sun Qianli 孫虔禮 (ca. 648–702). See Shupu
Sun Simiao 孫思邈 (581–682), 67
Sunzi 孫子 (trad. 544–496 BCE), 87
Suo Jing 索靖 (239–303), 125

Taishan 泰山 (Mount Tai), 55, 155, 203
Taizong, emperor of the Tang dynasty. See Li Shimin
talent, 31, 34–35, 40–41, 46, 55, 60, 73
Tao Hongjing 陶弘景 (452–536), 210n50
Tao Qian 陶潛 (365–427?), 145–52
Tao Qian, works of: "Da Pang congjun shi" 答龐參軍詩 ("Poem in Reply to Aide Pang"), 151; "Ji Chengshi mei wen" 祭程氏妹文 ("Sacrificial Offering to My Younger Sister, Madame Cheng"), 149; "Jin gu zhengxi dajiangjun changshi Meng fujun zhuan" 晉故征西大將軍長史孟府君傳 ("Biography of His Excellency Meng, Former Chief of Staff to the Jin Generalissimo for Subduing the West"), 148n90; "Ni wan'ge ci" 擬挽歌辭 ("Imitations of Coffin Puller's Songs"), 149; "Shi Zhou Zu Xie" 示周續祖謝 ("To Secretary Zhou, Zu, and Xie"), 150–51, 195; "Wu liu xiansheng zhuan" 五柳先生傳 ("Biography of the Master of Five Willows"), 149; "Yu zi Yan deng shu" 與子儼等書 ("Letter to Yan and His Other Sons"), 145–52; "Za

shi" 雜詩 ("Miscellaneous Poems"), 150; "Ziji wen" 自祭文 ("Sacrificial Offering to Myself"), 149–50, 155
teeth, 1, 55, 93, 95–96, 159, 163n129, 215
Thompson, Laurence G., 5
Three Bodies, of the Buddha (sanshen 三身; Skt. trikāya), 188–91
Three Character Canon. See San zi jing
Three Laughers at Tiger Brook (虎溪三笑), 149
Tian, Xiaofei, 16, 83, 148, 203n26
Tissot, Samuel (1728–1797), 66–67
Traditional Tales and Recent Accounts. See Shishuo xinyu
transcendence (xian 仙), 23, 27, 29, 94, 100
Turner, J. M. William (1775–1851), 145

Vimalakīrti: manifesting sickness, 19–20, 173, 176, 187–89; name, 212; performing miracles, 176–77; similes of the body, 189–93, 198–200, 215–16; teaching about illness, 186–93
Vimalakīrti Sutra: and Chinese poetry, 194, 197–202, 208–18, 221; commentary by Sengzhao, Kumārajīva, Daosheng, and Daorong, 124; content and narrative features, 176–78; on illness, 186–93; reception in China, 171–75, 216°18; reception in Japan, 175; sickbed visits, 19–20
Virchow, Rudolf (1821–1902), 9
vital breath or energies. See qi
vital essence. See jing

Waley, Arthur (1889–1966), 213–16
Wang Can 王粲 (177–217), 45n67
Wang Chong 王充 (27–ca. 100): nurturing life, 26–32, 75, 77, 220; overwork, 42–43, 52–53; self-writing, 92–96, 98, 100, 104, 106–7, 159, 163; as a slow writer, 45–46; on vigor, 54–56, 62, 68, 94, 96, 167; on Zengzi, 184n31
Wang Chong, works of: Lunheng 論衡 (Discourses Weighed in the Balance), 14n45; Yang xing 養性 (Nurturing

Inborn Nature), 27, 29, 32, 75, 93, 127; "Zi ji" 自紀 ("Records about Myself"), 27

Wang Huzhi 王胡之, 143n75

Wang Mang 王莽 (45 BCE–23 CE, emperor the Xin dynasty 梁簡文帝, r. 9–23 CE), 54

Wang Sengru 王僧孺 (465–522), 15n49, 107

Wang Wei 王維 (699–761), 213

Wang Xianzhi 王獻之 (344–386/88), 41, 137n56

Wang Xizhi 王羲之 (303–361): calligraphy, 41, 136–37, 142–45; letters, 5, 136–42, 151–52, 154, 168, 220–21

Wang Xizhi, works of: "Bu shen zun ti tie" 不審尊體帖 (aka "Heru tie" 何如帖), 139; "Chu yue tie" 初月帖 (aka "Xizhi lei shu tie" 羲之累書帖), 138; "Congmei jia ye tie" 從妹佳也帖, 139; "Dan fan tie" 旦反帖, 139; "Dan ji han tie" 旦極寒帖, 138; "De liren shu tie" 得里人書帖, 139; "Jin shu zhi ye tie" 近書至也帖, 139; "Sang luan tie" 喪亂帖, 142; "Wu zhi dongjie tie, 吾陟冬節帖, 139

Wang Xiuzhi 王秀之 (442–494), 194, 196, 206

Wang Yun 王筠 (481–549), 164

Wang Zhou 王冑 (558–613), 197, 209–12

Wei lüe 魏略 (Brief History of the Wei) (Yu Huan), 44n62

Wei Xiong 韋夐 (502–578), 165n36

Weimojie jing 維摩詰經 (Zhi Qian), 174, 188, 212

Weimojie suo shuo jing 維摩詰所說經 (Kumārajīva), 171, 174, 187–93, 199, 209–11, 214

wen 文 (refined literature): illness as subject of, 19, 21, 81, 155–56, 168–69, 219–21; in Wenxin diaolong, 35–36, 42; and wu 武, 99

Wen, emperor of the Song dynasty. See Liu Yilong

Wen, emperor of the Wei dynasty. See Cao Pi

Wen, king of the Zhou dynasty (周文王, fl. eleventh century BCE), 87

Wen xuan 文選 (Selections of Refined Literature) (Xiao Tong), 28, 51n86, 84, 128n32, 143n76, 145

Wenxin diaolong 文心雕龍 (The Literary Mind and the Carving of Dragons) (Liu Xie): on letters, 91; on memorials, 128–29, 155; metaphors, 15; on prefaces 84; "Shen si" 神思 (Spirit Thought), 25, 32, 34n35, 45–53, 78; "Yang qi" 養氣 ("Nurturing the Vital Breath"), 18–20, 23–78, 127, 168, 220–21

White Lotus Society, 148–49

Wittgenstein, Ludwig (1889–1951), 8

"Wo ji fu" 臥疾賦 ("Rhapsody Written While Lying Sick") (Pei Ziye), 196

"Wo ji Min Yue shu Jingming yi bing xu" 臥疾閩越述淨名意并序 ("Describing the Meaning of the Vimalakīrti Sutra While Lying Sick in Min-Yue, with a Preface") (Wang Zhou), 197, 209–12

"Wo ji qiong chou shi" 臥疾窮愁詩 ("Poem Written While Lying Sick and in Deep Distress") (Yu Xin), 197

"Wo ji xu yi shi" 臥疾敘意詩 ("Expressing My Intent While Lying Sick") (Wang Xiuzhi), 194, 196, 206

"Wo ji yuan bie Liu changshi shi" 臥疾怨別劉長史詩 ("Expressing My Intent While Lying Sick") (Jiang Yan), 196, 206

Woolf, Virginia (1882–1941), 3, 222

Wu, emperor of the Han dynasty. See Liu Che

Wu, emperor of the Jin dynasty. See Sima Yan

Wu, emperor of the Liang dynasty. See Xiao Yan

Wu, Pei-Yi (1927–2009), 80

Xi Kang 嵇康 (223–262), 28

Xiao Baojuan 蕭寶卷 (483–501, Marquess Donghun of the Qi dynasty 齊東昏侯, r. 498–501), 157

Xiao Baorong 蕭寶融 (488–502, Emperor He of the Qi dynasty 齊和帝, r. 501–502), 164

Index 261

Xiao Daocheng 蕭道成 (427–482, Emperor Gao of the Qi dynasty 齊高帝, r. 479–482), 133

Xiao Gang 蕭綱 (503–551, Emperor Jianwen of the Liang dynasty 梁簡文帝, r. 549–51), 196, 200, 203n29, 207n40, 208n43, 215n72

Xiao Gang, works of: "Baguanzhai ye fu si chengmen geng zuo" 八關齋夜賦四城門更作 ("Four Poems on Each of the Four City Gates Composed in Turns during the Night of an Eight Precepts Fast"), 203n29; "Liugen chanwen" 六根懺文 ("Confession on the Six Faculties"), 215n72; "Shi kong shi" 十空詩 ("Poems on the Tensimilies of Emptiness"), 200; "Wo ji shi" 臥疾詩 ("Poem Written While Lying Sick") (Xiao Gang), 196; "Xi ji liao shi" 喜疾瘳詩 ("Poem on the Joy of Convalescence"), 196, 207n40; "Yong ying shi" 詠螢詩 ("Poem on a Firefly"), 208n43

Xiao Tong 蕭統 (501–531, Crown Prince Zhaoming of the Liang dynasty 梁昭明太子), 28, 84, 145

Xiao Yan 蕭衍 (464–549, Emperor Wu of the Liang dynasty 梁武帝, r. 502–549), 107, 115, 156–61, 164–66, 200–201

Xiao Yi 蕭繹 (508–555, Emperor Yuan of the Liang dynasty 梁元帝, r. 553–555), 45, 53–56, 95, 106–15, 151n101, 167, 220–21

Xiao Yi, works of: *Jinlouzi* 金樓子 (*Master of the Golden Tower*), 45, 53–56, 106–15; "Zi xu" 自序 ("Self-account"), 106–15

Xiaojing 孝經 (*Canon of Filial Duty*), 86–89, 184–85

Xiaowu, emperor of the Song dynasty. *See* Liu Jun

Xie An 謝安 (320–385), 183

Xie Fei 謝腓 (439–506), 133

Xie Huilian 謝惠連 (407–433), 204–5

Xie Lingyun 謝靈運 (385–433): dream, 52, 144; inspiration to Yu He, 153–54, 156; and *Vimalakīrti Sutra*, 172, 197–200; sickbed poetry, 195, 200–207, 216, 221

Xie Lingyun, works of: "Bianzong lun" 辨/辯宗論 ("Discussion on Distinguishing What Is Essential"), 198, 201; "Chou congdi Huilian shi" 酬從弟惠連詩 ("In Response to My Younger Cousin Huilian"), 196, 204–5; "Chu zhi du shi" 初至都詩 ("When I First Arrived in the Capital"), 196, 202n25; "Deng chishang lou shi" 登池上樓詩 ("Climbing the Tower by the Pond"), 196, 202, 207; "Fo ying ming" 佛影銘 ("Inscription on the Buddha-Shadow"), 197; "Guo Shining shu shi" 過始寧墅詩 ("Stopping by My Villa in Shining"), 196, 202n25; "Huan jiu yuan, zuo jian Yan Fan er zhongshu shi" 還舊園作見顏范二中書詩 ("On Returning to My Old Gardens, for Perusal by the Imperial Secretaries Yan Yanzhi and Fan Tai"), 196, 202n25; "Lushan Huiyuan fashi lei" 廬山慧遠法師誄 ("Epitaph on Dharma Teacher Huiyuan of Mount Lu"), 197–98; "Ming xueshi jiang shu shi" 命學士講書詩 ("Commanding Scholars to Discuss Books [with Me]"), 196, 201; "Shan ju fu" 山居賦 ("Rhapsody on Living in the Mountains"), 198, 201–2; "Shibi jingshe huan huzhong zuo" 石壁精舍還湖中作 ("Written on the Lake on My Way Back from the Retreat at Stone Cliffs"), 153–54; "Weimojing shi pi zan" 維摩經十譬贊 ("Encomia on the Ten Similes of the *Vimalakīrti Sutra*"), 198–200; "You nan ting shi" 遊南亭詩 ("Visiting South Pavilion"), 196, 202n25; "Zhai zhong du shu shi" 齋中讀書詩 ("Reading in My Study"), 196, 200–201

Xie Tiao 謝朓 (464–499), 196, 203n29, 205

Xie Tiao, works of: "Chou de fu" 酬德賦 ("Rhapsody Requiting a Kindness"), 203n29; "He Wang changshi wo bing shi" 和王長史臥病詩 ("Companion Piece to a Poem Written While Lying Sick by Senior Administrator Wang [Xiuzhi]"), 196, 206; "Yi bing huan yuan shi qinshu shi" 移病還園示親屬詩 ("Claiming Illness, I Return to My Garden, Notifying My Relatives and Associates"), 196; "Zai jun wo bing cheng Shen shangshu shi" 在郡臥病呈沈尚書詩 ("Poem Presented to Minister Shen [Yue] While Lying Sick in My Commandery"), 196, 205

Xie Zhuang 謝莊 (421–466), 162–63

Xijing zaji 西京雜記 (*Miscellaneous Records from the Western Capital*), 51

Xin Kuang 辛曠, 133

Xin lun 新論 (*New Discourses*) (Huan Tan), 47–51, 76–78

Xu Mian 徐勉 (466–535), 156–62, 165

Xu Xiaosi 徐孝嗣 (453–499), 157

Xu Xun 許詢 (d. 361), 143

Xu You 許由, 132

Xu Zhuang 徐奘, 164

Xuan yan ji 宣驗記 (*Records Proclaiming Divine Manifestation*), 124–25

Xuanzang 玄奘, 174n8, 188, 212

Xun Yu 荀彧 (163–212), 97

Xun Yue 荀悅 (148–209), 29, 73

Xunzi 荀子, 22, 60, 182–84

Yan Hui 顏回 (521–481 BCE), 51, 53–56, 68, 96, 99, 110

Yan Kejun 嚴可均 (1762–1843), 47, 50–51

Yan Shigu 顏師古 (581–645), 64, 135n51

Yan Yanzhi 顏延之 (384–456), 147, 163n129, 195

Yan Zhitui 顏之推 (531–ca. 591), 27n8, 40, 69n149, 111–12

yangsheng 養生 (nurturing life), 23–78, 94–94, 127, 168, 220

Yangsheng yaoji 養生要集 (*Collection of Essentials about Nurturing Life*) (Zhang Zhan), 29, 62

Yang Xiong 揚雄 (53 BCE–18 CE), 45–51, 53, 56, 67, 77, 102, 110

Yanshi jiaxun 顏氏家訓 (*Family Instructions of the Yan Clan*) (Yan Zhitui), 7n19, 27n8, 111–12

Yao 堯, 132

Yao Sengyuan 姚僧垣 (499–583), 110

Yin Shi 殷師 (fourth century), 109

Yin Zhongkan 殷仲堪 (d. 399/400), 77n174, 109

Yiwen leiju 藝文類聚 (*Collection of Literature Arranged by Categories*), 43, 50, 200

Youzi 有子 (You Ruo 有若, trad. 508–457 BCE), 60

"Yu dong ri Puguang si wo ji zhi xue jian zhu jiuyou shi" 於冬日普光寺臥疾值雪簡諸舊遊詩 ("Poem Sent to My Old Companions from a Winter's Day in Puguang Temple Where It Was Snowing While I Was Lying Sick") (Huijing), 197, 207–9

Yu Fu 俞跗, 49

Yu He 虞龢 (fl. ca. 470), 152–56, 168

Yu Huan 魚豢, 44n62

Yu Xin 庾信 (513–581), 197

Yuan, emperor of the Liang dynasty. *See* Xiao Yi

Yuan Ang 袁盎 (d. 148 BCE), 185

Yuan Min 袁敏, 97

"Yuange xing" 怨歌行 ("Song of Resentment") (Ban Jieyu), 208

Yulin 語林 (*Forest of Conversations*) (Pei Qi), 143–43

Youming lu 幽明錄 (*Records of the Invisible and Visible World*) (Liu Yiqing), 49n83

Yueyi 月儀 (*Monthly Etiquette*) (Suo Jing), 125

Yuwen Tai 宇文泰 (507–556), 106

"Zeng wuguan zhonglangjiang shi si shou" 贈五官中郎將詩四首 ("Four Poems Presented to the Central Commander of the Five Guards") (Liu Zhen), 195, 203–6

Zengzi 曾子, 166, 184–85

Zhang bin 漳濱 (banks of the river Zhang), 203–4

Zhang Heng 張衡 (78–139), 45–46

Zhang Rong 張融 (444–497), 109

Zhang Zhan 張湛 (4th century), 29, 62–63

Zheng Xuan 鄭玄 (127–200), 62–63

Zhao Fei 趙匪, 109

Zhaoming, crown prince of the Liang dynasty. *See* Xiao Tong.

zhi 志 (intention), 31–41, 93–94, 101, 109, 114, 153

Zhi Qian 支謙 (fl. 220–252), 174, 188, 212

"Zhi shu Shi Sengzhao qing wei 'Banruo wuzhi lun' shi" 致書釋僧肇請為般若無知論釋 ("Letter to Shi Sengzhao Requesting an Explanation of his 'Discourse on *prajñā* as Not-Knowing'") (Liu Chengzhi), 122–25, 140

Zhi Yu 摯虞 (d. 311), 195, 207n40

Zhong Rong 鐘嶸 (467–518), 52, 145

Zhou Wen 周閱, 118n2

Zhou yi 周易 (*Changes of Zhou*), 64, 157n117, 206

Zhu Chaodao 朱超道 (fl. 520–539), 197

Zhu Fayi 竺法義 (d. 382), 49, 110

Zhu Weimojie jing 注維摩詰經 (*Commentary on the* Vimalakīrti *Sutra*), 124, 212n61

Zhuangzi 莊子: friendship and illness, 179, 185–86, 204–5; healing, 206; on heart *qi*, 108; nurturing life, 28, 32–33, 40–43, 56, 63n128, 72–76, 220; physical impairments, 105, 214n67; on pleading illness, 134

Zichan 子産 (Gongsun Qiao 公孫僑, trad. d. 522 BCE), 72–73

Zichong 子重 (sixth century BCE), 109

Zigong 子貢 (Duanmu Ci 端木賜, trad. 520–456 BCE), 60

zishu. See Masters literature

Zunsheng bajian 遵生八牋 (*Eight Notes on Pursuing [the Right Path of] Life*) (Gao Lian), 67

Zuo Qiuming 左丘明 (trad. 556–451 BCE), 62–63, 87, 109

Zuo Si 左思 (ca. 250–ca. 305), 45–53, 63, 102

Zuo Tradition. See Zuozhuan

Zuozhuan 左傳 (*Zuo Tradition*), 2, 61, 63, 68–69, 71–74, 127

Zürcher, Erik (1928–2008), 173, 189, 212

Harvard-Yenching Institute Monographs
(most recent titles)

85. *A Comprehensive Manchu-English Dictionary*, by Jerry Norman
86. *Drifting among Rivers and Lakes: Southern Song Dynasty Poetry and the Problem of Literary History*, by Michael A. Fuller
87. *Martial Spectacles of the Ming Court*, by David M. Robinson
88. *Modern Archaics: Continuity and Innovation in the Chinese Lyric Tradition, 1900–1937*, by Shengqing Wu
89. *Cherishing Antiquity: The Cultural Construction of an Ancient Chinese Kingdom*, by Olivia Milburn
90. *The Burden of Female Talent: The Poet Li Qingzhao and Her History in China*, by Ronald C. Egan
91. *Public Memory in Early China*, by K. E. Brashier
92. *Women and National Trauma in Late Imperial Chinese Literature*, by Wai-yee Li
93. *The Destruction of the Medieval Chinese Aristocracy*, by Nicolas Tackett
94. *Savage Exchange: Han Imperialism, Chinese Literary Style, and the Economic Imagination*, by Tamara T. Chin
95. *Shifting Stories: History, Gossip, and Lore in Narratives from Tang Dynasty China*, by Sarah M. Allen
96. *One Who Knows Me: Friendship and Literary Culture in Mid-Tang China*, by Anna M. Shields
97. *Materializing Magic Power: Chinese Popular Religion in Villages and Cities*, by Wei-Ping Lin
98. *Traces of Grand Peace: Classics and State Activism in Imperial China*, by Jaeyoon Song
99. *Fiction's Family: Zhan Xi, Zhan Kai, and the Business of Women in Late-Qing China*, by Ellen Widmer
100. *Chinese History: A New Manual, Fourth Edition*, by Endymion Wilkinson
101. *After the Prosperous Age: State and Elites in Early Nineteenth-Century Suzhou*, by Seunghyun Han
102. *Celestial Masters: History and Ritual in Early Daoist Communities*, by Terry F. Kleeman
103. *Transgressive Typologies: Constructions of Gender and Power in Early Tang China*, by Rebecca Doran
104. *Li Mengyang, the North-South Divide, and Literati Learning in Ming China*, by Chang Woei Ong
105. *Bannermen Tales (Zidishu): Manchu Storytelling and Cultural Hybridity in the Qing Dynasty*, by Elena Suet-Ying Chiu
106. *Upriver Journeys: Diaspora and Empire in Southern China, 1570–1850*, by Steven B. Miles

107. *Ancestors, Kings, and the Dao,* by Constance A. Cook
108. *The Halberd at Red Cliff: Jian'an and the Three Kingdoms,* by Xiaofei Tian
109. *Speaking of Profit: Bao Shichen and Reform in Nineteenth-Century China,* by William T. Rowe
110. *Building for Oil: Daqing and the Formation of the Chinese Socialist State,* by Hou Li
111. *Reading Philosophy, Writing Poetry: Intertextual Modes of Making Meaning in Early Medieval China,* by Wendy Swartz
112. *Writing for Print: Publishing and the Making of Textual Authority in Late Imperial China,* by Suyoung Son
113. *Shen Gua's Empiricism,* by Ya Zuo
114. *Just a Song: Chinese Lyrics from the Eleventh and Early Twelfth Centuries,* by Stephen Owen
115. *Shrines to Living Men in the Ming Political Cosmos,* by Sarah Schneewind
116. *In the Wake of the Mongols: The Making of a New Social Order in North China, 1200–1600,* by Jinping Wang
117. *Opera, Society, and Politics in Modern China,* by Hsiao-t'i Li
118. *Imperiled Destinies: The Daoist Quest for Deliverance in Medieval China,* by Franciscus Verellen
119. *Ethnic Chrysalis: China's Orochen People and the Legacy of Qing Borderland Administration,* by Loretta E. Kim
120. *The Paradox of Being: Truth, Identity, and Images in Daoism,* by Poul Andersen
121. *Feeling the Past in Seventeenth-Century China,* by Xiaoqiao Ling
122. *The Chinese Dreamscape, 300 BCE–800 CE,* by Robert Ford Campany
123. *Structures of the Earth: Metageographies of Early Medieval China,* by D. Jonathan Felt
124. *Anecdote, Network, Gossip, Performance: Essays on the Shishuo xinyu,* by Jack W. Chen
125. *Testing the Literary: Prose and the Aesthetic in Early Modern China,* by Alexander Des Forges
126. *Du Fu Transforms: Tradition and Ethics amid Societal Collapse,* by Lucas Rambo Bender
127. *Chinese History: A New Manual (Enlarged Sixth Edition), Vol. 1,* by Endymion Wilkinson
128. *Chinese History: A New Manual (Enlarged Sixth Edition), Vol. 2,* by Endymion Wilkinson
129. *Wang Anshi and Song Poetic Culture,* by Xiaoshan Yang
130. *Localizing Learning: The Literati Enterprise in Wuzhou, 1100–1600,* by Peter K. Bol
131. *Making the Gods Speak: The Ritual Production of Revelation in Chinese Religious History,* by Vincent Goossaert
132. *Lineages Embedded in Temple Networks: Daoism and Local Society in Ming China,* by Richard G. Wang
133. *Rival Partners: How Taiwanese Entrepreneurs and Guangdong Officials Forged the China Development Model,* by Wu Jieh-min; translated by Stacy Mosher

134. *Saying All That Can Be Said: The Art of Describing Sex in* Jin Ping Mei, by Keith McMahon
135. *Genealogy and Status: Hereditary Office Holding and Kinship in North China under Mongol Rule,* by Tomoyasu Iiyama
136. *The Threshold: The Rhetoric of Historiography in Early Medieval China,* by Zeb Raft
137. *Literary History in and beyond China: Reading Text and World,* edited by Sarah M. Allen, Jack W. Chen, and Xiaofei Tian
138. *Dreaming and Self-Cultivation in China,* 300 BCE–800 CE, by Robert Ford Campany
139. *The Painting Master's Shame: Liang Shicheng and the* Xuanhe Catalogue of Paintings, by Amy McNair
140. *The Cornucopian Stage: Performing Commerce in Early Modern China,* by Ariel Fox
141. *The Collapse of Heaven: The Taiping Civil War and Chinese Literature and Culture, 1850–1880,* by Huan Jin
142. *Elegies for Empire: A Poetics of Memory in the Late Work of Du Fu,* by Gregory M. Patterson
143. *The Manchu Mirrors and the Knowledge of Plants and Animals in High Qing China,* by He Bian and Mårten Söderblom Saarela
144. *A Historical Taxonomy of Talking Birds in Chinese Literature,* by Wilt L. Idema
145. *Health and the Art of Living: Illness Narratives in Early Medieval Chinese Literature,* by Antje Richter